The
BROKEN
WINDOW

ALBERT KRUEGER

The Broken Window

Copyright © 2023 by Albert Krueger

Paperback ISBN: 978-1-63812-706-2
Ebook ISBN: 978-1-63812-705-5

All rights reserved. No part in this book may be produced and transmitted in any form or by any means, electronic, or mechanical, including photocopying, recording, or by any information storage and retrieval system, without permission in writing from the copyright owner.

The views expressed in this work are solely those of the author and do not necessarily reflect the views of the publisher. It hereby disclaims any responsibility for them.

Published by Pen Culture Solutions   05/18/2023

Pen Culture Solutions
1-888-727-7204 (USA)
1-800-950-458 (Australia)
support@penculturesolutions.com

THE BROKEN WINDOW

AUTHOR'S PREFACE

"The Broken Window" is a description of the way perception is changing in the 21st century. Because the United States of America is the major player, still, in world affairs, and because I am an American, the manners in which citizens and not-yet citizens of the United States perceive reality is a governing factor in the present world transition.

A window is a regular opening in the wall of your house through which you can look at the outside world and light from the outside world can shine in. There are many ways in which that window is changing. It's easy to think that technological change is the driver of this transitional moment. The real drivers are changes in motivation, in the sense of personal identity, in the vision for humanity, and, most of all, in the entire apparatus of language and thought that has cocooned Christianity in the West over its entire long existence.

This book will not attempt to define Christianity. There is no definition of Christianity. It is, in the end, an institution, an integral part and member of the assortment of institutions we call "Western Civilization." It has been the mortar that keeps the bricks of the civilized wall solidly in place. In biblical language, it can be described as the plumb line envisioned in the Book of the Prophet Amos 7:7-9. The walls of the city are malleable: The spiritual gravity which governs the plumb is not.

Religion, as a testimony and as an institution, became the object of scientific inquiry sometime in the 16th and 17th centuries. When it did, Christianity as an institution was objectified in a way that had not been the case in preceding eras. Western Civilization eventually got to where it is today by objectifying everything. The only phenomenon left in the human cosmos to be objectified is feelings, and they are well on their way to succumbing to the process.

The window is the apparatus through which we associate our subjective reality with the assigned objective truth. The reduction of the subjective world to only a matter of feelings is the window's breaking. When our feelings become objectified by our world, we will no longer possess anything that traditional language has called a "soul": We will be objects ourselves.

Everyone, I perceive, "feels" this truth. This is why feelings have become so important in the late-Modern/early Postmodern Western era. It's the only personal possession, the only place of sacrosanct identity, we have left. The result is that we try, as a civilization or culture, to reduce all that was once considered to be non-objective, especially morality and faith, to a matter of feelings alone.

That the world, particularly the Western world, is in transition is undeniable. That this present transition is a big one is also undeniable. The Big Transitions are like evolution: You can't predict which species will become extinct and what new species will occupy their abandoned niches. This transition is apocalyptic. In the meantime, the world's best answer to the question, "How do you feel?" is "I don't know."

AUTHOR'S INTRODUCTION

The idea for this book began to germinate when the titles of the valedictory and salutatory addresses at my high school graduation were assigned by our English teacher, the beloved Katherine MacCauley. She took the defining title from Alfred Lord Tennyson's Morte d'Arthur, "The Old Order Changeth, Yielding Place to the New." My speech was to be titled, "Youth Faces Changing Fundamentals." The year was 1966.

Because I was a science geek at the time, I didn't take the time to research the titles. I thought I already knew what those changing fundamentals were. That's probably why she had me rewrite my speech at least six times. Now that I am 75 years old and a wizened old wizard, I can look back and be amazed at how prophetic and literarily astute Mrs. MacCauley truly was.

Life, like feelings, is undefinable. Within a year, I was listening intently to Jefferson Airplane singing "How do you feel?" and doing all such things as were standard op in that time. I didn't know how I felt then, and I only sort of know now. Feelings are like the wind; the wind is like God.

My fascination with God began with a course in symbolic logic. It was an easy way to fulfil a humanities requirement for a degree in astronomy. My mind was immediately captured, and my feelings followed suit. Before then, I hadn't even heard about real philosophy. I knew the scientists and the mathematicians, but until then, philosophy did not exist for me. Symbolic logic changed my life. It revealed a way to "cut to the chase" regarding the rather fuzzy ways in which meaning and truth are conventionally conveyed.

I neglected my studies in math and physics, favoring humanities add-ons from the philosophy department. The university I attended then presented a fecund garden of religious subjects and philosophies, and I consumed many of them. Many of the professors even had faith!

Eventually, I was ordained a priest in the Episcopal Church. I served my forty years and then retired. Now I'm back to the roots, philosophy, mathematics, science, and God. And God is good.

The thought-world, the noosphere, that undergirds what I am trying to get across in the following page, is a life-inspired stew of contemporary science, math, and philosophy interrupted, evaluated, and judged by a God-inspired lifetime of responsibility to proclaiming the word of God on public. I have always kept up my reading in the headier subjects, primarily because that's how God made me. I entered the ministry because that's what God compelled me do.

So, there is a bunch of philosophy, science, and mathematics in the following pages, not to mention a few twists on history. It's all theology, but I don't dwell much on the institutional stuff. I don't have very many religious heroes, but it's telling that my spiritual admiration goes out to John Wycliffe and William Tyndale. These are the brave ones who first translated the Bible into English.

Tyndale was the one who, before being burned at the stake under the auspices of King Henry VIII of England, said to a bishop, "If God spare my life, ere many years I will cause a boy who drives the plough to know more of the scriptures than you do." God didn't spare his life, but his holy threat has been abundantly fulfilled.

The philosophers and scientists whom I have quoted quite liberally in the following conversation are ones I have studied and appreciated for their mental acuity over the years. They are some of the true lights of our present mindset, even though most people are probably unaware that they ever existed. Western society has a way of soaking up ideas like a sponge. These days, they become operating systems primarily, these days, through the social sciences, and primarily, then, through theories of education.

My favorite five are Ludwig Wittgenstein, an ordinary language philosopher, Martin Heidegger, a philosophical metaphysician, Henry Margenau, a physicist, Morris Kline, a mathematician, and Barbara Tuchman, a historian. There are many more, but these are a few of my favorite thinkers. I'm heavy on quotes because I want the reader to hear the voices of my various and often contradictory mental OS sources rather than just me telling you, with much bias, what they "really meant" to say. Their voices are consistent and possess an integrity of meaning and intention that few of us can match.

The Prime Directive, as they say in *Star Trek*, of Western Civilization has been, from the civilization's inception in the 9th century, the vision of reconciling Reason with Revelation. It began with the rather unformed reminiscences of rationality that survived the Gothic and Merovingian eras and became a fully formed civilizational fetus under the expert intellectual midwifery of Saint Thomas Aquinas.

Thomas wished to show that what Reason can, will, and must discover is already revealed in the Christian Holy Scriptures. Therefore, Christian Society is virtually a finished product. This is the governing idea behind the scholasticism of the High Middle Ages. It's the idea that morphed into the iconoclasm of the European Reformation and the transposing of the role of the Bible with the role of Reason in Western Civilization.

Today, the Bible as revelation has been virtually eclipsed by Reason as the governor of all that is good, true, and beautiful. This inevitable eventuality can be seen as a tragedy or as a deliverance from tyranny, but it is very difficult if not impossible to see any hope of reconciliation between the two. Either the Bible is to be judged by the agreed-upon standards of Reason, or our reasons for doing things are to be judged by Revelation as it has been delivered to us through the Scriptures.

It requires a community and a world to sustain the meaning that language can convey, and when the way the language of the world conveys meaning becomes radically differentiated from the way the language of Scripture conveys meaning, the one language becomes barbarian to the perspective of the other. This is where Western Civilization is today. It's not a tragedy, however: It's a fulness.

If Reason is a train of ideas, right now is whereto the tracks have always led; if the Bible tells a transcendent truth that presages where the tracks of history will lead, right now is the telos, Kairos, and fulfilment of that truth. The Truth will out not by clearer definitions but by acting on Truth. The civilizational crisis abides in the increasing friction between the two monuments to Truth, and no one can serve two monumental masters.

Among the many Greek words I season the discussion with, the two biblical words *ginomai* and *gennao* stand out. *Ginomai* often appears in the biblical narrative in its past tense, *egeneto*. *Egeneto* is translated in the old texts as "it came to pass." *Gennao* is the combined moral, political, and physical process of childbirth. No civilization can exist in time without *gennao*, without literally generating a moral, political, and physical future.

In the 60s, we used to greet each other with the question, "Hey, man, what's happening?" This is a *ginomai* question. It can be answered by means of many language games, from Fate to Faith, but the one we are interested here is the God answer: What is coming to pass by the hand of God? The question is even more radical today than it was sixty years ago.

When seventy years have passed, we will surely know the answer, and the Bible is not only "still" worth reading: It's more worth reading today than ever before.

DEDICATION

This book is dedicated to the giants of the
Western Philosophical Tradition.

Contents

AUTHOR'S PREFACE i
AUTHOR'S INTRODUCTION iii
DEDICATION vii
Part One: EVERY GAME HAS BOUNDARIES 1
Chapter One: EPITAPH 1
Chapter Two: SUBJECTIVITY AND OBJECTIVITY 22
Chapter Three: I THINK, THEREFORE, I VANISH 40
Chapter Four: EXISTENCE DEPENDS ON APOCALYPSE 60
Chapter Five: HUMPTY DUMPTY 78
Chapter Six: THE DELAYED FUSE 99
Chapter Seven: ANTICIPATING THE SIGNS OF THE END ... 117
Chapter Eight: A COMING-TO-PASS SEPARATION 135
Part Two: PATTERNS OF TECTONIC CHANGE OR TRANSITION 159
Chapter One: JESUS WAS SILENT BEFORE PILATE 159
Chapter Two: LAWLESSNESS IS THE REJECTION OF ISRAEL 177
Chapter Three: FIRST AND LAST 201
Part Three: WHERE WE ARE 227
Chapter One: LEAP OF FAITH 227
Chapter Two: THE DESTINIES OF NATIONS 249

Chapter Three: A STATE WITHOUT BOUNDARIES 271
Part Four: NO DIRECTION HOME 293
Chapter One: THE TRAGIC AND THE COMIC 293
Chapter Two: I THINK, THEREFORE, I AM DROWNING 315
Chapter Three: THE NOAH POTENTIAL 342
POSTSCRIPT 367

Part One: EVERY GAME HAS BOUNDARIES

Chapter One: EPITAPH

If your fear is operating outside of the bounds, you're not. The boundary has been moved.[1]

EVERY GAME has boundaries; every prophet is out of bounds. If you play within the boundaries, you can win the game; if you don't play the game, you can never lose. Nevertheless, "if we live, we live for the Lord. And if we die, we die for the Lord. So whether we live or die, we are the Lord's."[2]

One of the most common political complaints you hear these days is the accusation that the "other side" has "moved the goalposts." To move the goalposts of the game you are playing is "to change the rules or requirements in a way that makes success more difficult."[3] If you are goal-oriented, this makes playing your chosen game very difficult, if not impossible.

Every member of every team of every game has a designated purpose. Even if your game is solo, the moves you can make are defined, fixed and ordered in time. If there are only two opponents, such as in the game of

---
1 *Sicario*, Lionsgate, 2015
2 Romans 14:8
3 Goalposts – https://www.merriam-webster.com move/shiftthegoalposts ; ref 11 Feb 23

chess, the pieces can be moved only in certain ways, and the game-board is a finite square of squares. You can't move your rook off the right side of the game board and bring it back behind the other player's queen. Such a move is so radical and out of bounds that it's too extreme even to count as an example of cheating.

Another political complaint that you hear quite often these days is "the game is rigged." If a game is rigged, it means that "it has been fraudulently manipulated by someone to get their desired outcome."[4] The winner has been designated before the game has even started. A game can be rigged to guarantee a designated winner, such as when a fighter is paid-off to deliberately get knocked down and lose the match. A game can be rigged in order to guarantee an advantage to one or more participants, such as when a competitor in a sport engages in doping and the referees or judges are paid to ignore that fact.

Sometimes, you hear the phrase "the game of life." For instance, one blogger has said that "Life is a game just like all other games. The only difference is that life is the only game that we don't realize is a game. Each of us has made up, largely unconsciously, a set of rules (our values) – based on our worldview and our beliefs – and we think our rules are right and inherently true."[5]

Sometimes you hear the phrase "the game of love." This phrase is particularly common in popular music. One podcaster proposes that "games are exhausting and they have zero to do with love. Instead of always thinking about your next move or trying to win, look inward and connect with your feelings ... Games stop when you open up and let go of control."[6] Then there's, "Tell me just what you want me to be; one kiss and boom, you're the only one for me."[7]

---

4   Rigged – https://www.quora.com_whatdoesriggedmeaninslang ; ref 11 Feb 23

5   Morty Lefkoe, The Blog, Aug 4, 2013, 05:41 PM EDT – https://www.huffpost.com_lifeisagameandyoumaketherules ; updated Oct 4, 2013, ref 11 Feb 23

6   Tracy Crossley, September 18th, 2018 – https://www.tracycrossley.com_#-287journeypofattachmentloveisnotagameofchess ; ref 11 Feb 23

7   *The Game of Love*, Santana, 2002

Sometimes, the accusation levelled is that someone is "gaming the system." Gaming the system is like rigging the game, cheating, bending the rules, or even breaking the system. It's "using the rules and procedures meant to protect a system to, instead, manipulate the system for a desired outcome."[8] Gaming a system can be as simple as choosing to abide by some rules while ignoring others or by imposing a hierarchy of rules on the game that no one else is aware of or would approve of.

The difference between a game and a system is one of scale. A system is a very large or encompassing game or a set of interfacing, interlocking, or intersecting games that work together to achieve an outcome or a purpose. To play an assigned game within a designated system is somewhat different than playing a role in a game. The game being played must segue or otherwise complement several other games, or all the other games being played, or the system does not work well. Project managers need to understand the different games that are involved in the project as a whole. Political leaders need to understand how virtually every game in a very large system that can be played can work in unison with all the others.

When a candidate for President of the United States used the phrase "It's the economy, stupid,"[9] he was indicating that in the grand scheme of American things at that time, the economy game needed to be given priority over the other games that also need to be played in order to keep a nation running and whole. Several different games and levels of games are played during a presidential campaign and debate. The goal of the campaign game, of course, is to get elected. The majority of the voting public liked Clinton's priorities, so H. W. Bush lost the campaign and election game.

I voted for G. H. W. Bush in that campaign. This was because I disagreed with Mr. Clinton's characterization of the issues of the day. I

---

8   Game the system – https://en.m.wikipedia.org_gamingthesystem ; last updated 16 November 2022, ref 11 Feb 23

9   Economy stupid – https://en.m.wikipedia.org_itstheeconomystupid : "A phrase that was coined by James Carville in 1992 … Carville was a strategist in Bill Clinton's successful 1992 presidential campaign against incumbent George H. W. Bush"; last updated 12 December 2022, ref 11 Feb 23

thought that Mr. Bush's focus on the changing world order should have been the priority. I still do. But since then, the game itself has changed. Virtually everyone these days has an opinion about how the American game has changed. Regardless of one's opinion of the matter, mine included, the psychological and political consensus clearly reveals a firm belief that there has been a significant change.

Voting itself is a game with many players. In a sense, each voter plays a solitary game, one that is honored by the principle of one-man-one-vote and the practice of the secret ballot. These two factors in the game of American voting are linked with the emergent question of conscience. The sanctity of the human conscience was one of the major ingredients in the creative cultural, legal, and philosophical mix that became the United States of America.

In the 19th century the term "the Great Game" was coined[10] and became very popular. This game "was a set of political, diplomatic and military confrontations through most of the 19th century and the beginning of the 20th century – involving the rivalry of the British Empire and the Russian Empire over Afghanistan and neighboring territories in Central and South Asia, such as Turkestan, and having direct consequences in Persia, British India, and Tibet."[11] The Game is still being played, but today we generally refer to it as "Geopolitics."

In the 21st century, the Great Game has exceeded even the implications of the term geopolitics. As the quote that characterizes this portion of writing, "The boundary has been moved." Virtually every boundary that was in existence in the 19th and early 20th century has been moved. New boundaries involve new borders, new rules, a new psychology, a new sense of commonweal, a new conscience, a new everything that goes into the

---

10 Danish Zahoor, TGP, April 4, 2021 – https://www.thegeopolitics.com_thegreatgametaleofacentury : "The Great Game is a phrase often attributed to Rudyard Kipling who immortalized it through his classic spy novel *Kim*. In fact, it was one of the earliest players of the 'game' Arthur Conolly – a valiant soldier and explorer in the service of the British East India Company, who coined the phrase"; ref 11 Feb 23

11 Great Game – https://en.m.wikipedia.org_greatgame ; last updated 5 February 2022, ref 11 Feb 23

mystical mix of ingredients that make up the human person as we know him or her ... or don't know him or her.

Pundits like to talk about "game changers" in their pronouncements regarding breaking news or unexpected discoveries on a grand scale. A game changer is "an event, idea, or procedure that affects a significant shift in the current manner of doing or thinking about something."[12] These game changers, wake-up calls, paradigm shifts, or otherwise sudden alterations of the perceived reality behind the game effect every game that can be played.

When a real and unavoidable game changer imposes itself on the system of games we have invented, created, or otherwise constructed for ourselves, especially one that is played within national or religious boundaries, your games must change as well, and my games must change. The change doesn't simply involve playing by different rules: If an event or discovery is a real, or authentic game changer, all the games in the system have to change.

When the game changers come onto the common geopolitical game as well as the individual psycho-spiritual game, the economic game, and so forth, all at once on a regular basis, it becomes impossible to not only play the game that becomes necessary, but it is impossible to even fathom what the game could actually be.

In the Middle Ages, a particularly snarky question was coined in direct criticism of the reigning philosophy and theology, Scholasticism: "How many angels can dance on the head of a pin?"[13] We had thought, as a civilization, to have resolved and transcended the obscurantism of the Roman Catholic Church because of the Renaissance, Reformation, and Enlightenment. We didn't. While most Christian denominations still cling to an obscurantism of their own, whether it be couched in medieval,

12 Game changer – https://www.languages.oup.com_gamechanger ; ref 11 Feb 23
13 Angels Dance – https://en.m.wikipedia.org_howmanyangelscandanceontheheadofapin : "The phrase was originally used in a theological context by 17th century Protestants to mock medieval scholastics such as Duns Scotus and Thomas Aquinas and the angelology of the period in particular"; last updated February 2023, ref 11 Feb 23

renaissance, reformation, or enlightened language, the obscurantism of the emerging Western culture has simply changed venues. It is now a secular obscurantism, and it makes the obscurantism of religion look amateurish by comparison.

"My way or the highway" is a difficult game to play successfully when the highways of cultural evolution have covered over the entire land of meaning, purpose, and intention. The Game can no longer be played at all. Every highway goes everywhere, but there is only one highway that will get you to where you want to go.

What we've got here is failure to communicate.[14]

LUDWIG WITTGENSTEIN is my favorite philosopher. I like to think of him as the one who asked the question "How do you mean what you mean when you say what you say the way you say it?" The question is complimented by this one, "How do you understand what someone says when they say it in the way they say it?" Wittgenstein's philosophical analysis, called Ordinary Language Analysis, was a game-changer in the field of professional philosophy. He said, "Systems of communication ... we shall call 'language games.' They are more or less akin to what in ordinary language we call games."[15]

According to the Encyclopedia Britannica, "ordinary language analysis (is) a method of philosophical investigation concerned with how verbal expressions are used in a particular, nontechnical, everyday language."[16] For instance, if I say to you, "Hey, what's the haps?"[17] you may or may not catch the drift of what I just asked you. This misunderstanding isn't a matter of stupidity, intellectual weakness, or

---

14 *Cool Hand Luke*, Warner Bros.-Seven Arts, 1967
15 Ludwig Wittgenstein, **The Blue and the Brown Books** (New York: Harper Perennial, 1960), p.81
16 Ordinary language – https://www.britannica.com ordinarylanguageanalysis ; ref 11 Feb 23
17 TheParser, Oct 21, 2015 – https://www.usingenglish.com whatsthehaps : "Young people often like to talk cool. Everyone, even I, knows the greeting 'What's up?' But I just learned a new greeting that I had never known: **What's the haps?** (= What's happening?)"; ref 11 Feb 23

feeble-mindedness: The problem is that you don't know to play the language game I am playing. In truth, there is no reason why you should know how to play that language game. It was rather time-and-place bound anyway.

The point is that a phrase such as "What's the haps" is more than just an inquiry into the present situation or even how one is feeling. It conveys a worldview and a privileged frame-of-reference toward reality, especially social reality, as well. It conveys, in a sense, who the speaker 'really' is, and it conveys a level of linguistic trust and fellowship to the person being addressed.

All ordinary language conveys all these things with every phrase, statement, inflexion, or word that is uttered during any conversation. We can call an entire verbal transaction a conveying of meaning, but MEANING is a very large word in this context. The level of meaning conveyed in ordinary language is, to use a currently very popular terms, existential. You exist as a player "in" that conveyed game or you do not. If you are not able to play some language games, your existence ceases to have meaning. In one of our current language games, it means that you have been cancelled.[18]

Language can separate or include. Even the language of inclusion, such as it has been promoted recently, can be a language of exclusion. Language can't be defined: That's generally why Wittgenstein chose to use the term "language game." We learn a language game by playing it. We don't learn a language game by defining its elements. Water for instance, can't be comprehended by knowing what oxygen and hydrogen are like in their separate basic states. Both oxygen and hydrogen are highly volatile: Water puts out fires.

---

18 Cancelled – https://en.m.wikipedia.org_cancelculture : "Also known as call-out culture, is a phrase contemporary to the late 2010s and early 2020s used to refer to a culture in which those who are deemed to have acted or spoken in an unacceptable manner are ostracized, boycotted or shunned"; last edited 8 February 2023, ref 11 Feb 23

One peculiar conundrum that is characteristic of the analysis of ordinary language is what is called "The Private Language Problem." The private language problem arises especially when we are investigating how a language conveys feelings, such as feelings of pain or feelings of confusion. There are words, such as "hurt" or "don't understand" that do convey something of what is going on inside the soul of the speaker, but the unavoidable fact is that what is going on inside of the speaker is entirely inaccessible to the listener.

One of Wittgenstein's questions regarding this strange thing called a private language is, "What would it be like if human beings did not manifest their pains (did not groan, grimace, etc.)? Then it would be impossible to teach a child the use of the word 'toothache.' – Well, let's assume that the child is a genius and invents a name for the sensation by himself! – But then, of course, he couldn't make himself understood when he used the word."[19] The point is that we do learn how to use language even when it does not refer to something that can be called objective in any way.

A language isn't defined by its use: It is characterized by its use. For instance, if I use the word "higher" to indicate "better' "superior to," I am using the word in a different language game than when I use the word to indicate an increase of physical elevation or altitude. Many, if not most, theological arguments revolve around a mix-up in the language games being played. Is a story metaphorical or literal? Is it historical or is it a fable? Whatever meaning is meant to be conveyed is conveyed within the language game being played. Meaning is holistic.

An essential characteristic of the cultural crisis of Western Civilization in the 20th-21st centuries is the stark differentiation between what is called "objective truth" and what is called "subjective truth." The private language problem isn't a problem with languages that only make sense to the speaker: It conveys the mysterious FACT that we can convey subjectivity in a way that can be objectively received by our hearers. When, for instance, I tell Mommy that my arm hurts, my Mommy knows

---

19 Ludwig Wittgenstein, *Philosophical Investigations* (Malden, MA: Wiley-Blackwell/Blackwell Publishing Ltd, 2009; original 1953), p. 98

what I mean, even though she cannot see, feel, taste, touch or here the "hurt."

Languages such as Klingon or Elvish can be constructed in a way that certain levels of meaning are conveyed. They aren't private languages, because different individuals can learn how to use them and communicate with each other. A private language is more like an animal's language: The animal communicates, but it is a struggle to translate the communication into a language we can understand. The best way to understand an animal's language is, then, to spend time with the animal. There might be some snarling, growling and even biting, but a deep level of trust and understanding can be developed. Meaning can be conveyed.

Wittgenstein's argument against private language was part of a technical philosophical campaign. His analysis of language in this instance was an attempt to understand how we can communicate purely subjective experience and know that we are sharing the same kind of experience when we do. For instance, if I say to you, "I have a headache," you know what I mean. It's a purely subjective phenomenon, but it is a real experience, and that experience can be shared.

He wasn't a theologian or a devout Christian, but he did indicate that the logic of "God" is legitimate and that God is real. For instance, he says, "It used to be said that God could create anything except what would be contrary to the laws of logic. – The truth is that we could not *say* what an illogical world would look like."[20] Farther on, in this earlier work, he states that "if a god creates a world in which certain propositions are true, then by that very act he also creates a world in which all the propositions that follow from them come true. And similarly he could not create a world in which the proposition 'p' was true without creating all its objects."[21]

---

20 Ludwig Wittgenstein, *Tractatus Logico-Philosophicus* (New York: Routledge, Taylor & Francis Group, 1974; original 1921), p. 11
21 Wittgenstein, *Tractatus*, p. 38

Wittgenstein grapples with three key elements of communication, science, and Creation. They are Truth, logic, and propositions. Propositions are statements made up of words, that is, language. His understanding of science-talk emerges from his understanding of how language works, how "talking" achieves its goal. He writes, "the whole modern conception of the world is founded on the illusion that the so-called laws of nature are the explanations of natural phenomena. Thus people today stop at the laws of nature, treating them as something inviolable, just as God and Fate were treated in past ages."[22]

He veers away from a strict, logical analysis of reality insofar as it can be comprehended by the use of language. In this position, he is opposed to those who philosophy refers to as the Logical Positivists. This movement was becoming popular at the same time as Wittgenstein was developing his early systematic thoughts about language. It was "a philosophical movement that arose in Vienna in the 1920s and was characterized by the view that scientific knowledge and that all traditional metaphysical doctrines are to be rejected as meaningless."[23] Vienna was the place to be before and after WWI: Everybody was there, including Freud, Jung, Hitler, Lenin and Stalin.

Finally, in his 1921 *Tractatus*, Wittgenstein says, "*how* things are in the world is a matter of complete indifference for what is higher. God does not reveal himself *in* the world ... It is not *how* things are in the world that is mystical, but *that* it exists."[24] Everything that Western philosophers and academics, whether theologians, mathematicians, scientists, or political theorists, had proposed in the previous centuries of the Western Enlightenment was "up in the air." It has remained up in the air, although proponents of various opposing worldviews and theories of meaning and truth continue to vilify each other as if they knew what they were talking about.

---

22 Wittgenstein, *Tractatus*, p. 70
23 Logical positivists – https://www.britannica.com logicalpositivism ; published Jul 20, 1998, last revised Apr 28, 2016, ref 12 Feb 23
24 Wittgenstein, *Tractatus*, p. 73

I once asked a noted, award-winning Astro-physicist at the University of Arizona what things like muons and other sub-atomic particles really are. He answered, "We have no idea." I asked him this in the context of a church coffee hour where he was a devout believer and contributor to the community of faith. I ran into him decades later at the same church. He was then the ranking lay-leader of the congregation.

I do not want to imply that every believer in Jesus Christ should study and thoroughly understand the philosophy of Ludwig Wittgenstein. As far as I can tell, now some forty years after I first became aware of his existence, no one can yet say that they understand Wittgenstein's writings thoroughly. I mention his thinking because it helped me, and still helps me, to navigate the current, and usually not very intelligent, arguments about the so-called conflict between science and religion.

Also, the very nature of the Gospel of God in Jesus Christ is in the fact that its meaning and content is delivered solely by means of words, of language. In point of fact, the very word, Word, is central to the entire meaning of the New Testament itself. When we argue about things such as Truth and Knowledge in the Postmodern world, or era, we tend to forget that these valued and meaningful categories are communicated in many different ways. To put it in simple terms, it is as meaningful to say, "Follow Jesus," as it is to say, "Follow the science."[25]

---

25 David Leonhardt, *The Morning*, Feb. 11, 2022 – https://www.nytimes.com_followthescience : "Many people have come to believe that expert opinion is a unitary, omniscient force. That's the assumption behind the phrase 'follow the science' and 'what science says.' It imagines science almost as a god – Science – who could solve our dilemmas if we only listened"; ref 12 Feb 23

Don Quixote[26] is the prototype of the subjective lunacy in which the passion of inwardness grasps a particular fixed finite idea. But when inwardness is absent, parroting lunacy sets in, which is just as comic...[27]

SOREN KIERKEGAARD, the author of the culturally astute remark quoted above, was a Danish thinker of the mid-19th century. Among professionals, he is best remembered by the line, "Truth is Subjectivity," the title of one of the chapters in one of his numerous very long books. It was a breakthrough work, primarily because Western thinkers were obsessed with the idea of "Objectivity" at the time. Many citizens of the West still are.

There is something to be said for objectivity in a world which seems to have accepted the idea that "my truth" can be different than "your truth." Whether you approach the question of my truth vs your truth by means of language analysis, especially a la Wittgenstein, or by means of Kierkegaard's "Truth as Subjectivity," Truth is still a unitary concept, not one which is divided and parsed out individually in different ways to different people.

If My truth can truly be different than Your truth, then logic itself goes out the window. Then again, both Wittgenstein and Kierkegaard can seem to be allowing for this abandonment of classical logic in that logic is seen as being inadequate to the task of finally determining what the truth or truth itself truly is. If there is a logic that connects My truth with Your truth, it remains to be discovered. The logic of Your truth might even be entirely different than, or even alien to, the logic of My truth. If so, then we can never truly communicate anything between ourselves including love and affection, and we cannot honestly and legitimately engage in any intentional cooperative tasks at all.

---

26 Don Quixote – https://www.sparknotes.com_donquixote : "Obsessed with the chivalrous ideals touted in books he has read, (Don Quixote) decides to take up his lance and sword to defend the helpless and destroy the wicked … On his second expedition, Don Quixote becomes more of a bandit than a savior … In the end, the beaten and battered Don Quixote forswears all the chivalric truths he followed so fervently and dies from a fever"; ref 12 Feb 23

27 Soren Kierkegaard, *Concluding Unscientific Postscript to Philosophical Fragments, Volume 1* (Princeton: Princeton University Press, 1992; originally 1846), p. 195.

On the other hand, to say that something or some perception or feeling about something is "only subjective," begs the question of what being a subject is all about. The idea that a personal report or determination can be only subjective usually implies pejoratively that it has nothing to do with reality at all. So, Truth is Subjectivity seems to indicate that there is no common reality and that truth itself moves from perception to perception like a wandering Aramean.[28]

Since Kierkegaard contrasts reality with subjective lunacy, we can be satisfied that he didn't mean to imply that there is no common reality. Nevertheless, he does want to honor inwardness as a separate and distinct realm of reality apart from what we call the objective world. We can glean from his thoughts that unless there is some kind of impact on the inwardness of the soul, some manner of impression beyond simply the continuing response to primordial sense impressions, it is senseless to talk about Truth. Truth is either a formative and constituent part of one's inward life, one's mental and emotional constructs, or there is no truth at all.

The idea that Truth is Subjectivity means, as well, that Truth is not an objective phenomenon. Objective phenomena are, by definition, things, or objects, that exist outside of or beyond your perceiving them: They are OUT THERE whether you perceive them or not. It was the goal of the enlightened philosophers of the 17th and 18th centuries to discover this Truth that is out there whether you sense or perceive it or not. This goal, or assumption about reality, is still part of our Western psyche or soul.

The idea of an objective world is that if we can describe what is real without any subjective bias, then we will be able to declare that we have true knowledge of it, knowledge that anyone can share. Shared

---

28 Sigma Faye Coran, D'var Torah, *Deuteronomy 26:1-29:8*, September 2003 – https://www.reformjudaism.org_myfatherwaslost : "Rashbam (twelfth century, France) tells us that Abraham was the Aramean in question. Abraham is from Aram and leaves his homeland in *Parashat Lech L'cha*. Abraham refers to his being lost when he tells Abimelech, 'So when God made me wander from my father's house . . . ' (Genesis 20:13). According to Rashbam, it is Abraham who says, 'I wandered afar like a lost [*oveid*] sheep" (Psalm 119:176)'"; ref 12 Feb 23

knowledge is something that distinguishes human beings from every other living creature.

For instance, mama beaver shows baby beaver how to build a domain of sticks with an underwater entrance, but Mama beaver has not shared knowledge with baby beaver: She has simply shown the child how to do what beavers must do. We cam call this phenomenon "instinct," but that label doesn't make it any less mysterious. By the word "mysterious," I mean that we don't really know how she does it. What you and I share that Mama beaver and her baby don't share are complex arrangements of words that go directly from one subjectivity to the other.

Kierkegaard didn't want to imply that Truth is merely "subjective." Subjectivity isn't a quality or state of existence: Subjectivity is where you live. If it wasn't for subjectivity, there would be no words that talk about something called "objectivity." Without subjectivity, no one would be concerned about objectivity. The objective world isn't our shared world: The world we all share is Subjectivity, not the subjective world, but subjectivity itself. Language is the essence of Subjectivity. Language is how we live together in the homeland of Subjectivity.

Keeping in mind that you don't have to understand Kierkegaard in order to get into heaven, the Don Quixote reference is key to what happens when Subjectivity is either ignored or exalted. If it's exalted, the question of personal identity becomes the "particular fixed finite idea." This notion touches on what the Existentialist thinkers were trying to get at altogether, that is, how does the human being deal with limits. The general term for this puzzle is the term "finitude." Finitude, for the Christian existentialist, is simply the overall impact of the realization that one is not God.

Finitude is so impressing upon the human soul that it is virtually impossible to even conceive of infinity, existence that is not bounded by limits. We resist limitations and do not naturally understand how to except our limitations as being able to generate a fulness of meaning and truth. Finitude causes us to continually feel that something is lacking, and no matter how much effort we put into relieving that feeling, it remains, not even diminished. Language is the vehicle by which we can find fulness and truth in the shared space of Subjectivity. Language is also the vehicle by which we can force a sense of emptiness or rejection on each other. Language, you see, is a double-edged sword: Either you want to share your Subjectivity with another, or you don't.

Kierkegaard criticizes the idea that we can create a system which will provide for this satisfying of the sense of emptiness and purposelessness for anyone and everyone. He says, "A system of existence cannot be given. Is there, then, not such a system? That is not at all the case ... Existence itself is a system – for God, but it cannot be a system for any existing spirit. System and conclusiveness correspond to each other, but existence is the very opposite. Abstractly viewed, system and existence cannot be thought conjointly, because in order to think existence, systematic thought must think it as annulled and consequently not as existing. Existence is the spacing that holds apart; the systematic is the conclusiveness that combines."[29]

Kierkegaard's thinking is entirely polemical, that is, it is qualifiedly NOT systematic. You almost must expel the temptation to systematize your thoughts in order to enter into his quite naked Subjectivity. It helps, however, to put his words into an historical context. The (and intellectual) context is this: The German idealist Wilhelm Georg Friedrich Hegel was Kierkegaard's nemesis.[30] Hegel was born 43 years before SK, so his dialectical philosophy had had time to become quite popular in Kierkegaard's time, especially in the Protestant churches.

---

29 Kierkegaard, ibid., p. 118
30 Paul Axton, *Walking Truth*, September 6, 2018 – https://www.forgingploughshares.org_kierkegaard'salternativetohegelianatonementtheorycuringthesicknessuntodeath : "One of the key contributions in human thought occurred in Denmark with the clash between the thought of Wilhelm Friedrich Hegel and Soren Aabye Kierkegaard (or SK). In that Hegel is summing up the possibility of human thought (not only the history of thought in philosophy in its various forms but its future) and SK is positing his own Christian understanding as the alternative to Hegel, it might be said that one has the choice of wither being Hegelian or Christian"; ref 12 Feb 23

Hegel is considered by many to be "one of the founding figures of modern Western philosophy."[31]

About the dialectical project initiated by Hegel, Kierkegaard writes, "The subjective thinker is a dialectician oriented to the existential; he has the intellectual passion to hold firm the qualitative disjunction. But ... if the qualitative disjunction is used flatly and simply ... then one can run the ludicrous risk of saying something infinitely decisive, and of being right in what one says, and still not say the least thing."[32] This quote alludes back to the Don Quixote remark, the crazed wannabe idealist challenging windmills to a duel.

In the end, Kierkegaard declares that there is no cure for the pathos of suffering and sin which separates one subjectivity from the other, except faith in Jesus Christ. No system can do the trick, and no dialectic can engineer or produce an acceptable solution to the problem. If the dialectic becomes the Gospel, as it were, then we all become parroting lunatics playing out a pointless comedy which, even in the short run, quickly ceases to amuse. We might think we have a soul, something of the inwardness of Subjectivity, but the idea is merely a self-congratulatory construct of habit, "full of sound and fury, indicating nothing."[33]

Reason is the comprehension of the divine work ... The claim of the World Spirit rises above all special claims ... The state is the divine idea as it exists on earth.[34]

GEORG WILHELM FRIEDRICH HEGEL transformed time into a system. Hegel was an idealist who set the stage for the romantic distortions of reason, religion, and politics that emerged in the 20th century. He "strove to address and correct the problematic dualisms of modern philosophy" and insisted "that reason and freedom are historical achievements, not natural givens."

---

31 Hegel – https://en.m.wikipedia.org_georgwilhelmfriedrich-hegel ; last edited 10 February 2023, ref 12 Feb 23
32 Kierkegaard, ibid., p. 350
33 William Shakespeare, *Macbeth: Act 5, scene 5, lines 16-17*, 1623
34 Georg Wilhelm Friedrich Hegel, *Reason in History* (Upper Saddle River, NJ: Prentice-Hall, Inc., 1997; original 1837), pp. 48, 53

An attitude like that, Hegel's dialectic, turns the classic principles of the Enlightenment into a kind of socio-political pretzel. His "philosophical system is divided into three parts: the science of logic, the philosophy of nature, and the philosophy of spirit. This structure is adopted from Proclus's Neoplatonic triad of 'remaining-procession-return' and from the Christian Trinity'" ... 'Reason itself has a history.'"[35]

Reason, as such, becomes more reasonable over time for Hegel. This becoming doesn't come without struggle. Human history is a struggle to become more reasonable, and the struggle participates in a grand dialectic that produces the ideals of human thought over time. In a sense, these ideals are only and always approached, rather than achieved, but Hegel's machinery for producing the final achievement, the *telos*, is the State.

There is a bit of everything in Hegel's phenomenology, from alchemy to the translation of the trinitarian hypostasis into the creation of the modern State. A more comprehensive philosophical system is impossible to find. Its appeal is virtually eternal, insofar as history tends toward eternity.

It was the overarching vanity of Hegel's system that so offended Soren Kierkegaard. Both Hegel and Kierkegaard claimed to be Lutherans. However, the transformation of Protestant sectarianism into the phenomenon of the State Church disturbed Kierkegaard but intrigued Hegel. For Hegel, the State absorbs the Church and causes it to be a subsidiary, although vitally contributing, element in the completeness of the State. For Kierkegaard, the Church has sold out.

If one extends the dialectic even a little bit into the future development, or dialectal evolution, of Reason, the State Church inevitably becomes the Church State. This development itself becomes the historical epitome of Reason and thus cannot be argued away. The State will have already co-opted all methods and processes of Reason as such. Reason becomes Politics in the fullest sense of the comparison.

---

35 Georg Wilhelm Friedrich Hegel – https://en.m.wikipedia.org georg-wilhelomfriedrichhegel ; last edited 10 February 2023, ref 13 Feb 23

Marxism, Marxist-Leninism, and even Naziism are the offspring of the Hegelian dialectic, the "system" as Kierkegaard calls it. The individual citizen becomes a non-individual, identified as a part of the system having no individual legitimacy whatsoever. In other words, for Kierkegaard, again a Christian existentialist, in the Hegelian the individual literally ceases to exist.

You don't need to be thoroughly learned in the thought processes of Hegel or Kierkegaard to see the many realized problems that have become manifest in Western society because of Marxism and Naziism. It's enough to know that there IS a vast and comprehensive philosophy of life itself behind these things and that it is this comprehensive worldview that energizes, motivates, and even procreates the cultural and civilizational progeny that created Stalin, Hitler, and Mao.

In many ways, the writings of Soren Kierkegaard blend together as one, seamless and intellectually impenetrable philosophical rant. His *ouvre* [36] is a kind of "run for your life" testimony in the prophetic sense, and his vision was that of an impending and universal destructive pathos emerging on the horizon of Hegel's history of Reason.

In a final comparison between the kind of religion which must come out of a Hegelian system and the kind of religion that traditionally places the individual sinner alone in front of the throne of God. The Subjectivity that is identified with Truth, for Kierkegaard, is also a Subjectivity identified with Truth for Hegel, but the identifying alchemy is directly opposed in its theo-political processes. In the end, Kierkegaard says, "what, I wonder, has Christianity become because we all are Christians of sorts as a matter of course?... the traveler is looking more at the wig than at the man."[37]

---

36 AUTHOR'S NOTE: I got this term from Foucault, whom I have just recently discovered. Foucault is, if you will, a non-Hegelian deconstructive postmodern philosopher of language and literature. An *ouvre* is "a substantial body of work constituting the lifework of a writer, artist, or a composer."

37 Kierkegaard, ibid. pp. 586, 616

The absorption of the individual sinner into the moral machinery of the State is the last frontier in Kierkegaard's argument/rant against Hegel. Once this happens, morality as such takes on a much different uniform in the postmodern era than it wore in the "Christian Era." Like the mathematician who wore the Napoleonic uniform after it was outlawed by the French State, simply because he had nothing else to wear, the traditional uniform will become, and is becoming, cause for incarceration.[38] This phenomenon is the natural consequence of the Hegelian or quasi-Hegelian system.

The way language works is of central concern for Hegel, although the direct analysis of language as such isn't his field of expertise. It is the historical development of language, in idealistic terms, that's of interest to him. The development of language, or languages, "has happened without real history ... it is ... a fact that with advancing social and political civilization this systematic product of intelligence is blunted, and language becomes poorer and less subtle ... Without language the exercises of memory and fantasy ae immediate (non-speculative) manifestations (that remain) veiled in the obscurity of a voiceless past ... The premature growth of language and the progress and dispersion of nations gains significance and interest for concrete Reason only in either the contact with states or the autonomous formation of states."[39]

In other words, for Hegel the ongoing development and use of language is the business of the State. The State is the originator of the processes and purposes of meaning. Ideally, then, Hegel being the pre-eminent idealist of history, authentic language can only be the language of the State. It is the duty and destiny of the State to create its own perfect language game.

For Kierkegaard, Subjectivity is still subject to the will and purposes of God; for Hegel, Subjectivity is entirely within the legal and existential domain of the State.

---

38 Galois – https://www.mathhistory.st-andrews.ac.uk_evaristegalois : "The 14th of July (1830) was Bastille Day and Galois was arrested again. He was wearing the uniform of the Artillery of the National Guard, which was illegal"; ref 13 Feb 23

39 Hegel, *Reason in History*, pp. 77, 78

In the face of the eternal power man is reduced to naught, together with his free choice and action. And the eternal power waxes immeasurable just because it fulfils its decrees despite the freedom of human will.[40]

RUDOLF OTTO was the last Christian mystic.[41] His writings are so mystical that it takes an expert to recognize its Christian roots. Otto was a "German theologian, philosopher, and historian of religion, who exerted worldwide influence through his investigation of man's experience of the holy." His span of influence brackets World War I, particularly by the publication of his 1917 work, *Das Heilige*, published in English in 1923 as *The Idea of the Holy*,[42] which is quoted above.

One of the most intriguing aspects of Otto's point of view is that he developed it during the advent of World War I, as did his neo-orthodox[43] theological counterpart, Karl Barth. Both theologians contributed significantly to the final mix of mysticisms, historicisms, and revelatory insights that have been the primary religious fertilizer for Christianity in the West in the 20th-21st centuries. Whereas Barth recognized the essential unholiness of World War I,[44] Otto must have recognized the

---

40 Rudolf Otto, *The Idea of the Holy* (New York: Oxford University Press, 1923, 1950, 1958), p. 89

41 Mystic – https://www.languages.oup.com_mystic : "a person who seeks by contemplation and self-surrender to obtain unity with or absorption into the Deity or the absolute, or who believes in the spiritual apprehension of truths that are beyond the intellect"; ref 13 Feb 23

42 Bernard E. Meland, *Britannica*, Jul 20, 1998 – https://www.britannica.com_rudolfotto ; last updated Sep 21, 2022, ref 13 Feb 23

43 Neo Orthodoxy – https://www.dictionary.com_neo-orthodoxy : "A movement un 20th century Protestantism, reasserting certain older traditional Christian doctrines"; ref 13 Feb 23

44 Karl Barth – https://en.m.wikipedia.org_karlbarth : "Barth is best known for his commentary *The Epistle to the Romans*, his involvement in the Confessing Church, including his authorship (except for a single phrase) of the Barmen Declaration, and especially his … *Church Dogmatics* … he became increasingly disillusioned with the liberal Christianity in which he had been trained … In August 1914, Karl Barth was dismayed to learn that his venerated teachers including Adolf von Harnack had signed the 'Manifesto of the Ninety-Three German Intellectuals to the Civilized World' (a complete theological approval of Germany's decision to go to war); as a result, Barth concluded he could not follow their understanding of the Bible and history any longer"; last edited 10 February 2023, ref 13 Feb 23

generally chaotic, ambiguous, and violent character of religious holiness in the news coming from the war itself.

Otto "became a member of the Prussian Parliament in 1913 and retained his position through the First World War ... He then served in the post-war constituent assembly in 1918, and remained involved in the politics of the Weimar Republic ... While his work started in the domain of liberal Christian theology, its main thrust was always apologetic, seeking to defend religion against naturalist critiques. (He) eventually came to conceive of his work as part of a science of religion, which was divided into the philosophy of religion, the history of religion, and the psychology of religion."[45] Between the theological ideas of Rudolf Otto and Karl Barth, we can discern the ever-widening cultural gap between liberal Christianity and Conservative Christianity in the West.

We began this discourse with a line from a recently distributed movie, *Sicario*. The movie is ostensibly about the problem of cartel activity on the border between Mexico and the United States. The substance of that movie is a questioning of the effectiveness of established legal methodologies in dealing with these activities and the people involved in them. The conclusion is that it is impossible to deal effectively with cartel activity and still remain within the bounds of established American legal procedure.

Sicario, after the fashion of the Jewish assassins of Roman soldiers and citizens during the Jewish Wars between 66 and 136 CE. The siege of Masada "was one of the final events in the First Jewish-Roman War (and) according to Josephus the long siege by the troops of the Roman Empire led to the mass suicide of the Sicarii rebels and resident Jewish families of the Masada fortress."[46] According to the director of Sicario, "the film asserts that the American War on Drugs is 'turning us into the very monsters we were trying to defeat.'"[47]

45 Rudolf Otto – https://en.m.wikipedia.org_rudolfotto ; last edited 10 February 2023, ref 13 Feb 23
46 Sicarii – https://en.m.wikipedia.org_siegeofmasada ; last edited 23 January 2023, ref 13 Feb 23
47 Sicario – https://en.m.wikipedia.org_sicario(2015film) ; last edited 10 February 2023, ref 13 Feb 23

The War on Drugs, as futile as it has appeared to be so far, is only as futile as the war that began the postmodern world, World War I. After WWI, "new boundaries involve new borders, new rules, a new psychology, a new sense of commonweal, a new conscience, a new everything that goes into the mystical mix of ingredients that make up the human person as we know him or her ... or don't know him or her,"[48] as well as the mix that makes up the foundational elements of a modern nation.

The intellectual ferment immediately prior to the advent of the Great War did not cross over intact into the 20th century: It died and was buried, like that mustard seed Jesus talked about.[49] Translated into a terminally nationalistic understanding of all the ideal, romantic and otherwise rational ideas of the prior several hundred years in Europe, WWI was offered to the masses as a fight to the finish that would justify in the mystical sense, a god-ordained hierarchy of national character which would establish the moral, social, and political City of God qua City of Man[50] for eons to come. Instead, it killed and buried all the values and progressive implications of those old ideas, values that are still struggling to be reborn in a poppy field of human history in which they cannot grow.[51]

World War I, the Great War, is the ultimate boundary marker. It marks a line in the history of Western Civilization can be crossed neither in a backward manner nor in a forward manner. Efforts to cross the boundary in order to establish some kind, any kind, of continuity with what this civilization once was or tried to be or vowed to be, are as futile as any mystical effort to penetrate the closed gates to the Garden of Eden. Both are guarded by cherubim with a flaming sword that turns in every direction.[52]

---

48 From earlier
49 Matthew 13:31-32
50 St. Augustine, *The City of God*, 413 CE
51 John McCrae, *In Flanders Fields*, 1918: "In Flanders fields the poppies blow between the crosses, row on row, that mark our place."
52 Genesis 3:24

The epitaph is written in the blood of millions, from then and on and on. It will always read, "He fell in October 1918, on a day that was so quiet and still on the whole front, that the army report confined itself to the single sentence: All quiet on the Western Front. He had fallen forward and lay on the earth as though sleeping. Turning him over one saw that he could not have suffered long; his face had an expression of calm, as though almost glad the end had come."[53]

---

53 Erich Maria Remarque, *All Quiet on the Western Front* (New York: Ballantine Books, 1982; originally 1928), p. 296

Chapter Two: SUBJECTIVITY AND OBJECTIVITY

Space and time are highly poetic subjects ... The awesome veneration of space and time has been continuous and has been continuously recorded, with the effect that even modern thought cannot entirely free itself from its mystic bondage to the past.[54]

DEATH IS WHEN YOUR PAST MEETS YOUR *TELOS*, your purpose in life. Until then, you spend your life trying to reinvent space and time. When the German 1st Army ploughed into the British Expeditionary Force at Mons, Belgium, Western Civilization realized its *telos*. It was the relentless force of the accumulated centuries that impelled that German Army to cross the border of neutral Belgium and take on an army that wasn't even Belgian.

Destiny is a very different kind of realized truth than Fate. Your destiny is fulfilled because you intended it to happen; Fate is just mechanical force enlivened by the mysteries of life.[55] Even though you must choose your destiny in order that it would be your destiny, to choose your fate is a pretense, and the shape of your destiny isn't yours to create. The shape of your destiny involves everyone else's destiny and fate from before all time and forever.

Destiny matures in the Great Subjectivity: Fate is entirely objective.

Who knows where in the Great Subjectivity Adolf Hitler lived when he was running messages on the Western Front? Who knows where Ludwig Wittgenstein's lodging was in the Great Subjectivity while he

---

54 Henry Margenau, *The Nature of Physical Reality: A Philosophy of Modern Physics* (Woodbridge, CN: Ox Bow Press, 1977), p. 123

55 Albert Krueger, Conundrums of the End: Fate, Destiny, and Apocalypse (Bloomington, IN: WestBow Press, 2020), pp. 55, 58: "The general study of fate in the affairs of humanity is called history. The general study of fate in the physical world is called science ... When the abstract horizon point of free will is compressed into a singularity, people will act out in certain ways because they no longer have any choice about it."

was fighting it out with the Russians on the Eastern Front? Even though they lived, as it were, through the maelstrom, the Great Subjectivity itself was dislodged from its mystical moorings: It began to free-float through a kind of not-yet-Sabbath time,[56] like an invasive balloon[57] attempting to violate a still dizygotic world soul.

Many believed they were putting the finishing touches on the grand project called 'civilization', but "the wisest were just the poor and simple people. They knew the war to be a misfortune, whereas those who were better off, and should have been able to see more clearly what the consequences would be, were beside themselves with joy."[58] The effort it took to prove the right and to preserve the good turned them all into uncivilized beasts (*therion*).[59] It should be pointed out that the beastliness was well-ordered and the line separating friend from foe was well-defined. Not-civilization doesn't necessarily have to look the part.

One is reminded of an officer's remark in a later war fought under the new regime of that floating Subjectivity, "It became necessary to destroy the town to save it."[60] Subjectivity itself didn't become such a cultural obsession until Schleiermacher (1768-1834),[61] Kierkegaard (1813-1855) and Otto (1869-1937) zeroed in on that vast aspect of human existence which had been completely overlooked, if not denigrated altogether, by

---

56 Abraham Joshua Heschel, *The Sabbath: Its Meaning for Modern Man* (New York: Farrar, Straus and Giroux, 2005; original 1951), p. 97: "When gazing at reality while our souls are carried away by spatial things, time appears to be in constant motion. However, when we learn to understand that it is the spatial things that are constantly running out, we realize that time is that which never expires, that it is the world of space which is rolling through the infinite expanse of time."
57 See footnote 64
58 Remarque, ibid., p. 11
59 *Therion*: Beast, as in Revelation 13:1
60 Peter Arnett – https://en.m.wikipedia.org_peterarnett : "In what is considered to be one of his iconic dispatches, published on 7 February 1968, [Peter] Arnett wrote about the Battle of Ben Tre: 'It became necessary to destroy the town to save it,' a United States major said today"; last edited 31 August 2022, accessed 15 Feb 23
61 Schleiermacher – https://www.quotefancy.com_friedrichschleiermacher-quotes : "Whenever I find a spark of that hidden fire that will sooner or later consume the old and create the new, I am drawn to it with love and hope, regarding it as a sign of my future home"; accessed 15 Feb 23

both the empiricists and the rationalists of the European Enlightenment. The Great War destroyed the City Built on Reason so it could save the primordial residence of humanity, "like Chaos, before the world was created."[62]

Sigmund Freud and Carl Jung zeroed in on Subjectivity as well. As much as does the Great War, the city of Vienna, too, is a boundary marker in history. Vienna was the edge of the universe, where the ocean of old things fell off the seamless precipice of subject-object indistinction into the misty world of uncertainty unfathomable depths below. Vienna was the City of the Fallen God: Paris was the City of a Lost God. Vienna produced Hitler and Karl Popper; Paris produced Ernest Hemingway and F. Scott Fitzgerald. Neither Moscow nor Washington, D.C. have been able to reset the Fallen God or rediscover the Lost God.

When we search the literature, the science, and the politics of the 19th century, what we find is an overweening sense of inevitability.[63] In between the two big wars, we find still a culture-wide sense of astonishment and surprise that something that had seemed so important for so many had indeed ended, even that it had failed completely. World War I had to happen: It was as inevitable an outcome of the Magna Carta[64] as was the creating of the United States of America. When Positivism mated

---

62 Schleiermacher – https://www.quotestats.com_friedrichschleiermacherquotes ; accessed 15 Feb 23
63 Barbara W. Tuchman, *The Proud Tower: A Portrait of the World Before the War, 1890-1914* (New York: Random House Trade Paperbacks, 2014; originally 1962, 1966), p. xv: "Although the fin de siècle usually connotes decadence, in fact society at the turn of the century was not so much decaying as bursting with new tensions and accumulated energies. Stefan Zweig who was thirty-three in 1914 believed that the outbreak of war 'had nothing to do with ideas and hardly even with frontiers. I cannot explain it otherwise than by this surplus force, a tragic consequence of the internal dynamism that had accumulated in forty years of peace and now sought violent release."
64 Doris Mary Stanton, *Encyclopedia Britannica*, Jul 20, 1998 – https://www.britannica.com_magnacarta : "English Great Charter, charter of English liberties granted by King John on June 15, 1215, under threat of civil war … By declaring the sovereign to be subject to the rule of law and documenting the liberties held by 'free men,' the Magna Carta provided the foundation for individual rights in American jurisprudence … The remarkable fact is not that war broke out between John and his barons in the following

with Romanticism, their children were as fated as the fall of Rome 1500 years earlier.

Then, of course, there was also Albert Einstein.

Einstein's Theory of Relativity wasn't just a mathematical expedition into seeing things from different points of view. His mathematics uncovered the way to seeing things from all points of view at the same time. Since Thomas Aquinas had defined and bounded omniscience as the one avenue of knowledge that is the sole prerogative of God, Einstein managed to prove that it is the destined prerogative of the human intellect.

The first theologian to grapple with the know-it-all-ness in a systematic and philosophical manner was St. Thomas Aquinas (1225-1274), a scholar at the University of Paris (founded 1150). He "holds that as far as temporal things are concerned, only present things exist. He also holds that God knows immediately, all at once, in a single act, the past, present, and future."[65] Einstein said that "coincidence is God's way of remaining anonymous." He also said that "technological progress is like an axe in the hands of a pathological criminal."[66]

As Chuck Berry composed his early rock 'n roll song, *Roll Over Beethoven*,[67] Einstein, who loved music and wrote his music down with the notes of higher mathematics, could have written a similar song, *Move Over Aquinas*. In the lives of Einstein, Wittgenstein, Freud, and Hemingway, and the others the purpose of Western Civilization was fulfilled. Then they went beyond that . . .

---

months but that the king had ever been brought to agree to the sealing of such a document at all"; last updated Aug 23, 2022, accessed 16 Feb 23

65 Kevin M. Staley, *Saint Anselm Journal 3.2*, (Spring 2006) – https://www.anselm.edu_omnisciencetimeandeternityisaquinasinconsistent ; referenced 29 Jan 23

66 Einstein – https://www.brainyquote.com_albertein-steinquotes ; accessed 15 Feb 23

67 *Roll Over Beethoven*, Chuck Berry, 1956

I dreamed I saw St. Augustine alive as you or me tearing through these quarters in the utmost misery with a blanket underneath his arm and a coat of solid gold searching for the very souls whom have already been sold.[68]

IN THE TWENTIETH CENTURY, the city of God became the pie in the sky. It had served as the cultural beacon and prototype for an entire civilization and half of the next. For eleven-hundred years, Jerusalem and Athens struggled to save their marriage, but in the end irreconcilable differences caused the judge to declare the relationship null and void.

A millennium is a long time. It's a long enough time to separate the ancient from the modern. It's a long enough time to liberate the evolved from the primordial. After a thousand years have passed, everyone rejoices in the new, and everyone has forgotten the old. It's the in-between that facilitates change.

World War I was an in-between worthy of being called a millennium. In those four horrifying years, what had seemed new just a decade earlier had become ancient and inaccessible. Whatever it was that Hegel was getting at with his fascinating synthesis between Christian theology and Greek political theory was buried beneath moral and ethical tons of unexploded ammo waiting to sprout from the desecrated ground of both eastern and western Europe. They would sprout, and each explosion would be reminiscent of a world that was lost and the growing civilizational despair of ever finding another one like it.

An entire generation of young men had vanished in an historical instant.[69] Like with the wandering horde in the desert of Sin, the familiar link between past and future was broken when an entire generation

---

68 *I Dreamed I saw St. Augustine*, Bob Dylan, 1967
69 Longley, Robert. "The Lost Generation and the Writers Who Described Their World." ThoughtCo. https://www.thoughtco.com/the-lost-generation-4159302 : "The term 'Lost Generation' refers to the generation of people who reached adulthood during or immediately following World War I. In using the term 'lost,' psychologists were referring to the 'disoriented, wandering, directionless' feelings that haunted many survivors of what had been one of the most horrific wars in modern history"; updated on March 02, 2022, accessed February 14, 2023

perished in the Wilderness.[70] Like the exiles who found themselves stranded in an alien world, a generation had been separated out and driven from their promised land.[71] They couldn't even remember what it had tasted like.[72] Like the sad band who attempted to resurrect the glories of the past by laying a new Temple foundation and strengthening walls that should have stayed unimagined, most of the builders never really knew why they were there, and those who could remember wept.[73]

It wasn't the City of God that was destroyed at the beginning of the twentieth century: That city had been untethered and released to float free some generations before then. When Descartes declared "I think, therefore I am,"[74] that famous *cogito ergo sum*, he hadn't discovered, like Archimedes, another Pi that would forever resolve the mysteries of boundedness in space-filled spheres.[75] The mind had been over-achieving ever since Thomas Aquinas had philosophized the Holy Scriptures. What Descartes said to Aquinas, in translation and transportation, was, "It's all in your mind."

The City of God still attempts to violate the boundaries of the post-Great War commonweal by appearing in the form of balloons, octagons,

---

70 Numbers 14:29-30: "In this wilderness your corpses will fall, and all who were numbered of you, according to your whole number, from twenty years old and upward, who have murmured against Me, you will not go into the land which I swore by My hand to cause you to dwell in it…"

71 II Chronicles 36:19-20: "So (the Babylonians) burned down the house of God, tore down the wall of Jerusalem, burned down all the palaces with fire, and destroyed all the precious items, Then (the king of the Chaldeans) carried into exile to Babylon the remnant, who survived the sword, and they were slaves to him and his sons …"

72 Psalm 34:7-9: "The angel of the Lord camps around those who fear Him, and delivers them. Oh, taste and see that the Lord is good; blessed is the man who takes refuge in Him. Oh, fear the Lord, you His saints; for the ones who fear Him will not be in need."

73 Ezra 4:12: "Now many of the older Levitical priests and chiefs of the fathers' households who had seen the first temple wept with a loud voice as the foundation of this temple was laid before their eyes, though many others shouted exuberantly for joy."

74 Rene' Descartes, *Discourse on Method*, 1637

75 Eureka – https://www.bellarmine.edu_abouteureka ; published 2023, accessed 14 Feb 23

cylinders, and other strange shapes, but it always gets blown up in the sky and its fragmentary remains fall once again to the earth.[76] Every balloon that gets tested also gets shot down. Even the balloons are "all in your mind."

Saint Augustine carried the neo-Roman civilization on his theological back from a time of great destruction and tribulation through to its fulfilment in the sixteenth century. When all the questions that could have been answered in his great, neo-Platonic system had been answered, and yet more questions arose to froth the sacred drink of holiness, the system began to fade from sight until it was finally driven from the felt memory of the masses. Saint Augustine's ghost comes back from time to time to haunt the hopes of those who continually weep at the new foundations of logic, truth, and justice, but very few believe in ghosts anymore.

Occasionally the ghost of Augustine appears in particularly fearsome and convincing form. Hegel's system was the first great appearance, and it was followed by an intriguing late-20th-century essay *The End of History and the Last Man* (1992), penned by Francis Fukuyama.[77] As a glorious paean to the modern expression of Western capitalism, it was heartily received by the neo-con faction and everyone else who thought that it was finally time for the New Jerusalem to begin descending from heaven.[78]

76 Eric Tupper, Associated Press, February 14, 2023 – https://www.apnews.com_usdefendsdecisiontoshootdown3unidentifiedobjects : "The White House defended the shootdowns of three unidentified objects in as many days even as it acknowledged that officials had no indication the objects were intended for surveillance in the same manner as the high-altitude Chines balloon that traversed American airspace earlier this month"; accessed 14 Feb 23

77 Jeffrey A. Engel, *When the World Seemed New: George H. W. Bush and the End of the Cold War* (New York: Houghton Mifflin Harcourt, 2017), pp. 74, 75: "Just one system remained. Democracy had won ... just as Bush believed the stream of history flowed toward an inevitable democratic end, Fukuyama argued that the democratic destination was not only in sight but unalterable as well. History had revealed its final point ... Western-style democracy ran on a straight path from the Athenian polis to the Roman Republic and then through the Magna Carta ... until ultimately landing in the United States ... Of all the statements in this book this one stands clear: Fukuyama's essay easily ranks among the best-selling studies of Hegelian philosophy ever produced."

78 Revelation 21:10-14

It didn't descend. Yet in a real sense the hopes and dreams of late 20th-century America amounted to a revisitation of the original Neoplatonism of Saint Augustine, made viable to pure Reason by virtue of Hegel.[79] The rejection of the non-empirical and the scientific reliance on mathematics and induction alone that had characterized the enlightened West for several hundred years was partially reborn in the guise of American Exceptionalism. Augustine's City of God was resurrected sans the troublesome inclusion of that ultimate moral authority in heaven, God.

If the Kingdom of Heaven can be thought, say the late 20th century descendants of Descartes, it will be realized. We think, therefore we are what we think, or "what we think, we become," *quod cogitamous, erimus*...[80] From now on, at least in the United States of America, the highest power governing Democratic Capitalism would be the Satisfaction Curve.

The higher men had awakened in Zarathustra's cave ... marshalled themselves for a procession to go and meet Zarathustra ... for they had found when they awakened that he no longer tarried with them. When, however, they reached the door of the cave and the noise of their steps had preceded them, the lion started violently; it turned away all at once from Zarathustra, and roaring wildly, sprang towards the cave. The higher men, however, when they heard the lion roaring, cried all aloud as with one voice, fled back and vanished in an instant ... Zarathustra ... left his cave, glowing and strong, like a morning sun coming out of gloomy mountains.[81]

THE HIGHER MEN of past centuries have disappeared into the all-embracing mists of relativity. Relativity itself has been culturally

79 Philip Stanfield, *Material, Mysticism and Art*, posted on September 22, 2014 – https://www.philipstanfield.com hegelmystic : "My thesis explores the relationship between Hegel's philosophy and Neoplatonism. In it, I will argue that Hegel's philosophy is not only mystical – Christian Neoplatonic – but Hermetic. A common understanding of 'mysticism' is that it is a belief that one can attain union with or absorption into a deity or an absolute, or spiritually apprehend knowledge – through the 'abandonment' of the self or through contemplation"; accessed 14 Feb 23
80 We think – https://www.mymemory.translated.net whatwethinkwebecome ; accessed 16 Feb 23
81 Friedrich Nietzsche, *Thus Spake Zarathustra* (London: Arcturus Publishing Limited, 2019; original 1883-1885), pp. 302, 303

appropriated out of the hands of the mathematical physicists into the hearts, minds and souls of the social justice warriors. The cave of ancient knowledge has been replaced by the great Sun governing the language of "Let's see what happened when we light the match." Even the old words can be left behind: The Higher Men can feed on them until they run out of meaning, and those Greater Intellects begin to starve.

I typically rest my thought systems regarding this 20th-21st-century exchange of truths on two vibrant and memorable intellectual experiences in the classroom. The first classroom accommodated a doctoral-level theology class at the Graduate Theological Union in Berkeley, California. This was in the late 1970s. The second classroom, but existing earlier in time, was an upper-division class in micro-economics taught at the University of Arizona in the mid-1970s.

The theology class was called *Theology Between the Wars*. The two wars in question were allegedly World War I and World War II. There was a mighty ferment of new theological investigation in those days, much of it in French. Since I don't read French, I didn't catch half the teaching, but even when it's in English, it's hard to catch even half the meaning in a modern theology class. There was even more German theology, and I don't read German either. German, however, translates into English in a much better deep-structural way that satisfied my genome than does French.

As people are wont to say when they survive an intellectual experience that verges on unintelligibility, "I learned a lot in that class." One thing I learned was that it wasn't my destiny to go on to do graduate work in theology after I got my MDiv. Too many languages! On the other hand, somehow, I pulled an "A."

The seminar was team taught by the Dean of the Graduate Theological Union, a Protestant theologian, and the Dean of the Dominican School of Philosophy and Theology, a thoroughly Roman Catholic theologian. Those were the days when inclusivity and diversity was just getting off to its start. The class lectures and discussions often reminded me of those early Donald Duck cartoons where the two imaginary ducks representing conscience stood on each of Donald's shoulder shouting and whispering advice into his right ear and his left ear.

The GTU Dean did the most whispering. In fact, it was difficult to conclude that he said anything at all. His reply to most queries and befuddlements from the class was, "I don't know. What do you think?" The good news was that he didn't seem to care what we thought as long as it represented a kind of thinking. The Dean of DSPT was the shouter, and he always shouted the same thing, "I think that eventually everyone will agree that St. Thomas Aquinas already said it all." It caused me to wonder which two wars he thought the class was supposed to be in-between: Perhaps he meant the Fourth Crusade and the Mongol invasions of the Levant,[82] but he was never clear on that.

Some of us go way, way back in order to establish the intellectual and cultural truth; some of us go so far ahead that Truth as such becomes something that is eternally just beyond the horizon. And here we are, "stuck in the middle with you,"[83] whoever that might be at any given moment.

I appreciated the class in micro-econ even more. I took it as a filler class after I had completed the requirements for a philosophy degree. I though that since I had grown up in a retailing family and even spent three years working the sales floor as my father's assistant manager, I would have something to contribute and something to learn. Well, again, "I learned a lot from that class." I learned that what I learned about merchandising from my dad, who learned the trade during the Great Depression and made money, was all wrong.

That was when I learned about the Satisfaction Curve. I had intuited such a thing when learning how to price goods for the salesfloor, but I

82 Wars in 1300s – https://en.m.wikipedia.org_listofwars1000-1499 ; last updated 14 February 2023, accessed 16 Feb 23
83 Stuck in the Middle with You, Stealers Wheel, 1973 – https://www.musixmatch.com_stuckinthemiddlewithyou : "Well I don't know why I came here tonight. I've got the feeling that something ain't right ... Clowns to the left of me, jokers to the right. Here I am stuck in the middle with you."

had no idea it could be construed in terms of higher mathematics. The math made mathematical physics look amateurish by comparison.

The Satisfaction Curve is "an indifference curve" that "shows a combination of two goods in various quantities that provides equal satisfaction (utility) to an individual" or business. "It is used in economics to describe the point where individuals have no particular preference for either one good or another based on their relative quantities."[84] To me it meant "price to sell." Sell at the price the market will bear. In our case, the market was a small and relatively isolated northern Arizona town of 8,000. We made money.

We were also terribly wrong. Maybe not wrong, but somewhat off-center. My micro-prof used his facility in higher mathematics to PROVE that there is no such thing as human need. There are only human wants. He did this by showing mathematically that if someone wants something badly enough, that person will find a way to get it. I had to admit that his thesis could explain some forms of shoplifting and burglary, even destruction, but it didn't relate to what I knew already about pricing.

The other thing the professor PROVED was that there is no such thing as a non-renewable, in fact, there would always be some commodities that would always be available. This is because as the availability of the non-renewable shrinks, the price of it will increase. Eventually, the price will be too high for anyone to afford: Thus, there would always be something of that commodity remaining. I learned a lot from that class.[85] Follow the numbers, as they say...

Zarathustra spoke loudly in the late 19th-century. He spoke with artillery and poison gases in the Great War. No one took notice, but he kept on speaking and is speaking even more loudly today. The lion

---

84 Caroline Banton, *Investopedia*, reviewed by Robert C. Kelly, fact checked by Kirsten Rohrs Schmitt – https://www.investopedia.com_indifferencecurvesine-conomicswhatdotheyexplain ; updated August 30, 2022, accessed 16 Feb 23

85 AUTHOR'S NOTE: The Philosophy Department at the University of Arizona has ranked in the top ten for public universities for many decades, as I understand it. I recommend it even today, although things there have changed mightily, too, in the last 47 years.

was fed, and all the Higher Men merely parrot Zara's grammar and his language games.[86] Follow your passion.

As I was walking among the fires of Hell, delighted with the enjoyments of Genius, which to Angels look like torments and insanity, I collected some of their proverbs ... so the proverbs of Hell show the nature of infernal wisdom better than any description of buildings or garments ... When I came home, on the abyss of the five senses, where a flat-sided steep frowns over the present world, I saw a mighty Devil ... with corroding fires he wrote the following sentence now perceived by the minds of men ... How do you know but every bird that cuts the airy way is an immense world of delight, closed by your senses five?[87]

EMPIRICISM is dead; so, too, is the classic American pragmatism. The five senses don't tell you anything but that you might need to defecate or that there is a large truck speeding right at you. Or that you don't like Brussels sprouts...

What about pragmatism? It "is perhaps America's most distinctive contribution to philosophy. Developed by Pierce, Dewey, and James in the late 19th and early 20th centuries, pragmatism holds that both the meaning and truth of any idea is a function of its practical outcome ... William James' view of pragmatism ... roughly equates truth and usefulness - if something is true it is useful, and if it isn't useful, then talking about its truth doesn't make sense."[88] Pragmatism, not science, was behind the development of the atomic bomb.[89]

---

86 Nietzsche, ibid., p. 37: "Once hadst thou passions and calledst them evil. But now hast thou only thy virtues: they grew out of thy passions ... All thy passions in the end became virtues, and all thy devils angels. Once hadst thou wild dogs in thy cellar: but they changed at last into birds and charming songstresses."
87 William Blake, *The Marriage of Heaven and Hell*, 1790 – https://www.ia803405.us.archive.org_themarriageofheavenandhell ; archived 1906, referenced 4 Feb 23
88 John and Ken, *Philosophy Talk*, American Pragmatism, Jan 14, 2007 – https://www.philosophytalk.org_americanpragmatism ; accessed 16 Feb 23
89 Kai Bird and Martin J. Sherwin, *American Prometheus: The Triumph and Tragedy of J. Robert Oppenheimer* (New York: Vintage Books: A Division of Random House, Inc., 2005), p. 220: "Even a skeptic like Bethe understood ... 'That once plutonium was made, it was almost certain that a nuclear bomb could be made as well.' Thus, the real news ... was that (the nuclear scientists) had a mission that could contribute enormously to the war effort. This fact alone lifted morale. Serber's first talk conveyed what Oppenheimer wanted:

There's nothing like the immanent threat of Evil to take over the entire world to stimulate the pragmatic spirit of a free nation. As with the Great War, there was something of the inevitable about the development of the bomb which vaporized Hiroshima and Nagasaki. The act itself illustrates the widening gap between what Tillich called *techne* and what he called *scientia*. Tillich was one of those theologians "between the wars" who survived Nazi Germany by fleeing to the United States.

Tillich writes, "Means become ends simply because they are possible ... the problem comes into the open if, after the satisfaction of basic needs, new needs are endlessly engendered in order to be satisfied. Technical possibility becomes social and individual temptation ... The production of means – of gadgets[90] – becomes an end in itself"[91]. Speaking of what was once *theoria* but is now practical knowledge, "man introduces another conflict, that between the intensification of potentialities and the unbalancing of the structure of smaller or larger parts of the universe. Here technical sublimation of matter includes its profanization. Such ambiguities lie behind the anxiety of myth-creating mankind about man's overstepping his limits and the anxiety of recent scientists about the same problem: a taboo is broken."[92]

The Doomsday Clock is now set at 90 minutes to midnight.[93] In the new language of science, the eternal motto is "If we CAN do it,

---

a sense of mission and a realization that they had the means to change history. But could they solve the technical problems before the Germans?"

90 Bird and Sherwin, ibid., p 287: "By late 1944, a number of scientists at Los Alamos began to voice their growing ethical qualms about the continued development of the 'gadget' ... the chief of the lab's experimental physics division ... put up notices all over the lab announcing a public meeting to discuss 'The Impact of the Gadget on Civilization.'"

91 Paul Tillich, *Systematic Theology, Volume Three: Life and the Spirit, History and the Kingdom of God* (Chicago: University of Chicago Press, 1963), pp. 62, 74.

92 Tillich, Volume Three, pp. 90-91.

93 Doomsday Clock – https://en.m.wikipedia.org_doonsdayclock : "The Doomsday Clock is a symbol that represents the likelihood of a human-made global catastrophe, in the opinion of the members of the Bulletin of the Atomic Scientists. Maintained since 1947, the clock is a metaphor for threats to humanity from unchecked scientific and technological advances ... the clock's original setting was seven minutes to midnight ... The farthest

we SHOULD." It's a bit of a twist on the old empirical "Is-Ought Problem":[94] it resolves the quandary between what is and what ought to be by simply equating possibility with the demand to know. Again, the Satisfaction Curve comes into play, not leastwise because someone has to pay for the inventing.

If you think something OUGHT to be, then it CAN be: Once it transcends the ethical it becomes part of the given and natural. Pragmatism has become the Mark of the Beast. So far it's an inner mark that qualifies and stimulates the cultural thought processes only, but, all things being equal, it has a life of its own and WILL match the catastrophic nature of actual historical things in the present moment eventually. 90 seconds is an absolutely brief moment of time in the general scheme of history: Who knows how much real time it will take to translate the metaphor into fact.[95]

Tillich never did find an intellectual and theological solution to the issues he raised in his own theology. The best he could do was invent a theological/historical/subjective construct called the Eternal Now. "Finite being," he wrote, "is a question mark. It asks the question of the 'eternal now' in which the temporal and the spatial are simultaneously accepted and overcome."[96] All modern Christians want to be overcomers, but how does this stuff play out in the postmodern world?[97]

---

time from midnight was 17 minutes in 1991, and the nearest is 90 seconds, set on January 24, 2023"; last edited 12 February 2034, accessed 16 Feb 23

94 Is-ought – https://www.academy4sc.org_isoughtgapfromfactstoval-ues : "The is-ought gap is a fallacy that attempts to make conclusions about the way things should be based on the evidence about the way things are ... there is no theoretical connection between facts about the world ethical facts. Appealing to nature in moral and political arguments cannot bridge the is-ought gap"; accessed 16 Feb 23

95 See footnote 93.

96 Paul Tillich, Systematic Theology, *Volume One: Reason and Revelation; Being and God* (Chicago: The University of Chicago Press, 1951), p. 209: "It asks the question of the 'ground of being' in which the causal and the substantial are simultaneously confirmed and negated."

97 John 16:33: "I have told you these things so that in Me you may have peace. In the world you will have tribulation. But be of good cheer. I have overcome the world."

What happens when we truly "open our senses five"? What are we actually overcoming?

When I look out my window, many sights to see, and when I look in my window, so many different people to be that it's strange; sure is strange ... must be the season of the witch.[98]

THE SUBJECT-OBJECT DUALITY is a remnant of a theory that must be described as "closed." A closed system is one that has boundaries of application. A closed theory is one that accounts for truth and falsehood within the bounds of a closed system. The classic comparison between a closed theory and an open theory is the one between Newton's theory and Einstein's theory.

Newton's theory of motion works quite well in a closed system like the surface of planet earth, but it does not work at all in an open system like "everything." Gravity takes on a much different shape, form and causal effect in Einstein's Theory of Relativity: The apple doesn't "fall down." In fact, nothing "falls" at all.

The key to the strange new questions raised by the Theory of Relativity and Quantum Theory is the idea of causality. Causality is the realm of how things happen the way they happen when they happen. In a closed system of causality, I trip you, you fall down, and you break your nose. You blame me for your broken nose. In a courtroom, the idea of causality is expanded. Did I cause you to break your nose? In terms of the universe as a whole, we don't really know what caused you to break your nose. I suppose we can blame everything on the Big Bang, but in the universe there are all kinds of broken noses, many of which do not involve anything or anyone falling down.

Gertrude Stein said, "A rose is a rose is a rose," and I suppose that a nose is a nose is a nose. Nevertheless, neither roses nor noses exist in the blackness of outer space, except, perhaps by metaphor or sealed in a climate-controlled space capsule.

---

98 Donovan Leitch, *Season of the Witch*, 1966

As our previously cited source tells us, "Were it not from the important fact that systems, finite in extent and in the number of constituent particles, are often known to have a fate which is independent of the rest of the universe, causality would be a futile subject. The availability of 'closed systems' is a precondition for causality to be meaningful ... Completely closed systems, however, are never found in nature and therefore display the 'fictive' character of idealizations ... All systems to which analysis can be applied are idealizations."[99]

Cause and effect have changed a lot since the days of Aristotle and Aquinas. Yet every theory regarding how things work relies on some sense of cause and effect. This includes political theories and psychological theories. The analytic problem for all theories in the postmodern world is that any theory which involves a definitive statement of cause and effect must be a closed theory, a theory with boundaries. When these boundaries are not clearly languaged, the theory becomes weird.

The scientific theories mentioned above are akin to the perceptual theory that Kierkegaard presented rhetorically in the 19th century, that Truth is Subjectivity. In his historical context, he was arguing against Hegel's allegedly objective theory of the State, an idealization in terms of modern physical theories. As an idealization, it must have a set of assumed boundaries, but those boundaries are not clear at all. When it comes to the elimination or ignoring of boundaries altogether, the inevitable result is the more postmodern political idealizations such as Fascism, Naziism, and Marxist-Leninism.

The old boundary that is most vulnerable to violation is the boundary between subject and object. This boundary is, in effect, the window through which we observe what we have become accustomed to calling "reality." A well-constructed window, one might surmise, keeps the weather out and the controlled temperature in. This is why we weatherize our windows and doors to keep out the heat of summer and the cold of winter. Similarly, our windows through which we observe this reality, as the mathematical physicists have realized, reveal very different characteristics of what we previously called the Real when the window

99 Margenau, ibid., pp. 388, 389

itself is removed, leaving only an open space. This is when the "weather" comes inside.

We started out this discussion, analysis, or perception, with a movie quote, "The boundary has been moved." When you remove the protective glass from your window, the boundary is not only moved: It becomes something entirely different than what it once was. You can even crawl through it.

The scientist puts it like this, "The act of reification of data involves more than integrations: it involves construction. Construction in accordance with rules. Objectivity emerges as a result of this procedure; to assert objectivity is our way of acknowledging the success of the transition from data to the rational wholeness of constructed objects ... objectivity, if it attaches to experience, is brought into the scene during our passage from the immediately given to what may here loosely be called concepts or ideas."[100] This is a very different understanding of objectivity than was the old understanding that said, "There is something out there."

Science is also not saying that there is nothing "out there," neither is it saying that "things" don't exist or that all concepts are futile. What we CAN say is that when we marry Kierkegaard's concept of Subjectivity with the physicists' concept of objectivity, we can say, "If there were no Subjectivity, there would also be not objectivity." We cannot say that there would not be an "objective" universe in the closed theoretical sense, but we need to be sure that we are defining the boundaries of our closed theory.

WE are the boundary. In order to assert with certainty that there is an "objective" universe which consists of valid truths which aren't subject to any subjective distortion or confusion, we ourselves have to cross the boundary line, not just in concept and idea, but as a self in its wholeness. No one can do this, mainly because even if one did no one could follow. Subjectivity would not allow such a discipling of others. If the crossing-over cannot be language without doing damage to the language of subjectivity and objectivity, then that language is meaningless.

100   Margenau, ibid., p 60.

All of our psychological and emotional and rational bearings are realized within the boundary between the subjective world and the objective world. When that boundary fades even just a little bit, we lose our bearings. We become "insane." We can even become a danger to society.

The discoveries of the late 19th century, discoveries that now shape our understanding of the "real," have caused humanity as a whole to lose its bearings on multiple levels of existence. It's this loss of a reliable sense of self-orientation that is the general cause of the general identity crisis through which individuals, governments, and nations are moving. In other words, as the song goes, "all the children are insane."[101] The corollary to this disturbing lyric is another lyric, "They're locking them up today. They're throwing away the key. I wonder who it'll be tomorrow, you or me ... We're all normal and we want our freedom, freedom, freedom."[102]

The songster here also sings, "I'll feel much better on the other side." We tried to make the suicidal feelings go away in the 1960s, but they linger on. As they become reified on the international scene once again, society itself begins to wonder what exactly IS the "other side." The analytic opposite to Subjectivity is Objectivity; the converse is Anti-Subjectivity.

---

101 *The End*, The Doors, 1966
102 *The Red Telephone*, Love (Arthur Lee), 1967

Chapter Three: I THINK, THEREFORE, I VANISH

We have had to change our ideas about space and time ... Just as one cannot talk about events in the universe without the notions of space and time, so in general relativity it became meaningless to talk about space and time outside the limits of the universe ... The old idea of an essentially unchanging universe that could have existed, and could continue to exist, forever was replaced by the notion of a dynamic, expanding universe that seemed to have begun a finite time ago, and that might end at a finite time in the future.[103]

IN THE BIBLE, Jesus is met by "two men possessed with demons." They come out of the tombs. They cry out, "What have we to do with You, Jesus, Son of God?" They fiercely reject the idea that their time has come. Indeed, their time has not yet come. When they saw Jesus, they thought that it had.[104]

The Greek idiom here is interesting. It reads, *Ti hehmin kai soi*, or "what to us and to you?" The demons are not to meet their destiny until the end of the world, but Jesus, who IS their destiny, is standing right in front of them. So it is with all of us, but the transformation of the situation here for the 21st century happens when we substitute the universe and ourselves for Jesus and the demons: What to us and to you?

We like to say things about the Universe, even to honor the universe by saying things like "this particular coincidence feels like a message ... the universe knows plenty of ways to get your attention."[105] This kind of language emerges from the fermenting thoughts, hopes and desires of all the sources cited in the preceding conversation and more. In a way, it is

---

103   Stephen Hawking, *A Brief History of Time* (New York: Bantam Books, 2017), pp. 18, 34, 35
104   Matthew 8:28-29
105   Barrie Davenport, *Live Bold & Bloom*, December 2, 2022 – https://www.theboldandbloom.com_21signstheuniverseistryingtotellyousomething ; accessed 17 Feb 23

paradigmatic of the way we customarily language our sense of purpose or intuition or insight in the America of the 21st century.

The ubiquitous spiritual habit of pre-Western Civilization, the one between Augustine and Luther, for over a thousand years was to pray to God. Variations of that realm of piety are many but not infinitely so. In the end, Jesus is the focus of and formula for our prayers, because He has been understood to be our gateway to God. God was understood to be the God of the Jews who was the same as the God and Father of Jesus. The God of the Jews was also the God of the Universe. With the negligence of the idea of Gode and the piety of Judeo-Christian Civilization comes the idea that if we pray at all we pray to the Universe as such.

One of the presenting aspects of modern piety, especially liberal Christian piety, is the renunciation of the concept of a personal God. When we ask the Personal God, "What to you and me?" He has plenty of answers. He is not a demon who has nothing in common with us, physically, morally, or metaphysically.[106] However, when we ask the Universe, "What to you and me", the universe acts like a cipher or a Greek oracle: Things are said that in and of themselves have no meaning at all, and this demon wants to convince us that we have everything in common with it.

The language of salvation as Western Civilization has inherited it belongs to a closed theory: There are limits and boundaries, there is the individual and there is the universal, and so forth. It is a well-ordered world, or set, as the mathematicians might say. The language of salvation as Western Civilization has analyzed it belongs to an open universe. The game has no boundaries, and there are no fixed rules and the playing pieces morph constantly.

We don't know whether the Universe is a demon, or demonic, or whether it is angelic, or positive in its intentions. As far as we call tell by means of our scientific methodology, the Universe has no intentions.

---

106   Luke 18:19: "Jesus said to (the rich ruler), 'Why do you call Me good? No one is good, except God alone.'"

Whether we interpret these intentions as being good intentions or bad intentions affects the resulting judgments we make regarding Good and Evil.

Descartes, the originator of our civilizational dilemma, proposed the possibility that a "malignant demon who at once is exceedingly potent and deceitful, has employed all his artifice to deceive me."[107] The demon presents "a complete illusion of an external world."[108] Descartes' task, in his own terms, was to reconnect the objective world with the subjective world. He finds a way to avoid the pitfalls of believing what this evil demon is telling him, primarily by believing that he "in truth ... have no ground for believing Deity is deceitful."[109]

It has been, and ought to be noted, that Descartes has changed the language game, here. In the Bible, a demon is a distinct entity, although knowledge of what kind of entity it IS is lacking. The entity is something that can be eliminated BECAUSE it is an entity. It can be eliminated, however, not by force of power but by force of authority.[110] Descartes malignant demon is not an entity, it is a concept, a sub-category of a more general theory of knowledge. This malignant demon cannot be "cast out" because it is neither inside nor outside, and because it isn't a "thing." However, the demon can be dealt with over time because of Deity.

You can see the flavor of the Biblical teaching in Descartes' rearranging of the language. Eventually, however, what you cannot see is the Deity, or God. God, too, becomes a concept, and it is Descartes' faith in thinking that leads him to believe that there is a deity. This j'adoube in his intellectual language game allows him to deceive the reader into going along with the new language game without even noticing. The

---

107 Rene' Descartes, *Selected Writings: Meditation One* (1641) (London: The Collector's Library of Essential Thinkers, 2004), p. 121.
108 Malicious demon – https://en.m.wikipedia.org_evildemon ; last edited 13 November 2022, accessed 17 Feb 23
109 Descartes, *Writings: Meditation Three*, p.137.
110 Mark 1:27: "They were all amazed, so that they questioned among themselves, 'What is this? What new teaching is this? With authority He commands even the unclean spirits, and they obey Him."

irony is that, in the long run, Descartes rational, or rationalized, gambits eliminate the language of the Bible altogether.

There seems to be a proof of the existence of God in his writings, one that has been much quoted and analyzed. It's a proof that might fool a non-philosophical bishop into thinking that Descartes still believes in God, but it's also a way for Descartes to honestly say that he doesn't really believe in God but that he dearly wants to Church authorities to think that he still believes in God.

We've already examined Descartes' transferring of heaven to the realm of the human mind. He did find it adventitious to leave Paris for a sojourn in Leiden and finally to Sweden where he died. "Tensions" had "mounted as a result of the public exchange and Descartes felt his way of life in the Netherlands to be threatened."[111] Causality has different ways of expressing itself, even in the life of someone who is attempting to analyze it.

Insofar as Descartes had attempted to understand how the mind and the body are connected, he failed. Subsequent Western philosophers attempted to redeem this failure, in a long and characteristic attempt to reconcile subjectivity with objectivity. It failed, too. In effect, the postmodern (if Descartes is modern) solution has been to break the glass window rather than to try to understand how you can see through it.

It's because of this breaking of the window that the Universe has lately come flooding into the soul in ways that had never been conceived as possible before. Without God to close the floodgates, the soul is beginning to drown. Even the "fountains of the great deep" are bursting open.[112]

---

111   Descartes – https://www.plato.stanford.edu_descartesli-feandworks ; first published Mon Apr 9, 2001; substantive revision Fri Sep 21, 2018, accessed 17 Feb 23.
112   Genesis 7:11

I saw the 'potamus take wing ascending from the damp savannas, and quiring angels round him sing the praise of God, in loud hosannas ... He shall be washed whiter as snow, by all the martyr'd virgins kist, while the True Church remains below wrapt in the old miasmal mist.[113]

ONE OF THE MOST ubiquitous cultural truisms in Western society is the saying, "History repeats itself." If so, we should have a pretty good notion of how history will go in the future. But we don't. Human foolishness repeats itself in many ways, but that relentless anthropological phenomenon isn't necessarily connected to what we call "history." History is our corporate self-awareness attempting to justify itself.

Our heroes are those who rise above history and then make it their own. If your name ends up in a book claiming to reveal how the machinery of history works, you have become a maker of history. You are an alchemist of time, one who turns old lead into new gold . . . or perhaps one who squanders all the gold. Winston Churchill once said, "Those that fail to learn from history are doomed to repeat it,"[114] but history is what those who didn't fail say that it was.

The famous historian Barbara Tuchman, already referenced earlier, said, "A phenomenon noticeable throughout history regardless of place or period is the pursuit of governments of policies contrary to their own interests."[115] This descriptive judgment is much more appropriate to the Hegelian concept of the State as "the divine idea as it exists on earth."[116] The phenomenon persists so demonstrably that one begins wo wonder what Hegel's idealism is really all about.

If the Divine Idea as it exists on earth can pursue a policy contrary to its own idealizing principles, i.e., its ideology, then the Divine is known only by means of its own intrinsic contradictions. In this case, true

---

113   T. S. Eliot, *The Wasteland and Other Poems: The Hippopotamus* (New York: Barnes & Noble Classics, 2005; original 1919), p. 50

114   Churchill – https://www.medicalconfidence.com thosethatfailtolearnfromhistoryaredoomedtorepeatitwinstonchurchill ; posted May 15, 2020, accessed 18 Feb 23

115   Barbara W. Tuchman, *The March of Folly: From Troy to Vietnam* (New York: Ballantine Books, 1984), p. 4

116   See footnote 34

foolishness consists of following the stated ideology of the State as if it was truly the Divine Idea. One must become accustomed to accepting the stark and often blatant contradictions as being, in effect, continuities that bind the soul, or psyche, to the State.

The psychological defense mechanism against the obviousness of the modern state's inherent foolishness is the belief that things historical are moving inexorably toward a resolution of those contradictions which will happen sometime in the foreseeable-in-theory future. This is where Tillich's picture of the gap between *techne* and *scientia*, or *theoria*, becomes virtually impossible to ignore. Technology provides the power, the authority, and the compelling finality of the Hegelian dialectic in the actions of states vying for the privilege of being identified as the Divine Idea on earth.

Elan Vital[117] died in the Battles of the Frontiers in 1914.[118] The hoped to be victorious advance of French troops into Germany became a slaughterhouse without benefit of profit. As the military sage once said, "Generals always fight the last war." Moral was a deciding factor in the Napoleonic Wars 100 years prior to the Great War,[119] but technology had transformed that key factor for victory into one of simply surviving on the battlefield. Moral became the purview of the generals and politicians after the first deluge of optimism had soaked the ground with blood.

117 Elan Vital – https://en.m.wikipedia.org_elanvital : "A term coined by French philosopher Henri Bergson in his 1907 book Creative Evolution, in which he addressed the question of self-organisation and spontaneous morphogenesis of things in an increasingly complex manner… The French army incorporated the doctrine … into its thinking during the leadup to the First World War by arguing that the spirit of individual soldiers was more important for victory than weapons"; last edited 28 December 2022, accessed 18 Feb 23.
118 Adrian Gilbert, *Encyclopedia Britannica*, Apr 19, 2017 – https://www.britannica.com_battleofthefrontiers : "(August 4, 1914-September 6, 1914) The commanders of the German and French armies had believed that the opening encounters of World War I would decide its fate. Both sides attacked with ruthless intensity, but French tactical ineptitude – massed infantry attacks against artillery and machine guns – nearly brought disaster to France"; last revised Jul 28, 2022, accessed 18 Feb 23
119 Napoleon – https://www.militaryhistorynow.com_thequotablebonaparte-nineofnapoleonsmostmemorablequipsexplained : "In war, moral power is to physical as three parts out of four"; published 2014, accessed 18 Feb 23

The blood sacrifice of World War I and the total unreality of the blood sacrifice of World War II has been authoritative enough to overshadow, or at least match, the hold that Jesus' blood sacrifice had on Western Civilization from its inception. Although Christianity was able to maintain its unitary hold on the moral and spiritual structures of this civilization until the end, in the end its grasp was loosened.

By the early 20th century, the term "unitary" as it applies to religion could only have been a variation of *theoria* detached from *praxis*, but it still evoked a kind of hope that things will someday work out. Clearly, it would take even more intense application of technological expertise to return Western Civilization to its original moral roots. The effort continues, but only as an after flash in the eyes of the Divine Idea after it has observed itself in the aura of atomic explosions.

In the "old language" of the New Testament, the word praxis meant "work." This kind of work could be the work of a human being or the work of God. The book Acts of the Apostles, is a revealing of how the acts of God, in the Spirit, coincide with the acts of the Apostles. In the Gospel according to Matthew, we read, "For the Son of Man shall come with His angels in the glory of His Father, and then He will repay every man according to his works (*praxin/praxis*)."[120] Works, or praxis, have to do with the End Times and the Last Judgment.

In Paul's Letter to the Colossians, we read, "Do not lie to one another, since you have put off the old nature with its deeds (*praxesin/praxis*)."[121] The Last Judgment is already accomplished in the putting off of the Old Nature, but the eventual act of judging, of concluding the moral story itself, has to do not with the deeds or works, but by how much the old nature has been retained in defiance or ignorance of the New.

Language changes along with everything else. It's not so clear whether everything else changes so that language must change or that language changes such that everything else takes on new appearances. To date, the language philosophers haven't unraveled that puzzle. What

120   Matthew 16:27
121   Colossians 3:9

we do know, because we are always caught up in it, is that the language we speak changes with the reality we think we know. Like Jesus, we are caught up in the clouds when we confess His name and are baptized,[122] but we only approach His throne in the flow of eons and remain in our own clouds of unknowing.

The word *praxis*, and along with it its meaning within a language game, became "practice" in English. I'll let the philologists fill in the factual and historical gaps in this analysis, but the word "pragmatic" also comes from the root *praxis*. *Pragmatohn* (*pragma*) were "those things which are most surely believed among us,"[123] but as we move through time into the 21st century, *pragma* involves computers and computer systems.[124] We live, as was said earlier, in a pragmatic Nation, and technology continues to widen the gap between Old Knowledge and New Knowledge.

In its long attempt to objectify the universe so that it could be more easily controlled or managed, Western Civilization has actually begun to merge its knowledge systems with the mystical expectations of old. Detached from the moral authority of the Original God and obsessed with the idea of cancelling the very idea of "God" from its vocabulary, the civilization thought it had progressed beyond archaic theology into a new realm of enlightened advantage over the created world.

Augustine's City of God was not so much "brought down to earth" as it was flung into space, freed from the centripetal tether that had kept the old priesthood from dying in the inner sanctuaries of Church authority. There are still a few ghosts left but it's only a matter of time until the ghosters get ghosted. The City of Man neither needs nor wants God, although the idea of the Divine is still very helpful. The Saint adorned

---

122   Acts 1:9
123   Luke 1:1
124   Pragma Systems – https://www.pragmasys.com_pragmasecure-factorswinsbangladeshsnationalclouddeployment : "More than 5000 companies around the world use Pragma Systems software: SSH Server, Telnet Server, secure file transfer (SFTP), SSH remote systems management and handheld client networks that meet their enterprise requirements and regulatory guidelines"; accessed 18 Feb 23.

the Empty Tomb with beautiful blooms of resurrection morality, but the blossoms have withered now that the Great War has been won.[125]

Was that Great War *praxis* or *Praxis*? History defeats itself.

Types and shadows have their ending. For the newer rite is here; faith, our outward sense befriending, makes out inward vision clear.[126]

WHEN *praxis* **COINCIDES** with *Praxis*, the moment is sacramental. One source describes a sacrament as "a religious ceremony or ritual regarding as imparting divine grace, such as baptism, the Eucharist and (in the Roman Catholic and many Orthodox Churches) penance and the anointing of the sick."[127] The Episcopal BCP defines the sacraments as "outward and visible signs of inward and spiritual grace, given by Christ as sure and certain means by which we receive that grace."[128]

Regarding the efficacy, or the power and authority, of the sacraments, "The merit and prayer of the just soul obtain the gifts of God *ex opere operantis*, by reason of the faith, piety, and charity of him who merits, but the sacraments produce grace *ex opere operato* in those who do not place an obstacle to it ... by themselves they produce grace from the fact that they were instituted by God to apply the merits of the Savior to us."[129] To be sure, for a sacrament of this type to be a sacrament, it must be administered by a sacramental person, unless it is the initial sacrament of baptism.

The sacramental system of salvation was the mainstay of Western Civilization even through the tumultuous years of the Reformation. It

---

125   See footnote 51
126   Thomas Aquinas (1225-1274), *Now My Tongue*, hymn– https://www.hymnary.org_nowmytonguethemysterytelling ; referenced 4 Feb 23
127   Sacrament – https://www.languages.oup.com_sacrament ; accessed 16 Feb 23
128   *The Book of Common Prayer and Administration of the Sacraments and Other Rites and Ceremonies of the Church*, according to the use of The Episcopal Church, Church Hymnal Corporation, 1979
129   Fr. Reginald Garrigou-Lagrange, O.P., *The Three Ages of the Interior Life: Prelude of Eternal Life* (Rockford, IL: Tan Books and Publishers, Inc., 1947), p. 141

was finally dismantled as a cultural given by the new reformers of the European Enlightenment. Since the theology of the sacraments could be construed as being neither empirical nor rational, that was the end of the sacramental worldview. Questions of transubstantiation[130] and consubstantiation,[131] the conventional boundary marker between Roman Catholic sacramentalism and early Protestant sacramentalism, became as archaic as alchemy.

In modern times, after the fashion of Hege's philosophy, the State becomes the ultimate sacrament. Whatever transubstantiation or consubstantiation might be construed to be taking place, it would be taking place within the soul of the citizen in order to perfect that one as a perfect citizen of a perfect State. In other words, the perfect citizen is one with the perfect State, after the fashion and pattern of the much older beliefs of the mystics. The State is Christ and we are its body and blood. Cancel "Christ" and replace it with "Savior, Lord, and King."

In the postmodern era, the human being is the ultimate sacrament, and action performed by a human being or humans in consort is a sacramental rite. The "newer rite" is, indeed, here. It just doesn't look anything like even the first religious humanists could have imagined. My truth is my truth, your truth is your truth, and we watch each other slowly, but rapidly gaining speed, drift away from one another. We are the expanding universe.[132]

---

130   Transubstantiation – https://www.languages.oup.com_transubstantiation : "The conversion of the substance of the Eucharistic elements into the body and blood of Christ at consecration, only the appearances of bread and wine still remaining"; accessed 19 Feb 23

131   Consubstantiation – https://www.languages.oup.com_consubstantiation : "Especially in Lutheran belief, that the substance of the bread and wine coexists with the body and blood of Christ in the Eucharist"; accessed 19 Feb 23

132   Alisa Harvey, Charles Q. Choi, *Space, The Evolution and Content of Our Ballooning Universe* – https://www.space.com_ourexpandinguniverseagehistory&otherfacts : "The universe did not expand into space, as space did not exist before the universe, according to NASA. Instead, it is better to think of the Big Bang as the simultaneous appearance of space everywhere in the universe. The universe has not expanded from any one spot since the Big Bang – rather, space itself has been stretching, and carrying matter with it"; last updated March 15, 2022, accessed 16 Feb 23.

When everything is sacramental, can anything be sacramental?

Paul Tillich was the last of the comprehensive dialectical theologians. His attempt to synthesize every aspect of theology and philosophy since Plato is a magnificent product of a heroic intellect. There's something of the mystical, the Hegelian, the Thomistic, the sacramental, the historical, the psychological, the anthropological and so forth in his thinking, and if he could have gone into prescriptive mode, we may have been able to benefit culturally and religiously from it . . . but there likely is no prescriptive mode for these things.

Tillich writes, for instance, regarding postmodern Protestant theology, "Classical orthodoxy established a kind of 'sacramentalism of the pure doctrine.' Under the title 'obedience to the word of God,' obedience was asked to the letter of the Bible, and, since the meaning of the Bible is not obvious, obedience to a special interpretation of the Bible by a special, historically dated theology was demanded (and is demanded in present-day fundamentalism). In many cases, especially a period in which critical consciousness has developed, this led to an intellectual asceticism or to the sacrifice of man's critical power. This demand is analogous to that made in monastic or Puritan asceticism, where all the vital powers are sacrificed."[133]

Tillich also grappled with the linguistic and theo-philosophical difference between a "sign" and a "symbol." The religious stuff doesn't "point to" anything beyond it, it becomes a "stand-in," venerated almost in the way the ancient gods were, something that has power in and of itself. Without getting into the comprehension of these fine-tuned differences which would require several more volumes of written density, one can trace the line of thinking that leads to this distinction all the way back to Augustine and its effect on how we use our own language as expressed in theories such as that of Wittgenstein.

For Augustine, language as such "points to" a reality beyond the words. For Wittgenstein, words aren't even symbols: They don't

---

[133] Paul Tillich, Systematic Theology, Volume Two: Existence and the Christ (Chicago: The University of Chicago Press, 1957), pp. 84-85.

"stand-in" for things. They convey meaning in the context of a mutually understood, learned, and accepted language game.[134] In a sense, the "mutual" aspect of the language isn't susceptible to analysis within the language itself. The analysis accompanies the speaking, thinking, and writing that is the expression of the language.

This process can be a bit dizzying at first. We have either learned, come to understand, and accepted our way of communicating in a common manner, or we haven't. Community and language exist together, and they cannot be separated without doing damage to one or the other. These differences in expression can seem tedious to the disinterested, but they have their place in the extended language game of any given church sect or denomination. For instance, the bread and the wine as "things" may be referred to as "elements," "tokens," "emblems," or other designations. These words aren't simply names for the "same thing." Within the doctrinal and pietistic language game of the community, they are decidedly NOT the "same things."

This "languaging" of things is the Achilles Heel of all attempts to create or sanctify a universal religion from the words and ideas of all religions. The Comparative Religions Fallacy assumes that the religious WORDS of each religion "point to" the same transcendent, mental, or otherwise invisible realities. Does the Buddhist word "nirvana" mean the same thing as the Christian word "heaven." To even begin to be able to answer a question like this, you must investigate everything else the Buddha and the Christ said as well as how people have understood what they said in community as well as what the psychology of belief is in Buddhism and Christianity.

To understand a word as it is used in religion-talk, you must swim in the sea of its language. If you can learn how to stay afloat, you have a fighting chance of communicating your experience to someone who is an Olympic swimmer in it. If not, you drown. Better to stay on the shoreline and share the little things, like the sand between your toes and the salt air stimulating your sense of smell. The psychological realm might be the appropriate common ground for conversation, involving

---

[134] Wittgenstein, *Investigations*, pp. 5-6.

as it does the emotions and hopes and dreams, but it also truncates the original assumptions of religion itself, that there is a transcendent reality into which we can arise.[135]

The only direct way to rise together into the sea of language above the *Stereoma*,[136] that dividing line or boundary between the waters above and the waters below, is by way of the mystical. You must transcend words altogether. Yet even so, when you try to understand that you do indeed understand each other, you must resort to words in a language. If you pursue that kind of language far enough without getting totally frustrated, enraged, or utterly confused or self-deceived, you will end up merely inventing your own language and community.

If the realm of the mystical isn't religious or spiritual, then it can be psychological. In this case, we may be licensed to talk about theological sublimation. The idea of theological sublimation leads directly to the idea of psychological sublimation. Sublimation in the psyche is "a defense mechanism in which unacceptable sexual or aggressive drives are unconsciously channeled into socially acceptable modes of expression and redirected into new, learned behaviors, which indirectly provide some satisfaction for the original drives."[137] When everything is Mind instead of Spirit, everything theological must be sublimated into the stratospheric reaches of the human intellect and emotions.

The mix-and-match, oceanic plethora of language games and their words is one of the defining characteristics of the postmodern world. The crux of the communication and fellowship matter is in the impact point between competing or entirely disparate languages. The language of mathematical physics does not easily correlate with the language of eating at a lunch counter. It can be done, but not without the invention of a higher meta-language which, in that case, is a new language. The mathematical language that fixes the earth as a body orbiting around the

135   AUTHOR'S NOTE: Appreciation to thinkers and writers like D. T. Suzuki, Carl Jung, and Eugen Herrigel, and Fritjof Capra.
136   Genesis 1:6-8: "So the evening and the morning were the second day."
137   Kendra Cherry, reviewed by Amy Morin, LCSW, *Verywellmind* – https://www.verywellmind.com whatissub,limationinpsychology ; updated on December 14, 2022, accessed 16 Feb 23

sun can also be expressed as the sun orbiting around the earth, or the entire universe orbiting around you or me.[138]

In the domain of the moral, the word "good" can take on meaning in a plethora of language games. Rather than the singular and indivisible Good of G. E. Moore,[139] everything "good" is now matter of sublimation. Truth is hidden in ultimate, but infinite, subjectivity. When we use language to communicate this hiddenness between and among ourselves, there is no predicting whether the Truth will reveal itself or become even more elusive. The Truth moves around while we speak.

The types are fluid, and the shadows increase. We have come a long way since Sigmund Freud said, "Sometimes a cigar is just a cigar."[140]

From the Greeks we have inherited a preoccupation for a sort of 'principle of being,' for some ultimate reality discoverable in, through, or beyond sensory experience but not identical with it ... There is this inherent diffuseness in all parts of the immediately given, and it is important that this be clearly recognized ... it comes about that historical reality, as it moves back into the past of our own experience, merges with physical reality and eliminates the need for a distinction.[141]

BEING MEETS IDENTITY in the human soul. The human soul IS the meeting place between Being and Identity. The language of religion is the language of this inner synagogue of Being and Identity. The language of the State is the language of proprietorship when both synagogue and Areopagus[142] become possessions of the whole. The Areopagus is language itself. The synagogue is where the languages gather.

---

138   See Morris Kline, *Mathematics: The Loss of Certainty*, 1982
139   G. E. Moore, *Principia Ethica* (Mineola, NY: Dover Publications, Inc., 2004; original 1903), p. 7: "'Good' is a simple notion, just as 'yellow' is a simple notion ... just as you cannot, by any manner or means, explain to any one who does not already know it, what yellow is, so you cannot explain what good is."
140   Freud cigar – https://www.medium.com_some-timesacigarisjustacigar ; accessed 19 Feb 23
141   Margenau, ibid. pp. 3, 56, 452
142   Acts 17:16-34

According to our philosophers, the immediately given is provided by, and only by, the five senses: Sight, hearing, touch, smell, and taste. My chemistry teacher in high school used to say: "If you don't know what it is, give it the taste test." I still wonder how many of my classmates burned their tongues off trying to follow his lead. I don't know what his point was, but when the five senses fail, the empiricist has no recourse. Whatever IT is, IT must be susceptible to the sight-hearing-touch-smell-taste test.

Over the centuries, especially in the 20th century, the parameters of the sight-hearing-touch-smell-taste test have been topologically[143] modified. The shape of sensation is not what it used to be. The immediately given has become diffuse. What you are experiencing by means of your senses isn't what you thought you were experiencing.

Some experts include the brain, or some aspect of cognition, as a sixth sense. This maneuver amounts to a kind of borderline mysticism, a mysticism which is, however, entirely appropriate to the surviving modern thought forms of the postmodern world. The mystic hasn't merged with the All, so far, but they are certainly trying. To complicate matters, the ALL has topologically morphed as well.

Other sources equate the Sixth Sense with the ability to see dead people.[144] Critics of Western Civilization as it has topologically morphed into postmodern American culture reduce all Western philosophy to a practice of seeing and hearing only dead white males.[145] This, too, a

---

143   Eric W. Weisstein – https://www.mathworld.wokfram.com_topology : "The mathematical study of the properties that are preserved through deformations, twistings and stretchings of objects. Tearing ... is not allowed. A circle is topologically equivalent to an ellipse ... the set of all possible positions of the hour hand of a clock is topologically equivalent to a circle ... What is a topologist? Someone who cannot distinguish between a doughnut and a coffee cup"; last updated Feb 14, 2023, accessed 19 Feb 23.
144   The Sixth Sense, *Buena Vista Pictures Distribution*, 1999.
145   Dead white males – https://www.dictionary.com_deadwhitemale : "one of a group of white male writers scientists, or other historical figures whose works have traditionally dominated the field or been a disproportionate part of school curriculum in the West"; accessed 19 Feb 23

manifestation of postmodern mysticism. Cognition itself is undergoing topological deformation.

Language, community, religion, identity and Being as such go together; they constitute a synagogue of meaning. Not one of these phenomena can be realized independently. They are as intertwined as are the five senses. If you remove one, the others become deformed.

These five primary expressions of existence shape and mold the human soul. Each in their turn is shaped and molded by the human soul. There is no such phenomenon as a soul without expression. There can be a soul with deformed expressions.

The sixth expression, the one that governs the five like the brain oversees the five senses, can be either God or the State. The mystical impulse which is the driving force of the human will toward self-transcendence, reaches upward to grasp either God or the State as its ultimate telos, or source of purpose.

All communities either strive toward the image of God or toward the image of the State. The ultimate community is approximated by such terms as "heaven," "brahmaloka,"[146] "paradise", and so forth. Tillich's "ultimate concern"[147] and Teilhard's "noosphere"[148] are examples of late rational attempts to qualify heaven as an existential potentiality.

146   Brahmaloka – https://www.britannica.com_brahma-loka : "In Hinduism and Buddhism, that part of the many-layered universe that is the realm of pious celestial spirits"; posted Jul 20, 1998, last fact-checked Nov 11, 2021, accessed 20 Feb 23

147   Tillich, volume one, p. 273-274: "When the invocation 'Almighty God' is seriously pronounced, a victory over the threat of nonbeing is experienced, and an ultimate, courageous affirmation of existence is expressed. Neither finitude nor anxiety disappears, but they are taken into infinity and courage. Only in this correlation should the symbol of omnipotence be interpreted. It is magic and an absurdity if it is understood as the quality of a highest being who is able to do what he wants."

148   Teilhard de Chardin, *The Phenomenon of Man* (New York: Harper & Brothers, 1959; original 1955), pp. 181, 182: "Psychogenesis has led to man. Now it effaces itself, relieved or absorbed by another and a higher function – the engendering and subsequent development of all the stages of the mind, in one word *noogenesis* ... Much more coherent and just as extensive as any preceding

The cognitively dissonant identification of God and State, Hegel's Divine Idea on earth, has roots reaching far back into human history, exemplified by the rule of Pharaohs and Shah-en-Shahs. The human and the divine have always been confused, conjoined, and/or co-mingled in the human mind and community. The only way to relieve the dissonance is to choose one manifestation of the divine over the other.

Rudolf Otto, characterized previously as the Last Western Mystic, invented the term "numinous" to displace the older tern "divine." He writes, "when this moment or element first emerges and begins its long development, all those expressions (qadosh, hagios, sacer, &etc) mean beyond all question something quite other than 'the good' ... it is worth while ... to find a word to stand for this element in isolation, this 'extra' in the meaning of 'holy' above and beyond the meaning of goodness ... For this purpose I adopt a word coined from the Latin *numen*. Omen has given us 'ominous', and there is no reason why from numen we should not similarly form a word 'numinous' ... This mental state is perfectly *sui generis* and irreducible to any other; and therefore, like every absolute primary and elementary datum, while it admits of being discussed, it cannot be strictly defined."[149] Both Tillich and Teilhard way in significantly on Otto's modification of the language of holiness and divinity.

Whereas Moore characterized "Good" as an unanalyzable singularity in the vocabulary and meaning of ethics, it was Otto's intent to go beyond ethics and morality into what would once have been called metaphysics. The attempt to restrain the divine from entering a kind of Teilhard-like noosphere is apparent in Otto's use of the term *datum*. The distinction between Subjectivity and the objectivity of mental data is obscure, and necessarily so because the distinction cannot truly be made.

To be clear, around the turn of the 19th-20th century, God, in Western thinking, became nestled in an upper room of the mind, safe and separate

---

layer, it is really a new layer, the 'thinking layer,' which, since its germination at the end of the Tertiary period, has spread over and above the world of plants and animals. In other words, outside and above the biosphere is the noosphere."
149   Otto, ibid., pp. 6-7

from all other empirical and psychological phenomenon, inviolate but also entirely incommunicable and noncommunicative. He was brought down that last minutiae of subjective space into a throne room cut off from both the subjective and objective worlds. God was not yet dead, but His tomb was being prepared.[150]

With God safely tucked away in the inaccessible reaches of the mind, history was free to have its way on the battlefields of Europe. It was time for the State to exert its divine destiny. God had been effectively demoted, His great and vast heart sealed in the walls of the human mind.

Like Poe's *Tell-Tale Heart*,[151] the beating of His heart can still be discerned, but only if you have a mind to listen very closely.

The duality of nature, Godly nature, human nature splits the soul; fully human, fully divine and divided. The great immortal soul. Split into pieces, whirling pieces, opposites attract; from the front, the side, the back, the mind itself attacks.[152]

BEREFT OF THE GOD who once reigned over it, the Christian mind resorts to suicidal thoughts and intentions. Western Civilization may think it can escape the bondage of transcendent authority by becoming

---

150   New World Encyclopedia contributors, "Death of God," *New World Encyclopedia*, https://www.newworldencyclopedia.org_deathofgod : "The theology of the Death of God, also known as Radical Theology, is a contemporary theological movement challenging traditional Judeo-Christian beliefs about God and asserting that human beings must take moral and spiritual responsibility for themselves. The term 'death of God' originated from the writings of Friedrich Nietzsche in the nineteenth century … Nietzsche's ideas were refined and carried forward in the philosophy of Martin Heidegger, and the theology of the Christian existentialists, who emphasized human moral and spiritual responsibility" … It first appears in his *The Gay Science*, but is found several times in Nietzsche's writings, most famously in his classic work, *Thus Spoke Zarathustra*"; accessed 21 Feb 23

151   Edgar Allen Poe, *The Tell-Tale Heart*, 1843 – https://www.poemmuseaum.org_thetell-taleheart : "True! – nervous – very, very dreadfully nervous I had been and am; but why *will* you say that I am mad? The disease had sharpened my senses – not destroyed – not dulled them. Above all was a sense of hearing acute. I heard all things in the heaven and in the earth. I heard many things in hell."

152   *Dime Store Mystery*, Lou Reed, 1989

a form of the Divine Idea after the fashion of Hegel's ideal State, but the Western mind is still "Christian," evolved, if you will, over centuries of interplay and mutual satisfaction among the five primary expressions. To finally "kill" God, the Western intellect must kill itself.

The capture of God by the human intellect is the final inquisition before adjudication and execution. It's the prelude to the Last Judgment. The zealots of Masada have nothing on the Western zealots of the postmodern world. The Sicarii of the Mind abound.

The mysticism of the Last Things is completely and utterly represented by the explosion of Oppie's "Gadget" in the deserts of New Mexico on July 16, 1945.[153] The explosive test was not for nothing named the "Trinity." That was the day St. Augustine's seminal contribution to Western Civilization was vaporized. That was the day Reason begat Chaos. It was the day Western Civilization came full circle, hungry, starving, bereft of the truly holy, to begin consuming itself. The Ouroboros of the alchemists is not "an emblem of wholeness or infinity":[154] It's a cosmic disappearing act.

According to the Greeks, the eternality of the soul is a given; according to Christian theology, eternity is a gift of God. When there is no God, the soul can't discern between Otto's *ominous* and his *numinous*. The one must do away with the other, else eternity become a jail cell from which there is no escape.

The reasonability of the Christian faith, discovered, invented, or otherwise constructed by St. Augustine from the evidence of the Bible and Greco-Roman civilization, has reached the boundaries of its own reasonableness. The Christian world, invented and constructed by human ingenuity, must turn against the Christian world, invented and constructed by human ingenuity. The one is the City of God; the other is the City of Man.

---

153   cf. footnote 89
154   Ouroboros – https://www.languages.oup.com uroboros ; accessed 20 Feb 23.

All the Augustinian constructs, or concepts, which have rigorously supported the Christian mind and society are up for an inquisition, adjudication, and execution. These include, but not exhaustively, such classic expressions as original sin, free will, predestination, just war theory, the sacramental, theodicy, heroic virtue, and so on.[155] They are caught between the final intellectual concepts of Good and Evil. They must decide, in a sense by themselves, which battlefront to join.

It is not simply ironic that the religion Augustine rejected, Manicheism, is the religion that is being rediscovered in America today.[156] The civilizational conundrum lies in the fact that the human mind, or intellect, has no intrinsic ability to decide which battlefront is the right one with which to ally.[157]

Western Civilization in the postmodern world is at the mercy of its own self-consuming moral and theological concepts. Augustine was the West's benefactor, but he is now only a dream.

I think, therefore I vanish. *Cogito ergo vanesco.*[158]

---

155   Augustine – https://en.m.wikipedia.org augustineofhippo ; last edited 19 February 2023, accessed 20 Feb 23
156   John Hubbuch, Wednesday Journal of Oak Park and River Forest, January 21, 2020 – https://www.oakpark.com themanichaeanstatesofamerica : "Manichaeism taught an elaborate cosmic dualism describing the struggle between a good spiritual world of light and an evil material world of darkness. Today Manichaeism seems to be making a comeback … in our democracy we citizens should stop slavishly supporting our political parties and mindlessly listening to paid, political, talking entertainers lest we remain citizens of our modern Manichea"; accessed 20 Feb 23
157   Jonah 4:10-11: "You are troubled by the plant for which you did not labor and did not grow. It came up in a night and perished in a night. Should I not, therefore, be concerned about Nineveh, that great city, in which there are more than a hundred and twenty thousand people, who do not know their right hand from their left …?"
158   AUTHOR'S NOTE: Pardon my French….

Chapter Four: EXISTENCE DEPENDS ON APOCALYPSE

We have laughed at the claims of the alchemists to be able to manufacture a lapis philosophorum [159] consisting of body, soul, and spirit, as impossible, hence we should stop dragging along with us the logical consequence of this medieval assumption, namely the materialistic prejudice regarding the psyche, as though it were a proven fact.[160]

THE OLD ALCHEMY, the one favored by such enlightened luminaries as Sir Isaac Newton, was transformed into the New Alchemy by the various Western thinkers mentioned in the previous chapter, including the psychoanalyst Carl Jung. The economist John Maynard Keynes re-visited Newton's alchemy and became the great alchemists of modern economics.[161][162] The New Alchemy is still being practiced in today's

---

159   Lapis Philosophorum – https://en.m.wikipedia.org_philosopherss-tone : "A mythic alchemical substance capable of turning base metals such as mercury into gold ... or silver. It is also called the elixir of life, useful for rejuvenation and for achieving immortality ... The transmutation mediated by the stone has also been interpreted as a psychological process. Idries Shah devotes a chapter of his book, The Sufis, to provide a detailed analysis ..."; last edited 16 February 2023, accessed 20 Feb 23.

160   CG Jung, *The Archetypes and the Collective Unconscious* (New York: Princeton University Press, 1969; original, 1933+), p. 58

161   Steve Paulson, *Wisconsin Public Radio*, Saturday, September 19, 2020, 9:20am – https://www.wpr.org_isaacnewtonssecretalchemy : "For historians, alchemy offers an intriguing glimpse into the origins of modern science. Take Isaac Newton, one of the founders of the Scientific Revolution. He wrote more than a million words on alchemy over his lifetime, conducting decades' worth of alchemical experiments. But he did it all in secret ... in 1936, most of Newton's alchemical papers came up for auction. The famous economist John Maynard Keynes bought them and later declared that Newton 'was not the first of the age of reason. He was the last of the magicians'"; accessed 20 Feb 23.

162   John Maynard Keynes – https://www.britannica.com_johnmaynard-keynesbritisheconomist : "The key to reducing unemployment was to increase government spending and to run a budget deficit. Governments, many of them looking for excuses to increase spending, wholeheartedly accepted Keynes's views ... The Keynesian model was a core part of economics textbooks from the late 1940s until the late 1980s. But as economists have become more concerned about economic growth, and more informed about

United States, albeit with many topological deformations of the language of economics:[163] "Meet the new boss; same as the old boss."[164]

The reversion to the medieval in the 20th century won't be complete until Western Civilization regresses completely to its own primordial state. The illusion that this can be accomplished by eliminating all influence of Christianity is accompanied by the delusion that Western Civilization can change its own mind without destroying it. Paul "disputed in the synagogue (and) then Paul stood in the middle of the Areopagus ... When they heard of the resurrection of the dead, some scoffed. But others said, 'We will hear you again concerning this matter.'"[165]

With the approach of the civilizational Eschaton, alchemy is stuck in the reified archetypes of its own determination. In order for anything new to come out of the present "now," there must be *metanoia*. But metanoia is problematic when God has been exiled to the dark, upper reaches of the human mind. The culture needs to invent a mystical upside-down room so that God can once again fall out from the top like salt from the salt shaker. Otherwise, the seasoning becomes one-dimensional.

In the meantime, things just keep getting curiouser and curiouser.[166]

Jung's archetypes may or may not be the definitive unconscious forms that will be most conducive to a crossing-over of Western Civilization to a new and as yet unimaginable civilization. The fact that Western culture is becoming more and more archetypal, or responsive directly to archetypal forms, is glaringly clear, but what they are is as ambiguously

---

inflation and unemployment, the Keynesian model has lost its prominence" (!); posted Jul 20, 1998, last updated Feb 15, 2023, accessed 20 Feb 23.

163   AUTHOR'S NOTE: If we can eliminate all meaningful international competitors, we will no longer have to worry about the deficit.

164   *Won't Get Fooled Again*, The Who, 1971 – https://www.azlyrics.com_thewholyrics : "I'll get on my knees and pray, we won't get fooled again"; accessed 20 Feb 23

165   Acts 17:17, 22, 32

166   Lewis Carroll, *Alice's Adventures in Wonderland*, 1865 - https://www.bookroo.com_lewiscarrollquotes - "Curiouser and curiouser! Cried Alice (she was so much surprised, that for the moment she quite forgot how to speak good English)"; accessed 20 Feb 23.

defined as Aquinas's fading types and shadows. They get defined in various disparate ways.[167]

An archetype is not "something" in the phenomenal, empirical, or even social sense. If you look for an archetype, you won't find it. Jung writes, "For our purposes this term is apposite and helpful, because it tells us that so far as the collective unconscious contents are concerned, we are dealing with archaic or ... primordial types ... with universal images that have existed since the remotest times ... The term 'archetype' ... applies only indirectly to the 'representations collectives' (of Levy-Bruhl),[168] since it designates only those psychic contents which have not yet been submitted to conscious elaboration and are therefore an immediate datum of psychic experience ... The archetype is essentially an unconscious content that is altered by becoming conscious and by being perceived, and it takes colour from the individual consciousness in which it happens to appear ... But if we try to establish what an archetype is psychologically, the matter becomes ... complicated."[169]

It is in this sense that I would characterize WWI as a type of Battle of the Titans, one that in effect took place between competing cultural archetypes. After 1918, the archetypes themselves became dizzying facsimiles of what they once were, and the cultural attempt to recover the feeling of archetypal security has plagued Western Civilization ever since then. Attempts to create the ideal State, such as with Fascism, Naziism,

---

167   Stewart Slater, *Areo*, 10/06/2022 – https://www.areomagazine. com_ancientarchetypesandmodernsuperheroes : "We live in an age of superheroes ... Should we bemoan the rash of (superhero) sequels or see them as continuing and updating literary tropes that have existed for millennia? ... That we can so easily find historical analogues for modern characters (such as Born Great: Superman; Achieved Greatness: Batman; Greatness Thrust Upon Him: Spiderman) should not be a surprise, for culture always builds on what has gone before"; accessed 20 Feb 23
168   Levy-Bruhl - https://www.britannica.com_lucienlevy-bruhl : "(1857-1939) French philosopher whose study of primitive peoples gave anthropology a new approach to understanding irrational factors in social thought and primitive religion and mythology"; originally Jul 20, 1998, updated Apr 15, 2022, accessed 20 Feb 23.
169   Jung, *Archetypes*, ibid., p. 5

and Marxist-Leninism, are purely and wholly archetypal in nature and in form.

Now we have Superman, Batman, and Spiderman.[170] The relative isolation of the United States of America following the moment of the Declaration of Independence lends a rather different assortment of unconscious archetypes to the American soul. Isolation and separation, as such, constitute a prototyping of archetypal foundations in the political and mythological origins of the USA. The current need to associate archetypal givens with comic-book heroes is evidence of the failure of postmodern American zeal to stay connected with its own existential and primordial sources.

American independence was made possible by the isolation and separation of the American homeland from its European heritage. On the other hand, there has always been a culturally felt need to revisit those old archetypes by means of more prototypical or paradigmatic connections with the Old Countries. Since the 18th century, isolation and separation have been in conflict with inclusion and welcoming. The Great Immortal Soul, divided,[171] slips away from its Chalcedonian[172] roots toward the Manichaeistic divisiveness of contemporary politics and religion. This phenomenon is most apparent in the ongoing popularity of the Star Wars Franchise.[173]

170 See footnote 167
171 See footnote 152
172 Rebecca Denova, World History Encyclopedia, 27 January 2022 – https://www.worldhistory.org_councilofchalcedon : "Was called in 451 CE by the Roman Emperor Marcian to settle disputes regarding the nature (*hypostases*, 'reality') of Christ … The question was whether Christ was human or divine, a man who became God (through the resurrection and ascension) or God who became a man (through the incarnation. 'taking on flesh'), and how his humanity and divinity affected his essence and being, if at all … The conclusion was reached that the two natures of Christ remained distinct in the union; neither nature was diminished in any way through their joining"; accessed 20 Feb 23
173 Star Wars – https://en.m.wikipedia.org_starwars : "The universe of *Star Wars* is generally similar to ours but its laws of physics are less strict … One result of that is a mystical power known as the Force which is described in the original film as 'an energy field created by all living things … [that] binds the galaxy together. The field is depicted as a kind of pantheistic god … The … powers (of the Force) are wielded by

The so-called Battle between Light and Dark is a thoroughly Manichaeistic myth. It should be pointed out that even in Manicheism the outcome is uncertain and virtually evenly balanced according to some. Christianity, on the other hand, does involve a "last battle," but the crux of the Good News is that the battle has already been won.[174] The starkness of postmodern Western alchemy, however, continues to be more and more apparent, both in homeland conversations and in view of the rest of the world.

Attention has been turned ... away from vast unities like 'periods' or 'centuries' to the phenomena of rupture, of discontinuity ... the great problem presented by such historical analysis ... is no longer one of tradition, of tracing a line, but one of division, of limits; it is no longer one of lasting foundations, but one of transformations that serve as new foundations, the rebuilding of foundations.[175]

EVERY CIVILIZATION has its myths. The myths are usually heroic, with variations of the Superman-Batman-Spiderman Trinity weaving in and out of the prehistoric stories.[176] No matter the characterization of civilizational beginnings "before anyone can remember," the stories are intended to reveal not simply the foundational elements, qualities, and values of the subsequent *polis* but that the *polis* if foundational to the meaning and purpose of the world as such as well to the entire cosmos or universe.

The Star Wars Franchise, mentioned previously, is a contemporary example of myth-making that started from a fantasy and became a cultural Bible. The original fantasy began with the written narrative, "A long time ago in a galaxy far away ..."[177] We could be looking back two major knightly orders at conflict with each other: The Jedi, peace-keepers ... and the Sith, who use the dark side by manipulating fear and aggression"; last edited 10 February 2023, accessed 20 Feb 23

174   John 1:5: "The light shines in the darkness, but the darkness has not overcome it."
175   Michel Foucault, *The Archaeology of Knowledge, and the Discourse on Language* (New York: Vintage Books, a Division of Random House, Inc., 2020, originally 1971), pp. 4, 5
176   See footnote 167.
177   Star Wars – https://en.m.wikipedia.org_starwarsopening-crawl ; last edited 21 January 2023, accessed 20 Feb 23.

from a far future time to a time that is also in our future, or we could be citizens of the virtual world which is replete with historical and pre-historical events that contributed to the formation of our own individual and social consciousnesses.

Myth is the connective tissue that holds the bits and pieces of consciousness together. We have small-scale family myths, clan myths, tribal myths, cultural myths, citywide myths, national myths and cosmic civilizational myths. Beneath the myths is the unconscious realm. The myth functions as a kind of archetypal sieve that filters bad myth from good myth so that the subconscious mind can decide subliminally which irrational elements of experience can become an essential part of Subjectivity and which are to be left behind.

When the conscious mind begins to lose the ability to manage the hidden myths of the subconscious sorting arena and the unconscious void, the archetypes follow the myths into the soul like vultures hovering over a soon-to-be lifeless prey.[178] It is then that the myths disassociate themselves from the carefully crafted conscious constructs of control and maneuver, beginning a long slide into a war in and of the soul with itself. When one's personal myths begin to lose this battle, insanity, or at least a pronounced social disconnect with respect to the constructs, comes into play; when a civilization's myths begin to war against each other, the result is apocalypse.

At some point, every civilization will enter its final bout with Lupus of the Corporate Identity. The little disconnects will not be noticeable at first, because they are mirrored by psychic disconnects in the citizenry and leadership. As the disconnects become more pronounced, they can neither be ignored nor accommodated. The general Biblical testimony regarding this increasing psycho-spiritual-historico-sociological disconnect is the Book of Revelation.

The Scriptures refer to this end, or demise, as a summation of idolatries, a disease all great civilizations and nations eventually contract.

---

178   Matthew 24:28 NIV: "Wherever there is a carcass, there the vultures will gather."

The prophet Isaiah has some pithy things to say about it, such as, "Their land is full of idols; they worship the work of their own hands, that which their own fingers have made. And the common man bows down, and the great man humbles himself; therefore, do not forgive them." The resulting psycho-social environment, becoming a direct matter of the Spirit, is described as well: "Enter into the rock, and hide in the dust from the fear of the Lord and from the glory of His majesty ... They shall go into the holes of the rocks, and into the caves of the earth ... to enter the caverns of rocks, and into the clefts of the cliffs..."[179][180]

The continuities of history are bounded. Like the mesmerizing head of a ready-to-strike cobra, they hypnotize us into standing still, caught in the deceit of our own self-constructed world. When the constructs are threatened, we freeze. We are unable to see the borders of our own identity, we are unable to look at ourselves indirectly, away from the cobra's glazed eyes, for fear that it is then that the serpent will strike.

Indeed, the serpent WILL then strike. Scripture has foretold it from the beginning, when it says, "I will put enmity between you (the serpent) and the woman, and between your offspring and her offspring; he will bruise your head, and you will bruise his heel."[181] With respect to the heel, it is the "'languaging' of things is the Achilles Heel of all attempts to create or sanctify a universal religion from the words and ideas of all religions."[182] Whether it's the collapse of a Tower of Babel or a bite on the heel from a poisonous snake, all empires of words come down in the end: Not even an appeal to the horrors and fascinations of the subconscious can redeem the fall.[183]

---

179   Isaiah 2:8-9, 19, 21

180   Malcolm Bull, *Seeing Things Hidden: Apocalypse, Vision and Totality* (New York: Verso, 1999), p. 287 "There are two sides of the same coin: how to treat others when identities are hidden; how you would like to be treated when your identity is hidden from you."

181   Genesis 3:15

182   See previous discussion.

183   Susanne Ricee, *Diversity for Social Impact*, September 8, 2022 – https://www.diversity.social/unconscious : "The subconscious mind is a secondary mind system that regulates everything in our life. In psychological terms, we define subconscious as the part of our mind that is not currently in focal

It's the discontinuities in the story that tell us how to survive as a People of God.[184] The holes of the rocks and caves of the earth and the caverns of rocks the clefts of the cliffs only serve to hide you from yourself as well as from God. Even the "higher men" flee back and vanish when the lion springs toward their cave.[185] The creatures of the apocalypse don't come from the subconscious: They come from a place that is both higher and lower than that.[186]

If it is to be the case that when the lasting foundations are found not to have lasted, transformations that can serve to rebuild foundations[187] may be the way to go. On the other hand, it depends on how you read your Bible. The required transformation will require a topological modification of everything that has gone into the civilization, especially the language. The shape of things to come[188] is unpredictable.

There are alternative transformations besides rebuilding the Temple. They are in the word of God. They are apocalyptic.

Do not be afraid, Daniel. For from the first day that you set your heart to understand this and humble yourself before your God, your words were heard, and I have come because of your words. But the prince of the kingdom of Persia withstood me for twenty-one days. So

---

awareness. In simpler terms, it's the barrier our mind makes because the brain is continually receiving information through our senses"; accessed 21 Feb 23

184　Albert Peter Krueger, *From the Fords of the Jordan to the Plain of Shinar* (Meadville, PA: Christian Faith Publishing, Inc., 2016), pp. 40-41: "To choose apocalypse as a starting point for an interpretation of the biblical narrative as a whole is to choose the discontinuities of that narrative over the many and varies implied continuities. Traditionally, the discontinuities in the text have been approached as logical gaps that need to be filled in with a reasoning process that requires continuity ... The assumption of a certain historical continuity guides one's decision as to when and how to mine the text. Nothing is gained over previous methods except yet another variation in the logic of discovery."

185　See footnote 84

186　Jung, Archetypes, p. 18-19: "Psychologically ... water means spirit that has become unconscious ... The descent into the depths always seems to precede the ascent."

187　See footnote 175

188　*Shapes of Things*, Yardbirds, 1966: "Come tomorrow, will I be older? Come tomorrow, may be a soldier; come tomorrow, may I be bolder than today?"

Michael, one of the chief princes came to help me, for I had been left there by the kings of Persia.[189]

ACCORDING TO THE BIBLE, angels are created. They are neither eternal forms nor pre-existing principles, although extra-biblical sources and wisdom might refer to them, or their ilk, in this way.[190] Angels figure significantly in the narratives of the Bible, especially when those narratives verge on and intercept with the apocalyptic.

From the above passage from Daniel, a thoroughly apocalyptic book, we see that the term "prince" when applied to the authority structure of a nation, empire, or civilization, is the equivalent of an archangel. A nation has character, and its character is drawn from its prince. A nation's prince can resist the will of God, but only temporarily, as in "twenty-one days." In that case, the chief "prince," the Prince-of-Princes as it were, comes in to unbalance, or "disequilibrate," the situation.[191]

The word "angel" means "messenger." Virtually every primitive pantheon accounts for messengers who flit between heaven and earth like God-particles maintaining mass.[192] Heaven is ethereal, earth is solid, and the distance between them is indeterminate. These are very fast creatures, like Mercury, the messenger-God of the Romans. The idea can be reduced to psychological terms as a mythological precursor to more brainy phenomena such as intuition or sudden insight.[193] Somehow, the "big picture" is conveyed to the immediate in such a way as to give gravitas to the less immediately discerned.

189 Daniel 10:12-13
190 AUTHOR'S NOTE: Plato's "forms" segue, over the centuries, into Hegel's "Divine Ideal on Earth," i.e., the State. In this sense, the laws of the state supplant the angels.
191 AUTHOR'S NOTE: You can see the Persian influence on the text, as in the sovereign title "Shah-en-Shah." The title also segues into "Lord of Lords."
192 Jim Baggott, *The Invention & Discovery of the 'God Particle': Higgs* (Oxford: Oxford University Press, 2012), p. xii: "The Higgs boson ... implies the existence of a Higgs field, an otherwise invisible field of energy which pervades the entire universe ... Without the Higgs field mass could not be construed and nothing could *be* ... this is one of the reasons the Higgs boson, the particle of the Higgs field, has been hyped in the press as the *God particle*."
193 See footnote 75

If you are taken to hiding in the rocks and crevasses of the earth, you are likely not going to hear from any angels. Angels take wisdom from the void where God IS and bring it to earth to enhance God's original plan in the soul-constructs of those who are willing and trained to listen. An angel, of course, is an anthropomorphic rendition of something that is just as real but not quite phenomenal. I prefer the term Archetype.

An archangel is a "type" of God, but only in part. If you were to assemble all the archetypes that have gone into the divine management of nations, you would have re-assembled only a fragmented God. Hegel's Divine Idea of God on earth must include an extra-quasi-phenomenal element that can only come directly from the Void. This is why existentialists reject his theories.

There is a metaphysics[194] to the biblical testimony, but the Western intellect has become so immersed in the characterization of metaphysical truth in the form of Greek ideas and myths that it cannot even conceive of a biblical psychology. There are plenty of ids and psyches to go around, but there are very few Elijahs, Abrahams, and Daniels-in-Persia. This realm has been commonly left to the conservative and fundamentalist evangelical preachers. For the most part they aren't welcome in the halls of academia.

The widening cultural gap between Liberal and Conservative Christianity in the West has been mentioned earlier. It's this gap which is of interest to the central thesis of this book. The cause of this gap, if one can be hypothesized, is somewhere in the far reaches of the origins of Western Civilization itself. In other words, it is built in.

One can see the gap, of course, in terms of the Protestant-Catholic divide that characterizes the historical origins of Western Civilization, and one can see it in the faux-arguments between science and religion. One can see it in the obstinate refusal of American Evangelicals, in general, to

---

194   Metaphysics – https://www.languages.oup.com_metaphysics : "The branch of philosophy that deals with the first principles of things, including abstract concepts such as being, knowing, substance, cause, identity, time, and space"; accessed 21 Feb 23

find common ground with American Pentecostals; one can see it in the divide between Latin-Mass Roman Catholics and Vernacular-Affirming Roman Catholics. One can see it in the doctrinal and dogmatic divide between Eastern Christianity and Western Christianity. One can see it in the ideological gap between Christian Republicans and Christian Democrats, not to mention the gap between Republicans and Democrats as such.

If any collective of words, a language, can characterize the conundrum of a divided Nation in the postmodern world, the United States of America specifically, it is that the foundational Christian substrate of American culture has become divided as like from a massive earthquake that rends one tectonic plate from another. Those words, such as tectonic shift and so forth, are used quite frequently to describe the problems of identity and cohesiveness in the culture. They will do here as well, only the blanket term for all of them in unison is Apocalypse.

The Apocalypse is most intimately felt in the deepest reaches of the soul. We FEEL the Apocalypse.[195] We feel it deeply, almost to the edge of the void that exists above and below our existential state and awareness. The slightest variations in the situation, in the language, and in the presentation of ideas can be sensed as an existential threat. This is because everything is becoming an existential threat. As with every other cultural and relational habit, Western Civilization has been objectifying for centuries, and it is not likely to break that habit in the foreseeable future. In the mind of the Western soul, there MUST be an objective source of the threat.

The FEELING of Apocalypse needs its OBJECT like the Princes need Nations. In terms of Western objectification of everything, the OBJECT becomes conflated with the PURPOSE, or *telos*. If the object is removed, the telos is accomplished.

The devil loves this kind of stuff. We all want to make bad things go away.

---

195   Krueger, *Conundrums*, p. 13: "The language of apocalypse is meant to be purely and wholly evocative."

Language, as the power of universals, is the basic expression of man's transcending his environment, of having a world. The ego-self is that self which can speak and which can by speaking trespass the boundaries of any given situation.[196]

THERE IS NO GOSPEL without speaking. That it might be imparted, implanted to the individual, implanted in the soul, or otherwise effectively transmitted in Spirit from the one who has to the one who has not, the Gospel must be spoken by one and heard by another.[197] Language is not just important: Language is critical to the propagation of the Good News of God in Jesus Christ. Language is critical to the very state of being in relationship with Jesus and to God, and it doesn't matter if it's a sign language without spoken words: The entire teaching of Jesus in the Gospels is sign language.

As I write this section, I am sitting in darkness. There is a fierce windstorm outside, and it has damaged the system that transmits electricity to every home. Without this transmission, when I turn on the light switch nothing else happens. All I hear is the click of the switch, but there is no light. It isn't that the lights are "out": The problem is that there is no transmission of the electrical message from the power source to my home.

King David once encountered a fierce windstorm when he was struggling to understand the word of God spoken to him and the word of God spoken to King Saul. There were, in fact and in truth, two kings, both legitimate in the eyes of God. The one king ruled by the decree of God, the other ruled by virtue of his descendants. Saul's descendants would not rule; David's descendants would rule. The right to rule had to be transmitted to David's descendants.

Saul was a "for the moment" king. He didn't originally have to be in such a state of authority, but his own actions had necessitated that it be so. David was, and was to be, the "forever" king, the one whose progeny would reign over every moment for all time to come. The same God who

---

196   Tillich, *Volume One*, pp. 170-171
197   Romans 10: 14: "How then shall they call on Him in whom they have not believed? And how shall they believe in Him of whom they have not heard? And how shall they hear without a preacher?"

had chosen Saul to reign had also chosen David to reign. The difference between the two reigns, because of sin, was realized in the realm of time. Had we lived in that time, we might have concluded that "only time will tell." We would be tempted to take one side or the other, but even David refused to take his own side against Saul.[198]

David said to Abishai, his tempter for the moment, "As the Lord lives, the Lord will strike him, or his day will come to die, or he will go down in battle and perish."[199] We live in this scenario every day, but sometimes the moment is pressing. Our hearts are energized and focused on what we know [200]MUST happen, and we want to MAKE it HAPPEN, but the Holy Spirit puts a check on the origins of our will, saying "You know the praxis, but you know neither the time nor the place."

The Spirit isn't asking for the will to act to subside: The intentions of your will have become permanent and eternal in the moment. The qualitative difference between your "get Saul" attitude and your "be David" identity is the difference noted before between *praxis* and *Praxis*. It's the work of God, God's mighty deed, that must take place, not your moral prerogatives.

You must be a moral person to be able to hear the word of the Lord clearly, but your morality does not accomplish the work of God. It's your obedience to the word of God through which the accomplishing takes place, or "happens." There is no systematic or objective dimension to spiritual obedience. As with any other need, it is an instantaneous need. Like the Buddhist said, "When hungry, eat. When tired, sleep."[201]

---

198   I Samuel 26:9, 11: "Who can stretch out his hand against the Lord's anointed and remain unpunished … The Lord forbid that I should stretch out my hand against the Lord's anointed …"
199   I Samuel 26:10
200   Matthew 25:13: "Watch therefore, for you know neither the day nor the hour in which the Son of Man is coming."
201   John Safer, PhD, *Masterpiece//Useless Life//True Self*, 1997 – https://www.users.rider.edu_whentired : "A student once asked his teacher, 'Master, what is enlightenment?' The master replied, 'When hungry, eat. When tired, sleep"; accessed 22 Feb 23.

It isn't up to the obedient servant to choose the object of his actions. The need and the desire to act are constant, and over time they both increase. Yet the moment of command remains in God's domain. Until that moment, *praxis* is not coincident with *Praxis*. Biblical morality is the art of seeking the moment when *praxis* is the equivalent of *Praxis*.[202] Nevertheless, the servant can still cry out, "How long, O Lord?"[203]

Language, as has been pointed out earlier, conveys meaning. Meaning floats in language like single-celled plants and animals float in the sea. There is a food-chain to language, one by which the larger, more powerful languages consume the more primitive and primordial languages. Eventually, one's own language and the understanding of meaning that it conveys becomes like the whale that swallowed Jonah.[204] The digester becomes the digested until he is spewed out into a foreign country and entrusted with the Word of God.

Elijah had his whirlwind[205] and Jonah had his stormy sea. This is how praxis becomes Praxis. The storm doesn't do it: Neither do the digestive processes of either Jonah or the big fish. But the action of the storm is part of *Praxis*, but when the mind chooses the storm, *praxis* does not coincide with *Praxis*. The word of God is a heart-to-heart transmitter. Through it, meaning goes directly from the source of meaning, the heart of God, to the heart of the obedient believer.

You can understand everything there is to understand regarding the various levels of meaning to the phrase, "In the beginning was the Word,"[206] but that fact in no way means that you have heard it. To hear it is to act on it. This is what the Bible means by Truth. This is what

202   See footnote 92
203   Psalm 13:1-2: "How long, O Lord? Will You forget me for good? How long will You hide Your face from me? How long will I harbor cares in my soul and sorrow in my heart by day? How long will my enemy loom over me?"
204   Jonah 1:12, 17: "Pick me up and toss me into the sea. Then the sea will quiet down for you. For I know that it is on my account this great storm has come upon you ... Now the Lord appointed a great fish to swallow Jonah."
205   I Kings 19:11: "The Lord passed by, and a great and strong wind split the mountains and broke in pieces the rocks before the Lord, but the Lord was not in the wind."
206   John 1:1

differentiates the deeds of the flesh, *praxis*, from the mighty deeds of God, *Praxis*. The origin of meaning is received only through hearing, not thinking, and "to all who received Him, He gave the power to become sons of God, to those who believed in His name, who were born not of the will of the flesh, nor of the will of man, but of God."[207]

The language of *praxis* never transcends one's environment: Only the language of *Praxis* can cross the established boundaries of the situation without trespassing the boundaries of meaning itself. The dialecticians are wrong.

It is, Heidegger suggests, not the difference between modern and pre-modern world pictures that defines the modern age, but "the fact that the world becomes a picture at all." For Heidegger, there is thus something close to an inverse relationship between Being and the objectifying gaze of modernity, for "Where anything that is has become the object of representing, it first occurs in a certain manner a loss of Being."[208]

WHERE APOCALYPSE and Reason meet is where predictability and comprehension cease. It's a "loss of Being" whether the approach is from the past or from the future. Everything stops, even while it keeps moving faster and faster. Being exists in the language game being played, and insofar as that language game is a language of praxis, Being is an investment of diminishing returns. John the Baptist indicate as much when he said of Jesus, "He must increase, but I must decrease."[209]

The obsession with Being as such is the obsession of the dialecticians, Marx included. Martin Heidegger represents the great pragmatic interim, the one who facilitates both Hitler and Tillich. Drawing from Heidegger's philosophy, Tillich writes, "finitude ... includes uncertainty ... it is an expression of the general insecurity of the finite being, the contingency of his being at all, the fact that he is not by himself but is 'thrown into being' (Heidegger), the lack of a necessary place and a necessary presence."[210] But Heidegger was a Nazi, evidenced by the fact that he maintained an

---

207	John 1:12-13
208	Bull, ibid., p. 172
209	John 3:30
210	Tillich, Volume Two, p. 73

official, state-sanctioned position in academia throughout the Hitler years.[211] His metaphysics fits well the Hegelian implication that the Being of the citizen is thoroughly interdependent on the Being of the State.

Tillich's "method of correlation"[212] depends heavily on Heidegger's metaphysics, although Tillich rejects both Naziism and Marxist-Leninism. He does, however, hover over socialism like the spirit hovering over the waters of chaos at the moment before creation. It is difficult to discern where else one can go to legitimate one's own sense of Being, of self, without some meaningful action that weds the soul to the State.

For Tillich, "Philosophy and theology ask the question of Being. But they ask it from different perspectives. Philosophy deals with the structure of being in itself; theology deals with the meaning of being for us."[213] His famous slogan is, "Philosophy asks the question: Theology provides the answer." He uses Heidegger's foundational question, "Why are there beings at all instead of nothing?" as the stimulus for his own theological answer [214],[215]

---

211 Michael Wheeler, *Stanford Encyclopedia of Philosophy*, Wed Oct 12, 2011 – https://www.plato.stanford.edu_martinheidegger : "(1889-1976)… Even if Heidegger had some sort of argument for the world-historical destiny of the German people, why on earth did he believe that the Nazi Party, of all things, harboured the divine catalyst? … the role of language in Being is at the heart of the issue … So the German *Volk* are a linguistic-historical, rather than a biological, phenomenon … Heidegger officially rejected one of the keystones of Nazism, namely its biologically grounded racism"; accessed 22 Feb 23.

212 Tillich, Volume One, pp. vii, 8: "The subject of all sections of this system is the method of correlation and its systematic consequences illustrated in a discussion of the main theological problems … The following system is an attempt to use the 'method of correlation' as a way of uniting message and situation." AUTHOR'S NOTE: Heidegger believed that there were only two languages capable of expressing spiritual things, German and Greek. Even if he rejected biological racism, it must be pointed out that under his umbrella of beliefs, Hebrew, the linguistic-historical language of the Jews, would be an inferior language. One has to really split existential hairs to free Heidegger from the charge of antisemitism in its most virulent form.

213 Tillich, *Volume One*, p. 22

214 Martin Heidegger, *Introduction to Metaphysics* (New Haven, CT: Yale University Press, 2000; original 1935), p. 1

215 Tillich, *Volume One*, p. 163

Since the Bible was written, the idea of *creatio ex nihilo*[216] has been the prime question regarding the role of God in the universe. In fact, it reduces the question of God's role in the universe to meaninglessness. God doesn't have a role "in" the universe: God is the *alpha* and the *omega*, the *ohn* and the *ehn*,[217] the *prohtos* and the *eschatos*,[218] *archeh* and *telos* [219] of the universe, its beginning, and its end. If this isn't the God we are worshipping, He isn't the God of the Bible.

Again, Tillich writes, "A ... problem in the organization of systematic theology is the position of apologetics. Modern theologians usually have identified it with philosophy of religion, while in traditional theology the section on natural theology contained much apologetic material. The exclusion of these two methods makes another solution necessary ... systematic theology is an 'answering theology.'"[220] In this instance, Tillich is absolutely right, and he speaks the truth. Christianity has been a matter of apologetics from the beginning, and as such it became an integral part and characteristic of Western Civilization.

Ever since Paul noticed the statue to the unknown god in the Areopagus, apologetics has addressed the questions of philosophy. Aquinas made the process legitimate by using the language of Aristotle; Tillich used the language of Martin Heidegger. Even St. Augustine used the language of Neoplatonism, going all the way back to the origins of Greek Civilization. The brilliance of one generation ignites the brilliance of the next. And so it is, and so it will be.

Once the transcendence of God is removed from the common language, the common language begins to fail. This is why language is so important, why the language game you are playing is so important, and why changing the language game becomes a critical component of civilizational change. If you want to remove the questions of philosophy from the answers of theology you must go back in conceptual time to the

---

216   *Creatio ex Nihilo* = Creation from Nothing
217   Revelation 1:8
218   Revelation 1:17
219   Revelation 22:13
220   Tillich, *Volume One*, p. 31

era before the first Greek philosopher, Thales of Miletus,[221] said anything at all. This puts you smack in the middle of ancient Persian philosophy, theology, and polytheism. That was when Darius of Persia proclaimed that Aramaic would be the official language of the western half of his empire.[222] You are now amidst the rebuilding of the Temple in Jerusalem.

Are you weeping or are you rejoicing?

Postmodern language falls off the edge of the world where dialectical language ends. Our own identity, our Being as such, falls with it. For the dialectical zealot, the one who would resurrect Marx to reign over the postmodern world, the being of the individual is entirely fashioned by the State. For the existential zealot, the one who would resurrect Kierkegaard and follow him into the void of Subjectivity, personal identity can be whatever you want it to be. It doesn't matter, because at the moment you don't exist.

Existence ultimately depends on the outcome of Apocalypse.

---

221   Patricia O'Grady, The Flinders University of South Australia, *Internet Encyclopedia* 2002 – https://www.iep.utm.eduthalesofmiletus : "Thales says that (the first principle) is water. 'it' is the nature, the arche, the originating principle"; accessed 22 Feb 23.
222   500 BCE – https://en.m.wikipedia.org_500bc ; last edited 28 January 2023, accessed 22 Feb 23.

Chapter Five: HUMPTY DUMPTY

He who does not enter by thew door into the sheepfold, but climbs up some other way, is a thief and a robber. But he who enters by the door is the shepherd of the sheep. To him the doorkeeper opens, and the sheep hear his voice. He calls his own sheep by name, and he leads them out.[223]

THERE ARE FIVE categories of theories of meaning: Substantive theories, Coherence theories, Constructivist theories, Consensus theories, and Pragmatic theories.[224] Meaning itself remains elusive. Meaning is found in Subjectivity. Even if you point to something you believe to be objectively true, the meaning of your pointing is entirely subjective. Although pragmatism is at the heart of the American way of life, most pragmatic theories of meaning render anything spiritual to be meaningless, merely a primitive way to language things more objective or empirical or verifiable. The meaning of the Bible is most problematic in a pragmatic culture.

The idea of a language game is not a theory about how language means what it means: It's a way of observing language while it is conveying meaning. The meaning conveyed is subject-to-subject, even involving the meaning of the word "objective." The observation is objective, because real spoken language is observed, but meaning is hidden in the transaction of speaking and hearing.

It isn't as complicated as it sounds, although those five categories mentioned above ARE very complicated. The idea of a language game simply highlights the notion that if you are talking about something, don't talk about something else. In contemporary political terms, this "talking about something else" is akin to gaslighting.

Gaslighting requires the subtle and hidden exchange of meaning within the words and phrases of a conversation. It is "a form of

---

223   John 10:1-3
224   Meaning – https://en.m.wikipedia.org_meaning(philosophy) ; last edited 16 February 2023, accessed 22 Feb 23.

psychological manipulation in which the abuser attempts to sow self-doubt and confusion in their victim's mind ... gaslighters are seeking to gain power and control over the other person, by distorting reality and forcing them to question their own judgment and intuition."[225] The words and phrases of the Bible are the culturally easiest words and phrases to use in gaslighting attempts and successes. This is because, as noted previously, the language of the Bible has always been voiced in terms of the language of the culture.

The language of the Bible consists of a singular language game. The language game of the New Testament has no intrinsic meaning unless the language game of the Old Testament conveys its own unique meaning. This consideration was one of the central theological battles fought out in the apologetic age leading up to the Council of Nicaea in 325 CE. You might compare the language game of the Old Testament and the language game of the New Testament in terms of a game of checkers.

In checkers, if you get a piece to the opponent's home side, it is "kinged." That is the Old Testament. Once the piece is kinged, it can move much more freely than the regular playing pieces. That is the New Testament. The language games are the same yet different. The difference between the Jewish game and the Christian game of meaning in this illustration is in the definition of the term "kinged."

The important thing to remember is that the language game of the Bible is singular, one game, and that is why it has endured. The game of checkers can apparently be traced back to 3000 BCE in the land of Ur of the Chaldees.[226] It's a basic, or fundamental game, that hasn't been and even can't be modified much beyond where it stands today. Since the testaments have also been passed down since the days of Ur of the Chaldees,[227] it stands to reason that the game can easily have remained

---

225 Gaslighting – https://www.newportinstitute.com howtotellifsomeoneisgaslightingyou ; posted November 4, 2021, accessed 22 Feb 23.
226 Checkers – https://en.m.wikipedia.org checkers ; last edited 14 February 2023, accessed 22 Feb 23.
227 Genesis 11:31

just the same as it was when it was first constructed. "Some things never change ... and some things do."[228]

The language game of the Scriptures is one which God has taught his people to play. It conveys meaning that is binding before the world was created and applies after the world will end. Everything in between is accounted for meaningfully within the boundaries of the biblical language game. Like other language games, too, it is learned by playing it.

The boundaries, or borders, of this vastly comprehensive language game are the beginning and the end. The playing pieces are the nations, and the shape of the playing surface is always the same, no matter how many deformations it undergoes. There is no knowledge beyond the reach of the biblical language game, and there is no truth that can be definitively expressed until the game is over. Truth is conveyed in the language game itself.

None of the five categories of theories of meaning can touch the meaning conveyed by the Bible's language game. It is sacrosanct, holy, untainted, and incorruptible. The four preceding five-fold chapters can't touch it, and no language-gamer can out game it.

Nevertheless, the only way the Western mind can conceive of the meaning of the words and phrases, indeed the totality of the Bible, is to begin with a language game that has been relayed to it by means of the presumptions of the culture, and those presumptions go back a long, long way. The centrality of certain language games from age to age deform the contours of the biblical language game. That is to say, the archetypal foundations of the civilization are shuffled around from time to time, giving history the semblance of ages and epochs.

---

228   The Matrix, Warner Bros./Roadshow Entertainment, 1999 - https://www.alt.movies.the-matrix.narkive.com_becausesomethings-neverchangeandsomethingsdo : "Morpheus looks down at Niobe and says, 'and some things do ... Niobe is referring to this when she volunteers the Logos to go after the Neb. Locke askes her 'Why?', acting as if she is personally betraying him. She says, 'because some things never change ... and some things do'..."; accessed 22 Feb 23.

The parameters of the archetypal pre-structure of meaning stay the same, and so we have a medieval period, a renaissance, a reformation, and an enlightenment. Sometimes the shift in cultural topology is more pronounced than in other times, such as during the times of the reformation and the subsequent enlightenment. But the general shape of things in the intellect and in the emotions stays constant, although often unrecognizable to the prior way of thinking. The angels of our civilization have always kept watch on its walls.

Until recently, the civilization has remained "Christian" in terms of both archetypal structures and precedents and in terms of the primary language game from which all political gaslighting proceeds. That America has always been Christian, and that civilization must be Christian to be valid and legitimate in view of reality as such is where the interface between philosophy and theology stands in the 21st century.

The divergence mentioned earlier, sometimes, if not always, characterized as a divergence between the liberal and the conservative worldview, is actually a divergence between those who recognize biblical language as a legitimate language game in and of itself and those who do not.

The doorkeeper may or may not recognize the Shepherd in the postmodern era.

Do not be afraid. I am the First (prohtos) and the Last (eschatos). I am He who lives, though I was (egenomehn) dead. Look! I am alive forevermore. Amen. And I have the keys of Hades and of Death. Write the things which you have seen (eides), and the things which are (eisin), and the things which will take place (genesthai) after this.[229]

BRACKETING THE WORLD into which God has caused us to be born are the Proto-world and the Eschato-world. Jesus the Logos is the authority who reigns from the throne of First Things and the throne of Last Things. The first things are the foundational realities that originate things, make things work, and continue things. The last things are the

---

229   Revelation 1:17-19

purposes, goal, conclusion, summation, and fulfilment of all things in time, the "where everything is headed."

When the First Things coincide with the Last Things, Jesus' words from the Cross, "It is finished," salvation will be ended, concluded, completed, or otherwise finally purposed. Then the New Jerusalem will come down from heaven as a bride adorned for her husband.[230]

The first heaven and the first earth will have passed away.[231] The world in which the resurrected faithful will be called to live in will share nothing in common with the world in which they died.[232] This is the crux of the Promise.

The Last Things are the down-slope equivalent of the First Things. They say that when you climb Mount Everest coming back down is the hardest part. Most climbers who die on the upper slopes die on their way back down. They never have the satisfaction of returning to the world they came from and seeing it with new eyes. They do have the satisfaction of seeing things from the summit. Concluding the expedition to the top is much riskier than beginning it. This is why the first chapter of Genesis looks so orderly and straightforward while the last book of the New Testament is filled with frightening things. All creation honors the same archetypal patterns, from mountaineering to living by faith.

When we talk about the "natural law" in the modern world, the one which is transitioning to the postmodern world as we speak, if we speak at all, we aren't talking about the natural law as St. Augustine or St. Thomas Aquinas would have conceived it. In fact, the entire concept of "natural" has undergone its own topological deformations since medieval times. Yet we still use the word with past meanings saturating present distortions.

In the Neoplatonic worldview of St. Augustine, the cosmos, the world, includes all things moral, social, political, and physical. The term

---

230	Revelation 21:2
231	Revelation 21:1
232	Revelation 21:3

"natural," in this context, indicates how all things work together, and how all things work together is the "world," the cosmos. There is little or no distinction between nature and things like politics and religion: You could say that everything is "nature." Everything has a nature and all natures must abide by the universal harmony in which they abide. Plato's ideal world, or world of ideas, was not an "abstract" world to him: It was the ultimate concrete world. Nothing is "just in your mind."

One of the "gifts" of the Middle Ages, so-called, to the modern world is the separation of the idea of natural law between what are physical laws "of nature" and the moral law which God has ordained for humanity. In the beginning of this separating journey, the inevitability of physical cause-and-effect began to be accepted, doing away with what the later critics called "superstition." The principle of cause-and-effect was not so easily applied to the Moral Law, which came to be known as Natural Law.

You might say that once the question of cause-and-effect was demythologized in the prototypical science of the Medieval world, the value of eliminating superstitious notions of cause-and-effect with respect to physical "laws of nature" shown a new light on the highly abstracted and institutionally mandated moral laws of the time. If the physical world follows fixed laws, then so, too, must the moral world. The moral laws of the time were still derived from a Neoplatonic worldview in which there is no real difference between the moral, the political, the personal and the physical, or material, or "natural."

The assumed connection between the moral law and the laws of physics and chemistry was severed by the British Empiricists. Even though his immediate predecessor in the field, John Locke (1632-1704), incorporated a vision of Natural Law into the realm of politics, a construct that finds its way into American jurisprudence via the Declaration of Independence, David Hume (1711-1776) discovered, or constructed, the so-called "Fact-Value Distinction." According to the fact-value distinction, or the "is-ought problem," "it is not at all obvious how we can get from making descriptive statements to prescriptive ... he advised against making such inferences, and this complete severing of 'is' from 'ought' is sometimes referred to as 'Hume's Guillotine.'"[233]

Hume's Guillotine has been much more effective and influential in the modern-postmodern era than Occam's Razor (14th century) could ever have been. Occam's razor is a late medieval principle of investigatory knowing that says "*pluralitas non est ponenda sine necessitate*, plurality should not be posited without necessity ... the simpler explanation of an entity is to be preferred."[234] Many contemporary liberal pastoral and dogmatic theologians cite Occam's Razor as a means to justifying the many changes in the moral law and code of the Church and of society, but they shy away from the Guillotine which declares, quite bluntly and clearly, that there is no such thing as a moral code that is anything like the laws of the universe.

In Hume, we see the most accurate picture of what has been pejoratively called Materialism. Materialism, as such, has nothing to do with greed or the economic and religious dark side of modern society. Materialism is essentially the declaration of a worldview that does not include principles of morality, justice, or any other non-naturally-cause-and-effect fact. Once morality, as such, is severed from the modern canon of cause-and-effect principles, it is virtually impossible to get it back. Morality becomes a matter of preference, and preference, then, as we go beyond materialism to Hegel's resurrected Neoplatonic idealism, is to be evaluated by the State and solely in terms of the practical needs of the State.

When we pass laws based solely on anyone's moral principles, they are laws that favor one group's moral PREFERENCES over all the others'. The laws of the State become the Natural Law, and to break this Natural Law is to transgress the identity and purpose of the State. There is no getting around this Final Principle of Government in the modern worldview in any way compatible with the thought-patterns, the archetypes of governance, that the United States of America has

---

233   Hume – https://www.philosophybasics_davidhume ; accessed 23 Feb 23.
234   Brian Duignan, *Encyclopedia Britannica*, Jul 20, 1998 – https://www.britannica.com_occamsrazor ; updated Dec 01, 2022, accessed 23 Feb 23.

inherited from the British Empiricists. We are all still English through and through.

According to our own principles as stated in our own founding documents, principles which indeed are the inheritance of centuries of thought, action, and conflict, the United States of America must and will inexorably tend toward a Hegelian future in which the Natural Law is universally agreed upon to be the laws of the State. It's like what the Borg says in the *Star Trek* Series, "Resistance is futile."[235]

In the end, we will all believe that this consequence is the coincidence of First Things with Last Things, but we will be wrong. Something else will have happened, and the world that has become will again be a world that God has caused.

In those days (egeneto) a decree (dogma) went out from Caesar Augustus that the entire inhabited earth should be taxed … So Joseph also departed from the city of Nazareth in Galilee to the city of David which is called Bethlehem.[236]

THE NATIVITY account of Luke is one of the most well-known stories in history. We all have pictures in our heads of the baby Jesus in the manger in Bethlehem, the City of David. The shepherds are there along with a host of animals honoring St. Francis of Assisi. In that one scene, the scriptures are fulfilled, time stops and then starts again, and the Way of Jesus the Christ begins.

The Germanic stable scene was and is actually a cave in the rocks near the ancient city of Bethlehem. The cave imagery courses throughout the Scriptures from Elijah to David to the fearful survivors hiding in caves at the end of time. Not much is made of this cave connection, although it is a generally consistent motif. It could be that the cave is not mentioned

---

235   The Borg – https://en.m.wikipedia.org_borg : "The Borg are cybernetic organisms (cyborgs) linked in a hive-mind called 'the Collective' … The Borg's ultimate goal is 'achieving perfection' … The Borg have become a symbol in popular culture for any juggernaut against which 'resistance is futile', a common phrase uttered by the Borg"; last edited 21 February 23, accessed 23 Feb 23.
236   Luke 2:1, 4

in the Bible, just the manger. The cave is part of the incarnation, the Word made flesh.

The Gospel according to Matthew is very good with pointing out when the scriptures are fulfilled. The fulfilment of ancient prophecy is one of the central characteristics of the birth of Jesus. Even the "Flight into Egypt," according to Matthew, is the fulfilling of a prophecy of Hosea.[237] Even at the End, scripture is fulfilled when the chief priests use the thirty pieces of silver, the price of betrayal, to buy the Potter's Field.[238]

Both Hosea and Jeremiah were prophesying much more than simply the passages remembered by Matthew to reveal the import and continuity of his testimony. There is history in that reminiscence, too, as well as a future, but most of all there is a character to the testimony, to the history, and to the future. This is what is proclaimed in prophecy, in any prophecy.

When the Pharisees try to entangle Jesus in a conundrum about paying taxes, He took a coin and asked whose image and inscription is on the coin.[239] The encounter seems to be about whether or not one should pay taxes, and this is how it has been interpreted from the beginning of Christianity. But it is not about paying taxes: It's about the Law. The Pharisees were mostly, if not entirely, concerned with the Law.

If it was a question about Caesar's law, then the answer is very clear: Pay the tax or be imprisoned. If the question is about God's Law, that is, the Law of Moses, then the question is quite different. It becomes a question about moral and cultural purity, of sinlessness. If it's a sin to pay taxes to the emperor, then everyone should immediately stop paying taxes or else offer a much greater quantity of sacrifices for sin in the Temple. It would also mean that the tax collectors are not only sinning for a living, but they are also forcing the populace to sin.

---

237 Matthew 2:14-15: "Out of Egypt I have called My Son." (Hosea 11:1)
238 Matthew 27: 9-10 (Jeremiah 32:6-9)
239 Matthew 22:15-22

In other words, the presence of the Romans is desecrating the entire country, from the Temple to the ground they are standing on. So, how does one escape the overwhelmingly sinful situation itself? If it's not okay to pay taxes, is it okay to smile at a Roman soldier? Is it a sin to be friendly to a Roman official, or is one required to make sure the Romans, every Roman, knows how despised and resented they are every time you see one.

The idea, after all, in the long run and the short run, is to rid the land of the Romans. If you pay Caesar's tax, you are financing the Roman occupation. After all, the representatives of the High Priest wouldn't even enter the Praetorium "so that they might not be defiled."[240] Good heavens, man, one might say, if you pay Caesar's tax you are paying not only Pilate's salary, but you are paying for the Praetorium which is defiling the very gates of Jerusalem![241]

I remember well the very first sermon I gave as an ordained preacher in an actual church to an actual congregation. It was on this very passage. I didn't choose the passage, because in the Episcopal Church the Bible readings are set forth in the lectionary. Okay, so here goes. The sermon was on "filthy lucre."

The term "filthy lucre" comes from Paul's letter to Titus. We read, "There are many unruly and vain talkers and deceivers ... whose mouths must be stopped, who subvert whole houses, teaching things which they ought not, for filthy lucre's sake."[242] I didn't preach on Titus, but I did remember the term "filthy lucre." Essentially, I taught that every penny, dime and one-hundred-dollar bill you have in your pocket has been tainted by dishonest gain long before it finds its way into your pocket. I don't remember the entire message, but I do recall that the congregation pretty much didn't like it.

I would preach it in a much better way, today, rightly dividing the Word in a more acceptable manner. That was forty-three years ago!

---

240 John 18:28
241 AUTHOR'S NOTE: By the way, while I write this section, it's tax time.
242 Titus 1:10-11 KJV

Anyway, if you read on, the scripture in Titus says, "to the pure, all things are pure. But to those who are defiled and unbelieving, nothing is pure."[243] All this money stuff and taxes stuff isn't about money and taxes: It's about purity of soul and how you get it and how you keep it. You neither get it nor keep it by obsessing over your checkbook, as many sincere and well-meaning gospel teachers will tell you. You get it and keep it by faith in Jesus Christ, and it is not a relative condition of the heart and mind unless you make it a relative condition.

Our entire economic system revolves around filthy lucre. As one faithful intellectual puts it, "A free political economy wears sin like a scarlet letter. Soft neon lights beckon, alas, to massage parlors and 'adult' (that is, adolescent) magazines. Democratic capitalist societies exhibit the lives of human beings not perhaps as they should be but as they are, for they have been conceived in due recognition of the errant human heart, whose liberty they respect."[244] As far as the tax system goes, pay it or pay the penalty that the system prescribes, but be sure you have your moral house in order when you refuse.

It's historically and exegetically interesting to note that the question the Pharisees asked which Jesus refused to answer is the one question every Christian theologian since Tertullian tries to answer in a yes-or-no rational fashion. This gives the Pharisees much more power than Jesus ever intended to give them, although His intention was never to reduce their power and authority in the community to nothing. He came to fulfill not just the prophets, but the Law as well.[245] The question is, "How do you fulfill the Law and the Prophets by faith?"

So, what is this fulfilment thing? The New Testament word for fulness is *plehrohma*, one of my favorite words. You'll see it usually spelled pleroma, so that's what I will do here. The Pleroma is The Fulness in systematic theology. We are called to live in the Fulness. The fulness is

---

243   Titus 1:15
244   Michael Novak, *The Spirit of Democratic Capitalism*
       (New York: Madison Books, 1982, 1991), p. 81
245   Matthew 5:18 KJV: "Till heaven and earth pass, one joy or
       one tittle shall in no wise pass from the law, till all be fulfilled."

that state or condition in which things are continuously being fulfilled, things of the Law and things of the prophets. To walk in the Fulness is to walk the path of fulfilling. Another way of putting this notion in Biblical terms is to walk in the Spirit. Also, to follow Jesus is the active and personal equivalent in meaning and use.

The most telling use of the word pleroma and its derivatives is found in Pauyl's Letter to the Galatians. We read, "now I say that as long as the heir is a child, he does not differ from a servant though he is lord of all. But he is under tutors and governors until the time appointed by the father. So when we were children, we were in bondage to the elements of the world. But when the fullness of time came, God sent forth His Son, born of a woman, born under the law, to redeem those who were under the law, that we might receive the adoption as sons. And because you are sons, God has sent forth into our hearts the Spirit of His Son, crying 'Abba, Father!' Therefore you are no longer a servant, but a son, and if a son, then an heir of God through Jesus Christ."[246] I quote the entire paragraph, here, because if we just look at the phrase 'fullness of time" we will be drawn off into a very long rabbit trail of parsings and promotions that may or may not have anything to do with The Pleroma. Suffice it to say that the incarnation of God in Jesus Christ took place in the fulness of all fulnesses such that there can be no subsequent fulness that is fuller than His birth.

The complete fulness of the fulness of time is precisely the main topic of the Gospels themselves. There is no more fulness to be researched, discovered, or constructed. Every moment of fulness from that time forward is a fulness that is full of all fulness for the faithful follower of Jesus. Legalistically speaking, it's a bit much to handle. But the starting point to understanding the fulness is revealed in the birth of Jesus in a manger in a cave in Bethlehem 2023 years ago.

Pleroma, as a term in the Greek language, is also the condition of expectation a mother is in in the moments just prior to giving birth. Birth happens in the fulness of time. Another way of saying this is "when the baby is ready, you need to be ready, too!" These two notions of fulness

246 Galatians 4:1-7

segue and coincide in the birth of Jesus. It is perhaps the most significant moment in the entire story of salvation.

When the writers of the New Testament, those who fulfilled the *logos* and *rhema* of God by recording their testimonies, te4stified to the fulness of time regarding the things happening in their time and in their midst, they used the word *egeneto*.[247] The word *egeneto* is a storytelling device in terms of the mechanics of specialized languages, and in the New Testament it becomes a sign meant to catch your attention. SOMETHING important is taking place here! When something "comes to pass," it means that God is doing something, and that something fulfils the law and the prophets.

Egeneto is when God is visibly, clearly, and unmistakably acting, or doing Praxis. In the case of all the events bracketing the birth of Jesus, praxis and Praxis are coming together mightily, even if some of the practitioners have no awareness of it at all. The disciples "hear" (*rhema*) the prophetic word (*logos*) when they SEE these things happening. They see the fulfilling of God's word and testify to it because they hear God fulfilling their understanding at the same time. God speaks directly to them without need of any rational intermediary.

And so, Caesar as Caesar is fulfilling the Law and the Prophets when he decrees that all the world should be taxed. In this instance, the taxing itself serves as a vehicle to the fulfilling of the Law and the Prophets. The least we can do is give Caesar his due.

Which leads us to the other conundrum about paying taxes. When Jesus says, "Whose is this image and inscription?" he uses the term "icon," the same term used to describe the creation of human being. I won't go on a rabbit trail of explanation for the use of icons in the Easter Church, but that use embraces the same idea that is behind the use of the word icon here and in Genesis 1:27. If you are created as an icon of God, then everything you are is God's, and that is your "God tax." You can't divide out your God tax like you can divide out the coins in your pocket.

---

247   Luke 24:18: "Are you the only foreigner in Jerusalem who does not know what has happened (*egeneto*) there is these days?"

This notion of fulness, or "everythingness," saturates the New Testament language. That question of the Pharisees was a question asked in the fulness of time. It happened, and in its happening it was Praxis as well as praxis, even though the people who were asking the question had no inkling that they were fulfilling anything. They didn't even think they were fulfilling the law, because their purpose in asking was to trip up Jesus, not to dialogue about the rules of living under which they all lived. But be advised, they weren't trying to trip up Jesus because they were bad people: They truly believed He was wrong and that his teaching had to be cancelled.

The exegetical, or interpretive, question to ask here is, "How did Matthew know that this was an *egeneto* occasion, a "coming to pass," that God was Practicing here?" He saw it because he recorded it. All kinds of biblical truths came together, as in "synagogue," on that occasion, from the Creation to the Temple. Jesus had just cleansed the Temple,[248] and Matthew noticed that, too.

We can't notice what God is doing by keeping our heads down, whether in the word or in perpetual thought and prayer: We have to look around in the manner that Jesus taught us, "I say to you, lift up your eyes and look at the fields, for they are already white for the harvest."[249] Something is happening, something is coming to pass, something is *egeneto*.

So, what are we to look for? We are to look for the reflection of the image of God in the moments into which God calls us. Since you and I are created in the image God, this task can be done without mediation. Look, and you will see.[250] What we are looking for is *egeneto*, not the fulness. We will never comprehend the Pleroma until God reveals the entire event to is in heaven. Then, we will fall into a faint flat on our faces because it will be too much for an individual existence to take in.

---

248   Matthew 21:12-16
249   John 4:35
250   Matthew 7:7-8

In the Letter to the Hebrews, we find another translation into our word image. It is called the "express image." This isn't the ultimate or complete image: It is the one that is expressed. It happens and it can be seen and heard. We read, "God, who at various times and in diverse ways spoke (*lalehsas*) long ago to the fathers through the prophets, has in these last days (*eschatou*) spoken to us by His Son, whom He has appointed heir of all things, and through whom He made the world (*aiohnas*/aeons). He is the brightness of His glory, the express image (charactehr/character) of Himself and upholds all things by the word (*hrehmati*/rhema) of His power."[251]

This pretty much sums the whole process up, except for "When He had by Himself purged our sins (cleansing of the Temple which is you), He sat down at the right hand of the Majesty on high,. He was made so much better than the angels as He has inherited a more excellent name than they."[252] In other words, in Jesus, no messengers are needed anymore. He is a direct route to the seeing of the coming to pass which is all around us.

We are looking for the character of God being revealed in all the events around us. We recognize this character through hearing the word of God and through knowing and following Jesus. We never recognize all the moments, but in Him we can recognize the moments He has called and appointed us to recognize.

As Jesus says, "Watch therefore – for you do not know when the master of the house is coming, in the evening, or at midnight, or at the crowing of the rooster, or in the morning – lest he come suddenly and find you sleeping. What I say to you I say to all: Watch!"[253]

Be a Gregory.[254]

In 1909 God moved two Christian laymen to set aside a large sum of money for issuing twelves volumes that would set forth the fundamentals

---

251	Hebrews 1:1-3
252	Hebrews 1:3-4
253	Mark 13:35-36
254	"Watch" = *grehgoreite*, or "gregoryate")

of the Christian faith, and which were to be sent free to ministers of the gospel, missionaries, Sunday School superintendents, and others engaged in aggressive Christian work throughout the English speaking world.[255]

IF YOU TAKE Hegel seriously, and I do because he invented history as we know it, it is apparent that the *egeneto* of creation is to be fulfilled, in his theory, by the State and by the State alone. Whatever "comes to pass" will be at the initiative and decree of the State. This includes both birth and death. The State will oversee the Incarnation itself. It will oversee who you are born to be. This should make you anxious. In church terms, the State will be your Bishop.

Alpha and *Omega* will be decreed by the State.

When R. A. Torrey wrote the words above, he used the phrase "God moved." God moved is *egeneto*, "it came to pass." In other words, *praxis* and *Praxis* coincided and the writing that comes from hearing took place. It was in this way that what is called Fundamentalism was born. This birth took place five years before the advent of WWI.

Torrey studied at the two great German universities of Leipzig and Erlangen. He was no foreigner to the academia of the late 19th century. He also graduated from Yale University and from Yake Divinity School. He was raised up in ministry under the example and tutelage of Dwight L. Moody, and Torrey became the superintendent of the Moody Bible Institute.[256] In other words, he was as much a product of the times as, for instance, Gottfried Leibnitz, Angela Merkel, Johann Wolfgang von Goethe, Friedrich Nietzsche, Richard Wagner, Emile Durkheim, Edmund Husserl, Ernst Junger, and many, many others, including Edward Teller, one of the creators of the atomic bomb.[257] Among notable Erlangen scholars are Ludwig Andreas Feuerbach, Hans Geiger, Georg

---

255   R. A. Torrey, *The Fundamentals, Volume II* (Grand Rapids: Baker Books, 2000; originally Los Angeles: The Bible Institute of Los Angeles, 1917) p. 5: Preface
256   Torrey – https://en.m.wikipedia.org_ratorrey ; last edited 23 February 2023, accessed 24 Feb 23.
257   Leipzig scholars – https://en.m.wikipedia.org_listofleipziguniversitypeople ; last edited 14 October 2023, accessed 24 Feb 23.

Simon Ohm, Louis Agassiz, Rudolf Otto,[258] Ernst Troeltsch, and Jurgen Kuczynski.[259] Rudolf Otto has already been mentioned.

Ernst Troeltsch was "a German liberal Protestant theologian, a writer on the philosophy of religion and the philosophy of history, and a classical liberal politician. He was a member of the history of religions school. His work was a synthesis of a number of strands, drawing on Albert Ritschl, Max Weber's conception of sociology, and the Baden school of neo-Kantianism."[260] Troeltsch influenced Paul Tillich, also mentioned earlier. He also "laid the groundwork for an inclusive perspective on world religions, tackling the problem of how one can acknowledge their shared elements and common values and also establish a legitimate standard measurement."[261]

We can see the roots of the divergence between liberal Christianity and Conservative Christianity in the emerging postmodern era through these examples of the ferment of ideas and subsequent intellectual and pastoral trends active in pre-WWI universities such as Erlangen and Leipzig. The University of Leipzig, founded in 1409, and the University of Erlangen, founded in 1743, were, and are, both top of the pyramid institutions of higher learning in Europe, the one being a product or construct of the Renaissance and the other being a product of the Enlightenment.

Because both Torrey and Otto, both being educated by the same system, represent the final thread of intellect and *praxis* that held the intellectual community of Western Civilization together before the advent of WWI. We can refer to the moments before WWI as *egeneto*, as a coming to pass, but we will find, after that time, a permanent discrepancy in what we can call *egeneto* in terms of praxis and Praxis.

---

258   See footnote 40.
259   Erlangen scholars – https://www.edurank.org_100notable-alumniofuniversityoferlangennuremberg ; accessed 24 Feb 23.
260   Erlangen, ibid.
261   Troeltsch – https://www.newworldencyclope-dia.org_ernsttroeltsch ; accessed 24 Feb 23.

At the very least, it is appropriate to say that R. A. Torrey, in supervising the collection of what is called *The Fundamentals*, saw the "writing on the wall … MENE, MENE, TEKEL, UPHARSIN" or "God has numbered your kingdom (twice) and put an end to it … you have been weighed in the balances and are found wanting" and "your kingdom has been divided and given to the Medes and Persians."[262] The "Modern" ended in 1914, having been divided and given over to the Medes and Persians.

Belshazzar is dead: Long live Darius! And so, the setting is set for the return to Judaea under the authority of the Persian Empire. But first, the exiles must fellowship with Persia. The Greeks are being Greeks, the Jews are being Jews, and the Persians are providing a bridge across the void.

But who ARE the Medes and Persians, and can we count on them to come through for us once again? When the city is rebuilt, it is much more likely to be Hegel's Divine Idea on Earth than it is to be Augustine's City of God.

Full "abandonment to God," unless guarded by the knowledge of the methods by which the Spirit of God reveals Himself, may open the life to the invasion of spirits of darkness … What the surrendered soul must pursue is the will of God as his chief and only aim, being watchful lest his mind be set on things which might promote carnality and be the issue of self-will.[263]

THE WELSH REVIVAL happened in Wales in 1904/1905. It began spontaneously and with a testimony, as all revivals do, its effect soon going "beyond Welsh borders and (becoming) the context from which Pentecostalism emerged."[264] The opening quote for this section is taken from the famous book that summarized the teachings heard and received in the Welsh Revival.

---

262   Daniel 5:24-28
263   Jessie Penn-Lewis/Evan Roberts, *War on the Saints, the Full Text Unabridged Edition* (New York: Thomas E. Lowe, Ltd., 1973, 1998; originally 1912), Introductory Chapter
264   Welsh Revival – https://www.wikisummaries.orgwelsgrevivalspreadspentecostalismsummary ; last updated November 10, 2022, accessed 24 Feb 23.

The Azusa Street Revival "took place in Los Angeles, California[265] ... led by William J. Seymour, an African American preacher. The revival began on April 9, 1906, and continued until roughly 1915."[266] As far as history can tell, nobody ran quickly from Wales to Los Angeles to tell Pastor Seymour "How to do it." It's a little less than 5,400 air miles from the one to the other. These virtually simultaneous events were the sparks that created the fiery piety which has become Pentecostalism.

One famous author in the realm of religious studies writes, "Among the many prefigurings of the future to appear at the turn of the last century, two in particular stand out. One was the great World's Columbian Exposition, which drew millions of people to Chicago in the summer of 1893v ... The second was a lesser-known Azusa Street Revival which took place a decade later in Los Angeles among a cluster of down-at-the-heels hymn singers and itinerant evangelists, but which marked the birth of the worldwide Pentecostal movement."[267] The exposition burned to the ground.

Harvey Cox was the Victor Thomas Professor of Religion at Harvard University who also wrote the famous/infamous book *The Secular City*.[268] In *Fire from Heaven*, Professor Cox effectively retracts the thesis of *The Secular City*. He writes, "I tried to work out a theology for the 'post religious' age that many sociologists had confidently assured us was coming ... Today it is secularity, not spirituality, that may be headed for

---

265   Azusa Revival – https://www.flickr.com_historicalmarker : "Historical plaque ... is located at Naguchi Plaza near the corner of Azusa Street and San Pedro Street"; accessed 25 Feb 23. AUTHOR'S NOTE: It's now in the middle of Little Tokyo.
266   Azusa Street Revival – https://en.m.wikipedia.org_azusastreetrevival ; last edited 11 December 2022, accessed 24 Feb 23.
267   Harvey Cox, *Fire from Heaven: The Rise of Pentecostal Spirituality and the Reshaping of Religion in the Twenty-First Century* (Menlo Park, CA: Addison-Wesley Publishing Company, 1995), p. 22
268   Harvey Cox, *The Secular City*, 1965 – https://www.press.princeton.edu_thesecularcity : "Since its initial publication in 1965, *The Secular City* has been as a classic for its nuanced exploration of the relationships among the rise of urban civilization, the decline of hierarchical, institutional religion, and the place of the secular within society"; accessed 25 Feb 23.

extinction."[269] Later in the book, he says, "large blocs of people became increasingly skeptical of inherited religious dogmas, and ecclesiastical institutions steadily lost their power to shape cultures. This is the part of the story many scholars expected, and I was one of those who accepted the appraisal. This is what gave the talk about secularization and the 'death of God' a certain plausibility. But something else was happening as well. Not only were large numbers of people becoming alienated from traditional religion, they were also losing confidence in the bright promises of science and progress."[270]

Professor Cox does an admirable and commendable job of re-assessing his own liberal assumptions gleaned from the 60s, and his description of the suddenly very visible "gap" between what was once called "liberal" and "conservative" is spot-on. Nevertheless, his analysis has been essentially ignored by the academic and liberal church communities.[271] Crossing the gap is no longer possible except by means of shouted epithets designed to reduce the other side to the status of comic book caricatures and strawman stereotypes that are easy to rhetorically cancel out from the realm of intelligent consideration.

Religion, even traditional religion, has been actively and vitally rediscovered and revivified since the 90s, such as with Hinduism in India and Russian Orthodoxy in Russia. Since these considerably impactful cultural transformations remain inaccessible to the old liberal categories of religion, morality, and political progressivism, they are largely ignored, derided, attacked, or otherwise completely anathematized by liberal Western thinking and piety. It is seen to be some kind of reversion or reversal of history rather than history's next instalment of transitional change.

---

269   Cox, ibid., p. xv
270   Cos, ibid., p. 104
271   AUTHOR'S NOTE: I suggested Fire from Heaven as a book study to a colleague in the Arizona Episcopal Church. He definitively poopooed the suggestion. Since the Charismatic Movement of the 60s through the 90s, the traditional liberal churches have vehemently and militantly opposed any consideration of Pentecostal truth and have reacted by becoming even more liberal than their 19th and 20th century predecessors could ever have imagined.

It's the change rather than the nature of the permanent that is of most concern to both religious and secular minds today,[272] the 21st century. Heraclitus[273] now rules the postmodern Greek Cosmos instead of Parmenides.[274] But the change is not so much a change from something to something else, or from something old to something new: The change is from something to bits of what might be something. This Humpty-Dumpty "new" world cries out for definition and reassembly, but the kingsmen are not up to the task.[275]

Can there be a revival for Humpty Dumpty?

---

272   See footnote 228.
273   Heraclitus (around 500 BCE)– https://www.plato.stanford.edu_heraclitus : "He is best known for his doctrines that things are constantly changing (universal flux), that opposites coincide (unity of opposites), and that fire is the basic material of the world"; Published Thu Feb 8, 2007, revised Tue Sep 3, 2019, accessed 25 Feb 23.
274   Parmenides (around mid-fifth century BCE) – https://www.plato.stanford.edu_parmenides : "Early Greek philosophy's most profound and challenging thinker ... A good many interpreters the ... paradoxical view that there exists exactly one thing, and for this lone entity's being totally unchanging and undifferentiated ... our normal beliefs in the existence of change, plurality, and ... our own selves (are) entirely deceptive ... Alexander Nehamas would ... propose that Parmenides employs 'is' in the very strong sense of 'is what it is to be'"; published Fri Feb 8, 2008, revised Mon Oct 19, 2020, accessed 25 Feb 23.
275   Humpty Dumpty – https://enb.m.wikipedia.org_humptydumpty : "(1868, 1869) Humpy Dumpty sat on a wall, Humpty Dumpty had a great fall. All the king's horses and all the king's men couldn't put Humpty together again"; last edited 14 February 2023, accessed 25 Feb 23.

Chapter Six: THE DELAYED FUSE

They went and entered a village of the Samaritans to make things ready for Him, but they did not receive Him, because He was set to go to Jerusalem. When His disciples James and John saw this, they said, "Lord, do You want us to command fire to come down from heaven and consume them, even as Elijah did?" But He turned and rebuked them and said, "You do not know what kind of spirit you are of. For the Son of Man did not come to destroy men's lives but to save them."[276]

THE DISCIPLES James and John were the "sons of thunder," that is to say, they were the loudmouths of the troupe. They would have loved to destroy the Samaritan village in order to save it.[277] The refusal by the Samaritans to offer hospitality to anyone who would want to go to Jerusalem is one of the signs of the complete disintegration of the Old Order in Jesus' day. The offer of the famous Sons of Thunder was indicative of one who has a newfound power and does not know how to use it responsibly.

Once upon a time, a long, long time ago, Samaria was the capital city of the Northern Kingdom of Israel while Jerusalem was the capital city of the Southern Kingdom of Judah. Since then, the Assyrian Empire had exiled the Ten Tribes of Israel followed by the exiling of the Three Tribes of Judah into Babylon. There are numerous historical rationalizations for why the residents of Samaria still hated the residents of Judah in the first century BCE, but suffice it to say, here, that the hatreds had grown into habits of the heart.

The disciples were, for the most part, from Galilee, north of Samaria. Both Samaritans and Jews from Jerusalem would have considered them to be either country yokels or of a region thoroughly compromised by

---

276   Luke 9:52-56
277   Philippe Theophanidis, *Communication*, August 8, 2012 – https://www.aphelis.net_itbecamenecessarytodestroythetowntosaveit : "(said by) an United States major, 1968. He was talking about the decision by allied commanders to bomb and shell the town regardless of civilian casualties, to route the Vietcong" … from *The New York Times*, February 8, 1968, p. 14; accessed 25 Feb 23.

cultural gentile incursions. These kinds of tensions between adjacent citizenries, even those living within the same national boundaries, are neither unusual nor fading in the 21st century. This is one presenting reason why the Gospel is still relevant.

If there is an evolutionary and progressive trend in the story of the human race, it is not becoming clearer but, rather, much more difficult to justify as a theory of human civilization. Granted, we have gas stoves and horseless carriages, now, but you can still use either or elements of either as a weapon to kill your neighbor, or even your friend. Too, people still want to kill their neighbors and their friends.

Two-thousand years after the life, death, and resurrection of Jesus Christ, it is getting acerbically difficult to say exactly what advantage His teaching and example has given to humanity as a whole and to Western Civilization as well. There are ways to rationalize this perception by means of metaphor, hopeful scenarios, and continuously refurbished political policies, but they remain rather unconvincing to the world, and as well, to the once universally Christian society in the West.

The future of Christianity is not, however, equivalent to the future of faith in Jesus Christ. Historical Christianity is an institutionalized form of religion that for centuries has held a privileged institutional position in the midst of other powerful Western institutions. When the institution became divided in the Reformation, the culture, too, became divided. The relationship between Church and State, previously one of primary national identities complementing a unitary primary Church, changed by necessity (or providence) into a more diversified and conflicted unity. The idea of being "Christian" still held across the boundaries of the nations, but the fact of one's being a Christian was now contested.

In the Medieval Western world, there was no such civilized phenomenon as being not-Christian. Religious faith and existence walked hand-in-hand. No one needed to identify as a "Christian" because the state of being Christian was simply a cultural given. How that faith was expressed on a micro-cultural level varied greatly, but the term "catholic" still meant universal rather than being the title of one of the many Christian sects.

Even with the fracturing, even fragmenting, of the Christian community into powerful and independent Protestant denominations, those denominations did not reject the heritage of being living aspects of the movement of Christianity in history. This heritage actually began to exert a much stronger pull on the hearts and minds of European Christians. With each claimant to the Christian throne claiming dogmatic and doctrinal supremacy over all the others, institutional Christianity became more like institutional secularity than it ever was before.

In the first decades of the 18th century, the competition between sects became uncontainable. Fire from heaven was called down upon every town, village, and principality that was considered to be Samaritan or less by some other town, village, or principality. In the Thirty Years' War, "an estimated 4.5 to 8 million soldiers and civilians died as a result of battle, famine, and disease, while some areas of what now modern Germany experienced population declines of over 50%."[278] The German people never forgot the devastation reeked on their principalities by the other nations of Europe.

One might say that the Napoleonic Wars were fought by Napoleon in the futile effort to establish a kind of secular/imperial rapprochement on the states of Europe. It didn't work, but it did set the stage for two great all-consuming efforts to improve on the effort, WWI and WWII. If the Thirty Years' War was a religious war, then Napoleon's grand effort was an anti-religious war. Crowning himself emperor without need of a Pope was the crowning act of his anti-religious campaign. It wasn't that religion, the Christian religion, needed to be eliminated: It simply needed to be subdued and rendered impotent regarding the affairs of the State. The Old Order disagreed, at least in word. The deeds of disagreement amounted to simply more war.

---

278   Thirty Years' War – https://en.m.wikipedia.org_thirtyyearswar ; last edited 25 February 2023, accessed 26 Feb 23.

It was in the Napoleonic Wars that fire from heaven became fire from a coalition of Nation-States. Hegel's vision of the future, penned during and immediately after the Napoleonic Wars, was starting to be fulfilled. The old western institutions of leadership, known by history as the *Ancien regime* was being transformed, but the transformation took on demonic proportions at the opening of the 20th century. It was in the 20th century that this civilizational transformation became a civilizational transition.

Because History began to take the place of God in the emerging secular theologies of the West, the ancient notion of God's action in the world became something other than what it was once assumed and believed to be. Words like "providence," "destiny," and even "hope," had to take on different meanings.

It was difficult to discern God's purposes in the rotten bodies that filled gas-drenched shell craters of WWI; it was even harder to discern God's purposes in the gassing of six million Jews during the Nazi holocaust. If the Medieval World vanished because questions like how many angels can dance on the head of a pin became silly even to the level of religious offense, the Modern world began to vanish when Hitler called his grand policy for purifying civilization his Final Solution.

There are many dimensions to the changes that began to take place in the domain of Western Civilization following WWI, but, like light when it gets too close, all of them disappear into a black hole that history can't pretend to escape. History defeats itself. Yet even though there is no rationality to the trends of history that are producing the postmodern world, we can still pretend. Pretension rests on self-deception like the elephants rest on the back of the turtle, and it leads inexorably to the establishment of the God/State that Hegel, Marx, Lenin, and Hitler longed for so dearly. If we become the Civilizational Black Hole, we will no longer need to fear falling into it.

The Black Hole quenches all fires and the light they produce.

Concerning the times and the seasons, brothers, you have no need that I write to you. For you know perfectly that the day of the Lord will come like a thief in the night ... Therefore let us not sleep as others do ... comfort yourselves together, and edify one another, just as you are doing ... Rejoice always. Pray without ceasing ... Do not quench the Spirit.[279]

WHEN PAUL and his companions came to the cities of Asia and Greece, they were met with hostility, both from the pagans and from the local Jewish leaders. They could please no one with their teaching. In Thessalonika, the complaint against them was, "These men who have turned the world upside down have come here also, and Jason has received them. They are all acting contrary to the decrees of Caesar, saying that there is another king, Jesus."[280] They turned their world upside down; in the 21st century it is being turned upside down again.

The upside-downing of the Christian West, although a necessary aspect of its lifetime destiny, began in full force in the decades immediately before WWI. We've mentioned the importance of that moment already and the demise of 19th-century liberal theology, the rise of historical theology, and the occasion of the Welsh Revival, the distributing of the Fundamentals, and the beginning of the Pentecostal Movement on Azusa Street in Los Angeles, California.

The variation in perspective between the Pentecostal and Evangelical worldview and the liberal/historical and higher-critical worldview is theologically breath-taking. The breath itself that is being both taken and given was first inhaled in the centuries preceding ours. It is as if all the conflicting elements, sects, denominations and private versions of Christianity were holding their manifold breath until they could hold it no longer. WWI was the Great Exhale, and it revealed that Western Civilization was suffering from terminal halitosis.

From Pentecostalism to the very liberal stance of Ritschl, Wellhausen, and Bultmann, the once-magnificent Christian unity of Western Civilization was gassed into a stupor by an overdose of noxious and disconnected theologies. Some tried to prove that Christianity is

279   I Thessalonians 5:1-2, 6, 11, 16, 19
280   Acts 17:6-7

"scientific," some professed that Christian doctrine and the Bible are to be interpreted relative to ancient and modern cultural beliefs; some divided a theology of literalism and inerrancy with regard to the very words of the Bible; some relegated Christianity to the status of being one among many valid religions, sometimes the "most" valid and sometimes not even as valid as some of the others.

The extreme radicalness of these changes within Christianity's self-understanding and self-awareness of itself cannot be overstated. The flood of variations in what is expected from the faithful, in terms of mind, heart, and body has been one of the chief, if not the leading factor, in the postmodern world's strange quest to rediscover its identity, even identity as such. From the prenatal to the very old, from the individual to the international, identity is the game of the postmodern era. To identify as a "Christian" no longer has any common or singular meaning.

The language games in which the word "Christian" finds its meaning are as manifold as the opinions musicians arguing about the nature of physics. There is no possible sense of harmony in it or state of harmony that can be reasonably promoted through its use in the language. Plato's ideal world has been rendered permanently, or eternally, defunct. And ... if Plato's ideal world is permanently defunct, so are any of the other worlds that have been fashioned on that foundation.

As the famous British philosopher Alfred North Whitehead (1861-1947) once put it, "All Western philosophy is but a footnote to Plato."[281] Whether it is Augustine's Neoplatonism or Hegel's dialectics, Plato has been revealed to be the feet of clay to Daniel's giant, imaginary ruler.[282] The historians and liberal theologians like to believe that Daniel's vision was fulfilled in the person and office of the Roman Caesar, but it is an apocalyptic vision, therefore eternal. While it ought not be applied willy-nilly to any series of events someone doesn't like, it applies quite directly in apocalyptic times. The ontological and existential ground on

---

281   Whitehead – https://www.laphamsquarterly.org_plato ; accessed 26 Feb 23.
282   Daniel 2:31-35

which we stand in these times is shaking, and our civilization's clay feet are refusing to keep us standing upright. These are the earthquakes.[283]

Meaning strains to escape the prison-like language games in which Western Civilization has enclosed it. The word "Christian" frantically flails its ancient arms while being sucked into a whirlpool of contradictory currents, returning to the primordial sea from which its origins first emerged. At best, the word Christian means "good citizen"; at worst, it means "enemy of the State." If there is any longer a choice for religious affiliation in the Western world, it depends on how you use the word "Christian." Comparing the language games in which the word has found meaning is of no use: They share no common syntax.

The Evangelical Tradition is the cornerstone of the Reformation. Today's Lutheran Church in America merged with several other branches of Lutheranism into the Evangelical Lutheran Church of America in 1988.[284] Martin Luther's *sola scriptura* and *sola fide* changed the topology of Western Christianity. Partly because many, if not most churchgoers were unlettered, even with the aid of the printing press to spread Luther's message, it took generations to truly work out the implications of his break with *Sola Ecclesia Cattolica*.[285] With the Bible in the hands of anyone who wanted to pick it up, William Tyndale's hope that "ere many years I will cause a boy who drives the plough to know more of the scriptures than you do," speaking to a local bishop, would eventually be realized.

It was Karl Barth's church mentor who signed the *Manifesto of the Ninety-Three German Intellectuals to the Civilized World*[286] and it was the Lutheran University of Halle in effect began the trend toward the higher critical approach to the scriptures which has produced the plethora of liberal theologies in the 20th and 21st centuries.[287] Not to fix responsibility

---

283   Mark 13:8
284   LCA – https://en.m.wikipedia.org_lutheranchurchinamerica ; last edited 21 September 2022, accessed 26 Feb 23.
285   AUTHOR'S NOTE: I made up this term.
286   See footnote 44.
287   Ray Dyer, PhD, *The Victorian Web* – https://www.victorianweb.org_thehighercriticsananointedchronology1710-1917 : "1710. Halle, Germany. A Bible group begins distribution of low-cost Bibles to the poor (1804).

for all the theological and ecclesiastical changes which have taken place following those days, but it is fair to quote the famous truism "What goes around comes around." I was raised in the Lutheran persuasion, and as far as I can tell, Luther's Small Catechism owes nothing to the higher critical method of interpreting the Bible![288]

All this focus on the theological ferment in the years immediately, and not so immediately, preceding the turn of the 19th-20th centuries is intended to highlight the fact that the fundamental theological AND philosophical foundations of Western Civilization, from Augustine to Aquinas to Ockham to Luther and so on came to an abrupt end and began to crack into thousands of separate pieces. Tyndale's hope was realized, that anyone can pick up a Bible and read it, but he could have had no idea what the long-term ramifications of that gift to humankind would eventually be.

Not everyone who reads it believes it; not everyone who studies it believes it has anything to do with the transcendent God. Even so, often when a denomination or body of scholars refer to the Bible as the "word of God," the entire meaning of the phrase "word of God" has been irrevocably deformed. Once Spirit became Reason, the phrase "quench the spirit" itself can mean almost anything.

It could even mean treason.

To believe in the New Testament Holy Spirit and follow his groanings[289] could even be called treason.

University of Halle founded as <u>Lutheran</u> foundation 1694, 'the first modern university'. Had renounced religious orthodoxy in favor of objective-rational science and investigation. Canonical texts were replaced by systematic lectures, and German replaced Latin as the language of instruction"; accessed 26 Feb 23.

288 AUTHOR'S NOTE: On the other hand, when I was younger, my family attended an Evangelical Lutheran Church, but when I was of confirmation age, our local Lutheran option was the very conservative Wisconsin Lutheran Church.

289 Romans 8:26-27: "The Spirit helps us in our weaknesses, for we do not know what to pray for as we ought, by the Spirit Himself intercedes for us with groanings too deep for words. He

Moral intuition presupposes what Taylor[290] terms "a given ontology of the human" ... As individuals. And especially as moral individuals, "We are selves only in that certain things matter for us. What I am as a self, my identity, is essentially defined by the way things have significance for me." Self-interpretation in this sense is inescapably a linguistic activity, and as language requires a community, not just to provide a language, but to provide the social meanings of selfhood within which any self-interpretation is articulated.[291]

THE EXTENDED modern intellectual task is to rediscover, reclaim, or newly discover a reason to be moral. Considering the vast immoralities of the 20th century, this task is virtually impossible, its answer being hidden in the ambiguities of misconstrued selves. Church, State, Political factions, revolutionary groups, think tanks, advocacy groups, and so forth, have all been seasoned with fragmented versions of morality custom designed to suit their ideological ends.

Ideology and morality coincide only in the sense that morality is deformed to meet the demands of the ideology. All ideologies come from an assumption of past moralities uniquely and indivisibly intertwined with the totalities assumed by the ideology. It is in this way that ideology, and its application on State and international levels, becomes the beginning and the end of morality and the sole determiner of all moral principles.

The only recourse the individual soul has to counter this nationalizing of morality, within the context of the concepts and principles allowed by rational Modernity, is anarchy and even nihilism. If the individual is constrained by the Modern conscience to adapt either anarchy or nihilism to the foundational needs and desires of the self, the individual

---

who searches the hearts knows what the mind of the Spirit is, because He intercedes for the saints according to the will of God."

290   Charles Taylor, born November 5, 1931 – https://en.m.wikipedia.org_charlestaylor(philosopher) : "A Canadian philosopher from Montreal, Quebec, and professor emeritus at McGill University best known for his contributions to political philosophy, the philosophy of social science, the history of philosophy, and intellectual history ... *Sources of the Self: The Making of Modern Identity*, Cambridge, Massachusetts: Harvard University Press. 1989"; last edited 20 February 2023, accessed 27 Feb 23.

291   Bull, ibid., p `. 258

must then choose to identify with the prescribed national characteristics of the State.

The definition of self, quoted above as, "the way things have significance for me," appears as the last stand of modern social science and its intrinsic wisdom regarding whether or not there can be said to actually BE such a thing as a personal self, or identity, in the Modern world, apart from the dictates of the State. This is why the author coins the phrase "ontology of the human." In short, science in the form of the social sciences has lost track of what once was commonly understood to be "human." This is an odd predicament for a trajectory of thought, belief, and concern which was initiated by a cultural phenomenon that is still referred to as Humanism.

It is historically and intellectually interesting to note that the central interests of William of Ockham, the inventor of the so-called Occam's Razor, were natural philosophy, metaphysics, epistemology, theology, and most notably, ontology.[292] His razor has shaved the theological person's face so closely over the last 700 years that the shaving is beginning to cut the spiritual person's theological throat. After that, the State will provide life-support, if the individual merits it according to the ideology of the State.

The ancient and culturally ubiquitous question, "Who am I?" is the fundamental question of all individuals in society. Even before learning a language, the infant asks it by means of crying, gurgling, screaming, and so forth in order to become oriented in that very basic society which consists only of mother and child. The question "who am I?" is always shadowed by its complimentary question, "Who are you?" The differentiation between the two questions forms the primordial basis of all societies, cultures, and civilizations.

The need to ask the question never subsides. The fundamental need to find a reliable answer to live by never ceases to challenge the human soul. Drugs, surgeries, wars, political campaigns, the obtaining

---

292   William of Ockham – https://en.m.wikipedia.org_williamofockham ; last edited 8 February 2023, accessed 27 Feb 23.

of advanced college degrees, and so forth are all singular and corporate attempts to answer the question, but when the question seems to have been answered, it simply acquires a new language game in which the answer can be both imbedded and effectively hidden.

Tillich tried to answer the defining concept of self as being what matters to us when he invented the theological term "ultimate concern." His ultimate concern, however, needed to be a universal human concern, an existential concern. He struggled with the idea of dialectic truth in order to arrive at some kind of synthesis which would make sense both of the Bible, the accumulated theology and philosophy of the West, and the declarations of various versions of State ontology and existence in the 20th century. He failed.

"Ultimate Concern" is both too abstractly vast and too limited in scope. There is no plurality to it because it is presented as an ontological and phenomenological whole which embraces all the totalities of the past and anticipates all the totalities of the future.

In the end, as Modernity marches toward its own future and *telos*, my ultimate concern will always be ME . . . and it will be more and more ME as the decades flow by. It will become so much ME that I won't be able to either comprehend or act out of the Truth of ME without the help and even control of the larger ME, the State. In this way, Tillich and the dialecticians' God is ME, but I am not God. I just think I am. In a postmodern deformation of the founder Descartes' phrase, "I think I am God, therefore I am not God."

The last scene in the classic movie, *2001: A Space Odyssey*, is a rather prophetic imaging of this idea. The machine, in the form of A.I., acts as the midwife in the birthing process of a New Humanity, or a new civilization. The archetypal imprint of this great movie still clings to the unconscious mind of everyone who watches it. It's like something waiting to happen that will, eventually, and soon, happen. On the other hand, by today's cinematic standards, the movie can be quite boring. We are left waiting still as we leave the theater.[293]

Birthing and "eventing" are the two archetypal realities that come together in the birth of Jesus. In the language of the Bible, the event is the coming-to-pass that fulfills God's plan which was established at the beginning in and for creation. Generating of generations is the social and relational expansion of the coming-to-pass. People are born; events signify or anticipate new birth. Together, they constitute the unfolding of God's plan of salvation. They are often confused.

The gift of birth protects and enables the ontology of "self": the gift of *egeneto* protects and enables the ontology of community. How they go together is the long message of both Testaments. The structure of Biblical morality is determined and revealed by the synagogue of the two.

When I look over my shoulder, what do you think I see? Some other cat looking over his shoulder at me, and he's strange, sure is strange; you've got to pick up every stitch …[294]

IN A PREVIOUS CHAPTER, I said that "being meets identity in the human soul." The human soul IS the meeting place between Being and Identity. The language of religion is the language of this inner synagogue of Being and Identity. The language of the State is the language of proprietorship when both synagogue and Areopagus[295] become possessions of the whole. The Areopagus is language itself. The synagogue is where the languages gather." The languages can gather as the vultures gather over a carcass, or the languages can gather as the Nations gathered before Zion.[296]

---

293   Ben Hardwick, *CBR* - https://www.cdr.com_ararestanleykubrick-interviewexplains2002aspaceodysseysending : "He then found himself in a cleanly lit room and watched himself rapidly age into an old man. As David lay withered in bed, he reached out to the monolith and became a baby. 2001: A Space Odyssey's final shot showed this child floating above planet earth … the climax's deeper meaning is still open for debate"; last updated Feb 4, 2023, accessed 27 Feb 23.

294   *Season of the Witch*, Donovan Leitch, 1966 - https://www.genius.com_seasonofthewitch ; accessed 27 Feb 23.

295   Acts 17:16-34

296   Isaiah 66:18: "For I know their works and their thoughts. The time shall come to gather all the nations and

Egeneto is when God is visibly, clearly, and unmistakably acting, or doing Praxis. In the case of all the events bracketing the birth of Jesus, praxis and Praxis are coming together mightily, even if some of the practitioners have no awareness of it at all. The last Coming-to-Pass is the gathering of the nations. Only then will every individual realize one's identity, or self, in Christ.[297] After this moment, the last moral and social adjudication follows. The Old Creation is realized, completed, and then forgotten, giving way to the New Creation.[298]

The New Creation is neither a modification of the Old Creation nor a moral substitute for it in principle: It is something utterly new, something that has been neither conceived nor seen nor experienced before, for "eye has not seen, nor ear heard, nor has it entered into the heart of man the things which God has prepared for those who love Him.[299] But God has revealed them to us by His Spirit."[300]

The window into the shape and form of the New Creation is the word of God.[301]

In the movie, *Annihilation*, the protagonist, Lena, encounters "a pulsing Mandelbulb that absorbs blood from (her), creating a humanoid that mimics Lena's motions. Unable to escape the creature, Lena tricks it into accepting a phosphorus grenade as it transforms into her doppelganger. Lena flees, but her doppelganger calmly allows the grenade to burn it along with the lighthouse. The Shimmer collapses. Back at the facility, Lena tells an interrogator that the Shimmer did not seek to destroy, but to 'make something new.'"[302] The movie can either be an apocalyptic

---

tongues. And they shall come and see My glory."
297   I Corinthians 13:12: "For now we see as through a glass, dimly, but then, face to face. Now I know in part, but then I shall know, even as I also am known."
298   II Corinthians 5:17: "If any man is in Christ, he is a new creature. Old things (*archaia/arche/*archetype) have passed away. Look, all things have become new (*gegonen kaina/egeneto*)."
299   Isaiah 64:4
300   I Corinthians 2:9-10
301   See footnote 98.
302   *Annihilation*, Paramount Pictures, 2018 – https://en.m.wikipedia.org_annihilation(film) ; last edited 26 February 2023, accessed 27 Feb 23.

horror film or an intriguing look into the future of the cosmos and humanity. At any rate, Lena, played by Natalie Portman, saves the day ... sort of. As are all postmodern apocalypses, the ending is ambiguous. It can either be a psychological thriller or a sci-fi horror flick: Viewer's choice.[303]

Annihilation could also be about Western Civilization's annihilation of itself due to the ontological loss of self in the machine-like evolution of the state. Anarchy and nihilism, in this version of interpretation, do not destroy the State: They actually form the fundamental attitude of the New State. The Apocalypse is commandeered by the State, and the State becomes the Beast.[304] Evil has its own allure. The self is destroyed and then resurre4cted through the power of the State.

The language game being promoted by the State will make all the difference in the interpretation of present cultural reality's interpretation of its own existential situation. The end-times conundrum of the self in search of itself is magnified by the coming-to-pass that "in modernity roles and identities were uncoupled so that someone with a single identity could play multiple social roles; there seems no intrinsic reason why social identities should not be similarly uncoupled from somatic continuity ...We do not really know who we are or who we are dealing with, not because we are confused, but because we cannot know."[305] Modern humanity has lost touch with its own origins in humanism. Even the physical body is up for grabs in terms of what IT is all supposed to mean.

The postmodern situation is a bit like the times of Jesus, or the times of Augustine, or the times of the mini-apocalyptic breaks in the story of Western Civilization. Only more so, of a exponential magnitude: We should have known by now, but we don't. Knowing, in the truest sense of the word, has slipped our grasp. The Tower of Babel is being constructed

---

303 AUTHOR'S NOTE: Personally, I see the story as an inside look into Lena's soul as she melts down from guilt and shame over her sexual betrayal of her husband. In the end, they don't know each other at all.
304 See footnote 59.
305 Bull, ibid., pp. 283, 288.

on the foundation of the Areopagus. The gathering of nations is forced to climb to the top where the Universal Nation resides.

Being and Identity both are to become the possession of the Universal Nation, and personal transition provides the steps for the New Stairway to Heaven.[306]

The apocalyptic features of late modernity are those we take for granted ... As in apocalyptic, taboo has ended, sacrifice has ceased and the scapegoats have returned. Small wonder, therefore, that the social developments of late modernity have been accompanied by a barrage of excited commentary from the apocalyptically minded of all religions. The social character of late modernity actually is apocalyptic; every breakdown of sacrifice, every infringement of taboo, brings the polluting undifferentiation that is the reversal of the mechanisms that maintain order in traditional societies.[307]

THIS ATMOSPHERE of undifferentiation is a matter of language. It's a matter of language games that have lost their own boundaries: There are very few borders to meaning, and those that still abide are getting buried in blizzards of ideology. We began this book with a quote from a currently popular, or notorious, movie, "If your fear is operating outside of the bounds, you're not. The boundary has been moved"[308] and qualified it with the statement, "Every game has boundaries, every prophet is out of bounds."

The prophet's words and phrases may make no sense, but their meaning goes deeper than the will or perception. The language of the Bible is entirely prophetic. Sometimes the prophet sets boundaries, often political, ritual, or moral boundaries, but there are specific times in the economy of God when there is no more setting of boundaries, only declarations of the inevitable.

---

306   Stairway to Heaven, Led Zeppelin, 1971 – https://www.musixmatch.com_stairwaytoheaven/lyrics : "And its whispered that soon if we all call the tune, then then piper will lead us to reason, and a new day will dawn for those who stand long, and the forests will echo with laughter"; accessed 27 Feb 23.
307   Bull, ibid., pp. 291-292.
308   *Sicario*, Lionsgate, 2015

As a language game of its own, the language of the Bible sets its own boundaries, and it erects its own boundary markers. The ability to discern these boundaries and boundary markers is directly proportional to how far into the language game you are willing to go. This is the aspect of Bible-talk, or God-breathed words, that makes it so preachable. The meaning is transmitted direct from heart to heart. It doesn't bypass the mind, but if the kind is paying attention to the changes of heart which the words and phrases accomplish, the mind itself will be wholly attentive to the language.

The author quoted above concludes his analysis of the present apocalypse in the West with these words, "One consequence of this account is that it suggests that the apocalyptic hiddenness of contemporary society is not an unwanted by-product of the Enlightenment project but a testimony to its success ... the increasing hiddenness of the world comes from the spread of recognition and the lighting up of the necessarily hidden – in which this apocalypse has to be seen not as a sudden implosion of the world, but, rather, as Joachim[309] and Hegel envisaged, a gradual progress toward contradiction brought about by the subtle but irreversible dawning of new aspects on the aspect-blind."[310] If there are no aspects to the self to be discerned, there is no judgment that can be made regarding the efficacy and legitimacy of those aspects.[311]

The conundrum of this end is that the dialectic has only gone so far as creating the two antagonists, the thesis and the antithesis, and there is no way to language any meaningful kind of synthesis. In this case, "while it shares the gradualism and egalitarianism of utopia, our apocalypse is also characterized by just that epistemic undecidability which the utopian

---

309   Marjorie E. Reeves, *Encyclopedia Britannica*, Jul 20, 1998 – https://www.britannica.com_joachimoffiore : "(1130-1201) Italian mystic, theologian, biblical commentator, philosopher of history ... He developed a philosophy of history according to which history develops in three ages of increasing spirituality: the ages of the Father, the Son, and the Holy Spirit"; updated Dec 30, 2019, accessed 28 Feb 23.
310   Bull, ibid., p. 294
311   AUTHOR'S NOTE: We have already seen some of the long term continuity with Joachim of Fiore in theology in the previously quoted work by Garrigou-Lagrange, *The Three Ages of the Interior Life*.

thinkers have so often sought to exclude, for its epistemic abjection is the token of its dialectical progress. We should hesitate before we proclaim every symptom of our ignorance to be pregnant with utopian promise..."[312]

Utopia is "a place of ideal perfection especially in laws, government, and social conditions." It can also be construed as "an often imaginary place or state of utter perfection and happiness." Some synonyms for utopia are paradise, nirvana, wonderland, empyrean, promised land, Shangri-la, Garden of Eden, dreamworld, Elysium, Camelot, and New Jerusalem.[313] Some of these synonyms borrow from the biblical language game and deform the meaning somewhat, but it is good to keep in mind the "perfection" is one of the translations of the Greek New Testament word, *telos*, which also means "end" and "ultimate purpose." Movie-goers will recall mention of Elysium, for instance in *Gladiator* [314] and in the movie of the same name, *Elysium*.[315]

Telos is what God has planned for us. The fulfilment (re: *pleroma*) of God's Plan of Salvation is The Telos. This word has troubled Western Christianity from the beginning. *Telos* saturates the meaning of the language of the Old and New Testaments. This is why it is necessary to understand that every word and phrase has its purposeful place. Nobody made it up, it was passed on from generation to generation, just like any other language.

The curious thing about the dissolution of the Western intellect and the parallel "polluting undifferentiated" characteristic of modern communication of all kinds is that the fragmenting of ancient and trusted narrative prescribed by the deconstructionists is actually an aspect of salvation rather than of the dreaded undifferentiation. The old narratives merge into each other, trespassing the boundaries of meaning such that

---

312   Bull, ibid., p. 294.
313   Utopia – https://www.merriam-webster.com_utopia ; accessed 28 Feb 23.
314   Gladiator, *Dreamworks Distribution*, 2000 – https://www.amer-icanrhetoric.com_gladiator(2000) : "If you find yourself alone, riding in green fields, with the sun on your face, do not be troubled, for you are in Elysium, and you're already dead!"-accessed 28 Feb 23
315   *Elysium*, Columbia Pictures, 2013

to do away with them is the only recourse to which the late modern intellect can turn.

The old narratives are the narratives of church, especially church history, culture, morality, science, and so forth. The crisis faced by the civilization as such lies in the emerging fact that even such previously disparate language games such as science and history have become indistinct both with respect to each other and in themselves. The most observable cultural efforts to redeem this situation amount to the equivalent of putting Humpty Dumpty together again.[316] It's not going to happen.

The only apparent alternative to the woebegone task of reinventing and reassembling Humpty is that of letting the fire fall so that it can consume everything, all the totalities, as a free will sacrifice to one god or another. The language of ritual sacrifice is so ambivalent now that it is becoming more and more questionable whether the god we are worshipping is the God we once worshipped.

There are the fires of nuclear destruction and there is the Fire of the Holy Spirit. They may be blended in confusion too much for rational intelligence to separate them, but they will come as utterly different manifestations of destiny, even if they happen concurrently.

There have always been delaying actions, too, but the delayed fuse is coming close to its explosive conclusion.

---

316   See footnote 275.

Chapter Seven: ANTICIPATING THE SIGNS OF THE END

The history of ideas ... follows the genesis, which, on the basis of received or acquired representations, gives birth to systems and ouvres. It shows, on the other hand, how the great figures that are built up in this way gradually decompose: how the themes fall apart, pursue their isolated lives, fall into disuse, or are recompensed in a new way. The history of ideas ... is the discipline of beginnings and ends, the description of obscure continuities and returns, the reconstitution of developments in the linear form of history. But it can also, by that very fact, describe, from one domain to another, the whole interplay of exchanges and intermediaries...[317]

WWI WASN'T AN IDEA: It blossomed from an entire garden of ideas. Those ideas had been tried, tested, and synthesized for over a thousand years. That synthesizing is what I am calling Western Civilization. The final synthesis of Western Civilization, Hegel's imaginations notwithstanding, was and is World War I. There is no coming synthesis, no union of opposites, no thesis-antithesis-synthesis: There is only thesis vs antithesis which results in dissolution. Hegel's prescription and mystical description degenerates into Thesis-Antithesis-Chorathesis (xorathesis), or Separation.[318]

Hegel's State, his construct-synthesis, is reified xorathesis, or separation. Its fundamental structure requires a separation of self from self on the unconscious level. The invented and politically submissive self effectively replaces the created self, fashioning a synthetic New Creation. Because the created self has been eclipsed by the invented self, the invented self can have no idea regarding the truth/knowledge substance or content of the synthetic New Creation.

---

317   Foucault, *Archaeology*, p. 137
318   cwris – https://en.m.wikipedia.org_cwris : "From cwra (khora), coros (khoros, 'place') + is (-is), initially meaning 'in another, separate space or place' ... without, otherwise ... cwrizo (choridzo): to divide, separate"; accessed 3 Mar 23

In other words, the once-Christian civilization will believe that Jesus has returned, even if it had of late pretended to not believe in such things anymore. By the breaking of the window between the subjective and the objective and refusing to see the connection between the two in the light of the Gospel, the Gospel itself, in terms of its words and phrases, will become the anti-Gospel in the minds of the citizens of the synthetic New Creation. The Battle for the Mind will have been won, not by changing minds or replacing old ideas with new ideas, but by a kind of State-initiated trans-morphosis by which the *meta* of metamorphosis, meaning above and beyond the present morphology, becomes *trans*, meaning "on or to the other side of" the present morphology. The shape of creation is turned inside out: Its topology becomes a-morphology.

The world is turning upside-down again.[319]

There is no way of knowing what a civilization turned inside-out might look like. Essentially, it can look not at all like a civilization, even one in the making. Nevertheless, it likely wouldn't look like an "uncivilized" world because the meaning of uncivilized rests on the meaning of civilized. In other words, it will be totally unfamiliar and unrecognizable in terms of any of the "old" language games.

Remembering that a language game is how truth and meaning are conveyed between selves, this means that truth and meaning will no longer be communicated between selves. How a society might function, if at all, when even the expression of a threat or of love cannot in principle be understood is beyond imagination.

This emerging situation should come as no surprise with respect to the history of ideas that undergirds Western thoughts and sentiments. The mystical ideal, whether of Hegel or Al-Ghazali or St. Theresa of Avila, involves the annihilation of self.[320] This ideal follows a cultural

---

319   See footnote 280.

320   Barbara Newman, *Chicago Journals*, 27 February 2016 – https://www.journals.uchicago.edu_annihilationandauthorshipthreewomen-mysticsofthe1290s : "One of the most startling tenets of late-medieval mysticism is its call for self-annihilation. The human soul, with all its powers of knowing, willing, and loving, must be reduced to nothing

trajectory all the way back in time to the 13th century, but its general presenting idea would not be foreign to, say, the Greek philosopher Heraclitus or earlier holy people in virtually every historical culture and society.

As has already been mentioned, Heraclitus rules the postmodern cosmos, not Parmenides: Change over permanence. This return to mysticism in Western thinking participates in the origins of the Western identity via its appropriation of the Greek worldview. Mysticism, then, as a comprehendible philosophical or theological position disintegrates into the previously mentioned undifferentiation.[321]

Given Whitehead's true-enough but slightly facetious remark that Western philosophy from start to finish is just a series of footnotes to Plato,[322] it is possible to begin a discussion in terms of the beginnings and ends that Foucault prescribes. That he was a so-called deconstructionist or postmodernist, and his lifestyle was somewhat less than status-quo, can be forgiven by the fact that he was speaking truth to power: The power of an entire civilization.

As a reminder from the previous discussion, "The mysticism of the Last Things is completely and utterly represented by the explosion of Oppie's "Gadget" in the deserts of New Mexico on July 16, 1945. The explosive test was not for nothing named the 'Trinity.' That was the day St. Augustine's seminal contribution to Western Civilization was vaporized. That was the day Reason begat Chaos," and "this atmosphere of undifferentiation is a matter of language. It's a matter of language games that have lost their own boundaries: There are very few borders to meaning, and those that still abide are getting buried in blizzards of ideology. We began this book with a quote from a currently popular, or notorious, movie, 'If your fear is operating outside of the bounds, you're not. The boundary has been moved' and qualified it with the statement, 'Every game has boundaries, every prophet is out of bounds.'

---

and merge with God without remainder, sacrificing its unique identity in indistinct union with the Beloved"; accessed 3 Mar 23.
321　　See footnote 307.
322　　See footnote 281.

Foucault and the other deconstructionist and/or postmodern academics are diabolically correct, and their visions of what **IS** ought not to be ignored by conventional voices.

The deconstructionists are not tearing down the tower: It is collapsing of its own accord, and they are just a witness and a participant in the collapse. There is no other practical direction in which the civilization can go. The civilization's trajectory reached its apogee and "what goes up must come down." But the Wisdom of the Age demands that down become up and up become down so to save the entire civilizational edifice from its natural end. Just as death is built into every cell of the body, so, too, the end of every civilization is postulated by its beginning. The dying lion is in its most dangerous state.

There is a transition, but it, too, is discontinuous both from what was and what is to be. It's a transition "from one domain to another, (a) whole interplay of exchanges and intermediaries." Therefore, it isn't unwise to discount the deconstructionists and the postmodernists, but it is wise for the classical Christian to take not of the Bible and its depictions of the same kinds of archetypal changes that Western Civilization is experiencing in the Postmodern world.

As *they* say, "When in Rome do as the Romans do."[323]

(Returning) briefly to the time-honored question of absolute vs. relational space. It can be put in this form: Would there be space if there were no objects?... the advocate of absolute space bases his attitude on the simple fact that he can intuit three-dimensional space even when it is vacant of objects ... it is not the space which scientists have adopted. It is not the kind of space which functions as a valid construct in the face of the requirement laid down (in preceding chapters). These requirements to not contain a postulate of intuitability...[324]

---

323   When in Rome – https://www.gingersoftware.com_when-inromedoastheromansdo : "The origin of the idiom ... was first seen in print in 1777, in Interesting Letters of Pope Clement XIV" (regarding the traditional Italian afternoon siesta) ... "examples (date) from as early as the late 1500s"; accessed 3 Mar 23.

324   Margenau, ibid. p. 153.

THE ROME WE LIVE IN is not the historical city of Rome; neither is it Augustine's City of God. It is fair to say, however, that it is not Augustine's City of Man, either. It isn't even Rome, and we don't really live there. Therefore, what we do in Rome is an entirely open question.

If anyone chooses not to accept this radical change in existential AND ontological fact, let that person stand next to an atomic explosion: The vaporization of the self will be instantaneous. It isn't just a big bomb: It is, as Oppenheimer said, a product and gift of Vishnu, who said in the Gita, "Now I am become death, the destroyer of worlds."[325] The nations are still trying to arm themselves with death. Vishnu has finally self-transformed into Shiva. He is to be followed by his neo-consort, Kali.[326]

Oppenheimer knew this, but he discovered too late that it was too late to opt out of the transition to a quasi-Hinduism in the West and return to the symbols and language of Christianity. Self-annihilation, destruction of the structures of civilization, and the ascent of feminism were all guaranteed by the atomic bomb.[327] The unfortunate caveat is that it is virtually impossible to shift a dualistic culture over to becoming a non-dualistic culture. The window must still be broken, and the result is not a kind of Western Hinduism: The result is the present return to Manichaeism[328] with its consequent historical "xorathesis."

---

325 Bird and Sherwin, *American Prometheus*, p. 309:
326 Hindu Trinity – https://www.bigthink.com_trimurtimeettheholytrinityofhinduism : "The Hindu trinity is also known as the Trimurti, Sanskrit for 'three forms,' and it includes Brahma, Vishnu, and Shiva. The deities are responsible for guiding the cycles of creation and destruction in the Universe … Brahma is responsible for bringing the Universe into existence, Vishnu maintains its balance, and Shiva is called on to end the cycle of creation and destruction … while Shiva's role is to destroy, this is for the purpose of constructive transformation … Kali, the goddess of death and destruction … the image of Kali standing over Shiva symbolizes the supremacy of Nature over man, or the triumph of the divine feminine energy, the creative force, over divine masculine energy"; posted January 11, 2023, accessed 3 Mar 23.
327 Bird and Sherwin, *American Prometheus*, p. 462: "Since Hiroshima, Oppenheimer had lived with … a peculiar sense that someday his own 'beast of the jungle' would emerge to alter his existence. For some year … he had known that he was a hunted man."
328 See footnote 156.

When matter is entirely transformed into energy, there is no more objective reality, only invisible energy. When there is no matter, there are no objects. When there are no objects, there is no space. Certainly, 'things' have changed much more radically than any of us could ever had expected. A spaceless world has no locations, and thus it has no boundaries. There are no "things." When the window between the subjective and the objective is broken, this becomes the situation in the mind as well. The noosphere itself becomes undifferentiated.

The undifferentiated world is the world of chaos. Cause and effect, along with the logic of cause and effect, become vaporous and nebulous. The Cloud of Unknowing becomes the Cloud of Uncertainty. The only thing one can know is that one is uncertain and is living in an uncertain world.

What happens in a world that can neither be known by intuition nor by direct observation? Its boundaries must be set by moral and intellectual fiat. If you say you know what a sub-atomic particle is, you are lying; if you say you know what is the right thing to do, you are lying. A world without boundaries is a world that increasingly demands boundaries.

What we face in the Postmodern era is not self-annihilation by atomic bomb: We face the certainty of the coming void that the existentialists tried to conquer. It's a void through which the high-pressure wind of the objective storms into the low-pressure domain of subjectivity; it's the void through which the high-pressure wind of subjectivity storms into the low-pressure realm of objectivity. In the broken window itself, the perfect storm develops. The general counter facing situation cries out for a savior.

But the savior of the world is no longer a civilized given: He has been de-civilized, cast out. His authority has been stripped away, just like it was in the beginning. With nothing to cover the wounds we have inflicted on His naked body, we shrink away from even ourselves in horror. We want to be somebody else.

Even so, the Scriptures say, "Let us therefore go forth to Him outside the camp, bearing the reproach that He bore. For here we have no continuing city, but we seek one."[329] When it's time to break camp, the Ark goes forth first. To follow the Ark when sunrise approaches is to enter the void we have always feared. When the Ark rests, the Lord returns.[330]

The sacred space in the Bible is defined by movements and the transition to and transformation of worlds. Without movement, there is no space. There is movement through a world and there is movement from one world to the next. The movement within a world is constituted in terms of praxis coincident with Praxis; the movement between worlds is an expression of Praxis alone. When praxis coincides with Praxis, it results in a coming-to-pass in time and space. God determines when praxis coincides with Praxis, yet the free will of the participants is never compromised. As we have seen, this can take some doing, as exemplified by the accounts of the nativity of Jesus.

Sacred space is defined by movement, then, and it has four dimensions, just like space-time. In effect, everything is moving relative to everything else from the moment of Creation to the Last Judgment. The Holy Spirit of God manages this movement, so the finite participants find themselves participating in the whole. When Elijah moves, for instance, that movement affects us as well; when Joshua moves, that movement affects us as well.

When we move in the Spirit, that movement accords with, and effects, the movement of Joshua, Elijah, and all the other resurrected saints. This is that "great cloud of witnesses"[331] in which the fellowship of the saints is contained. It's bounded by faith, *sola fide*, faith alone. This, too, is not the space scientists have adopted. That space is the void

---

329 Hebrews 13:13-14
330 Numbers 10:33-36: "When the ark set out ... Moses said, 'Rise up, O Lord, and let your enemies be scattered, and let them that hate You flee before You.' And when it rested, he said, 'Return, O Lord, to the multitude of thousands of Israel.'"
331 Hebrews 12:1

into which we are marching. The void is always at the end of the march because the New Creation is incomprehensible to us.

Then I saw four angels standing at the four corners of the earth, holding the four winds of the earth, that the wind would not blow on the earth or on the sea or on any tree. And I saw another angel ascending from the east, having the seal of the living God. He cried out with a loud voice to the four angels who had been given power to harm the earth and the sea, saying, "Do not harm the earth or the sea or the e, until we have sealed the servants of our God on their foreheads."[332]

CHRISTIAN THEOLOGY within the bounds of its civilization is like the firmament, or expanse, that divides the waters above from the waters below.[333] In the Book of Genesis, it's called Heaven. In the language of the Septuagint, it's called the *stereoma*. It divides, *diachohridzon*, the waters. This is the same type of dividing that involves the end of Christian civilization as it has chosen to end, the Thesis-Antithesis-Chorathesis.

The *Stereoma* is put in its place by means of *ginomai*:[334] It simply came, and comes, and will come to pass. As a coming-to-pass event or moment in space-time, it is eternal. It ALWAYS comes to pass: It comes-to-pass on the Second Day, the Day Christians call Holy Saturday. The Second Day immediately precedes the Day of Resurrection. The Cross of Christ is a type of *Stereoma*. All Christian theology must follow this type or pattern of revealed truth, or else it is not Christian theology.

The four corners of sacred space-time are also types of *stereoma*: They divide one side of the square, or one world, from the next. The waters above and the waters below are once again harmonized so that life can once again be realized and fecund for the People of God. This truth is readily apparent in the prophet's call to the people when they are going into exile: "Build houses and dwell in them; and plant gardens and eat their fruit. Take wives and beget sons and daughters; and take wives for your sons and give your daughters to husbands, so that they may bear

---

332   Revelation 7:1-3
333   Genesis 1:6-8
334   Genesis 1:6: *Kai eipen ho theos Genehthehtoh stereohma en mesoh tou hudatos kai estoh diachoridzon ana meson hudatos kai hudatos.*

sons and daughters; so that you may increase there and not diminish. Seek the peace of the city where I have caused you to be carried away captive, and pray to the Lord for it; for in its peace you will have peace."[335]

Saint Augustine's theology is a boundary condition. When the waters below and th3e waters above overwhelm its foundational patterns of thought and belief, the world turns its corner. Saint Augustine's foundational patterns of thought and belief are already overwhelmed. There is nothing to separate the waters above from the waters below: The *diaxoridzo* requires a new *Stereoma*. The New Stereoma is the coming of the Son of Man, commonly referred to as the Return of Messiah.

Augustine compares and contrasts God's continuing judgment with regard to morals and faith with the Last Judgment. He writes, "I shall speak, as God permits, not of those first judgments, nor of these intervening judgments of God, but of the last judgment, when Christ is to come from heaven to judge the quick and the dead. For that day is properly called the day of judgment, because in it there shall be no room left for the ignorant questioning why this wicked person is happy and that righteous man unhappy. In that day true and full happiness shall be the lot of none but the good, while and supreme misery shall be the portion of the wicked, and of them only."[336] But the Progressive mindset cannot abide a Last Judgment, although continuous judgments emerging from its ideology are perfectly acceptable.

Sacred space is foursquare; progressive space is linear. The ideal of progressive space is modification; the ideal of sacred space is completion. The transition from one world to the happens (*egeneto*) when there is no more possible modification. When this moment or event of era occurs, the world itself changes.

To understand what the Bible reveals to us regarding the crossing-over from one world to the next, it doesn't help to examine the moral and social changes that are clearly exhibited in the narrative. These changes

---

335   Jeremiah 29:5-7
336   Saint Augustine, *The City of God* (New York: The Modern Library/Random House, Inc., 1993; original CE 413), p. 711.

take place within a world, not in transition from one world to the next. These are changes such as the falling of rain in the antediluvian world, the drunkenness of Noah, the assembling in the Spirit of the family of Jacob, the exile and suffering of Joseph and the final conclusion of his story and his reconciliation with his family, the battles for Canaan, the era of the Judges, the moral and military actions of David, the neglect of the Temple by the Southern Kingdom and its renunciation by the Northern Kingdom, the rebuilding of the Temple and the rise of the Maccabean family of Levi to authority in the in-between realm of Judaea.

Crossing over always involves a void. The void faces the People of God, as the singular family of Noah, when it starts to rain and flood; the void faces the People of God when Pharaoh forgets Joseph; the void faces the People of God when the Assyrians and then the Babylonians close in on them; the void faces the People of God in history when Jesus is crucified, the Temple is utterly destroyed, and the City is raised to the ground.

Each time a world of the People of God ends, there is the crossing of the void in order to arrive at a beginning. This crossing-over imitates, or is a type of, the Creation itself when the void is ended and there is, then again, something rather than nothing. This is the question Heidegger grappled with when he began his metaphysics with the question, "Why are there beings at all instead of nothing?"[337]

Heidegger fills the void by assembling all the great philosophical concepts of the West in an attempt to wrest a *pleroma* from emptiness, but the fulness he creates too easily merges with a kind of fulness no one ever really wants.[338] When this wresting, initiated and fashioned by

---

337 See footnote 214.
338 Heidegger, Metaphysics, p. 47: "A basic characteristic of a being is its *telos*, which does not mean goal or purpose, but end ... 'end' means completion in the sense of coming to fulfilment. Limit and end are that whereby beings first begin to *be*. This is the key to understanding the highest term that Aristotle used for Being: *entelecheia*, something's holding- (or maintaining) – itself-in-its-completion – (or limit). What was done with the term 'entelechy' by later philosophy (cf. Leibniz), not to mention biology, demonstrates the full extent of the decline from what is Greek. Whatever places itself into and thereby enacts

the intellect, reaches its limit, its only salvation lies in its submission to Hegel's transcendent State. No more wresting of meaning from the void is the secular equivalent of the sacred Sabbath rest of holiness.

As the great Jewish theologian Abraham Joshua Heschel puts it, "The seventh day is the armistice in man's cruel struggle for existence, a truce in all conflicts, personal and social, peace between man and man, man and nature, peace within man ... For the Sabbath is a day of harmony and peace ... On the seventh day man has no right to tamper with God's world, to change the state of physical things."[339] The Sabbath prefigures weekly the turning of the corner into a new world. The Sabbath seals the work week and declares it to be finished, and yet, the Sabbath is the beginning of the new work week.

And so, how is it that the People of God are sealed?

They asked Him, "Teacher, when will these things be, and what will be the sign (sehmeion) when this is about to happen? (ginesthai)' ... There will be signs in the sun and the moon and the stars; and on the earth will be distress of nations, with perplexity, the sea and the waves roaring; men fainting from fear and expectation of what is coming on the inhabited earth. For the powers of heaven will be shaken.[340]

WE'VE ALREADY NOTED that "heaven" and the firmament, or *Stereoma*, are equivalent. Jesus, as the divider, or *diachoridzo*er of history, as we call the flow of human times, becomes the *Stereoma* as the defining character of the Second Day of Creation. He is the mediator, the in-between guy, the one who holds the waters above and the waters below in tension so that life can emerge and thrive. This is what Jesus recapitulates on the Christian Holy Saturday: His Praxis constitutes the location of light in the world, that light to be copied later by the creation of the sun, the moon, and the stars on the Fourth Day. He restores the firmament between His crucifixion and His resurrection.

---

its limit, and thus stands, has form, *morphe*. The essence of form, as understood by the Greeks, comes from the emergent placing-itself-forth-into-the-limit."
339   Abraham Joshua Heschel, *The Sabbath* (29,31
340   Luke 21:7, 25-26

A world is defined, bounded, or limited, semiotically. We find ourselves in the world by means of semiotic behavior. Our behavior is a sign that there is a self underlying that behavior. That behavior also points to the character of that self. The signs of the times are most apparent at the beginning of the times and at their end. We live between the signs of beginning and the signs of end.

There are signs that a world is ending, and there are signs that a world is beginning, but there is always a gap between one world and its successor. We call this gap the Dark Ages in customary history of the West language. It's an age in which the rules of the earlier age no longer apply directly, and the new set of rules have not yet discovered and realized their archetypal foundation. Augustine's theological mind reached into the new archetypal arrangement that became Western Civilization: Augustine's obsolescence marks the end of that arrangement.

Apocalyptic literature, such as is found in Ezekiel, Daniel, and Revelation, is poignantly evocative. To evoke means to "bring or recall to the conscious mind" or to "elicit a response."[341] The things brought or recalled to the conscious mind are, logically, things of the subconscious and unconscious mind. In the case of apocalyptic language, knowledge and familiarity, as well as acceptance and belief in, the Gospel that comes forth to temper whatever else might be drawn out of one's subconscious or unconscious mind.

The evocative signs and symbols of apocalyptic language evoke a soul-response that ranges between incomprehension to rage to satisfied complacency to a sorrowful sense of ultimate justice to rejoicing that victory is at hand. In other words, the language itself brings the content and intent of one's own deepest self into the light. Nothing is either added or subtracted from the gospel by apocalypse: It is simply completed or punctuated in the recollections of the soul.

Ultimately, the threats, astonishments, and pressures of the apocalypse are rendered impotent to the Christian soul because whoever hears Jesus' word and believes in Him who sent Him has eternal life and "shall not

---

341   Evoke – https://www.languages.oup.com evoke ; accessed 5 Mar 23.

come into condemnation, but has passed from death into life."[342] The Last Judgment has already happened for that soul, and the advent of the New Heaven and New Earth is already just beyond the horizon of faith.

The down-here-on-earth sociology and psychology of apocalypse is as complex as the human soul, but the Existentialists' favorite word, "anxiety," or *angst*, is adequate enough to describe it. *Angst* is defined as "a feeling of deep anxiety or dread, typically an unfocused one about the human condition or the state of the world in general."[343] In the Age of cellphones, the internet, and social media, there is very little cultural wiggle room regarding the permeation of the soul with *angst*.

The politics of *angst* is self-destructive.

Angst is both a poetic and a mystical phenomenon, i.e., it isn't accessible solely by means of the power of reason. Apocalypse is when reason fails in its appointed role and refuses to rise to it ever again. The poet says, "When the historical process breaks down and armies organize with their embossed debates the ensuing void which they can never consecrate, when necessity is associated with horror and freedom with boredom, then it looks good to the bar business."[344] It's not only good for the bar business but also for every type and brand of intoxicant that is or will be available.

War is the greatest intoxicant. And so, "you will hear of wars and rumors of wars."[345] In the words of General George S. Patton, "Accept the challenges so that you can feel the exhilaration of victory."[346] You can feel the exhilaration verging on intoxication. Watching the war in

---

342   John 5:24
343   Angst – https://www.languages.oup.com_angst ; accessed 5 Mar 23.
344   W. H. Auden, The Age of Anxiety: A Baroque Eclogue (Princeton: Princeton University Press, 2011; originally 1947), p. 3.
345   Matthew 24:6: "See that you are not troubled. For all these things must happen (*genesthai*), but the end is not yet."
346   Quote – https://www.brainyquote.com_georgespattonquotes ; accessed 5 Mar 23.

Ukraine is like watching an apocalyptic football game.[347] Good and Evil vie for supremacy over the world, and voters couch their votes in those terms. Sadly, were it true that any war in the immediate present is even the beginning of Armageddon then it's too late to change your spiritual mind about anything: a voice comes "out of the temple of heaven, from the throne, and says, 'It is done!'(*gegonen/ginomai*)"[348]

Evil isn't done away with until it becomes clear to everyone that Jesus already defeated evil on the Cross. Until then, there is nothing in any war except Evil compounding Evil.

But wait, the conventional Western theologian might say, according to Augustine Evil is just the lack of Good. It was Augustine, remember, who coined the phrase "just war." After all, Augustine of Hippo invented Christianity. He did the right thing at the right time in the right place. The Christian Church calls him Saint Augustine because of his unsurpassed pastoral, theological and Biblical offering to the Church. Even History calls him St. Augustine; Hippo is forgotten, but St. Augustine lives on. At least, he did until quite recently. When we began to think and plan in Manichaean terms, we gave up St. Augustine to the dustbins of history. The narrative has changed.

Perhaps it isn't too late: We can still salt the events of the world with Good and thus mitigate the effects of the lack of Good. In the 20th century, this vain hope would require a ton of salt, more than there is in the sea and in the caves of Austria. The salt has lost its savor.[349] Will the "real" Christian please stand up?

---

347 Maximillian Alvarez, Jocelyn Dombroski, Marc Steiner, Bill Fletcher, Jr., *The Real News Network*, March 31, 2022 – https://www.therealnews.com_howthemediaturnswarintoaspectatorsport : "From the moment Russian troops invaded Ukraine on Feb. 24, people in the West have been glued to their TV, computer, and phone screens, furiously consuming news about the war and posting their reactions online … it's become clearer than ever that our corporate and social media ecosystem has not given us the tools to critically navigate the incessant militaristic propaganda, nor has it provided many pathways for people to do anything besides watch and post"; accessed 5 Mar 23.

348 Revelation 16:16-17

349 Matthew 5:13: "You are the salt of the earth. But if the salt loses its saltiness, how shall it be made salty? It is from then on good for noth-

The powers of heaven have been and are and will continue to be shaken. The firmament is becoming porous, and the stars are falling through it. The Son of Man never said He would save anybody: The Son of Man is the commander of Apocalypse: "When the Son of Man comes, will He find faith on the earth?"[350]

In the foursquare world of the Old Testament, we can learn of apocalypse by examining the previous ages of anxiety that not only seemed terminal, but they were terminal. When things are ending, even though no one wants to acknowledge it, everybody feels it.

In the biblical and apocryphal apocalypses, what is revealed at the end of the world frequently turns out to be what is hidden at its foundation ... Apocalyptic, taboo and sacrifice all appear to be concerned with the opposition between undifferentiation and difference, mixture and separation, chaos and cosmos, and all explore the boundary that divides them.[351]

IN THE NEW TESTAMENT Greek, the foundation of the cosmos, the world, is the *archeh*. Genesis 1:1 reads, "In the beginning God created the heavens and the earth." In the Septuagint Greek we read, *ev archeh epoiehsen ho theos ton ouranon kai tehn gehn*. This is a foundational statement, not a statement pointing to something that happens or happened in time. The preliminary and foundational fashioning for creation is archetypal; the heavens and the earth are archetypal before they are realized, empirical, objective.

In the New Testament, John 1:1 reads, "In the beginning was the Word, and the Word was with God, and the Word was God." In the *koineh* Greek, we read, *en archeh ehn ho logos, kai ho logos ehn pros ton theon, kai theos ehn ho logos*. Again, the action or situation revealed is archetypal. It isn't a situation that existed forever before the world was created: It's a situation that IS before there is anything to be called existence.

Behind these rather torturous statements lies the void that the theologians and philosophers grapple with. They didn't make it up: It's

---

ing but to be thrown out and to be trampled underfoot by men."
350 Luke 18:8
351 Bull, *Things Hidden*, pp. 76, 77

the void over which the Spirit of God brooded . . . and broods.³⁵² The Holy Spirit, in this sense, is that hen settling over her eggs so that her warmth will make them hatch.

The brooding of the Holy Spirit is a characteristic of all creation. When Jesus says, "O Jerusalem, Jerusalem, you who kill the prophets and stone those who are sent to you. How often I would have gathered your children together as a hen gathers her chicks under her wings, but you would not!"³⁵³ He indicates that even Jerusalem, the Holy City, is a pre-creational archetypal and foundational reality. The Holy Spirit even brooded over Mary to "hatch" Jesus. In such a manner, the New Jerusalem will come down from heaven.

What we see in these two first sentences is the fundamental pattern and type which characterizes anything that comes-to-be. *Ginomai* precedes *gennaoh*, except in the case of Jesus who is eternally begotten of God. This pattern is inviolable.³⁵⁴ It's the source of all of God's Praxis, and without it there is no praxis that can become coincident with that Praxis. The seed of all Truth is brooded over by the Holy Spirit before time and space are created. If all Western philosophy is merely a series of footnotes to Plato, all creation is simply a footnote to Jesus.

At the end, or conclusion, of each Hebrew/Jewish world are many archetypal inevitabilities that are build into the story. The most apparent is "sin," but we tend to reduce the notion of sin to be the doing of bad things of which God and decent human beings disapprove. Sin is a characteristic of our existence in creation. We are culpable of sin through choice, so much so that no matter HOW we choose, we choose to sin. But the word "sin" is so far-reaching that it becomes almost meaningless to postmodern ears. It's like the word "reality" or the word "truth." Tis is because its ultimate meaning is archetypal: It is a necessary condition that oversees, as it would, God's plan of salvation.

352   I Gordon, Bible Study Series: The Beginning and the End – Genesis and Revelation – https://www.jesusplusnothing.com_thebroodingandworkofthespirit ; accessed 5 Mar 23.
353   Matthew 23:37
354   Genesis 1:3: "God said, 'Let there be (*genehthehtoh*) light,' and there was (*egeneto*) light."

If there is no sin, there is no need of salvation. To separate the meanings of the two words is like trying to separate heads from tails on a coin. It's like trying to separate breathing in from breathing out: If you don't do either one or the other, there is no life in you. Life thrives in the overcoming of sin.

In the following discussion, I won't try to do a thorough hermeneutic and exegesis on the biblical word "sin." It is better to leave that to the biblical language game itself. That language, as we have noted, is learned and understood by practice. Instead, we'll see how five conceptual constructs appear at the end of each world: The *Stereoma*, the subject/object window, undifferentiation, the boundaries of language, and the meaning and significance of self. Then we will be able to spot them in our present situation and thus be able to read the signs of the times. They have their own language and speak a consistent language game.

It's helpful to note that the evidence of sin, as far-reaching as the word may be, is revealed in the act of hiding. The Bible says, "Then they heard the sound of the Lord God walking in the garden (*paradeisoh*/paradise) in the cool of the day, and the man and his wife hid among the trees of the garden."[355] The general characteristic of individual, social and national identity in the fallen world is in this hiding from God. This is the praxis that makes apocalypse necessary because apocalypse is the coming-out-of-hiding, the tearing of the veil. The most starkly revealed phenomenon in the subject/object world at the time of apocalypse is the human soul.

Every true conversion is an apocalypse. Salvation is initiated in the garden, however, by the Praxis of God in calling out the prototypical couple and covering their nakedness Himself.[356] They still know their nakedness, but they are no longer constantly ashamed in the presence of their maker and of each other.

---

355 Genesis 3:8
356 Genesis 3:21

All civilization can be reduced in character to that of an oversized and communal fig leaf.[357] Only God's proffered clothing can cover the shame and relieve the angst, and that covering is exemplified in the end by the symbolic and evocative nature of the garments of salvation.[358] The first archetypal apocalypse is illustrated by the hiding in the trees of the garden and the attempt to self-clothe in order to hide guilt and shame. All moral systems, too, are fig leaves. This is a type of apocalypse that carries through in *Kairos* [359]moments that are given definition by the boundaries and expectations of worlds in the process of completion, of the coming-to-pass.

The next section will be an examination of those worlds in their final stages of completion, those cultural moments just before the void reappears to swallow them up, like Jonah's whale, into the renewed purpose of God.[360] This examination won't be comprehensive, just a skimming of signage that anticipates the signs of the End.

---

357   Genesis 3:7
358   E.g., Zechariah 3; Revelation 7:14
359   Kairos – https://www.languages.oup.com_kairos : "a propitious moment for decision or action"; accessed 6 Mar 23. E.g., Luke 4:13: "When the devil had ended all the temptations, he departed from Him until another time (*kairou*)."
360   AUTHOR'S NOTE: Perhaps Jonah's big fish was a porpoise. Hahahahahaha!

Chapter Eight: A COMING-TO-PASS SEPARATION

And God said, "Let there be (genehthehtohsan/ginomai) lights in the expanse (stereohmati) of the heavens to separate (diaxoridzein) the day from the night, and let them be signs (sehmeia) to indicate seasons (kairous), and days, and years. Let them be lights in the expanse of the heavens to give light on the earth." And it was (egeneto) so;[361]

THE PASSAGE ABOVE is the first passage in the Bible to involve the word *kairos*. Kairos is "a propitious moment for decision or action."[362] Kairos is an element of coming-to-pass, subject to it and significant only in terms of it. This is the Fourth Day when Kairos is introduced by means of the lights in the sky. Kairos, in this context, indicates the separation that stands between the waters above and the waters below. The Fourth Day is the Day of Signs.

The Fourth Day, of course, is a building block, or foundational element, in the First World of the Hebrews. The question for apocalypse is, "What was the situation before the First World came to be?" The days of creation are all moments of *egeneto*, or the coming-to-pass. Before then, there is no coming-to-pass: There is only *Archeh*, the archetypal reality and the void.

The First Apocalypse, then, is the occasion of Heidegger's famous question, "Why is there something instead of nothing?" This is a very Western question, because some religions imply and even practice the notion that everything is nothing anyway.[363] Modern science comes close to announcing the same Truth.[364] If Heidegger had been a Vedantist

---

361 Genesis 1:14-15
362 See footnote 359.
363 Nothing – https://en.m.wikipedia.org_maya(religion) : "In the Advaita Vedanta school of Hindu philosophy, *maya*, 'appearance', is 'the powerful force that creates the cosmic illusion that the phenomenal world is real"; last edited 14 February 2023, accessed 6 Mar 23.
364 Margenau, *Physical*, p. 61: "Of course, we *can* refrain from seeing a light and constructing it into an object, as we do in the dim conscious-

thinker, he might have asked "Why is there nothing that seems to be something?"[365] But then there would be no "there" there. We could go on like this forever....

Heidegger, and all modern Western metaphysicians, engages with the question of something rather than nothing, and they do it in Western ways. But it is also true that the heart of comparative religions fails at the get-go regarding Judeo-Christian theology at the beginning. Hinduism and Buddhism are answers to "what is there before something." The answer is inevitably Nothing. The nothing takes on a life, a totality of its own, and true existence is found only when the nothing becomes your reality. At any rate, Heidegger, because his mind is a Western product, must ask the question "why is there something" instead of "what is the nothing."

The What and the Why meet only in *kairos* and by means of the coming-to-be. They aren't dissolved in the Not. This is the constructional heart of Western mysticism AND science, the fact that the What and the Why seem to negate each other, leaving the intellect with the choice of one or the other in terms of understanding anything, or the crisis that occurs when they are independently fulfilled and must be transformed into a union of opposites. So, the scientists try to answer the What while the metaphysicians are stuck with trying to answer the Why.

In this contest of fundamental meaning, the What and the Why do not come together in the magical synthesis of GWF Hegel: They destroy each other. They must separate or cease to be at all. A marriage of sorts can be forced by means of the ideal State, which is the divine idea on earth, or the marriage can represent the End of a world. The reasonable life then continues in the divine ideal on earth, the State, but only in an inviolate coincidence between the State and the soul. The other choice is to anticipate the new world solely by faith, or sola fide.

    ness of half waking. It is quite possible that in other cultures, among the orientals for instance, the transition is performed in a different way or is not performed at all. Could it be that Hindu's nirvana, reputedly so unattainable to Western man, is its (reifrication's) willful suppression?"

365   AUTHOR'S NOTE: Perhaps the *dasein*, the thing-in-itself, would be the *nichtzein*, the not thing.

Sola fida attributes purpose to the void that surrounds the phenomenal world. Science does not. Purpose belongs solely to the God who broods and is the archetypal substrate of God. Purpose (*telos*) IS the *hypostasis*. In terms of our five earthly and metaphysical categories of apocalypse, what ends at the moment of Creation is not-undifferentiation, not subject/object window, not-boundaries of language, not-*stereoma*, and not-meaning and significance of self.

The only way to penetrate through understanding the vast void that embraces reality or the phenomenal and moral world, is by faith which realizes that it is purpose which surrounds, embraces, and permeates everything that IS. Otherwise, there is the modified thesis-antithesis encounter which morphs into eternal separation, or 'chorathesis.' This is an ornamental and metaphysical way of saying you will go to hell.

It can be hell on earth, or it can be a hereafter hell. It doesn't really matter because those distinctions will both be gone. This is WHY it's important for the Christian to pay attention to *Kairos* and the signs of the time.

The earth was corrupt before God and filled with violence. God looked on the earth and saw it was corrupt, for all flesh had corrupted (adikias) their way on earth. So God said to Noah, "The end (Kairos) of all flesh is come before Me, for the earth is filled with violence because of them. Now I will destroy them with the earth."[366]

WE DON'T ENCOUNTER *Kairos* again until the sixth chapter of Genesis. At this juncture in the narrative, it gets translated as End. It isn't an end of time as much as it is fulfilment, a fulfilment of the nature of all flesh. As such, it is the inevitable consequence of the fall, of sin, sans any further intervention from heaven on earth. The intervention comes when God looks and sees Noah.

Between the Fourth Day of Creation and when God sees Noah amidst the corrupt world of the flesh is an extended moment of Kairos. The entire First World is, in effect, but one moment. It isn't a coming-to-pass. It isn't a dividing point between a past and a future. It just IS,

366   Genesis 6:11-13

or should we say, it just WAS. But what it was is forever because it is Kairos. This recognition of the Kairos of all flesh due to its inherent *adikias*, or unrighteousness or corruption, is a universal moment of self-understanding without benefit of true understanding.

From this moment of Kairos on, in time, beginning with the origins of the genea, or generations, of Noah, *gennaoh* and *ginomai* will be travelling together, and the Kairos moments will be those moments when this fact is recognized by the godly. They will recognize the moment because God sees, or recognizes, the moment. In truth, there is no Moment unless God recognizes it as such. In this way, righteousness and recognition are joined at the hip, and the human potential to recognize is at the heart of the subsequent Promise.

The next biblical moment of *Kairos* is when God promises, once again, a son to Sarah, saying, "I will establish My covenant with Isaac, whom Sarah will bear to you at this set time (*kairos*) next year."[367] In this way, *Kairos*, or the propitious moment, the moment of decision and action, is eternally linked with *gennaoh*, or the procreational existence of a line of descendants. This linkage continues all the way through to its completion in the birth of Jesus of Nazareth.

The Flood is virtually directly linked in time and space with the void. The void becomes the Great Deep, the Sea. In the vernacular of the 20th century, it becomes the unconscious mind or realm. It becomes the unconscious because that's the name given to it by modern philosophy, psychology, and theology. But it's all the same stuff. We now think, because of this transposition of the language, that the unconscious mind is a "place" of some kind, but it is not a place. Rather it's a moment in time and space in which there is neither time nor space, just like the void.

So, let's look at our five categories of apocalypse:

1. **The Boundaries of Language**: What can be said about a time and place that no longer exists? We don't even know which language Noah spoke, because the term "semitic" comes from

---

[367] Genesis 17:21

his first son, Shem. It's almost as if there were no languages, or there was no language, before. Maybe they all communicated by means of grunts, coughs, shouts, and pointing. Whatever language that first family spoke, it was a family language. In the previous world, the language was the language of patriarchal domains. The patriarchal domains of the antediluvian world[368] seem to be consistent. Noah lives in a primordial linguistic exile.

2. **Undifferentiation**: This quality certainly applies to a world that is suddenly and completely destroyed. Nobody even has time to say good-bye. This world doesn't even understand what the instrument of destruction is. What we do know from much later speculation, if you can call speculation a form of knowing, is that the entire world sank back into the unconscious realm. It became a world of memory without experience. Noah and his family were the differentiation, and that is only because he was obedient to the unfathomable word of God. In effect, his praxis was entirely Praxis. He was just doing what he was told. It would be fair to say that the quality of life in the antediluvian world was just to do what you are told. In the end, God had to speak once more, this time to a man who was simply "blameless among his contemporaries." One is left to wonder what justice could have been in a world that was entirely corrupt.

3. **The Subject/Object Window**: Subjectivity is entirely reified into a totality when the First World is inundated. It becomes a source of skill as well as immorality, or corruption, that no one can quite identify in any specific way. In the beginning of the Second World, neither Noah nor his sons know what they are doing. Subjectivity, which in its more refined form is indelibly linked with language, isn't linked with anything objective. Everything is subjective, and the subjective is entirely unknown and unknowable. The objective world will need to be spoken into existence, and the first thing said is when Noah condemns Canaan for seeing his father's nakedness.[369] In this way, even the fall in the garden is carried over archetypally into the second

---

368 Genesis 6:9
369 Genesis 9:24

world as Noah tries to express why it is that he suddenly feels separated from his youngest son. He can't hide in the trees of the Garden, but he CAN banish Canaan.

4. **The Stereoma**: The firmament was entirely obscured in the deluge of waters coming down from above the *Stereoma* and the waters coming up from underneath the earth. If one looked up from the ark, all one would see was water; if one looked down, all one would see was water. The waters would become indistinguishable, covering over both the *Stereoma* and the Light of the First Day. In effect, the ark was suspended on and by the firmament, a very thin surface between the waters which dominated everything else.
Some Bible scholars claim that Noah could look up and see God. He could not. His relied absolutely on the fact that the ark had been constructed to float on the *Stereoma*. Since God had instructed him as to the exact dimensions and constructs of the ark, his faith in God kept angst away. Otherwise, the angst would be overwhelming, because he had no way to orient himself in this world or to navigate or to even be sure what was up and what was down. All Noah could be sure of was the Ark.

5. **The Meaning and Significance of the Self**: Noah was the First Self. He was required by necessity and God to define himself through action. It was his action alone that made it possible for the Old World to transition to the New World. In the Old World, he had free will in the context of an entirely corrupt world. The task of righteousness was to NOT be like anyone else in that world. Everything about his status before God was relative to his standing among his contemporaries. Before Noah, the self has not yet reached the level of personal identity. From Adam to Lamech, people are essentially identical: They are parts of a totality that reaches completion only as the 'descendants' of Adam, as in, "This is the book of the generations (*geneseohs*) of Adam."

The image of God is passed on from generation to generation, but the process is accounted for by the term *ginomai*. On the other hand, the birth of the next generation is accounted for with the term *gennaoh*. The blessing of being an aspect of the coming-to-pass and being a "son of" comes together in Noah. God does not like the version of His image that He sees when He looks on the world as a totality, but He does like what He sees when He looks on the mirror image of Noah. The fact of God's looking and seeing is what makes all the difference between Noah and everyone else before him.

When Noah arrives at dry land, he does three things: He builds an altar, he plants a vineyard, and he gets drunk. The stage is set for all selves and personal identities that follow, and the praxis of worship, work, and intoxication.

The name Noah means "rest" or "repose." In Noah, God can finally rest, thus fulfilling the Seventh Day.

Then the Lord spoke to Moses, saying, "Sanctify unto Me all the firstborn (prohtotokon prohtogenes) ... Moses said to the people, "Remember (mnehmoneuete) this day, in which you came out of Egypt ... Nothing unleavened shall be eaten ... It shall be as a sign (sehmeion) to you on your hand and as a memorial on your forehead, in order that (genehtai) the Lord's law (nomos) may be in your mouth. For with a strong hand the Lord brought you out of Egypt. You shall, therefore, keep this ordinance at its appointed time (kairous) from year to year.[370]

IF THE COMING-TO-PASS of the self and personal identity are exemplified in Noah, Moses represents the effects of betrayal of friendship and cultural alienation. At this moment, Kairos, the generations of Abraham are complete; the *ethneh* (ethnicities) have populated the entire region. The Promise has been declared over Abraham, Isaac, and Jacob, and Jacob has become (*ginomai*) Israel. Our examination continues:

1. **The Boundaries of Language**: Moses was raised in the court of Pharaoh and was accepted as virtually a legitimate member of the royal household or family. He spoke the Egyptian language,

---

370   Exodus 13:1, 3, 9-10

and it was the language games of the court and family. In other words, Moses knew the language of power and authority.

It's highly unlikely that Moses knew or spoke Hebrew. He had nothing to do with the Hebrews slaves until he realized he was one of their *genea*. He wouldn't, however, know how to use the language game of slaves. The deeper meanings carried from person to person in that language game would be hidden from him. It would take an apocalypse for him to be able to truly understand what they were saying, thinking, and feeling, even if they were speaking in Egyptian. Moses lived somewhere around the 13th century BCE.[371] According to current scholarship, "the Hebrew language developed out of the Canaanite language, and some Semitist scholars consider both Hebrew and Phoenician to have been essentially dialects of Canaanite. The language variety in which the Masoretic biblical text is written is known as *Biblical Hebrew* or *Classical Hebrew* (c. 10th century BCE+)."[372] The spoken language of the slaves in Moses' time could have been a kind of proto-Hebrew or come other pre-Hebrew language altogether. Some scholars connect the ancient designation *apiru* to the development of the Hebrew language, and that "the word 'Hebrew', like Habiru, began as a social category, and evolved into an ethnic one ... Habiru or Apiru is a term used in 2nd-millenium BCE texts throughout the Fertile Crescent for people variously described as rebels, outlaws, raiders, mercenaries, bowmen, servants, slaves, and laborers ... Apiru (means) 'dusty, dirty.'"[373]

In the time of Moses, there likely was no "Hebrew" language. The language spoken by the slaves was a slave language. Without a doubt, it bore resemblance to the language or languages spoken by the Twelve Tribes of Israel, but these languages weren't necessarily exact replicas of each other. Even after the conquest, one tribal member could recognize a member of an-

---

[371] Moses – https://en.m.wikipedia.org_moses ; last edited 25 February 2023, accessed 7 Mar 23.

[372] Hebrew – https://en.m.wikipedia.org_ancienthebrew-writings ; last edited 23 January 2023, accessed 7 Mar 23.

[373] Apiru – https://en.m.wikipedia.org_habiru ; last edited 1 October 2022, accessed 7 Mar 23.

other tribe by the dialectical variation in the spoken vernacular.[374] In other words, the form of life of the slaves, to 'speak Wittgensteinian,'[375] was so much at odds with Moses' form of life that misunderstanding would have been the absolute norm rather than the exception. At the very least, Moses does not need to either know or understand how to respond to an immediate order given to him by a slave-master with a whip.

The language gap between Moses and his own people is vast.

2. **Undifferentiation**: The Hebrew, or "dirty and dusty" *Apiru*, slaves existed as an undifferentiated slave mass in the eyes of their masters. Male or female, child or adult, intelligent or not-so-bright, they were all the same. One life was as expendable as the next, as long as the pyramids got built. There would have been some differentiation in the 'hidden' *Apiru* culture with some memetic quality of family and clan still extant in the language. It would have been very difficult to maintain this remembrance of the order of family, clan, and tribe that once was. It is likely that many of the *Apiru* had forgotten the Old Order entirely. Considering that the time of slavery predates the time when Hebrew first appeared as a language in itself, it's also likely that a kind of slave jargon was the only language game that maintained any sort of corporate identity. This language would be undifferentiated as such, a kind of work-language. The apocalypse to come would necessitate a common language that respected what was left in memory of the Old Order. Not only would the fleshpots of Egypt need to be entirely forgotten, but the form of life that constituted the language games themselves

---

374 Judges 12:4-6: "Then Jephthah assembled all the men of Gilead and fought with Ephraim. The men of Gilead struck Ephraim down, for they had said, 'You Gileadites are fugitives in Ephraim, living in Ephraim and Manasseh.' Gilead captured the fords of the Jordan River leading to Ephraim, Whenever an Ephraimite fugitive would say, 'Let me cross,' the Gileadite men would say to him 'Are you an Ephraimite?' If he said, 'No,' then they would say to him, 'Say 'Shibboleth!',' yet he would say 'Sibboleth', for he could not pronounce it correctly."

375 Wittgenstein, *Investigations*, pp. 8, 11: "I shall also call the whole, consisting of language and the activities into which it is woven, a 'language game' … to imagine a language means to imagine a form of life."

would have to be entirely forgotten. The people as a whole would start out in the wilderness as an undifferentiated totality.

3. **The Subject/Object Window**: The objective world in the time of Moses before the Hebrews became separated from the Egyptians was the Egyptian World. The Hebrew World would have been almost entirely Subjective a world shared only in the deep recesses of Subjectivity itself. There would be no crossing over, even for Moses once he had realized his true genealogy. Moses, in fact, would be virtually unable to see through the window in either direction. His own Subjectivity and his accustomed Objectivity would be seriously, even irredeemably divided. The window would be opaque. The Hebrew people would need to learn a New Objectivity. This Object World would need to be reconstructed, or newly constructed, entirely from fading memory, from the stories and their personalities of the past. It would be a New Order with an enhanced memory, subject to memory and the Godly authority of Moses' divided soul situation. Moses, as a leader, would be stranded psychologically, with neither an effective and communicable Subjectivity nor an Objectivity that meant anything at all. After all, they had been led into a wilderness, a place with no semiotic character and no mnemonic value.

4. **The Stereoma**: The firmament had once again been obscured. When Pharaoh forgot Joseph, forgetting became the mode of existence for both the Egyptian authorities and the Hebrew tribes. There would be no First Day Light until they had been gifted a pillar of light by night and a pillar of smoke by day. In this way, the People of God could begin to practice, or praxis, the Fourth Day dividing line between night and day, to distinguish it from the boundary between Good and Evil. There would be signs and a developing form of life in the Wilderness. The purpose of the Wilderness was to ensure that the People would know where these signs and this form of life came from: God. They did NOT come from the Egyptian World. They were utterly new and utterly formative. They

would re-form the People of God, as well as Moses. Not even Moses would be able to anticipate or even read the signs of the times. Every moment would be a moment in *Kairos*.

The People of God would cross through the waters below when they crossed the Red Sea on dry land. They would recapitulate the journey of Noah across the endless and formless ocean until dry land once again appeared. The *Stereoma* itself, that firmament dividing the waters above from the waters below was transformed ritually, mnemonically, and semiotically into the Wilderness. In effect, the Wilderness itself became the New *Stereoma*. It would forever separate the waters of the past from the waters of the future.

5. **The Meaning and Significance of Self**: In the Wilderness, the New *Stereoma*, the Twelve Tribes, having been reduced to a state verging on the abject and undifferentiated, became (*ginomai*) a Nation. The Hebrew self had been reduced to a state of insignificance with no redemption in sight. Egypt was the whole world for them: How to you escape the World? When the World tells you who you are, and you believe and accept that identity, you are lost. Moses was a privileged but synthetic self. He had no idea who he really was. His family was not his family, and his people were not his people. Moses, in other words, was the complete antithesis to Egypt. He did not know or realize this essential characteristic of his personal identity until he saw and felt one of his own being mistreated. This was the crisis, or dividing and separating judgment, that propelled him out of the Old World toward the New World. In the meantime, he would always be from then on pretty much "out of his mind." The only phenomenon of social significance that would pass through the waters and the wilderness would be that *Kairos* moment called "The Passover." The celebration of the Passover at the right time and the right place, prescribed by God, would always be a *kairos* moment. It would be a guaranteed Kairos experience, a sacramental moment if you will.

The celebration of the Passover and its significance, its semiotic value, would change the character of the nearly cancelled Twelve Tribes into the Nation it was always meant to become (*ginomai*). It would be a permanent sign in the always repeating of signs that constitutes the sun, the stars, and the moon. In this way, the light would always be with the Nation.

The name "Moses" means "to pull out or draw out of water." He is a type of Noah, drawing his people out of the sea of chaos that embraced their form of life in Egypt and placing them on dry land in order to build a new kind of altar, plant new vineyards, and, as well, get drunk again. The Flood has been re-enacted, recapitulated with power that matches family, clan, and tribal relationships.

What had been what amounted to a cosmic betrayal, a betrayal of the people by the only world they knew, became a time of resurrection when they crossed the Jordan River on dry land. However, this would necessitate the complete disconnection of the Old Generation from the New Generation. The New Generation would have no tangible memory of the form of life in Egypt or of the signs and wonders that had been performed there.

Memory would become story, and the Sabbath (rest) would cross over into the next world.

At that time (kairoh) the servants of Nebuchadnezzar king of Babylon came up against Jerusalem, and the city was under siege. Nebuchadnezzar king of Babylon came up to the city while his servants were besieging it, and Jehoiachin king of Judah went out to the king of Babylon, he, his mother, his servants, his princes (arxontes), and his eunuchs. The king of Babylon took him in the eighth year of his reign.[376]

THE TRANSITION of authority from King Jehoiachin of Judah and King Nebuchadnezzar of Babylon and the transfer of sovereignty from the lineage of Judah to the empire of Babylon, was a *Kairos* moment. It was perhaps the most consequential *Kairos* Moment of all time, excepting, for Christians, the incarnation of God in Jesus the Christ.

---

376   II Kings 24:10-12

The testimony of Chronicles has a slightly different, but not contradictory in the sense of the overall language game, take on Kairos. We read, "So all the service (*leitourgia*/liturgy) of the Lord was carried out that day to have the Passover, and to offer the burnt offerings on the altar of the Lord according to the command of King Josiah. And the sons of Israel who were present had the Passover at that time (*kairoh*) and the Feast of the Unleavened Bread for seven days. And no Passover had been made (*ouk egeneto*) like this in Israel since the days of Samuel the prophet..."[377]

The Passover had become a permanent and liturgical *Kairos* moment immediately prior to the crossing of the Red Sea. Josiah's renewal of the Passover came at the last minute: He would be dead and the People exiled very soon after this celebration. The Land in those days was being contested by Egypt and Babylon, as was the eternal custom in that part of the world. Babylon eventually won the prize of Jerusalem.

The times had, of course, all the characteristics of a coming apocalypse, even though King Josiah couldn't have known this:

1. **The Boundaries of Language**: The narrative in Chronicles tells us that representatives of both Israel and Judah were present at the Last Passover. It was, then, an inclusive celebration involving two branches of the extended tribes who had been at war with each other or in a tenuous alliance for many generations. The language game of Israel was radically different from the language game of Judah. Also, the Northern Kingdom of Israel had already been taken captive by Assyria, and Assyria had been virtually absorbed not too long before by Babylon. The language of the Passover, that remembrance of having to depart from Egypt with unleavened bread to eat, and the death of all the Egyptian first-born, exemplified the entire situation of this concluding end to the kingdom-ish existence of the Twelve Tribes. The families and tribes had their own language games and their own dialects of the common language. They may

---

377   II Chronicles 35:16-18

even have spoken languages that didn't seem the same, like Irish and Scottish English. They had broken tradition by coming together (synagogue) to celebrate the Last Passover under their own authority. The only language game that mattered, then, was that of the liturgy of the Passover. It would be the priests who salvaged, maintained, and preserved the Hebrew language in the exile and beyond. The common language would either revert to, or had long or always been, Syrian or Aramaic. Hebrew was about to become (*ginomai*) a sacred, or Holy, language, one that was believed to have come down from heaven direct from God. Hebrew became a language unto itself, a closed and self-sustaining, self-regulated language game that exemplified a form of life that was, that is, and that would be, but which was not in the power of the Nation or the priests to live out.

2. **Undifferentiation**: The undifferentiated character of the Nation is marked by the celebration of the Passover. The Passover brought the people together in a time of diabolical and existential threat. The threat did destroy their commonweal and every action or work that could be expressible through their language, but the memory of the Passover provided the bridge to a new identity, one that was undifferentiated as such but one that was differentiated precisely because it was entirely different from both the world and from what the People had once been. It is in this sense that the Exile was actually a resurrection, though the times immediately following were a recapitulation of the Wilderness experience, not only in terms of cultural surroundings but in terms of language itself. No matter how one looks at the moment, however, it was apocalyptic.

3. **The Subject/Object Window**: The besetting problem for the People of God in Exile was to learn the language of objectivity into which they had been called while maintaining their own language both in terms of Subjectivity but, in terms of a sure and certain future, Objectivity as well. The Objectivity of their faith became something other than the Objectivity that had

symbolized and sustained it. It wasn't the prescribed Objectivity of Babylon, but through the window the Objectivity of faith could clearly be seen. Eventually this comparative Objectivity would be realized in the rebuilding of the Temple, a task which likely seemed to the Kahn of Persia to be a tribute to his own God as represented by the liturgical subservience of the Jewish God. Nevertheless, the rebuilt Temple provided the Objectivity of faith that had been lacking for seventy years, even if it was an Objectivity grounded in a practical (*praxis*) partnership between Gods.

4. **The Stereoma**: The waters from above and the waters from below once again came together in the coming-to-pass of the Exile. That it was a God-ordained coming-to-pass is not any less arguable than was the occasion of the Flood. It was also a prophetically announced coming-to-pass (*egeneto*) that mimicked (semiotic and mnemonic) the escape from Egypt. The event itself (*egeneto*) declared the inconclusiveness of the original Exodus and the lessons of the Wilderness, and decreed a re-enactment that would finalize the substance of the Promise in the hearts and minds of the People of God. The people themselves would become the ultimate sign of God's grace and goodness.

    The celebration of the Passover would not be a sign of anything: It would be an actual Kairos Moment forever. Every time the Passover was celebrated at its assigned *Kairos* time, the people would be reminded that the *Kairos* was eternally present in the People themselves. The *Stereoma* was reified as the Passover. It would always separate the waters above from the waters below.

5. **The Meaning and Significance of Self**: The self in the Fourth Hebrew World reached an existential apogee during the reign of King Solomon. It didn't last but a Kairos moment. David, the warrior King, had died, leaving a legacy that no King of Judah or in any historical sovereignty would ever surpass. We read, "Now the acts of David the King, first to last, are written in the book of Samuel the seer, and in the

book of Nathan the prophet, and in the book of Gad the seer with all his reign and his might and the times (*kairoi*) that overtook him, and Israel, and all the kingdoms of the lands."[378] *Kairos* is not mentioned again until the dedication of Solomon's Temple, but then and there a very strange thing happens. When the propitious and appointed time for the priests to enter comes, they cannot enter: The glory of the Lord is so intense, filling the Temple, that they are inhibited from entering. It reads, "when Solomon finished praying fire came down from the heavens and consumed the burnt offering and sacrifices, and the glory of the Lord filled the temple. And the priests were not able to enter into the house of the Lord for the glory of the Lord filled the Lord's house."[379]

The ability to stand in the presence of the Glory of the Lord isn't apparent in a single human being until the arrival of the prophets Isaiah, Ezekiel, and Jeremiah. In their time, the Exile is immanent, although Isaiah, the earlier prophet, still offers a chance at redemption. Jeremiah is the "last chance" prophet, and Ezekiel witnesses the departure of the Glory from the Temple.[380] Ezekiel is perhaps the most "insane" of all the Old Testament prophets. His demeanor before the city, his visions, and his encounters with God are all reminiscent of David's pretense of insanity when he was exiled, or hiding, in Gath.[381] The coming exile is a type of hiding, a preliminary condition, or state of soul, for apocalypse. In effect, Ezekiel tells the proud tribe that could take credit both for David and Solomon and for the Temple that the Glory of God will be with them in exile even though, or perhaps precisely because,

---

378   I Chronicles 29:29-30
379   II Chronicles 7:1-2: The phrase *en toh kairoh ekeinoh* is left untranslatable in both the MEV and the KJV. The temple was already filled with the glory of the Lord.
380   Ezekiel 10
381   I Samuel 21:12-13: "David greatly feared Achish the king of Gath. Therefore he changed his behavior before them and pretended to be insane in their hands."

the Temple is no longer a necessary house for the Lord.[382] The entire Ezekiel narrative is a coming-to-pass time. The first verse reads, "In the (*kai egeneto*) thirtieth year, in the fourth month, on the fifth day of the month, as I was among the captives by the river of Kebar, the heavens were opened and I saw visions of God." His entire life, his very existence, is a matter of the coming-to-pass. Ezekiel is a priest,[383] and he epitomizes the final soul transformation taking place the community of faith that will fulfill the Law of Moses when, giving voice to God, he said, "You will be to Me a kingdom of priests and a holy nation. These are the words you shall speak to the children of Israel."[384] Ezekiel embodies and ensouls the Apocalypse. His prophecies enshrine it. He is caught up in the Glory of the Lord so much so that he cannot help himself. Everything he says and does is in *kairos*, but this entrance into a permanent and abiding appointment and propitiousness requires exile and the loss of everything near and dear to him, especially the Temple where he once fulfilled the very meaning and significance of his life.

The priest has no inheritance but God.[385]

If the Exodus was necessitated by the betrayal of friendship with the world, the Exile was experienced as a betrayal by God. You can feel Ezekiel's agony and grief throughout his testimony. He cannot comprehend anything that he is being told to do or say, and the fact that the entire Nation is being dragged away in chains is too heartbreaking to endure. Nevertheless, he doesn't flee from God or deny God. Rather, he outdoes even Job, who's suffering merely prefigures the suffering endured by Ezekiel and the People of God under the yoke of Assyrian and Babylon.

---

382   Ezekiel 10:18-22
383   Ezekiel 1:3
384   Exodus 19:6
385   Numbers 18:20: "I am your territory and your inheritance…"

Ezekiel is thoroughly chosen: For him, time and space have gone away.

Ezekiel is even given a vision of restoration and of the New Temple.[386] But there is no prophesied *Kairos* for these things.

Then he said to me, "Do not seal the words of the prophecy of this book, for the time (kairos) is at hand. He who is unjust, let him be unjust still. He who is filthy, let him be filthy still. He who is righteous, let him be righteous still. He who is holy, let him be holy still."[387]

THE SEVENTY YEARS of exile is the fulfilment of the Forty Years in the Wilderness. Every kind of transition that is possible in the corporate and individual lives of a people takes place during this time. Nevertheless, the subsequent Return isn't the prophesied Return. It is a prefiguring of return, at best, and a pretense of return at worst. But just as the height of Jewish identity, that of the priesthood, is revealed at the nadir of the Hebrew story rather than at its apogee, the low point, the pretense, and the high point, the Glory, become indistinguishable.

The People of God enter a permanent *Kairos* following the return to Judaea and the rebuilding of the Holy City. This *Kairos* is fulfilled during the time (*kairos*) of Jesus. This is why the term "at hand" is used in the New Testament to describe the nature of *Kairos* and of the Kingdom.[388] The Kingdom of God had been at hand since the days of Ezekiel.

The attempt to rebuild the Kingdom as it once WAS was always doomed to fail. It was pretense, but not intentional pretense. What was revealed, not in Sacred Text but in history, was that the attempt to rebuild on earth or materially would only lead to endless repeats of what had already been endured. First, the Persians gave way to the Greeks, and the Greeks desecrated the Temple. Then the Greeks gave way to the Romans, and the Romans destroyed the entire commonweal of the Jews.

---

386 Ezekiel 39:25-48:25
387 Revelation 22:10-11
388 Matthew 3:2

The Kairos between the return and the time of the Roman occupation was time to learn. This learning was through experience and through the finalizing of the sacred texts. *Kairos* became incarnate in the Hebrew Scriptures, and the day-to-day evidence of *kairos* became uninterpretable. The appointed time and place became "all the time in every place" while being, also, "at no time and in no place." This spiritual and religious situation anticipates both the mysticism of the late Middle Ages and the present as well as Hegel's anticipated Synthesis which will never happen (*ginomai*).

The analysis of the five apocalyptic signs becomes concrete at the moment Jesus is crucified and the moment that the Second Temple is entirely destroyed brick by brick. Things can now be understood in terms of recorded history, in terms of chronological sequences, and in terms of human decisions that may or may not be examples of the coincidence of praxis and Praxis:

1. **The Boundaries of Language**: The significance of the boundaries of language is summed up by the question, "How can we talk to each other?" Can meaning be conveyed by means of the language games we have, or is the attempt to cross boundaries of culture, heritage, personal identity, and National character a futility of the nth degree? When everything is questioned, can there really be answers? The Bible, as the first and foremost example of this conundrum, was finalized in the Hebrew language. It was translated into Greek, and the New Testament was originally in Greek. The Romans took over the world, and Latin became the lingua franca. The Romans absorbed all manner of ethnicities, from the Germanic to the Celtic, and many of them became Latinized. In terms of Wittgensteinian language games, the question of the Bible is the question of whether or not the form of life conveyed in its language game can be conveyed in any other language game and whether or not anyone can find meaning in the Bible's language game today. The post-Wittgenstein philosophical world struggles with this question, and this is a struggle which

characterizes the 20th and 21st centuries of Western Civilization. In short, there is neither assurance nor evidence of *kairos* or *ginomai* in the "real" world without the language game of the Bible. The "appointed time" might as well be opening and closing time for a local business and the coming-to-pass is simply anything that happens. Up until recently, there was, however, a sustaining trust in *gennaoh*.

2. **Undifferentiation**: The use of the word "undifferentiation" is taken, in the context of this writing, from the previously quoted book, *Seeing Things Hidden: Apocalypse, Vision and Totality*. The word "totality" is used in the sense that Foucault uses it in *The Archaeology of Knowledge and the Discourse on Language*. They are uses of these two words that take some getting used to. We find that "As in apocalyptic, taboo has ended, sacrifice has ceased and the scapegoats have returned ... The social character of late modernity actually is apocalyptic; every breakdown of sacrifice, every infringement of taboo, brings the polluting undifferentiation that is the reversal of the mechanisms that maintain order in traditional societies ... Here, perhaps, is the key to late modernity's peculiar symbiosis with apocalyptic religion; by continually furnishing the evidence to confirm apocalyptic expectations, modernity may also serve to re-legitimate the values that it dissolves, and so reinforce modernity's specifically apocalyptic appearance."[389] This "specifically apocalyptic appearance" is the central thesis of my book *Conundrums of the End: Fate, Destiny, and Apocalypse*: If everyone is convinced that apocalypse is immanent, it IS immanent.[390] The evocative language of the Book of Revelation, or any other apocalyptic literature, will create the mental images and sensations that confirm the nearness of apocalypse. When that confirmation is total, then people will act out of their apocalyptic convictions. Their praxis will be entirely apocalyptic. As such, then it will also be Praxis.

---

389   Bull, ibid., pp. 291-292.
390   See footnote 195.

3. **The Subject/Object Window**: Modern science has broken the window between the subjective world and the objective world. Empirical science in the form of Einstein's Theory of Relativity and Heisenberg's Uncertainty Principle haven't smashed the window, but they have put an expanding fissure in it that is expanding into a definite hole. It's a break that no earthly Safelite[391] can repair. The postmodern ambiguity between what was once absolutely ascribed to the human condition as a soul in a body is irreversible. The train of ideas from the beginning of Western Civilization to the present moment has led to modern and postmodern conclusions. There is no way to "go back" to the time when the subject/object divide provided a workable approach to the understanding of the Real without going all the way back to pre-Augustinian times. This is, in fact, what is happening, as is illustrated by the contemporary affinity for Manichaean principles and its worldview.

4. **The Stereoma**: The dissipation of the subject/object divide, equivalent to the polluting undifferentiation to which Bull's book refers, is neither different from nor more critically threatening to the existential state of both Western Civilization and its citizenry than was the coincidence of the waters from above with the waters from below in Noah's time (*Kairos*). If the present culture can find a type of Bechtel or Red Adair Company to cap the wells of the Deep,[392] the problem would be solved. Yet, to accomplish this would mean to reverse everything that IS Western Civilization, how we think, what we expect from life, and what we like or don't like about life as we are living it. In other words, it's not going to happen, and their will also be no gigantic umbrella to keep the waters from above away from our City.

---

391 Safelite – https://www.safelitesolutions.com_anextensionofyour-teambrand&culture : "As an industry leader, Safelite Solutions provides comprehensive end-to-end claim management solutions for more than 200 insurance and fleet clients"; accessed 8 Mar 23.

392 Capping wells – https://en.m.wikipedia.org_kuwaitioil-fires ; last edited 1 February 2023, accessed 8 Mar 23.

In the Postmodern world, the *Stereoma* is once again a thin dimensionless reality on which only a God-purposed ark can float.

5. **The Meaning and Significance of Self:** That the entire feel and shape of the human self has and is still radically changing is the primary fact of life in Western Civilization today. One professional analysis compares this transformative moment to the use of the Johari Window: "Ironically – and poignantly – the Johari Window, as a guidebook for this transitional period, is still relevant today."[393] This 'Window' "is a framework for understanding conscious and unconscious bias that can help increase self-awareness and our understanding of others ... It is composed of four quadrants in which people ... can identify what they know about themselves and what other people know about them. This results in four areas of understanding: Open area ... Blind area ... Hidden area ... Unknown area."[394] Another professional approach involves the notion of self-fragmentation. This vision of postmodern society segues nicely, and not surprisingly, into Foucault's disdain for literary and historical totalities. The idea of "uncentered people" is accounted for in this way: "Because of rapid economic and political innovations, changes in the nature of the family, and the decline of religion, the individual or essential self is suffering a breakdown, such that individual or fragmented selves are being created, namely combinations of belief and emotional involvement, each which could readily be abandoned for another. This process is exacerbated by the movement towards a mass capitalistic society in which individual selves have little input into the collective, in contrast to tribal societies..."[395]

---

393 William Bergquist, *Library of Professional Psychology*, present – https://www.library.psychology.edu thenewjohari-window#6thepostmodernself ; accessed 8 Mar 23.

394 Johari Window – https://www.gartner.com gartnerglossary ; accessed 8 Mar 23.

395 Fragmentation – https://www.encyclopedia.uia.org fragmentationofthehumanpersonality ; accessed 8 Mar 23.

The Unknown self in this scenario undoubtedly longs for the Hegelian solution by which the psychological life and the social and political life merge to become one. This condition would have been, and was called, a pathology in the evolving Modern world view, but it has quickly and suddenly become a norm. This is a sign of apocalypse. In Old Testament terms, one might be asking the question, "Should I go the Egyptians, surrender to the Babylonians, become consumed in mystical awareness, or simply die on the parapets of the Holy City?"

Where is Ezekiel when we need him? The *Kairos* itself could be anything and anytime. Humpty cannot be put back together once he has lost track of his own soul: By what means would he be able to do this? Humpty Dumpty is no longer a "good egg."

The Old Languaging of the current advanced state of Western Civilization is epitomized in the creation of and establishment of the United States of America. Nevertheless, the passage of nearly 250 years has made as much a difference in the Nation's self-perception as did the Flood, or the Exodus, or the Exile. The Old Language and its very games of meaning and use won't patch up the expanding crack in the subject/object window. The flood is already beginning to pour through it, and if one's ark isn't already ready to float, it will be a miracle if it can be made to do so.

A coming-to-pass Separation is taking place.

Part Two: PATTERNS OF TECTONIC CHANGE OR TRANSITION

Chapter One: JESUS WAS SILENT BEFORE PILATE

Our culture has built a shrine to the real, a shrine supported by the three pillars (the enduring, the thing-like, and the efficacious) ... among them we are accustomed to worship, though often without much discrimination ... For most of us, there is no higher instance of appeal.[396]

THE COMPARISON between patterns of tectonic change, or transition, in the Old Testament and patterns of transition in the history of the West shows us that Western Civilization is entering the time of its End. Our times, in the West, are eschatological. That the Apocalypse was prefigured at the beginning of Christianity is a sign that points to the finalization of that Apocalypse in our time. In terms of "world," or cosmos, the Last World of the Hebrews, the Exilic/Postexilic world, was divided mid-world by the incarnation of Jesus Christ.

"Cosmos" is a unifying word that brings together the visible universe, the inner life of human beings, and the spiritual character of the whole. Whereas there was a dividing line between the visible, or "objective," aspect of the cosmos and the psychological, or inner, aspect, that dividing line was not the fixed and inviolate threshold that was set by Western science in the days of the Enlightenment.

---

396   Margenau, *The Nature of Physical Reality*, pp. 3-10.

The cosmos, then, is both the visible world and our perceptions of it and our responses to those perceptions. It's from this combinatory milieu that the more arguable aspects of culture, such as justice, truth, integrity, character, and so forth, arise. The gods of ancient times were the mediators, influencers, and disruptors who reigned in the vast and mysterious boundary between the perceived world and the perceiver.

In many ways, modern science, especially considering Relativity Theory and Quantum Theory, has returned to this more unified view of the "world" or "cosmos." It is no longer just billions and billions of stars: It includes and involves our perception of those stars and our judgments and thoughts that originate in those perceptions. In effect, the idea of the "cosmos" and the idea of our place in it are congruent: You can't have one without the other.

On the other hand, once you have erected an impenetrable barrier between objectivity and subjectivity, the cosmos can no longer reveal any truth to the subjective world that has anything significant to do with how Subjectivity ought to work in order to fit into the world as a whole. This is why Objectivity became such a critically important aspect of Western culture: Without objectivity, it was believed to be impossible to set boundaries to the moral life. It was assumed that those boundaries needed to be "objective."

Once the gods had been relegated to the dustbins of intelligent history, there were no longer any mediators between the Subjective and the Objective worlds, or world aspects. The interior world was relegated to the status of mere observer, a mysterious cosmic interloper who just happens to be placed in a position to be outside of the material world but who has no definite shape, form, or substance. In this context, the word "mind" has a much more active, or verbal, use than it does a nominal, or naming, use. "The Mind," in effect, doesn't really exist.

In Descartes' original philosophy, and it was entirely original, he started with personal identity. This was probably because unless he started there, his philosophy could go nowhere. Once he decided that "mind," or thinking, is the main event in the cosmos, the emerging conundrum was the question of how this "thinking" is connected so intimately with what is observed. His initial speculation was that the Pineal Gland[397] marked the answer to this secret. He decided that the Pineal Gland must be the locus of connectivity between Mind and Matter.

As you can see, virtually every rational endeavor that has characterized the culture of the West, such as medicine, has been inspired by the method Descartes used to find the Truth. This method is called Rationalism. In professional philosophical circles, it's called Continental Rationalism, because it was the long-favored approach to The Truth on the continental states of Europe.

The British love their island sanctuary, and so, too, do the British thinkers love to disagree with their continental counterparts. The empirical method of finding The Truth became most popular in the British Isles, all of them, and so the professionals refer to this method of investigation into the cosmos as British Empiricism. British Empiricism is essentially the Patriarch of modern science, because its primary directive is to make no assumptions about reality until enough experiments have been successfully completed that show conclusive evidence of reliable and continuing cause-and-effect relationships between substances and elements of the physical world.

To further illustrate the gap between the Rationalistic approach to Truth and the Empirical approach, a popular postmodern term has been invented. This is the "thought experiment." A Thought Experiment is "a hypothetical situation in which a hypothesis, theory, or principle is laid out for the purpose of thinking through its consequences"[398] or "they are a way to craft free experiences in our mind, designed to answer a question

---

397 Pineal Gland – https://my.clevelandclinic.org_pinealgland : "Your pineal gland is a tiny gland in the middle of your brain that helps regulate your body's circadian rhythm by secreting melatonin"; last reviewed 06/22/2022,l accessed 11 Mar 23.
398 Thought experiment – https://en.m.wikipedia.org_thought-experiment ; last edited 23 February 2022, accessed 11 Mar 23.

or validate a hypothesis we have about human nature without imposing any demands on us for physical resources, time, or risk-taking."[399]

To be sure, if there are no demands for physical resources, no time restrictions, and no taking of risk, then we have already eliminated "human nature" as a meaningful term in our experiment. No reliable evidence can ever be produced by a thought experiment. Nevertheless, the idea of such a thing being real enough to merit a name is a sign of the times. Western Civilization is still seeking that mystical and magical connection between thought, or Mind, and action, or the material world. It is a type of hybrid frame of reference that tries to embrace both the empirical and the rationalist methods of finding The Truth.

The philosophical school, or discipline, called Phenomenology is another intellectual attempt to connect he rational project with the empirical project.[400] Phenomenology is "the science of phenomena as distinct from that of the nature of being, an approach that concentrates on the study of consciousness and the objects of direct experience."[401] The discipline of phenomenology is another 20th-century phenomenon (pardon the pun) affecting a real sea-change in the frames of references of many disparate academic and medical pursuits.

The aforementioned Martin Heidegger and Paul Tillich owe a metaphysical debt to phenomenology as does, most significantly, the modern discipline of psychology. Derrida, who developed the philosophy of deconstruction, and Sartre, as in "hell is other people,"[402]

---

399   Hitendra Wadhwa PhD., *Psychology Today*, June 8, 2022 – https://www.psychologytoday.com_thepowerofthoughtexperiments ; accessed 11 Mar 23.

400   AUTHOR'S NOTE: Like Splinter in *Teenage Mutant Ninja Turtles* (Paramount Pictures, 2007), "I made a funny." Both the purely rational and the purely empirical involve psychological "projection" . . . hahahahaha!

401   Phenomenology – https://www.languages.oup.com_phenomenology ;accessed 11 Mar 23.

402   Brandon Ambrosino, *Vox*, Nov 17, 2014, 1:20pm EST – https://www.vox.com_hellisotherpeople...misquotingphilosophers : "The line comes from a 1944 existentialist play by French philosopher Jean-Paul Sartre called *Huis Clos*, or *No Exit*. In the play, three people are trapped in Hell – which is a single room – and ultimately, while confessing their sins to one another, end up falling into a bizarre love triangle"; accessed 11 Mar 23.

were influenced by Husserl's phenomenology as well. And so . . . the Postmodern era comes into being (*egeneto*).

The upshot of this inevitable trend in late Modern Western thinking, planning, and psychologizing, is the accompanying impossibility of ever revealing or discovering the phenomenal connectivity between thinking and doing, between thought and physical reality, without breaking through the barrier separating Objectivity from Subjectivity which has been considered to be inviolate in all forms of Western thinking and analysis. It can't be done without undoing the entire edifice of enlightened civilization.[403]

This should be as frightening as the possibility of Apocalypse, which is the de-integration of the cosmos. But it should also be encouraging at least to the faithful. By faith, we can see and understand from the patterns of Holy Scripture, how navigating through the interim space and time between worlds is and can be done. And if you don't like long sentences, blame it on the influence of Heidegger and Plato, not to mention the Apostle Paul, on my own point of view.

If thought experiment is the prescribed way to go in the Postmodern interim, then, amen, let it be so. Every New World begins with the Holy Spirit hovering and brooding over the dark and deep waters of pre-existing chaos. If the saints before us did it, so can we.

The Cosmos IS heaven, earth, and the *Stereoma*, or Firmament: Let Apocalypse be our Thought-Experiment. Apocalypse is our Court of Higher Appeal.

Then, out of the box came Thing Two and Thing One! They said, "How do you do? Would you like to shake hands with Thing One and Thing Two?" And Sally and I did not know what to do. So we had to shake hands with Thing One and Thing Two. We shook their two hands, but our fish said, "No! No!"[404]

---

403   AUTHOR'S NOTE: Both Relativity Theory and Quantum Theory are, in character and in effect, universal thought-experiments.

404   Dr. Seuss, *The Cat in the Hat* (New York: Random House Children's Books, 1957, 1985), pp. 33-34.

SCHRODINGER'S CAT is back in the box, but we still wear his hat. The hat is Old Science in the Old Cosmos; the Apocalypse is the random event. [405] Thing One and Thing Two are our apparent choices of friendship. They look alike, but they aren't alike at all. The choice is entirely unregulated and non-rational.

The realm of the Stochastic[406] is the realm between worlds. That is to say, the cause-and-effect relationships and principles are God's cause-and-effect relationships and principles. They aren't discoverable either by rational thought or by empirical experiment. But then again, neither is Reality these days. If we include the earth-bound wisdom of Charles Darwin, then we are evolving in an entirely random manner,[407] if we are evolving at all. There is no guaranteed effect that must result from any of our "causes."

If "we," are evolving as the result of an entirely stochastic process, then entropy is the normative evolution of civilizations, just as most species, according to Darwin, fail to survive in the long run. Modern archaeology seems to confirm this principle. Yet the People of God survived a series or a coincidence of apocalyptic moments that changed the nature of the species and the world toward which its survival had evolved. The narrative of Jewish survival, the Hebrew Scriptures, follows the principles of Darwin's theory of Natural Selection in the sense that "offspring ... will thus have a better chance of surviving, for, of the many individuals of the many species which are periodically born, but a small number can survive ... We have seen that man by selection can certainly produce great results, and can adapt organic beings to his own uses, through the accumulation of slight but useful variations, given to him by

---

405   Schrodinger's Cat – https://en.m.wikipedia.org_schrodingerscat : "In quantum mechanics, Schrodinger's cat is a thought experiment that illustrates a paradox of quantum superposition. In the thought experiment, a hypothetical cat may be considered simultaneously both alive and dead, while it is unobserved in a closed box, as a result of its fate being linked to a random subatomic event that may or may not occur"; last edited 19 February 2023, accessed 11 Mar 23.
406   Stochastic – https://www.languages.oup.com_stochastic : "randomly determined: having a random probability distribution or pattern that may be analyzed statistically but may not be predicted precisely"; accessed 11 Mar 23.
407

the hand of Nature. But Natural Selection ... is a power incessantly ready for action, and is as immeasurably superior to man's feeble efforts.as the works of Nature are to those of Art."[408]

Like Thing One and Thing Two, Darwin's Theory of Natural Selection can lead either to racism[409] or the emerging reliance on stochastic processes.[410] This is as far as rational/empirical science can go, and Thing One and Thing Two are both troublemakers out to destroy the entire house of wisdom. A reliance on stochastic processes leads inevitably to the occurrence of pyroclastic flows. Again, the world ends in fire. At present, the allure of stochastic processes still leads to both racism and inevitable uncertainty.

Morris Kline, a noted mathematician, writes, "We know today that mathematics does not possess the qualities that in the past earned for it universal respect and admiration. Mathematics was regarded as the acme of exact reasoning, a body of truths in itself, and the truth about the design of nature ... Unfortunately, mathematicians had abandoned God and so the Divine Geometer refused to reveal which of the several competing geometries He had used to design the universe ... The recognition that mathematics is not a body of truths has had shattering repercussions ... Whom the gods destroy they first make mad ... Clearly, different bodies of mathematics will result from the multiplicity of choices. The recent research on foundations has broken through the frontiers only to

---

408   Charles Darwin, *The Origin of Species* (New York: The Modern Library/Random House, 1993; original 1859), pp. 88-89.

409   Social Darwinism – https://www.britannica.com socialdarwinism : "the theory that human groups and races are subject to the same laws of natural selection as Charles Darwin perceived in plants and animals in nature ... Social Darwinists held that the life of humans in society was a struggle for existence rules by 'survival of the fittest' ... "; accessed 11 Mar 23.

410   Stochastic – https://www.wallstreetmojo.com whatisstochasticprocess : "Stochastic process refers to a series of events where each event through random occurrence has an inbuilt pattern ... a probability model that describes a set of time-ordered random variables representing the potential impact of a dynamic process in a single instance ... The random process has wide applications in physics and finance ..."; cpr 2023, reviewed by Dheeraj Vaidya, CFA, FRM, accessed 11 Mar 23.

encounter a wilderness."[411] His use of the word "wilderness" is apropos to our present discussion on Apocalypse. The Old Gods are driving us mad.

Because this is a discussion about what is revealed in the patterns of the biblical narrative as a whole, as a totality, the relationship between the coming-to-pass, or *ginomai*, which is history as we can perceive it, and *gennao*, which is the procreational process, the one Darwin tries to understand as a totality, the coming together (synagogue) of *ginomai* and *gennao* must be understood as a type of reconciliation between the Christian faith and the Jewish World. Institutional Christianity cannot accomplish this necessary apocalyptic process because all institutions operate on the principle of self-preservation.

Christianity and Judaism are the two foundational "things," or spiritual and institutional phenomena, of Western Civilization. The term Judeo-Christian still resonates in the heart of Western humanity. But these two historical realities are not Thing One and Thing Two in our cosmic metaphor: Thing One and Thing Two point to the division, or foundational crisis, that affects religious, or spiritual, America in the 21st century.

What HAS come-to-pass in the 20th and 21st centuries? Is it all just random, tending toward civilizational entropy? Only revelation can guide the way through the transition of the world: The other choice is to never know if Schrodinger's cat is still dead or alive. Perhaps if we break the windowpane some more, we'll be able to find out.

Come down off your throne and leave your body alone; somebody must change. You are the reason I've been waiting all these years; somebody holds the key: Well, I'm near the end and I just ain't got the time, and I'm wasted, and I can't find my way home.[412]

---

411   Morris Kline, *Mathematics: The Loss of Certainty* (New York: Oxford University Press, 1980), Preface, and pp. 86, 98, 273, 276.
412   *Can't Find My Way Home*, Blind Faith, 1969 – https://www.lyricfind.com_cantfindmywayhomelyrics ; accessed 12 Mar 23.

THE 60s ENDED both chronologically and *"ginomatically"* in 1969. Until the world ends, the 1960s will be ripe for the picking for commentators of all stripes. There are many highlights, events, and remarks that can still serve to characterize the 60s in America, even for those born long after that time and that space. For anyone who was coming into maturity in those years, that time and space was a threshold.

A threshold is "a point of entry or beginning ... the magnitude or intensity that must be exceeded for a certain reaction, phenomenon, result, or condition to occur or be manifested ... a limit below which a stimulus causes no reaction ... a level, rate, or amount at which something comes into effect."[413] When you arrive at and/or then cross a threshold, you know it. There is a sense of excitement and soft dread, a knowing that you have never been there before and that if you cross the threshold you might never come back.

One of my "small group's" regular thresholds was a place called Gates Pass just west of Tucson, Arizona. At night, you drove up a narrow canyon road with sudden sharp turns and deceptive straightaways. In the dark, you could see the little park structure settled up ahead in the pass, in between two very rocky, cactus-blanketed mountains. There was always a bit of light behind the view, coming from farm equipment or the moon.

You parked below the structure and walked uphill for maybe one-hundred feet. There, from within the park structure, you were at the threshold. The structure was built right on the edge of the threshold, a descent of at least a thousand feet, nearly straight down to the floor of the Sonora Desert, stretched out for miles ahead. It was nothing but empty space from where you stood at Gates Pass, and the road going down the west side was steep and straight.

There was another threshold that you couldn't see directly, but you could feel it as an almost living force cocooning you in an anticipation of endings. In the distance, one could see some of those "little blue lights"

---

413   Threshold – https://www.languages.oup.
   com_threshold ; accessed 12 Mar 23.

that ringed the city at a distance, always there, always waiting for their moment. They marked the locations of missile solos, many, many missile silos, harbingers of the almost guaranteed nuclear holocaust to come.

The two thresholds never ceased to thrill. Even today, you can visit a decommissioned silo just south of town. The thrill is slightly different, but the combined effect of memory and current anticipation is enough to bring back an even more threatening sense of soft dread. The thresholds represented by Gates Pass have not ended. They are part of a coming-to-pass that is still being experienced by the entire planet and every world in it.

Back on campus in the late sixties, you could never escape one constant reminder that you were living in a threshold time of soft dread that could reify into rock hard certainty at any moment. The campus of the University of Arizona lies directly in the flight path for Davis-Monthan Air Force Base, and the F4C pilots being trained for war flew low and slow over the red brick buildings at a ceaseless rate, two by two, morning, noon, and night.

They were very, very loud. If you were in a classroom near the flight path, the class would have to stop. The Top Guns of Dickie Goober[414] were taking the techniques of America to Southeast Asia for demonstrations of cultural superiority. As a nation, we are still trying to demonstrate this thing, to finally cross the invisible threshold beyond which everybody will know that the United States of America is the Chosen Nation.

We will all have sunk deep into the same amount of trouble, or as the Bible calls it, tribulation, regardless of the direction that takes us through and beyond that threshold. Chosen for what, actually? What exactly IS American exceptionalism? Where IS America, "my home sweet home"? It's a beautiful piece of geography, but what is its topology?

---

414 AUTHOR'S NOTE: My roommate, an Air Force brat, called it Dickie Goober. I don't know if his dad was ever stationed in Kansas City, but of there was a NORAD station there it's possible.

The concept of American exceptionalism includes the idea that if the United States of America is lost, the whole world will be lost. Because the USA is the crown of Western Civilization, if the Cat's Hat, that crown of exceptionalism, is removed, then civilization as such, even its future possibility, will fail. We felt this going into the 60s- it was still, felt after that decade, but the feelings changed and intensified in many and various ways.[415]

Because the West can no longer distinguish between the voice of history and the voice of God, our feelings regarding what is being said are mixed and indistinguishable, too. Thanks to Thomas Aquinas, Spirit became Reason,[416] and thanks to Hegel, Reason became the State in the form of the Spirit of God on earth. Whether or not the State becomes (*egeneto*) Marxist or Fascist or some variation of the theme, human evolution terminates with the emergence of the perfect State. After that, the idea of "human being" changes radically. It just depends on to which lesser spirit you ascribe holiness. The part becomes identified only by means of the whole. The idea of stochastic reality is just the beginning.

The Last coming-to-pass began in 1914. To discern the fulness of that *egeneto* would require a close and accurate examination of every Kairos Moment since Augustine wrote his famous City of God. The transitional moment between the Modern Age and the Postmodern Age is a threshold of its own. When you look over the precipice, you can see those little blue lights twinkling in the darkness of a vast desert.

You'd like to go back home, but the canyon has swallowed your winding road in the deep darkness. You can never go back to your Old City, whether it might be Sodom and Gomorrah,[417] Rome, or Plymouth Colony. The only movement possible, the only movement that is ever possible, is forward, and forward trends toward the deep darkness of the desert and those little blue lights twinkling in the distance.

415   Hebrews 1:1-2: "God, who at various times and in diverse ways spoke long ago to the fathers through the prophets, has in these last days spoken to us …"
416   Aquinas – https://www.brainyquote.com_thomasaquinasquotes : "Reason is rather like God in the world"; accessed 12 Mar 23.
417   Genesis 19:26

The throne sits on the edge of the threshold.

Words are proximally present-at-hand ... we come across them just as we come across Things; and this holds for any sequence of words, as that in which the logos expresses itself ... In the logos an entity is manifest, and with a view to this entity, the words are put together in one verbal whole ... every logos is both sunthesis and diaresis, not just the one (call it 'affirmative judgment') or the other (call it 'negative judgment') ... The goddess of Truth who guides Parmenides, puts two pathways before him, one of uncovering, one of hiding ... The way of uncovering is achieved only in krinein logo – in distinguishing between these understandingly, and making one's decision for the one rather than the other.[418]

SUNTHESIS (SYNTHESIS) and *diaresis* are the "putting together" and the "dividing." Heidegger calls these affirmative judgment and negative judgment, or "Yes" and "No." Apocalypse, the "uncovering," is a manifestation of both so that the yes-or-no decision can be made. This he calls the action of *krinein logo*, dividing or judging by or of the word. Heidegger deviates from Hegel in this way, by revealing that there is both a "putting together," or synthesis, and a "dividing," or *diaresis*, whenever any Thing is revealed, or disclosed.

I have used the word *diachoridzo*, which means separation, as it agrees more succinctly in intent and description with the essential separating God does when declaring justice or ending one world to facilitate the beginning of another. Nevertheless, dividing is the usual reified description of God's judging action, as in when the waters of the Red Sea are divided. In this sense, the Last Judgment is the separating of the entire Old Heaven and Earth from the New Heaven and Earth. After this dividing, or judging, there is no more need for the *Stereoma*: It's always the First Day. It constitutes the *xorathesis* that actually comes after the thesis and the antithesis discover that they can't really get along in eternity.

Returning to words more intelligible than those of Martin Heidegger, once the thesis and antithesis have been given expression, Thing One

---

418   Martin Heidegger, *Being and Time* (New York: Harper & Row Publishers, Incorporated, 1962; original 1926), pp. 201, 265.

and Thing Two must go their separate ways. Heidegger, after all, is most concerned with the idea of "thingness."

The two Things that are separating are two variations of traditional, or conventional, institutional Western Christianity. There is as yet no distinct topology to either variant, that is to say, no perfect form, or telos. The dividing and separating is indicative of the Eschaton, or Last Things. The two Things both claim the legitimacy of being substantively allied or covenanted with past Christianity, but that past Christianity is thoroughly mitigated by the fact that it did not receive form, or topology, until St. Augustine gave it such in words.

The increasing separation between the two Western Christianities is an End Time phenomenon, one that points directly to the *Telos*, the perfected end purpose of God. The separating, or *diachoridzo,* of the two Things, causes an increasing conviction of the coming Apocalypse, because it involves the soul as well as the Spirit. It's a purifying process, and nobody enjoys being purified by fire. Jesus uses a word that indicates pruning, as in cutting off useless or dead branches.[419]

The particular mode of separating in the case of Western Civilization involves the dividing of the tenets laid down by St. Augustine in terms of the word of God and reasoning on the word of God. It's a separating that can't be done by studying Augustine's writings, because the way of studying those words is the long-term consequence of abiding by the words in the first place. It's like cutting off a branch from the tree while you are sitting on the point farthest from the tree. You will fall with the outer part of the branch.

God does the separating through the instrumentality of angels.[420] We leave the weeds mixed in with the wheat, because we don't have the pure knowledge it takes to separate them on our own. Only the word can do this.[421] The word does the pruning, the angels do the separating. In the

---

419 John 15:3: "You are already clean (pruned) through the word which I have spoken to you."
420 Matthew 13:40-42
421 Matthew 13:24-30

meantime, on hearing the word of God, many are already separating themselves from the fellowship.

Finding the word of God in the reasoning on the word of God is no simple task with Augustine: With Modern and Postmodern Christian writings, it's virtually impossible. Reasoning is built on reasoning to the point at which you do need, as Foucault suggests, a kind of archaeology in the search for what might have been original in the moment. What can be said positively is that Western Civilization is built on the foundation of the revealed word of God, but there must also be the unfortunate caveat that layers and layers of intellectual, ontological, and existential structures have been built over that foundation and on top of each other.

A trained eye and intellect can discern fragments of the un-modified word of God in theologians such as Paul Tillich and Karl Barth, and one can even discern topologically deformed evidence of the word of God in Heidegger's writings. Connecting the dots from what is written contemporarily and what was heard originally is problematic to the point of uselessness. What results is a kind of free-form Christianity that looks erudite and applicable, but which is so distant from the original word as to be over the increasingly distant horizon of salvation.

Like Waldo in those *Where's Wally* pictures, God is often in the picture, but you can't easily distinguish God from all the other gods. It's such a joy to find Waldo in even one picture that one is tempted to cling to that one picture as the definitive picture of one's entire situation.

Eventually, the two Things must diverge perpendicularly, at a 180-degree variant. One Thing will consist of Bible teaching only; the other will consist of reasoning on reasoning on reasoning on reasoning on the word. Because the variance between the two is extreme enough already to merit the accusation of deviance between one Thing and the other, the Manichaean character of the current political and moral and religious divide in America can only become more intense.

That this variance in the Christian divide is the natural or determinative result of the will of God is something most Christians on either tangent would vehemently deny. God's will must be pleased with either the one or the other. God must say "Yes" and "No" just like everybody else. God, in short, must choose between them. This is what in Bible language is called the Last Judgment.

The sheep and the goats[422] don't represent the immoral and the moral or the just and the unjust in political terms as much as they represent the transcendence-favoring versus the immanence-favoring, the ones who favor the pure word of God for all learning and teaching and those who prefer reasoning on reasoning on reasoning on the word of God. This is the divide that separates belief from unbelief, the only divide that will make any difference in the End.

God's decision creates the Great (Tectonic) Divide[423], the one from which all water flows either east, toward the rising sun, or west, toward the setting sun.

If one recognizes in science only the linear accumulation of truths or the orthogenesis of reason, and fails to recognize in it a discursive practice that has its own levels, its own thresholds, its own various ruptures, one can describe only a single historical division, which one adopts as a model to be applied at all times and for all forms of knowledge ... All the density of the disconnexions, the dispersion of the ruptures, the shifts in their effects, the play of the interdependence are reduced to the monotonous act of an endlessly repeated foundation.[424]

THE CURRENT BATTLEGROUND between science and religion isn't a fight over Truth or even the Source of Truth: It's a cage fight between two unwarranted language-game hybrids. The modern language game of Western Religion attempts to splice science-talk into or onto religion-talk; the modern language-game of science attempts to remove religion-talk from its own epistemological source. This splice-fight characterizes the conversations regarding religion in the Modern West.

---

422   Matthew 25:31-46
423   Continental Divide – https://en.m.wikipedia.org_continentaldivideoftheamericas : "The Continental Divide extends from the Bering Straight to the Straight of Magellan, and separates the watersheds that drain into the Pacific Ocean from those river systems that drain into the Atlantic and Arctic oceans..."; last edited 28 February 2023, accessed 13 Mar 23.
424   Foucault, *Archaeology*, p. 188

Insofar as the illusion persists that politics is, or can be, a science, the conversation, such as it is, between science and religion spills over into the conversation between Church and State. To be sure, each church has its own deformative language game, and each partisan political group has its own deformative language game, and they both try to justify their deformations in terms of what is erroneously believed to be the Original Language Game of the United States of America.

Because of this linguistic seepage between these various levels of language-game-cage-fights, the general activity of political discourse and campaigning becomes more of a mob scene than of a rational debate between equally esteemed contenders. The Lincoln/Douglas Debate could never happen in Postmodern America: It will always degenerate into a postmodern version of the duel between Aaron Burr and Alexander Hamilton. Their encounter sounds very contemporary.[425] It seems almost foundational.

There is an archaeology to this late Modern inevitability, as Foucault suggests, but the levels of meaning are virtually civilizational, not national. Because the pathology of Modern/Postmodern conversation effecting nearly all levels of meaning and conviction is rooted more deeply in the character of the Western citizen rather than simply the character of the American citizen, to resort to strictly American archetypal foundations in the attempt to resolve or win the conversation are futile. It's the momentum of the civilization itself that impels us toward a Greet Divide.

---

[425] Burr-Hamilton – https://www.nps.gov_hamiltonburrduel : "Hamilton opposed Burr for elections and used his influence to keep Burr from holding office. 'I feel it is my religious duty to keep this man from office,' wrote Hamilton in 1792 ... in April 1804 (in the Albany Register) a letter ... referenced a conversation between Hamilton and other dinner guests in which Hamilton mentioned that Burr is a 'dangerous man, and not to be trusted.' The letter also references a 'more despicable' statement made by Hamilton about Burr ... Burr insisted on an apology from Hamilton, but Hamilton refused ... he claimed to have no personal ill-will towards Aaron Burr, although their differences lie in political matters ... He explained that he could not apologize ... because he meant what he said ..."; accessed 13 Mar 23.

More simply put, one player tosses the basketball: The other player swings a bat. Nobody can ever really find out who's on first.[426] Who is on first, but who is on first? The one language game claims its precedence in the Bible, while the other claims precedence in the value and power of reason. At this point, history can only be depicted as a regular-singular point[427] on the timeline toward which a certain continuity can be imagined but beyond which the line is entirely discontinuous. The conversation can neither go "backward" nor "forward": It can only be resolved by the decisive fiat of each player.

A regular singular point is one to which you can calculate an approach, but you cannot find a way to depart. If you want to get from your "here" point to the next "there" point, you may find that either there is no "there" there or that there is a multiplicity of "theres." Character of divergence at this point is what will determine where the possible there's are, but because the function has no continuity at that point, none of the options can be analytically calculated.

At such a point, to use a previous illustration, matter becomes energy, and location in time and space exceeds the limits or boundaries of your universe. In the United States of America, Western Civilization has reached its custom-made cultural discontinuity, its threshold, its Foucaultian Fissure. The continuities of Western Civilization, insofar as they could be legitimately itemized to produce a reliable totality, become discontinuous today, divergent, even extremely divergent. They will never meet again, and they only actually ever came VERY CLOSE to meeting.

---

426 Who's On First – https://en.m.wikipedia.org_whosonfirst : "a comedy routine made famous by … Abbott and Costello … Abbott is identifying the players on a baseball team (but) the player's names can simultaneously serve as the basis for questions (e.g., The first baseman's name is *Who*), leading to repeated misinterpretations and growing frustration between the performers"; last edited 12 March 2023, accessed 13 Mar 23.

427 Regular Singular Point – https://www.encyclopedia2.thefreedictionary.com_regularsingularpoint : "A regular singular point is a differential equation is a singular point of the equation at which none of the solutions has an essential singularity"; accessed 13 Mar 23.

All the language games of Western Civilization are falling like acid rain on the thirsty land of its self-defining culture; like radio-active fallout that's carried on the winds of time to the four corners of the earth. The seven woes give us a sufficient definition of the situation, but all the interpretations are divergent.

Even Jesus was silent before Pilate.[428]

---

[428] Matthew 27:12-14: "When He was accused by the chief priests and elders, He gave no answer. Then Pilate said to Him, 'Do You not hear how many things they testify against You?' But He never answered him a word, so that the governor was amazed."

Chapter Two: LAWLESSNESS IS THE REJECTION OF ISRAEL

Neque enim quaero intelligere ut credam, sed credo ut intelligam – fides quaerens intellectum...[429]

IT WAS BETWEEN the days of St. Augustine and the days of Thomas Aquinas that Anselm, who became the Archbishop of Canterbury, said, "I do not seek to understand in order that I may believe, I believe in order that I may understand" and coined the phrase "faith seeking understanding." He also gave Western Civilization the famous Ontological Argument for the existence of God, and the Satisfaction Theory of the atonement.

The Ontological Argument goes: "God (is) a being than which no greater can be conceived. And ... such being must exist in the mind, even in that of the person who denies the existence of God ... if the greatest possible being exists in the mind, it must also exist in reality, because if it existed only in the mind, then an even greater being must be possible."[430] One can see at a glance how all the theological, metaphysical, and even scientific questions we know arose from this very clever argument.

It's easy to misconstrue scientific hypotheses to make them fit one's current metaphysical, religious, or political ideology, but Anselm's argument, moved ahead into a Modern context, is like asking, "If the universe has limits (or boundaries), is it really The Universe?" The famous mathematical physicist Stephen Hawking had some things to say in this direction. For instance, "An event is something that happens at a particular point in space and at a particular point in time ... Space and time are now dynamic quantities: when a body moves, or a force acts, it affects the curvature of space and time – and in turn the structure of space-time affects the way in which bodies move and forces act. - Space

---

429   Anselm of Canterbury (1033-1109) – https://en.m.wikipedia.org_creadoutintelligam ; last edited 26 June 2022, accessed 13 Mar 23.
430   Ontological Argument – https://en.m.wikipedia.org_ontologicalargument ; last edited 30 December 2022, accessed 13 Mar 23.

and time not only affect but are also affected by everything that happens in the universe ... it became meaningless to talk about space and time outside the limits of the universe."[431] An event is, in other words, a singularity, and the entire universe is deformed by each and every event. Hawking covers the entire gamut of language games from the material to the metaphysical to the expressive or thought game and all the accompanying universes that might be emergent in each case.

Are there other universes? Are there other gods? Are we really saying anything meaningful when we ask questions like this? Anselm would say, "Yes", unless, of course, he said "No."

The Satisfaction theory goes like this: "Anselm believed that humans could not render to God more than what was due to him. The satisfaction due to God was greater than what all created beings can do, since they can only do what is already required of them ... only a being that was both God and man could satisfy God and give him the honor that is due him ... The Protestant reformers shifted the focus of this satisfaction theory to concentrate not merely on divine offense but on divine justice. God's righteousness demands punishment for human sin."[432]

Anselm's Satisfaction theory becomes very Roman Catholic whereas its modification designed to satisfy the need to "pay" for sin becomes a central dogma of Protestantism. Both variations stem from the New Testament revelation that Christ's sacrifice, His shedding of blood, satisfies the cost of sin, which is life itself. Life is in the blood. The blood sacrifice of Christ on the cross ties together and satisfies the prices that had to be paid by God and everyone else for the deliverance of the people time and again. They are summed up by the celebration of the Passover which then becomes the Pascha of Christ.

St. Augustine's City Theology is much more formal and discursive and does not try to find linkage between the patterns of life in the City of Man with the patterns for life in the City of God. They are kept apart,

---

431   Hawking, *Time*, pp. 24, 34
432   Satisfaction theory – https://www.theopedia.com_sat-isfractiontheoryoftheatonment ; accessed 13 Mar 23.

but in the early Middle Ages of the West, they began to come together.[433] For Augustine, Rome was gone; for the Medieval theologians, Rome was being renewed by the patterns, or archetypes, of the City of God.

At any rate, by the time Anselm proposed his *credo ut inteligam*, the distinction between the direct text of the Bible and the process of reasoning on the word and language of the Bible was already obscured. Was he understanding the biblical testimony, or was he understanding a given understanding of the language of the Bible? In effect, Anselm created an understanding that stood in for the original. He did this in his own mind, and Mind and Spirit, *psyche* and *pneuma*, have been at odds ever since. He was believing his own understanding, and his understanding told him what to believe.

Anselm thought he had thought the thought that was beyond all other thought, but don't we all? It wasn't therefore the scientific reformers of the Enlightenment who eliminated the need to think about God as a pathway to the Truth: It was Anselm. Everything else was inevitable . . . except maybe the mystery of the Pineal gland.

The publication of the Fundamentals in 1915 represents a kind of last-gasp theo-intellectual attempt to stay the advance of the waters of higher-critical rationalism before they flooded the entire civilization. It was the last formal publication by conventional Christian theologians to maintain and promote the Christian intellect's reliance on and dependence on the content of written revelation, i.e., the Holy Scriptures.

There are to prime hermeneutical directives governing the Modern interpretation of Scripture: One, Reason has the final word on what the

---

433   See footnote 50, et al.

words of the Bible mean,[434] and, Two, the Bible interprets itself.[435] In an age when reason can't give you the final word on what reason itself has concluded, it's culturally problematic to put one's trust in any reasonable interpretation of the Holy Scriptures. Eventually, the words themselves are only momentary signs or triggers to an utterly different point of view. The frame-of-reference of the interpreter completely overwhelms whatever frame of reference can be gleaned from the words of Scripture themselves.

In Postmodern Western Civilization, the Bible has become a religious artifact, a ritual object, good for use only as a symbolic reminder to oneself that one is a "good" person. Even this use, a language-game use, is rapidly going out of style, because the general population is becoming convinced that the civilization never was good, and that, therefore, no one who is participating in it can be called "good" either. This is a totally Manichaean point of view, one that disjoins the civilization from its own roots.

Postmodern Manichaeism takes the Good/Evil dichotomy out of its Gnostic roots and transplants it into anthro-political origins.[436] It

---

434   Interpretation – https://en.m.wikipedia.org_historicalcriticism : "Also known as the historical-critical method or higher criticism … investigate the origins of ancient texts in order to understand 'the world behind the text' … to discover the text's primitive or original meaning in its original historical context … In the 21st century, historical criticism is the more commonly used term for higher criticism, and textual criticism is more common than … 'lower criticism' … where historical investigation was unavailable, historical criticism rested on philosophical and theological interpretation … historical criticism became refined into … source criticism, form criticism, redaction criticism, tradition criticism, canonical criticism …"; last edited 23 February 2023, accessed 14 Mar 23.
435   Interpretation – https://www.thewayinternational.com_thescriptureinterpretsitselfintheverserightwhereitiswritten : "God never meant for us to interpret the Word for ourselves; we do not need to, nor should we. Instead, we can learn how the Scripture interprets itself in three main ways: (1) In the verse, (2) In the context, and (3) Used before"; posted April 30, 2018, accessed 14 Mar 23.
436   Gnosticism – https://en.m.wikipedia.org_gnosticism : "Gnostic cosmogony generally presents a distinction between a supreme hidden God and a malevolent lesser divinity (sometimes associated with the Yahweh of the Old Testament) who is responsible for creating the material universe …

undergirds all forms of racism by attributing good to one assortment of anthro-political elements and evil to the other assortment. Because religion in the West had become thoroughly historicized, history becomes the Good God of the gnostic worldview, the one who reveals the evil minions of the Evil God. The solution to the Good vs Evil problem in the postmodern age, then, is to eliminate the Evil minions. It is NOT to rise in one's consciousness to a higher plane at which knowledge merges with truth and divinity. An Evil minion can't rise.

Oddly enough, the transition between pre-Augustinian Manichaeism and Postmodern American Manichaeism consists of the reduction of the worldview to a non-transcendent context. The theology becomes a spiritual philosophy that can use the words of the Bible to justify its reduction of the Gnostic format to an entirely pragmatic one. One sees this format in political statements such as, "My administration has a job to do and we're going to do it. We will rid the world of the evildoers."[437]

Segue suddenly some twenty years later, and you find statements such as, "MAGA Republicans post a clear and present danger' to American democracy." The President went on to say, "I believe America is at an inflection point, one of those moments that determine the shape of everything that's to come after ... MAGA forces are determined to take this country backwards."[438] If one can't see the Gnostic/Manichaean religious substrate (hypostasis) in these comments, one is choosing to be willfully blind.

You can feel it. Some people like the feeling; some do not.

Manichaeism conceives of two coexistent realms of light and darkness that become embroiled in conflict"; last edited 12 March 2023, accessed 14 Mar 23.

437   Manuel Perez-Rivas, *CNN Washington Bureau*, September 16, 2001 4:54 PM EDT – https://www.edition.cnn.com_busgvowstoridtheworldofevildoers : "'We've been warned there are evil people in this world. We've been warned so vividly,' Bush said. 'And we'll be alert. Your government is alert ... As I said before, people have declared war on America and they have made a terrible mistake'"; accessed 14 Mar 23.

438   MAGA – https://www.cnbc.com_bidenwarnstrumpsextrememagarepublicansareclearandpresentdanger tousdemocracy : "'I believe America is at an inflection point, one of those moments that determine the shape of

The most revealing aspect of Postmodern American spirituality is that the historical interpretation of the Bible, although reduced to a potpourri of various academic conclusion reasonably arrived at, is the exact spiritual equivalent of the Biblical apocalypse. Virtually everyone senses this, but few are willing to point it out. The apocalypse is supposed to be symbolic, not ostensive!

This bifurcation of American citizens and citizens of the world into a company of Good Human Beings and a company of Evil Human Beings is the most manifest sign of the times. It involves a spiritual reversion, a rejection of the Christian values and worldview that provide the moral AND historical foundation of Western Civilization, as well as a synthetic and hidden re-interpretation of spiritual Gnosticism into pragmatic, doable terminology, or language.

Consider the currently popular euphemism "regime change."[439] It sounds very academic, like a legitimate abstraction in the language of political science. Yet, it really is neither abstract nor an example of systematic analysis: It means quite simply to get rid of the leader of the regime. Do this, and the Evil will be gone, such as what happened (*egeneto*) in Iraq.[440]

Except Evil doesn't go away: It morphs. When Evil morphs into its end-time shape and form, the situation is like that in Masada at the

---

439   Kevin Ward, Encyclopedia Britannica, current – https://www.britannica.com_regimechangepoliticalscience : "refers to the overthrow of a government considered illegitimate by an external force and its replacement with a new government according to the ideas and interests promoted by that force"; last updated Sept 19, 2022, accessed 14 Mar 23.

440   Kenneth Katzman, Library of Congress Washington DC Congressional Research Service- ADA474703, 2004-02-23 – https://www.apps.dtic.mil_iraqusregimechangeeffortsandpostsaddamgovernance : "Operation Iraqi Freedom accomplished a long-standing objective the overthrow of Saddam Hussein. But replacing that regime with a stable, moderate, democratic political structure has run into difficulty ... escalating resistance to the U. S. – led occupation has complicated U. S. efforts to restore stability, accomplish economic reconstruction, and build and transfer authority to Iraqi political and security bodies"; accessed 14 Mar 23.

end of the Old Era.[441] The people begin to consume each other. The interpretations begin to devour each other like Langoliers consuming past reality.[442]

These things bring to mind a passage from the New Testament, one that interprets itself, "Remind them of these things, commanding them before the Lord that they do not argue (*logomachein*) about words, which leads to nothing of value and the destruction (*strophe*)[443] of those who hear them. Study to show yourself approved by God, a workman who need not be ashamed, rightly dividing (*orthotomounta*)[444] the word of truth."[445] When apocalypse arrives, the arguments have already been fulfilled.

When the Word is rightly divided, the world is rightly divided.

Now the sons of Eli were corrupt. They did not know the Lord ... the men treated the offering of the Lord with contempt ... Eli was very old, and he heard all that his sons were doing to all Israel ... they did not listen to the voice of their father ... Samuel was ministering to the Lord before Eli. And the word of the Lord was rare in those days ... Eli called Samuel and ... said, "What is the thing that the Lord has spoken to you? Do not hide it from me ... Samuel told him (that the iniquity of Eli's house shall not be atoned for with sacrifice nor offering forever) ... (Samuel) said, "It is the Lord; let Him do what is good in His eyes."[446]

---

441   See footnote 46.
442   The Langoliers – https://en.m.wikipedia.org_thelangoliers(miniseries) : "Based on the novella by Stephen King ... originally aired May 14-15, 1995, on the ABC network ... As they board (an airplane) the group witnesses strange creatures consuming everything including the ground ... The plane takes off just as the Langoliers consume the airport ... Dinah (a protagonist) dies while recalling 'everything was beautiful, even the things that were dead' ... The passengers are concerned (after they land in Los Angeles) ... they may be a few minutes ahead of the present"; last edited 2 March 2023, accessed 14 Mar 23.
443   Krueger, *Conundrums*, p. 23: "The logic of the historical situation points to the logic of catastrophe in the Bible ... The Biblical tradition didn't reveal a clear path through catastrophe, only that God always redeemed the people from such by leading them literally into another world altogether."
444   *Orthotomounta*, cf. "ortho-doxy" – https://biblehub.com_ortho-tomeoh : "to cut straight, correctly apportion"; accessed 14 Mar 23.
445   II Timothy 2:14-15
446   I Samuel 2:12 - 3:18

THE TIMES OF ELI and Samuel were Kairos Times. You might say that when Eli heard what Samuel had to say to him from God, Eli experienced a Kairos Moment. We don't know how Eli experienced that message, but we do know how he responded: He responded with an 'Amen.' He also knew the difference between Good and Evil, even when the evil was the product of his own house.

Samuel's mother was Hannah, the famous typological forerunner of Mary the mother of Jesus. Eli was a priest. Eli was, then, of the House of Levi; Hannah, we read, is married to a man of the House of Ephraim. We recall, here, that Joshua, the great deliverer, was also of the House of Ephraim. Prophetic truth is being manifested here, even in the sense of first emerging. There is not yet a temple, and there is not yet a king.

Eli was the last Judge. Each judge has been hand-picked by God to lead the people in times of trouble. There was no tribal precedent for the honor of being chosen: In this case, Eli just "happened" (*egeneto*) to be of the House of Levi. The evil in Eli's house was not initiated in his soul or spirit: His sons initiated it. Yet, Eli "honored (his) sons above (the Lord,"[447] even though their behavior indicated that they rejected his authority as well as God's authority.

There is much that can be unpacked in the story of Eli and Samuel, existential stuff, Being stuff, authority stuff, and so forth. The presenting stuff, as it is in most of the Old Testament, is tribal stuff. It's important to note which tribal generations are in play. So Samuel who is to become (*ginomai*) the first anointed prophet within the authority structure of mature Israel, is of the House of Ephraim. Ephraim eventually becomes (*ginomai*) one of the Ten exiled northern tribes. But that's a bigger kind of dividing.

The Eli-Samuel divide is between one system of governance and another. The system under which judges were chosen was one presided over directly by God. It was a system that accounted for whatever contingency or threat might face the People of God. That system did

---

447   I Samuel 2:29

NOT rely on the anointing of a particular family to lead: All the families were eligible. Eligibility blanketed all the twelve tribes.

What becomes of Ephraim and the other eleven northern tribes is an open question even today. What became (*ginomai*) of the Age of the judges is a closed subject: It came to an end. Samuel, to be sure, was a type of judge-prophet, but with the assigning of kingship to a specific person from a specific family, Saul of the House of Benjamin, to be king, the judge part of Samuel's calling was dropped. The house of Benjamin, the house of Levi, the house of Judah and some of the house of Simeon were granted revelational continuity by God; the others were not.

Samuel was an interim leader, between the time of the Judges and the time of the anointed kings. This transition from Judge to King was not, however, apocalyptic: It owned its own sense of continuity. Judge became (*egeneto*) judge-prophet became Prophet alongside King. The kings were thereafter be designated strictly by generation, by *gennaoh*: The prophets, however, remained chosen and anointed by God directly.

This Kairos moment, the Moment of Samuel, is important. Without the intervention of the prophets, initiated by the intervention of God, the kings would always stray. They would stray just like the sons of Eli. Even King David strayed, in as evil a way as had those two sons. When the king strayed, the entire commonweal became (*egeneto*) open to Evil. The anointed descendants of the anointed king would always need a prophet chosen specifically to critique and judge and re-align that king's application of godly authority.[448]

Anselm of Canterbury is a type of theological Judge-Prophet. The gap between the systemic foundations of Western Civilization before Anselm and those foundations following him is large, although not apocalyptic. It guarantees the later apocalypse, but it is not the final catastrophe itself. Anselm declares the headship of belief over human understanding, but then he employs human understanding to formulate his theories of the

---

448 AUTHOR'S NOTE: King Saul's sin was not in the doing of Evil as much as it was in the embracing of Evil. When evil didn't produce his desired results, he chose Evil in order to complete those desired results.)

existence of God and of the stoning victory of Christ. The archetypal foundations of his arguments are intellectual and cultural.

Western culture needed a king in those days. What happened (*egeneto*) over time (*Kairos*?) was the emergence of a plurality of kings and sovereignties. The sovereign God was represented by the Pope in Rome. Many kings played the role of Holy Roman Emperor until the empire's dissolution under the sword of Napoleon in 1806. Many kings reigned over many principalities, then nations, and then councils and parliaments ruled under laws created by themselves. But there was one emerging king: Academia.

St. Thomas owed an intellectual debt to St. Anselm and others in the intervening two centuries. Among them were the Muslim teachers Avicenna, Al-Gazzali and Averroes as well as the Christian teachers Anselm, Albertus Magnus, and Peter Lombard, and also the great Jewish scholar Maimonides. Although suspect at first, because his affection for the pagan philosopher Aristotle betrayed his non-revelational roots, and subjected to a kind of proto-inquisition, Thomas Aquinas became (*egeneto*) a saint of the Church, and he "influenced all of subsequent Western philosophy and Catholic theology."[449]

In the West, academia has been at odds with all designated authority since the days of St. Thomas Aquinas.

Types and shadows don't specifically correlate to historical events in the way that Margenau's Rules of Correspondence and Constructs relate Subjectivity to Objectivity, or the Spontaneous and Reflective, or the Mental and the Physical,[450] in order to produce a workable and

---

449 Aquinas – https://en.m.wikipedia.org_thomasaqui-nas ; last edited 14 March 2023, accessed 14 Mar 23.
450 Margenau, *Nature: Chapter 3: What is Immediately Given; 4: Departure from the Immediate; Constructs*, pp. 33-74: "It is found that the spectator-spectacle relation is difficult to maintain in the face of the newer knowledge of science, primarily because the knowing subject intrudes itself unpreventably into the objective scheme of things ... The rules of correspondence ... are not eternally grounded in the nature of things, nor are they immediately suggested by sensory experience; they are important parts

relevant picture of reality, but the connections between what went before in the story of the Old Testament and what has gone before in the story of Western Civilization is not so obscure as to deserve being relegated to mere foolishness and mystical conjecture.

If humanity could learn from history, there would be no history: History loves itself like a face before a mirror loves its reflections. The history of Western Civilization can't be compared to the events of the Bible because the Bible's language and points of view have saturated the Western intellect: The history of Western Civilization bears close resemblance BECAUSE it is Christian, and the resemblance can be understood only in terms of the original face in the mirror, the story of the Jews, or "salvation history."

The only way to rid the civilization of this law of correlation and the constructs that support and express them is to rid the civilization of both the Bible, the source of our fundamental language game, the Christian Church, the source of our standards and patterns of morality, and the Jews, the source of every identifying characteristic of humanity that we have. This attempt is the great last attempt of Western Civilization to rid itself of its debt to God and to Christ, and to recreate itself in its own image.

Heritage is one of those "unseen" things that is vital to the continuance of a civilization. We see objects that are emblematic of our heritage, such as old pieces of furniture or fading photographs of ancestors, but we don't "see" our heritage. We ARE our heritage which is "the full range of our inherited traditions, monuments, objects, and culture ... the range of contemporary activities, meanings, and behaviors that we draw from them ... it is both tangible and intangible."[451]

The inheritance of Eli's sons came to an abrupt termination. Because of one priestly family's sin, the entire structure of Hebrew society had to be changed. Eli, as a father, was unrighteous, and his sons disconnected

---

of every theory of nature and receive their validity from the consistency, the internal neatness and success of the entire explanatory scheme."

451   Heritage – https://www.umass.edu_whatisheritage ; accessed 15 Mar 23.

entirely from their heritage. When such a thing happens (*egeneto*), the entire heritage of the nation changes. The culture changes, and the meaning inherent in everyday communication or language, changes.

When (*egeneto*) sons were sent to war in 1914, the heritage of the West changed.

When all Israel saw that the king did not listen to them, the people responded to then king, saying, "What portion do we have in David? We also do not have an inheritance in the son of Jesse. To your tents, O Israel, and see to your own house, David!" So the people departed to their tents. [452]

SOME CHANGES are neither good for the Nation nor bad for the Nation: They simply change the entire shape of the Nation. If King Rehoboam had not destroyed his father's work and derailed the wisdom that had made the unified kingdom as great as it was, things could have unfolded differently. That this disjuncture in the history of Israel festered into an all-encompassing, ongoing cultural regret is evidenced in the prophecies regarding the restoration of the unified kingdom and the coming of Messiah. Because it is a prophetic regret, it expresses God's regret as well.

How does this work?

The first instance of God's regret is found early in the Scriptures. In the Book of Genesis, we read, "The Lord regretted that he had made man on the earth, and his heart was deeply troubled."[453] In other translations, we read that the situation "grieved God in His heart." These attributions to the heart of God cut across the Modern Era's distaste for anthropomorphisms, but they, and others like them, are very much an inseparable part of the narrative.

The antediluvian accounts in the Bible become fixed archetypes in the succeeding culture. Adam and Eve are ALWAYS being expelled from the Garden, Cain is ALWAYS killing Abel, and God is always grieved in His heart by an unsatisfiable regret. This regret is waiting to

---

452   I Kings 12:16
453   Genesis 6:6 NIV

be satisfied in the New Creation, and its satisfaction is guaranteed by Jesus' sacrifice on the cross.

These archetypes become resident in the darkness of the human unconscious. Created in the image of God, the human being cannot escape the fact that creation begins in darkness and formlessness. In this manner, all human inventiveness and creativeness incorporates a seed of regret. The seed will always grow into a very large tree. God Himself hangs on that Tree.

The Flood didn't eliminate the patterns, decisions, and sins of the antediluvian world: It incorporated them into the plan of salvation. In the unconscious realm, every human being knows that he or she exists just prior to a great deluge. Every human being has the option of being a Noah or of being drowned. This pattern, too, extends into modern times, and as the unconscious mind of humanity becomes more prominent in the affairs of humanity, the Truth of all the apocalyptic moments in the story of the Hebrews will arise to become closer and closer to the surface of the waters.

The Existentialists believed, and believe, that the void has been bridged by salvation, but it has not: It has been incorporated into the message. Nothing escapes the glance of God, not even abject darkness. God lives in darkness and is surrounded by darkness. When we try to invade heaven, we enter darkness.

The entire message of the Gospel with respect to darkness is not that darkness has gone away but that God chose to exist in the first day of creation, in the darkness, as Light. He "shines in the darkness, but the darkness" can't overcome Him.[454] But this was always so, because the Light was God and was with God from the beginning. The Word is the Light, and the Word is everything that is said and done in the Holy Scriptures.[455] This is why the Bible calls Jesus "The Word."

---

454   John 1:5
455   John 1:1-4

Every word in the Bible points to every other word, and the pointing is like the pointing of God toward Adam in Michelangelo's famous painting "The Creation of Adam." The Bible as a complete testimony is the painting of the pointing. We can see the subtle colors and forms take shape when we hear, read, mark, learn, and inwardly digest[456] the words and phrases of the Biblical language game.

The promise of the New Creation can only fail to satisfy God's intentions if the Old Creation becomes eternal. Every apocalyptic moment in the Bible is like the bringing down of the Tower of Babel. When one unified language of a civilization threatens to overcome the acceptable language of salvation, the tower must come down. To be caught without the language game of salvation is to be trapped in a land of perdition forever. Reason on reason on reason on reason can only result in a weight so massive that no human being can carry it.

When the Unified Kingdom of David and Solomon became divided, the tower of Solomon's wisdom came tumbling down. The two kingdoms, Israel and Judah, could never again communicate with each other effectively. They could not "speak life" into a reunification of the divided soul of the Nation of Israel. Israel chose the language of early beginnings, of the setting up of altars in special places; Judah chose to venerate the Temple.

Once the Second Temple was raised to the ground, leaving no stone upon stone, the entire meaning of "temple" was radically changed. Rome and Greece still had their Temples, but faith in the One God was no longer resident in them. Civilizations since then have built their own temples, Western Civilization included. They won't last: They will be buried under the fillings-up of successive cultures and civilizations, just like the temples of old.

God's archetypal regret will never cease to animate the rearrangement of civilizational archetypes, of the emergence and reemergence of cultural and social archons, until it is time to complete the entire project when the final Kairos comes. Nevertheless, even as Jesus said, "when the son

---

456   Book of Common Prayer, *Proper 25*, p. 236

of man comes, will He find faith on earth?"[457] If not, the Tribulation will never pass.

God does not want to settle back into the pre-creational void. The void itself involves a regret that surpasses all regrets, a regret that can only be overcome by the Light of Truth. Every sin is propelled forward in time by a host of regrets. The entanglements they cause are the source of every effort to create a Nation or empire that reaches, and even exceeds, the blessings and promises of God as presented to us meaningfully in the Holy Scriptures.

Reasoning on the promises of God does nothing to build the City of God: The City of God is the source of Reason. The dividing of a kingdom may seem unreasonable to the mind of its citizen, but we know that no divide, as like the River Jordan or the Red Sea or the River Kebar, can keep the People of God from crossing over into their Promised Land. The dividing, in other words, is Good: It leads to a true knowledge of the last, Great Divide.

Except in the moment, God did not choose Judah over Israel. God exiled them both, one to a seemingly irrevocable exile of identity, the other to a reformative passing through a wilderness of culture and language that threatened to drown identity altogether. Israel remained united in the mind of God. Reunion is the overcoming of God's regret. It is mystical, historical, and National. It's when the meaning of meaning finally means what it has always meant to mean.

Do not grieve the Holy Spirit of God, in whom you are sealed for the day of redemption. Let all bitterness, wrath, anger, outbursts, and blasphemies, with all malice, be taken away from you[458] ... Do not despise the discipline of the Lord ... Pursue peace with all men, and the holiness without which no one will see the Lord, watching diligently so that no one falls short of the grace of God, lest any root of bitterness springs up to cause trouble, and many become defiled (stained) by it...[459]

---

457   Luke 18:8
458   Ephesians 4:30-31
459   Hebrews 12:5, 14-15

TRUTH IS THE WINDOW we look through; meaning is generated from knowing Jesus. Truth is transmitted by means of meaning; meaningful truth is characterized and shaped by language.

If we do not look through the window, Truth is not Subjectivity: It simply vanishes. Insofar as one does not know Jesus, one does not know the Way, the Truth, and the Life: Jesus cannot be seen unless one looks through the window of the Holy Scriptures. The words, the meanings conveyed by the words, and the truth imbedded in the meanings when they are heard, cleans the window between Subjectivity and Objectivity.

Pure Subjectivity is not Self, rather, it is not-self; true objectivity is not empirical: It is an objectifying Subject. When the subject eternalizes by means of objectifying, the subject becomes objectified. Then there is no Subject. The broken window allows Subjectivity and Objectivity to blend. There is always the blending that results from uncertainty; it's the blending of certainty that kills the spirit.

The only language game that can convey the certainty that is both subjectivity and objectivity is the language game of the Scriptures. Everything else is ideology. Ideology is graceless; love doesn't break the window. When the window is broken, we project, and we transfer. Projection[460] and transference are the psycho-social means by which we widen the breech in the windowpane.

Projection is when you project your unwanted feelings in a situation of communication onto the intentions of some other communicator. You believe that the "other" has intended to cause you to feel the bad feelings, connected to bad thoughts and memories, that you are feeling. Transference is when you redirect your feelings about someone else onto the spiritual or psychological authority to whom you are in meaningful submission. Countertransference is when the authority redirects his, her or its feelings onto you.[461] Anway, these are handy psychology terms

---

460   See footnote 401.
461   Transference – https://www.webmd.
    com_transferencewhatitisandhowtodealwithit

that apply to virtually every transmission of language from one soul to another by means of language, pseudo-language, or assumed language.

Projection and transference involve their own language games, but the meaning of the truth assignments is akin to Wittgenstein's "beetle in the box" or even Schrodinger's Cat. In other words, meaning and truth become entirely private in the processes of projection and transference. We all project and transfer feelings from time to time.[462] It happens frequently in churches and other communities of intimacy. It happens when we try to conjure up connections with each other that aren't really there, primarily because we think, and feel, that we are obliged by faith, dogma, or doctrine, to have those connections.

The church becomes a self-defining ideology.

With projection and transference, the Cat-in-the-Hat goes back into the box, but Thing One and Thing Two continue to wreak havoc, taking on different disguises from moment to moment until, no one can distinguish one from the other. Ideology is the ultimate defense mechanism against this increasingly complex confusion, because it reifies a certain universal or ubiquitous set of feelings and causes attributable to them and universalizes them by intellectual constructs onto the whole, whether that whole might be a church, a family, eve,. A community or a sovereign state.

In an ideologically understood world, the language game is always the same. The Self vanishes into the language game and becomes the part of the whole that the ideology demands. The window between Subjectivity and Objectivity is maintained by the seeming elimination of Subjectivity.

---

462   Kimberly Holland, *Healthline,* May 28, 2019 – https://www.healthline.com_whatistransference : "Projection and transference are very similar. They both involve you attributing emotions or feelings to a person who doesn't actually have them. The difference between the two is where the misattributions occur ... (with) projection ... you may begin to see 'evidence' of those feelings projected back onto you ... Individual behaviors act as 'proof' of your theory ... the therapist can work with you to end the redirection of emotions and feelings ... 'Projection does what all defense mechanisms are meant to do: keep discomfort about ourselves at bay and outside our awareness'"; accessed 16 Mar 23.

Every-"thing" then becomes objectified. When things are all Objective, they can be easily manipulated in ways like how we manipulate physical objects. We arrange them the way we want to.

According to Jung, unresolved transference contributes to the creation of symbols that serve as a bridge between the conscious mind and the unconscious mind.[463] He mystifies projection by considering it to be more deeply connected to an unconscious identification with objects, such as polytheistic idols, that is, "the subject transfers itself to an object, so that it seems to belong to that object."[464] This kind of Deep Projection can permeate value systems, such as those of patriotism, of love, and of purpose.

Ancient Gnosticism, a general term for a religious infatuation with Intimate Knowing, mentioned earlier,[465] is the most compromising expression of projection and countertransference, because it identifies the object world with thoughts themselves and terms of religious language. Gnosticism becomes a kind of masturbatory religion in which the pious provides all the satisfaction needed to justify the claim to ritual purity. The rituals are all internal, and they are shared only in the sense that the "beetle in the Box" is shared. That is to say, the sharing is bogus.

Gnosticism at its worst, in the form of Manichaeism, exports dissatisfaction to an external realm of Evil. The moral and spiritual satisfaction which is desired then is believed to be possible only by relieving the soul of the external influence of and constant oppression by external Evil. By the time Manichaeism becomes the spiritual norm of a culture, both projection and transference have become so reified by ideology that there is no way to even chip away at the pseudo-objectivity that has been fashioned, even created.

The only recourse for gaining or even being able to perceive the possibility of ritual purity is to flee from such a system altogether. Jesus said, "When you see the 'abomination of desolation,' spoken of by Daniel

---

463   Jung, *Archetypes*, p. 289
464   Jung, *Archetypes*, p. 60
465   See footnote 437.

the prophet, standing in the holy place, then let those who are in Judea flee to the mountains. Let him who is on the housetop not go down to take anything out of his house. Let him who is in the field not return to take his clothes."[466] The desolation is a complete disconnection between the Self and itself. It's when the ideological self loses sovereignty over its own imaginations.

Enter the Dragon.[467]

The prophet Jeremiah calls this syndrome The Imagination of the Heart. He calls out to the People after evoking an imagery of Exile, "After this manner I will destroy the pride of Judah and the great pride of Jerusalem. This evil people, who refuse to hear My words, who walk in the imagination of their hearts, and walk after other gods, to serve them, and to worship them, shall be even as this waistband which is good for nothing. For as the waistband cleaves to the loins of a man, so I have caused the whole house of Judah to cleave to Me, says the Lord, so that they might be (*genesthai*) to Me a people for renown, and for a praise, and for a glory, but they would not listen."[468] He goes on to say, "If you will not listen ... my soul will weep in secret places for your pride; and my eyes will weep sorely and run down with tears, because the flock of the Lord is carried away captive."[469]

We see an allusion to this imagery in the gospel when Jesus washes the disciples' feet with "the towel in which He was wrapped,"[470] and again when the young man flees from the Garden of Gethsemane naked, "so he left the linen cloth, ands fled from them unclothed."[471] In the time of exile, the people were forcibly removed from the city and the land naked, with neither Temple nor sovereignty to cover them. In this manner, they crossed the Euphrates River into Babylon. There, "by the rivers of

---

466 Matthew 24:15-18
467 Revelation 12:3-4 (AUTHOR'S NOTE: Not to be confused with the 1973 Warner Bros. movie of the same name)
468 Jeremiah 13:9-11
469 Jeremiah 13:17
470 John 13:5
471 Mark 14:52

Babylon, there we sat down and wept when we remembered Zion,"[472] and "all who honored her despise her, for they have seen her nakedness."[473]

Yet, Naomi's bitterness is not removed by fiat. It would be removed in time for all the people when the righteous king took the throne. "Do not call me Naomi (*sweet, pleasant*)," she said. "Call me Mara, because the Almighty has brought great bitterness to me. I was full when I left, but the Lord has caused me to return empty," but her daughter, Ruth, found her husband that to preserve the name of her husband from Moab for his inheritance. Then Ruth gave birth to Obed, the grandfather of David.[474]

Truly, truly (Amehn, amehn) I say to you, unless a man is born again (gennehtheh anohthen), he cannot see (idein) the kingdom of God … unless a man is born of water and the Spirit, he cannot enter the kingdom of God … The wind blows where it wishes. And you hear its sound, but you do not know where it comes from or where it goes. So it is with everyone who is born of the Spirit.[475]

WHEN JESUS SAYS "AMEN" before a statement, He is declaring the coming-into-being (*ginomai*) of an aspect of the New Creation. His voice enters the chaos of pre-creation and brings the light into it. To the church in Laodicea, He refers to Himself through the angel as, "the Amen, the Faithful and True Witness, the Beginning of the creation of God …"[476] He does this a lot in John's Gospel, and this is the First Time He does it.

The Great I Am is also the Great Amen.

This biblical concept of a threshold between one world, or universe, and another is the beating heart of this essay. It's by means of Jesus' "Amen, amen" that we are introduced to the way of crossing that threshold. The Amen is Noah's ark and the Ark of the Covenant, the staff and person of Moses, the transposition of the prophet Ezekiel, the destruction of the Second Temple, the City of Jerusalem, and the dispersal of the Jews in the first century CE. The Amen is the expression

472 Psalm 137:1
473 Lamentations 1:8
474 Ruth 1:20-21, 4:9-10, 16-17.
475 John 3:3,5, 8
476 John 3:14

of fulness, the purpose, and the finality of the Kingdom of Heaven. It's when there is no longer the need for a firmament, a *Stereoma*, to separate the waters above from the waters below. *Amen* is when the beginning begins.

The Amen is the ascension of Jesus after He TRULY died on the cross. The Amen is when He said, "Go ... and make disciples of all nations, baptizing them in the name of the Father and of the Son and of the Holy Spirit, teaching them to observe all the things I have commanded you"[477] and when He said, "you shall receive power when the Holy Spirit comes upon you."[478] The Amen is when the Spirit of God is finished brooding over the dark waters of the deep.

To be born again is to become the anticipation of the New Creation on earth. It is a first and final deformation of the soul which reshapes it to be fitting for the New Heaven and the New Earth. The Old Heaven and the Old Earth provide the faithful with plenty of metaphorical and analogical material with which to express and envision the New Creation in language that can be understood, but the language game of the New Creation is the Gospel and the Gospel alone.

The New Song has been sung by the saints of the Word for 2000 years, now. The New Song proclaims from the heart that Jesus, by His blood, has redeemed a New Fellowship out of every tribe (*phulehs/phylum*)and tongue (*glohssehs*) and people (*laou*) and nation (*ethnous*).[479] The New Fellowship, or koinonia, is not a replacement fellowship: It's the Anticipatory Fellowship of the Kingdom. That's why the generational impact of baptism doesn't extend beyond a first generation. If it did, it would be a replacement genealogy (*genea, gennaoh*), a replacement People of God: It is not, and it never has been (*ginomai*).

From every tribe, tongue, people, and nation, Jesus draws them all up by means of the gospel, and the whole world, from beginning to end, has had the opportunity to be drawn up as well in the anticipation of the

---

477	Matthew 28:19-20
478	Acts 1:8
479	Revelation 5:9

redemption of Israel, Israel's "Ruthness." "Ruth" means "compassionate friend."[480] Through this seal of the Promise,[481] Christians have shared the name of Abraham, which means "friend of God."[482]

The Christian Fellowship has always been, from the Beginning and to the End, simply the steward of the franchise of God, the holder of the Promissory Note, the guarantee of the redemption of the Jews following the extended time of exile. That note is meaningless UNLESS and insofar as the Jews, and the Hebrew ancestors, are redeemed in history. It's only by means of this Promissory guarantee that the Gentiles will be able to recognize who the Jews are and be able to choose whether to honor the promise or to reject it.

The mission of Christianity is, or ought to be, not the conversion of every individual to the religion of Christianity but to open the eyes of the tribes and the ears of the languages, and to restore the identities of the peoples and the purposes of the nations. There is only one nation that is privileged to be the steward of Mt. Zion, the ultimate Ascent[483], and that is Israel. In our time, Ascent, or Aliyah, is accomplished by means of immigration to Israel.[484] When that mission is complete (telos), "it is the

---

480   Meena Azzolini, *Verywellfamily-Baby Names*, February 18, 2022 – https://www.verywellfamily.com ruthnamemeaning ; accessed 18 Mar 23.
481   Ephesians 1:3-14: "In Him ... you were sealed with the promised Holy Spirit, who is the guarantee (down payment or earnest) of our inheritance until the redemption of the purchased possession..."
482   James 2:23
483   Robert Kremnizer, Chabad, – https://www.chabad.org yeridah(descent) foraliyah(ascent) : "Every Jewish *neshomah* (soul) in its *gilgul* (life cycle) in a particular body has descended in order to afford it the opportunity to do certain *mitzvos* and thus realize its potential. Its *yeridah* (descent) is for the sole purpose of a subsequent *aliyah* (ascent) and ... as everything physical is a reflection of its spiritual counterpart, so it is with everything. Every descent is for the purpose of an ascent ... there is no ascent without a *prior* descent. This is true of souls, of nations and of each individual in his own life. This is staggering information ... when (that person) reaches Eretz Yisrael and finds new life and new happiness, he may understand that without the descent which was for the purpose of the ascent there could have been no ascent"; accessed 18 Mar 23.
484   Aliyah – https://www.jewishunpacked.com makingaliyahshouldistayorshouldigo : "Simply, it means a Jewish person in the Diaspora moving to Israel ... 'The State of Israel will be open for Jewush immigration

power of God for salvation to everyone who believes, to the Jew first, and also to the Greek ... all Israel will be saved, as it is written, 'the Deliverer will come out of Zion...'"[485] Paul agonizes over this reality, because he is a Jew who is called to be a Greek. He is the ark of Christianity. As such, his soul was divided from itself for the Gentiles' sake.

Traditional Christianity has held that the Jews will not be saved unless they confess Christ, but Jesus says "Do not think that I have come to abolish the Law (*nomon*) or the Prophets. I have come not to abolish, but to fulfill (*plehrohsai*). For truly (*amehn*) I say to you, until heaven and earth pass away, not one dot or one mark will pass from the law until all will be fulfilled (*genehtai*)."[486] It is of serious note that the word used to indicate the fulfilling of the Law is a derivative of *ginomai*, the coming-to-pass.

The Law is *nomos*, a term from which our word "antinomian" is derived. Antinomian means "lawless." Christians are privileged to be antinomian, but only in anticipation of the End in which all Law will be fulfilled. In Bible-talk, then, **the return of the Son of Man is equivalent to the final fulfilling of the Law.** The Law and the Prophets WILL be fulfilled through Israel. Those who are of the generation of the Spirit, a privilege granted by the sacrifice of Jesus on the cross, bear witness to this Truth.

In the meantime, the hope of Israel remained hidden until the 20th century, when the Great Divide began to become (*ginomai*) what it has always been destined to become. Christian theologians have long recognizes the interim nature of Christian becoming (ginomai), but it has almost always been interpreted to be symbolic only, never historical. Even the End Times prophecies of these last days tend to relegate the evocative imagery of the Book of Revelation to a reification of symbolic eschatological forms, like statues rather than events or moments in the actual and actualized world.

---

and for the Ingathering of the Exiles,' declares the country's Declaration of Independence"; originally Jan 22 2023 05:36AM EST, accessed 18 Mar 23.
485   Romans 1:16, 11:26
486   Matthew 5:17-18 (see footnote 245)

Reified symbolic eschatological forms can terrify your nightmares, but they don't really serve to reveal the signs of the times as directly as one would hope. The signs can be symbolized, but they can't be seen except by faith.

To renounce the ultimate role of Israel in the Promise is to become historically lawless.

Chapter Three: FIRST AND LAST

Do not listen to the words of the prophets who prophesy to you. They lead you into vanity; they speak a vision of their own heart and not out of the mouth of the Lord. They still say to those who despise Me, "The Lord has said, 'You will have peace'"; and they say to everyone who walks after the imagination of his own heart, "No evil will come upon you."[487]

ELI'S SONS transgressed their calling in 1914. When Queen Victoria died, the functioning high priesthood of Western Civilization died with her. The Old Order was not only interrupted: It vanished forever. The leaders of the European nations who were the successors to the 19th century giants were incapable of doing the right thing. The kings and queens, all related to each other like one big family, had decided to work out their family differences by slaughtering their respective subjects on the battlefields of Modernity. Nobody stopped them.[488]

What was proven by the Great War was not the superiority of any one or two nations or national cultures over some others: What was proven was the spiritual paucity, indeed, vacuity, of the entire civilization. What spiritual strength there was became expendable in the fight. The faith of the young, the faith they believed had been passed on to them by their fathers, would die with them. The faith they thought was real was a chimera.

Western Civilization ran out of breath, the kind of breath that the Bible calls Spirit. Nothing in the four or so years after August 1914 revealed anything hinting of the presence of, let alone the approval of the Holy Spirit of God. It was like Ezekiel watching the Presence depart (exodus) from the Temple in Jerusalem, bound for exile with the remnant of Judah.

The United States, virtually winning the war for one side after both contenders were paralyzed with national and social exhaustion, claimed

---

487   Jeremiah 23:17
488   AUTHOR'S NOTE: This is the gist of Tuchman's *Proud Tower*.

the moral high ground and incorporated that claim into its sense of identity, self, and purpose. Military victory was translated into a national and foundational absolute, a total reification of the momentary historical advantage which benefited the United States of America for the next half century or so. The Spirit of America forgot that the very same thing has always happened in the mindset of every victorious empire . . . as long as the victories are sustained. And more and more, these victories must be military, because only force can do the reifying necessary to maintain the Self image and the National spirit.

All great civilizations aka empires are destined to rule . . . until they are not. Most great civilizations are destroyed, not by outside forces but by internal vanities. More often than not, these vanities are collectively referred to as "national pride," but the kind of pride that motivates and sustains the individual becomes something quite different when it saturates an entire Nation. It turns a nation upside-down, an inversion by which the people no longer maintain their nation through pride of self, but, rather, the nation maintains the people through corporate vanity.

Hegel would be proud: He saw how this all works. His only mistake was believing that what he saw is Good, even Very Good.[489] When a nation sees itself as being by nature Good, then there must, by logic, be nations that are Evil. A good nation cannot remain good in the eyes of its faith unless it continues to oppose evil nations. It is in this way that the Great War provided the transition from a world in which nations competed according to national interests into a world in which nations compete in order to prove their goodness.

Modern Manichaeism differs from ancient Manichaeism in this way: The ancient form was gnostic and oriented toward the person, the individual, by means of ritual and religious language; the modern form is statist. The religious language is the language of the State, and the individual is non-existent except by means of the decrees of the State and the definitions of ideologies. This is the Modern mindset. It isn't Christian.

---

489   Genesis 1:31

Western Civilization never rid itself of its Roman roots, in spite of the infusion of ancient and Hellenistic Greek thought in its Renaissance. The Greek forms of life could have pre-empted the Roman, but the Roman mindset had already stabilized the crumbling interim hillside with its web of deeply penetrating roots. It seemed appropriate at the time of civilization's founding, but Rome means "conquest,"[490] and that mindset will always remain where there is a Western Civilization that is worthy of the name.

Conquest is the last crucial archetype in the deep structure of Western Civilization, and it demands reification if the civilization is to survive. It's our cultural imperative. It applies to every activity of Postmodern American activity, or *praxis*. It applies even to the remnant of Christian fellowship, although it remains disguised as *Praxis*. Whatever voice claims that Christianity can be separated or removed from the culture is delusional. The imagination of the heart does wondrous things on the downside of a culture.

Paul tells us that "the weapons (*hoopla*/hoplite) of our warfare (*strateias*/strategy) are not carnal, but mighty through God to the pulling down of strongholds, casting down imaginations and every high thing that exalts itself against the knowledge (*gnohseiohs*) of God, bringing every thought into captivity to the obedience of Christ, and being ready to punish disobedience (*ekdikehsai*) when your obedience (*hupakon*/obedience, compliance)is complete (*plehrohtheh*)."[491] Our compliance is complete, or full, when every jot and tittle of the Law is fulfilled. The thing that exalts itself against the gnosis of God is the Antichrist.

The Antichrist looks so much like the Christ that it becomes very difficult to see the "anti" in our own expectations. This is why imagination must be cast down. They won't fall by themselves because they have already been reified in the national soul. People feel this, but tearing

---

490   Julius Caesar: "I came, I saw, I conquered",
    Veni, vedi, vici has a nice "ring" to it….
491   II Corinthians 10:4-6

down actual statues won't accomplish anything regarding the imagination of the heart. The imagination of the heart is self-replicating.[492]

When the "nation" in "imagi-nation" sees itself as the only Good, it becomes evil. The imaging is no longer of God, who alone is good:[493] The imaging is of darkness.

Then if anyone says to you, 'Look, here is the Christ,' or 'There He is,' do not believe it. For false (pseudo-)christs and false prophets will arise and show great signs (semehia) and wonders to deceive, if possible, even the elect ... So if they say to you, 'Look, He is in the desert,' do not go there; or, 'Look, He is in the private chambers (erehmoh),' do not believe it.[494]

THIS STATEMENT FOLLOWS the warning regarding the Abomination of Desolation that is suddenly seen "standing in the holy place."[495] The word "standing," here, doesn't mean standing like a statue: It's the wrestling term that Paul uses when he says "Stand therefore, having your waist girded with truth, having put on the breastplate of righteousness, having you feet fitted with the readiness of the gospel of peace, and above all, taking the shield of faith, with which you will extinguish all the fiery arrows of the evil one. Take the helmet of salvation and the sword of the Spirit, which is the word of God. Pray in the Spirit always with all kinds of prayer and supplication.""[496] It's what the wrestler does when the opponent taps out: It's a victory stance.

When the Abomination of Desolation stands in victory, it is a pseudo-victory, but it will feel and seem like a defeat of the faithful. It will be all you can see, all that to which you can point.

---

492   Self-replication – https://en.m.wikipedia.org self-replicatingrobot : "A **self-replicating machine** is a type of autonomous robot that is capable of reproducing itself autonomously using raw materials found in the environment, thus exhibiting self-replication in a way analogous to that found in nature"; last edited 11 February 2023, accessed 20 Mar 23.
493   Mark 10:18
494   Matthew 24:23-24, 26
495   Matthew 24:15
496   Ephesians 6:14-18

As was stated earlier, "The desolation is a complete disconnection between the Self and itself. It's when the ideological self loses sovereignty over its own imaginations." The place, or *topoh* (topology, topography), is your own heart. That's why no one can point to it and say, "There."

The pointing is that ostensive definition we talked about earlier, and it's the pointing that we are all caught up in in these Last Days. The topological term "deformation" is very appropriate in these times[497] because our hearts have been deformed by our civilization. The beetle is trapped in its box, and the system wants to keep it there. It's by this means that the system controls your own imagination: You can imagine nothing else but what is prescribed for you.

To be sure, when you stand in victory, which is "to stand upright, to stand near, to stand before a judge, to make firm, to place oneself, to be kept intact, to ratify, to stand immutable and/or to make oneself public or seen,"[498] the slings and arrows of the enemy tend to confirm the desolation he desires for you. You make yourself a target at the same time as you make yourself holy. The holiness that has no "there" is a holiness that can't be targeted. It can't be tainted with sin.

What the system requires of you in these last days is to imagine conquest. As the only civilizational archetype left standing, so to speak, it's the only one that inculturated/enculturated minds and hearts will recognize. The other Western archetypes, such as the typically and foundationally American ones like "freedom" and "justice," bow down in submission to "Conquest." They acknowledge in worship the *Praxis* of Conquest.

The American rituals of freedom and justice will always obey the demands of conquest. Rome will never fade away until we stand and challenge Rome to do what it will. For all practical (*praxis*) purposes, Rome has conquered the Church, but the heart of the faithful is unconquerable. Even if a powerful lie can seem to be the ideal systemic solution to all of one's problems on earth, the redeemed soul resists it: The word says,

---

497   See footnote 143.
498   *Histemi* – https://www.biblehub.com_histemi ; accessed 20 Mar 23.

"Where do wars and fights among you come from?... 'God resists the proud, but gives grace to the humble' ... Therefore submit yourselves to God. Resist (*antistehte*) the devil, and he will flee from you."[499] But to the world, it will look like you are the one who is fleeing.

There is a psychology to all this, but it isn't the psychology that was invented immediately prior to the advent of WWI.[500] Modern psychology utilizes models, or archetypes, that either come from primitive cultures or interim reifications that come from classical Greek culture. Because our civilization has chosen (if a civilization can 'choose) to construct its governing edifices and commonweals on the basis of the same, even though they seem to have evolved, the processes, formulas, assumptions and algorithms of modern philosophy are necessarily form-fitted to the evolving governing forms. It is in this way that modern therapeutic models are compelled to produce selves that fit the forms prescribed by contemporary society.

The interplay between psychological and sociological expectations is as subtle as that between muons within a lepton group.[501] It has become (*ginomai*) so fundamental to our Western way of life and the language that expresses it, that we generally don't notice the interchanges at all. If you ascribe validity to the Hegelian version of God-on-earth as The State, this interaction of subtle foundational noologies (thought systems) will seem to be the right and good and best thing that could happen (*ginomai*). If everyone is "fit" for the contemporary mode of society, there will be no more crime, there will not even be sin as we have understood it.

<u>When our muons and leptons unite, we will be "free".</u>

499 James 4:1, 6-7
500 Modern psychology – https://www.sciencedirect.com modernpsychology : "(William Maximillian Wundt (1832-1920) was a pioneer of modern psychology ... Modern psychology has spawned three major theoretical paradigms: cognitivism, behaviorism, and depth psychology, all of which continue longstanding philosophical traditions"; copyright 2023 Elevier B.V., accessed 20 Mar 23.
501 Muon – https://www.energy.gov muon : "The **muon** is one of the fundamental subatomic particles, the most basic building blocks of the universe as described in the Standard Model of particle physics. Muons are similar to electrons ... part of the lepton group. Leptons are a type of fundamental particle"; accessed 20 Mar 23.

Let's deform the analogy without stretching it to its biblical breaking point.[502] The analogy of subatomic particles, little active things, can be stretched to include the analogical realities of the subconscious self and the unconscious. They are analogical realities because they can't be directly observed. They can only be observed by means of their effects, and their effects can only be judged by the standards of the society that observes them. They are "spaces" that aren't spaces in which things that aren't things move, and we don't know what those things are.

We do, after all, live in deformative times.

The system wants to dispossess you of your own unconscious assets by filling your subconscious with assumptions about yourself that you cannot accept.[503] You repress the prescribed assumptions and then act out their denial. Your *praxis* of denial then becomes visible, and your standing before the court becomes condemnatory. These assumptions are virtually impossible to NOT Accept or at least receive. They are protected and promoted by the cultural language you already speak.

Thye method used in this implantation and impartation of unacceptable assumptions about yourself is what is nominally called Fear. In the Greek, and in the Bible, Fear is *phobia*. The therapy for a phobia is "exposure therapy." The process by which the system compromises your subconscious mind, or self, is the impartation of phobias by cultural accusation. Your fear of the system, that which is greater than you, overcomes your fear of God,[504] that than which no greater can be conceived.[505] The mind is compromised, and the soul slips into cultural bondage.

Phobia as a word is not equivalent to terror. *Phobia* is "to be alarmed by"; terror is extreme alarm. To be alarmed by the Lord prior to the advancement of the world into your soul is to be pre-alarmed to resist

502   Luke 5:37
503   See footnote 183.
504   Proverbs 9:10: "The fear of the Lord is the beginning of wisdom"-*archeh sophias phobos kuriou.*
505   See footnote 430 and look up Ontological Argument for the Existence of God.

the terrors of force and social marginalization. If you are pre-alarmed by God, you will not be alarmed by the world. Nevertheless, the world wants you to embrace an entire field of phobias, all of which are powerless in your heart of they are preceded by the fear of the Lord.

The evocations in the Book of Revelation, when reified in the mind, are all terrifying, the Beast, the dragon, and so forth. To be caught up in Babylon is, and was, terrifying. The prophets understood this, especially the prophets of the apocalypse. Joel's most famous passage reminds us of this truth, when he says, "Blow the ram's horn in Zion, sound the alarm on My holy mountain! All the inhabitants of the earth will tremble, because the day of the Lord has come, because it is near – a day of darkness and gloom, a day of clouds and thick darkness."[506]

The darkness is represented in the semiotic world by your unconscious mind. It is the preceding, sustaining, and succeeding void out of which God speaks. This re-examination of the psychological self is a revelatory re-representation, a re-deforming of the modern conceptuality into a biblical conceptuality. The first and most important biblical Truth to remember is that the First Thing God speaks out from and into the void is Light. This re-deformation of the mind is the result of confession and repentance and turning.

It is significant to note that the word for "beginning" in that famous proverb has nothing to do with a start of something: The word is *archeh*, the foundation of all things. The fear of the Lord is foundational, a character trait without which there can be no wisdom at all. It's one of those primordial archetypes that was once an integral and prioritized construct of the foundations of Western Civilization. Being no longer part of that assortment, the assortment is reduced to Conquest, and Conquest is substantiated by terror.

The word of God was expelled from our private chambers, our erehmoh, before we were born, as in *gennaoh*, or generation. Nobody has taught it to us as it was meant to be taught, in a way that requires no teacher. At best, it's taught as an overlay or courageous replacement of the

506   Joel 2:1-2

noology (thought system) that we absorb automatically from our parents, schools, and government. This overlaying of Logoi is a temporary, but necessary and helpful, stopgap, but in the end, it won't keep the dam of the waters of history from breaking.

Not even the hermit, the eremite, the isolated self, can keep the flood from overwhelming. The art of faith in the Postmodern world is the science of breathing underwater.

When I think in words, I don't have 'meanings' in my mind in addition to the verbal expressions; rather, language itself is the vehicle of thought ... One cannot guess how a word functions. One has to look at its application and learn from that ... A mental image is the image which is described when someone describes what he imagines ... Grammar tells us what kind of object anything is.[507]

NOAN CHOMSKY is one of the leading students of language in the 20th century. Wikipedia describes him as "an American public intellectual: a linguist, philosopher, cognitive scientist, historian, social critic, and political activist."[508] It is right and fair to describe him as a "Renaissance Man," one who possesses a level of professional and information expertise in all the vital fields of knowledge in his time. We don't live in the Renaissance, however: We live in the Postmodern Age.

Among those thinkers who influenced Chomsky are Rene' Descartes, Galileo, David Hume, Immanuel Kant, Bertrand Russell, Ludwig Wittgenstein, John Dewey, Peter Kropotkin, Rosa Luxemburg, John Locke, John Stuart Mill, George Orwell, Jean-Jacques Rousseau, and Adam Smith. Among those luminaries who claim him as a major influence are Christopher Hitchens, Michael Moore, and Arundhati Roy. These names are the major influences on anyone who takes modern philosophy seriously. They are the Enlightened Ones. They are the philosophers: The Lovers of Wisdom, or most of them, anyway.

---

507   Wittgenstein, *Investigations*, pp. 113, 116, 122, 123
508   Chomsky – https://en.m.wikipedia.org_noamchomsky
 ; last edited 19 March 2023, accessed 20 Mar 23.

Chomsky invented the philosophical discipline known as Transformational-Generative Grammar, which "became the dominant syntactic theory in linguistics for two decades ... derived from the work of the Danish structural linguist Louis Hjelmslev, who introduced algorithmic grammar to general linguistics."[509] I owe a debt to Chomsky via my Professor of New Testament Greek in seminary[510] who utilized a transformational-generative apparatus to teach us koine' Greek.

Chomsky, who "aligns with anarcho-syndicalism and libertarian socialism ... posits that language consists of both deep structure and surface structure ... (and) now focusses on the mechanisms the brain uses to generate these rules and regulate speech."[511] The sinister aspect of this theory is that it is suggestive of the possibility of altering the physical brain in order to produce a desired language and conceptuality. Fortunately, the brain is far too complex for this kind of manipulation to succeed.

At any rate, the idea that all human languages organize along the same deep structure is the main point, here, and, besides, learning a language this way, or at least getting minimally comfortable with it, was fun. The memorizing dimension of learning the language is seriously truncated, although one still needs to learn words. That there may be a grammatical deep structure that is the same for all human languages suggests that the source of language goes deep, even into the unconscious mind.

A language game, such as is described by Wittgenstein, would be a surface segment, or portion, of a language that shares deep structure with all other languages. The language game limits the field of meaning, so that if one is familiar with and has a practical knowledge of the field of

---

509   Ibid.
510   Edward Craig Hobbs (1926-2018) – https://www.wellesley.edu_edward-craighobbs : "Faculty emeritus, Ph.B., S. T. B., Ph.D., University of Chicago ... came to Wellesley College in 1981 as Professor of Religion ... and to Harvard University as Sometime Frothingham Professor of New Testament ... Between 1958 and 1981 ... Professor of Theology and Hermeneutics at the Graduate Theological Union, Berkeley, California, Professor of New Testament Theology at the Church Divinity School of the Pacific..."
511   Chomsky, ibid.

meaning, one can speak the language, can "use" the rules of the game appropriately. The proper syntax of the language remains common, but the game itself is highly intentional. Language games, then, are special structures that express meaning as intention and intentional action, or *praxis*.

He writes, "Don't I know ... which game I want to play until I *have* played it? Or is it, rather, that all the rules are contained in my act of intending?" Again, "the existence of a custom, of a technique, is not necessary (to intention) ..."[512] It's difficult to analyze your own meaning while you are speaking. The meaning conveyed may or may not be the meaning you intend. Nevertheless, meaning does not exist in a secret garden in the middle of your mind. Meaning happens (*ginomai*) in communication.

So, is playing the Bible Language Game like playing a game of chess? That would be the Wittgenstein-ish question for text-critical students of the Scriptures. The answer is: Yes, but the language game is much more complex than chess. The moves are all life-or-death moves, and the game-board changes from resurrection to resurrection. The game ends where it begins, and all the different moves are the same move. And if you don't play the game, you will never truly exist.

Christianity is the default of Judaism: If you are not a Jew, you need to be a Christian. The reduction of the game to Jewishness vs Christianness, introduced and perfected by Western Civilization, is what transformed the little game of first century pieties into the Game of Thrones we call the History of the West. The deep structure of the language game itself, the system of words and phrases that convey ultimate meaning, is with God and is God:[513] The Logos.

For the Greeks, the Logos was "the unchangeable principle that underlies Heraclitus' ideas on change (and)the world is a collection of unified things that are in a structure arranged by *logos*. Human wisdom is tasked with understanding this principle as all our actions depend on

---

512 Wittgenstein, *Investigations*, pp. 86, 88
513 John 1:1

the participation in this divine *logos* ... (for Plato) *logos* is perceived as the true, analytical account ... the characteristic of true knowledge is the ability to give account, *logos*, of what one knows ... Aristotle understood *logos* as reason and rationality, especially in the ethical sense."[514] Western Civilization is founded on an epistemic (knowledge/wisdom) alloy of the Greek approach to reality and the New Testament witness to it in Jesus Christ. To miss this absolute Truth and Condition of Western Society is to not see it at all.

All Western European languages partake of this alloyed sense of true wisdom: They developed in order to express it, to convey meaning grounded in analytic reason and in New Testament revelation. In this historical and developmental sense, these languages double alloyed with the traditions of the tribal cultures from which they originated. When you say "Hello" in English, the meaning you communicate is an alloy of New Testament, Greek, and comprehensive Latin/tribal senses of reality. The deep structure of anything said in English (or German, or Spanish) is a structure that binds these archetypal precedents into a communicable whole. Language is logos.

The language of the New Testament seasoned the cooking and simmering of the other original languages involved, brought to a level of rare, medium rare, medium, medium well, or well in the sense of the differentiation between the various Western European languages. The Latin provided a conceptual connection with the earlier Greek, but the Latin of St. Augustine represents and stands-in for a deterioration of culture that harkened back to a time before the deterioration began. His conceptuality, then, is labelled Neoplatonic.

There is a sense of nostalgia built into Augustine's summation of the Christian faith in culture. This sense of nostalgia always lends flavor and texture to any Western philosophy or theology. The nostalgia isn't for Augustine's Moment: It's a longing for the societal continuities that connected Augustine's Moment over time with the momentous origins of civilization itself. This nostalgia was poignantly and abundantly

---

514   Visnja Bojovic, *Classical Wisdom Newsletter*, January 20, 2021 – https://www.classicalwisdom.com_logos ;

evidenced in the so-called Romantic Era from around 1798 to 1837.[515] Romanticism was effectively eclipsed by Bismarck-ish blood and iron,[516] but it factored majorly into the cultural impetuousness of WWI, as a kind of Frankenstein-ish conglomerate of the romantic and the steely, of the relational and the machine-like.

As the Dark Age followed St. Augustine's Moment, so did a darkness at noon[517] follow the dismemberment and parceling out of Augustine in the 20th century. It was the crucifixion of Western Civilization.[518] God was, and is, there in His completeness and fulness, "for darkness shall cover the earth and deep darkness the peoples ... for in My wrath I have struck you, but in My favor I have had mercy on you."[519] And still the highly-anticipated resurrection has not taken effect: The civilization has tried to rise and shine over and over again, but the light has not yet come.[520] We have yet to behold the New First Day.

As you can see from the above paragraph, and many expressions throughout this essay, the language of both the Old Testament and the New Testament can be of good use (*praxis*) in the language of assigning purpose and meaning to not-so-distant past events. Westerners of all languages once talked like this every time a great speech was made or a significant historical event was analyzed, or a profound work of literature

---

515   Romanticism – https://www.easternct.edu_theromanticperiod ;accessed 21 Mar 23
516   Bismarck – https://en.m.wikipedia.org_bloodandiron(speech) : "The name given to a speech made by Otto von Bismarck given on 30 September 1862, at the time when he was Minister President of Prussia, about the unification of the German territories"; last edited 25 January 2023, accessed 21 Mar 23.
517   Arthur Koestler, *Darkness at Noon*, 1940: "The principle that the end justifies the means is and remains the only rule of political ethics; anything else is just a vague chatter and melts away between one's fingers."
518   John 19:34: "One of the soldiers pierced His side with a spear, and immediately blood and water came out ... Nicodemus, who at first came to Jesus by night, also came"; Mark 15:33: "When the sixth hour had come, there was darkness over the whole land until the ninth hour" (noon to three).
519   Isaiah 60:2, 10
520   Isaiah 60:1

was published. There is still a chaplain of the United States Congress, although that office has been becoming (*ginomai*) a bit "iffy."⁵²¹

The language of the Christian faith has become so pluralized that it is sometimes impossible to comprehend what meaning the words and phrases once conveyed. For example, during the Second Intifada I made my way to the Armenian section of Old Jerusalem. Just outside the city wall is one candidate for the Mt. Zion area, where I found myself in the presence of a cadre of yeshiva students praying at the Tomb of David. One of the students guided me to a rooftop from which you can see the entire Old City before you, and the rooftop is situated between a mosque, and Church and a Synagogue. At least that's what he told me just before demanding payment for the tour.

The presence of those three places of worship presents a profoundly concrete symbol of the kind of unity of faith that ecumenism and pluralism seeks and exalts, but its symbolic power remains diminished. In U.S. law today, "to be a 'church' a religious organization must engage in the administration of sacerdotal functions and the conduct of religious worship in accordance with the tenets and practices of a particular religious body."⁵²² This definition is appropriate for tax purposes, especially because it sidesteps the need to change all the tax laws to include all manner of religious language ranging from the various forms of Hinduism to Scientology.

Actually, the designation of Scientology as a "church" remains iffy due to interpretive difficulties on the part of lawmakers and religious influencers. Once a religious organization is designated "church," and its buildings thus become "churches," it is eligible for tax benefits as befit

---

521   Brian Kaylor, *Roll Call*, January 5, 2021 – https://www.rollcall.com_the-democraticsinofcongressionalchaplains : "On the last day of 2020, Speaker Nancy Pelosi announced that for the first time in history a female minister would serve as the new chaplain for the U.S. House of Representatives. But if Pelosi had wanted to make real progress, she should have just abolished the position … my prayer is the next speaker will make a truly historic move and end the antiquated position of government chaplain"; accessed 21 Mar 23.

522   Church – https://www.irs.gov_definingchurch+theconceptofacongregation ; accessed 21 Mar 23.

the long-standing place of the Church in the American way of life. But what is that way of life? As Wittgenstein put it, language games express a "form of life," but the languages games of these religions don't appear to be the same in their surface-language expressions.

One must do violence to the language games of the different religions so that the word "church" can be used in reference to their character and presence in society. Whether or not this violent action (*praxis*) does justice to either the surface-structure or the deep structure of the various religious language games is entirely open to question. Originally, "church" was *ecclesia*, or "the assembly of citizens in a city-state." It was to segue from this secular, or Greek, idea of ecclesia directly to the Christian idea of the gathering of the faithful as citizens of the emerging City of God that the term appeared in the New Testament.

The use of the term *ecclesia* in the New Testament, a reflection of its use in the nascent Christian community of the first century CE, was intentional. For instance, "by the time Pliny (CE 23-79) had come into contact with Christianity, most Christians had adopted the word ecclesia ... to refer to themselves ... The Romans did *not* use the term ecclesia to refer to the new movement. They simply called it Christian ... Pliny, too, calls them *Christianii* ... Had Pliny heard the term *ecclesia*, he would have been puzzled, for in common usage in Greek and Latin ecclesia referred to the political assembly of a people of a city, as contrasted with the smaller group of elected officials who comprised the council."[523]

The theo-historical question for a situation like this is: Was the use of the word ecclesia by the new Christians an example of *praxis* or of *Praxis*? If both, it indicates a Kairos Moment in cultural history. The language game being developed is an expression of a form of life, but it uses words that express a different form of life. This is the moment the church/state issue began to be a problem.

The Church/State problem was temporarily worked out in Western Civilization in two ways: First, most States established a particular

---

523   Robert L. Wilken, *The Christians as the Romans Saw Them* (New Haven: Yale University Press, 1984), p. 33

church to be the State Church, and second, the foundational impact and motivation on the human soul arising from church concerns and state concerns was formally separated in the Bill of Rights. In this present situation, these concerns must be translated one to the other for conversation to remain meaningful. The interpreted impact is an integral part of American history, but the vehicle of impact has changed with the advent of religious pluralism beyond the old Judeo-Christian influence.

The meaning of this sea-change in American political and religious society and culture must be conveyed by language, but the creation of a new or more adequate language has yet to be accomplished. If it could be done in a continuous and evolutionary sense, peace would prevail with respect to the First Amendment; if not, peace will not prevail with respect to the First Amendment: The various religious languages are too disparate. Further, the newer languages must adapt to the political language which is itself saturated with Judeo-Christian assumptions, words, and expressions.

Lacking a viable vehicle for promoting an evolutionary change in the religio-political language of the United States, only the kind of crude linguistic violence such as is illustrated by the IRS' use of the word "church," can accomplish the kind of synthesis that does not require an overturning of the entire system and a subsequent reinventing of something systematic that works. In any case, the confusion of language games can only continue to promote a confusion of national and religious identity that demands a new kind of religious certainty that not only supersedes the old certainties but condemns them altogether.

It's virtually impossible for a Nation to evolve itself. When the proposed evolution requires a complete seismic break from its previous identity, only violence can assert the shift from one tectonic socio-political state to the next. If the violence is in effect a totality of totalities as such,[524]

---

524   Foucault, *Archaeology*, pp.3-4: "What link should be made between disparate events? How can a causal succession be established between them? What continuity or overall significance do they possess? Is it possible to define a totality, or must one be content with reconstituting connexions?) ... in what large-scale chronological table may distinct series of events be determined?"

there will be no next evolved species of State. Heidegger is victorious over Hegel. The door is held wide open to the welcoming of fascism, Naziism, Communism or some other conceivable form of authoritarian ideology.

This is neither a mystical nor an esoteric problem: If the citizens of a Nation cannot effectively convey meaning in conversation, the Nation itself will become (*ginomai*) meaningless. That Nation will have no Logos.

As a shepherd seeks out his flock in the day that he is among his sheep that are scattered (diakechohrismenohn), so I will seek out My sheep and will deliver them out of all the places where they have been scattered (diesparehsan/diaspora) in a cloudy and dark day.[525] *"If I say, 'Surely the darkness shall cover me, and the light shall be as night about me,' even the darkness is not dark to You, but the night shines as the day, for darkness is like light to You."*[526]

WE HAVE SEEN the use of the Greek word *diachoridzo* in a previous section. Separating is the fundamental and archetypal way that God orders Creation. In Genesis 1:6, we see how separation is critical to the function of the *Stereoma*, or the Firmament, which divides the waters above from the waters below. [527] The place to which the separated or scattered are scattered is called the Diaspora.

The shepherd imagery of the Gospel derives from this notion of un-separating, or un-scattering, the citizens of the City of God who are living in other cities. Depending on the nature of one's metaphysics, we might also refer to this action as the non-separating or the non-scattering. In either sense, it is an historico-apocalyptic action of God, a final series of events that together constitute *ginomai*.

Related to the meaning of un-separating is its apocalyptic compliment, in-gathering, or harvest. Also related to the meaning of ingathering is the meaning of the term *aliya*, mentioned earlier. The Jewish festival of Shavuot is a celebration of the in-gathering, or harvest. It is coincident with the Christian celebration of Pentecost. The word *sunagohgehs*

---

525   Ezekiel 34:12
526   Psalm 139:11-12
527   See footnote 143.

(synagogue) is used to mean in-gathering in Exodus 34:22. These words all hang together in a family of meaning.

Within this family of meaning, the action of separating, or dividing, is assigned a type of holiness in character. God does both. When there is a dividing by God, and God alone, there is a Kairos Moment and there is a sequence of *ginomai*, or coming-to-pass, occurrences. There is an ingathering, a Great Ingathering, happening (*ginomai*) in our time as well as a dividing. The ingathering is God's assignment for the modern Nation-State of Israel; the dividing is God's assignment for the United States of America. Both the ingathering and the dividing together (as in synagogue) constitute an extended Kairos Moment called the Apocalypse, the Last Coming-to-Pass.

Dividing is reminiscent of both Exodus and Exile. Also, between Noah of antediluvian reality and drunken Noah on the shores of the New World is also a dividing, world from world, game from game. Dividing is also what God did between the inheritors of the Jewish promises and the inheritors of the Christian promise. As we have seen, the Jewish promises extend from generation to generation, whereas the Christian promise never applies to a second generation, only the first.

Dividing is also what God does among the Nations in the End Times. All dividing is the same dividing, because it's the same God who does the dividing, and God does not change. The original dividing (in the beginning, or *archeh*) is the dividing between the darkness and the Light.[528] God's dividing is the most central element of the archetypal structure of creation, or the archaeological constructs of the revelation we call the Holy Scriptures. Every earthquake is a prefiguring, or proto metaphor, of the Last Dividing. All earthquakes are archetypal, an unavoidable, foundational, and inevitable characteristic of geological reality. So, too, with apocalyptic earthquakes.

The United States of 2023 is divided. From this judgment there is little or no reasonable dissent. In one post from the University of Southern California, the experts say, "'We believe that polarization is

---

528 Genesis 1:4

a communications problem ... We aim to model and advance a politics where we respect each other and we respect the truth ... Amid the rise of conspiracy theories and violence, the country has seen an unprecedented number of claims and court challenges questioning election outcomes ... It's hard to imagine polarization getting worse – and yet it does..."[529] And yet it does.

The study is correct insofar as it concludes that "What we've got here is failure to communicate."[530] As they say in the vernacular, "It doesn't take a rocket scientist." Just imagine, for a moment, that you are stepping into the street, and you see off to your right an out-of-control automobile coming at you at a speed far exceeding the posted limit. Do you stop to calculate how long it will take before the car hits you? Do you do a quick calculation to determine whether or not the impact will kill you? Likely not.

The empirical method, even the stochastic kind of computational investigation that powers such academic research into causes and effects of things in Postmodern society, is far too slow to account for appropriate management models and decision-making algorithms in the world today. To refer your impending impact with the speeding and out-of-c0pntrol car is not just impractical (*praxis*): It's insane.

The extreme polarization of American society in the 21st century is not just a problem with communication: Communication is both the cause and the effect of the polarization. The attempt to point out and isolate "miscommunication" or "misinformation" simply feeds the communication issue and the polarization themselves. The control rods of the American cultural nuclear generator have been removed.[531]

It's the hidden source of the communication problem that is the cause of the problem. That it is a communication issue is true enough,

---

529   Emily Gersima, *USC News*, November 23, 2021 – https://www.news.usc.edu_whyisamericasodividedresearchersfindfakenewsaboutcontroversialtopicscontribut estopoliticalpolarization ; accessed 22 Mar 23.
530   See footnote 14.
531   See footnote 1.

but it is a much deeper **language** issue. Not only does the computer not speak or think in human language but that which has been garbaged into it,[532] the polarized subsets of citizenry speak entirely different languages.

American society in the Postmodern era is governed by a divergent socio-historical algorithm, a hypo-deep-structural source of knowing and languaging that is unapproachable by means of any surface grammar. The surface grammar of the opposing subsets of citizenry can even look the same with respect to syntax and vocabulary, but the deeper grammar and the meaning which is conveyed by it is categorically NOT the same.

One might say that the problem with communication in 21st century American talk lies in the fact that the essential assumed relationship between deep-structure and surface structure has been inverted: Now the common language is on the surface, but underneath, the entire realm of meaning is conveyed in opposing forms.

An inversion is "a situation in which something is changed so that it is the opposite of what it was before, or in which something is turned upside down ... a situation in which an organ, or part of an organ, is turned inside out."[533] A particularly disturbing example of what such a thing could look like in terms of biological or cultural inversion is in that scene from the remake of the movie *The Fly*.[534] The mad scientist creates a matter-transfer machine, and its first test on a living creature uses a monkey. The monkey comes out at the other end of the transfer beam inside out, skeleton in/organs out.

There seems to be a glitch in the cultural algorithm: Garbage in/garbage out, GIGO.

---

532   GIGO – https://en.m.wikipedia.org_gigo : "In computer science, **garbage in, garbage out (GIGO)** is the concept that flawed, or nonsense (garbage) input data produces nonsense output ... The principle applies to all logical argumentation: soundness implies validity, but validity does not imply soundness; last edited 28 February 2023, accessed 22 Mar 23.

533   Inversion – https://www.dictionary.cambridge.org_inversion ; accessed 22 Mar 23.

534   *The Fly*, 20th Century Studios, Warner Bros., Universal Pictures, 1986

A more palatable example of inversions can be seen in mathematical fractions, e.g., ½:2/1, 19/100:100/19, or 3/87:87/3. These inversions produce radically diverse results. Another example of inversion comes from the weather. An inversion layer during which warmer air is held above cooler air can cause violent changes in the weather, such as thunderstorms or freezing rain. It can also trap smog in ever increasing densities low to the ground.[535] Translate these metaphors into observed social change, especially in terms of communication, and you can see how diversity becomes divergence when it reaches a certain, shall we say, stochastic[536] point of no return.

The deeper communication problem pre-dates the cacophony of irreconcilable differences which characterize Postmodern American society. They originate in the pre-20th century drift from using (praxis) the Bible as a foundational norm for meaning as it is conveyed vie spoken and written language into a final, and ultimate infatuation with the abstraction we call Reason. In a sense, it's like going off the gold standard, a metaphor that many have used to describe many different forms of divergence in 21st century society. There is no solid foundation for the enculturated common language, because the inculturation has been torn asunder.[537]

In the Bible we read, "No one sews a piece of new cloth on an old garment, or else the new piece that covered it tears away from the old, and the tear is made worse. And no one pours new wine into old wineskins, or else the new wine bursts the wineskins, and the wine is spilled, and the wineskins will be marred. But new wine must be poured into new wineskins."[538] This passage has traditionally been interpreted by institutional Christianity as referring to the faith and trust gap between

---

535 Inversion layer – https://en.m.wikipedia.org_inversion(meteorology) ; last edited 11 February 2023, accessed 22 Mar 23.
536 See footnote 407.
537 Vatican, *International Theological Commission*, 1988 – https://www.vatican.va>cfaith_faithandinculturation : "The term inculturation includes the notion of growth, of the mutual enrichment of persons and groups, rendered possible by the encounter of the Gospel with the social milieu"; accessed 22 Mar 23.
538 Mark 2:21

Old Judaism and New Christianity. But in the larger context of the Bible language-game, it must point to the teaching about being born again. The Old Wineskin is everything that you are, your entire story of *gennaoh*. What is required is the *gennehteh anohthen*.

The Old Garment is the cultural covering that consists of reasoning on reasoning on reasoning and so forth: The patch is the Bible as such. No attempt to re-patch the culture with Bible-talk can effect further change, progress, or evolution in Western Civilization. The patch has already torn away, making the tear worse, and the new wine is being spilled on the ground like the blood of the saints.[539] What goes around, as they say, comes around: The present situation is what it has always been, what it has been from the beginning. That is to say, "As a shepherd seeks out his flock in the day that he is among his sheep that are scattered (*diakechohrismenohn*), so I will seek out My sheep and will deliver them out of all the places where they have been scattered (*diesparehsan/diaspora*) in a cloudy and dark day."

I charge you therefore before God and the Lord Jesus Christ, who will judge (krinein/crisis) the living and the dead at His appearing (epiphaneian/epiphany) and His kingdom: Preach the word (logon), be ready in season and out of season (eukairohs akairohs), reprove, rebuke, and exhort, with all patience and teaching (didache). For the time (kairos) will come, when people will not endure sound doctrine, but they will gather to themselves (anexontai/annex) teachers in accordance with their own desires, having itching ears, and they will turn their ears away from the truth and turn to myths.[540]

A MYTH (*MUTHOS/MYTHOS***)** is "a widely held but false belief or idea ... a misrepresentation of the truth ... (and/or) an exaggerated or idealized conception of a person or thing."[541] By this token, a mythology is "a collection of myths, especially one belonging to a particular religious or cultural tradition ... (and) the study of myths."[542] The history of Western

---

539   Genesis 4:10: "The voice of your brother's blood is crying out to Me from the ground"; Revelation 16:6: "For they have shed the blood of saints and prophets…"
540   II Timothy 4:1-4
541   Myth – https://www.languages.oup.com_myth ; accessed 22 Mar 23/\.
542   Ibid., mythology

Civilization is a mythology. The Zeus of that mythology is the United States of America.

The Old Mythology of the United States of America incorporates the Bible as a source of transcendent and transcending knowledge without which the earthly, or immanent, sources of knowledge convey no ultimate sense of meaning.[543] The New Mythology discorporates the Bible from the evolved intellectual and cultural body of Western Civilization from its inception to the present moment. What was once considered to be transcendent knowing is now relegated to the basement of the subconscious and the unconscious. One might call it descendant or descended knowledge.

Descendant knowledge is beneath civilized consideration. It arises from the subconscious mind as unresolved moral conflict and from the unconscious mind as archetypal misapprehensions and primordial archetypes themselves. Insofar as these archetypes are no longer acceptable to the surface, or expressed, culture, their emergence from time to time is considered an affront to human identity. From this comes new surface language terms such as "unconscious bias" and "implicit association."

One source tells us that "unconscious bias is far ore prevalent than conscious prejudice and often incompatible with one's conscious values" and that "certain scenarios can activate unconscious attitudes and beliefs." The recognition of and the investigation of unconscious bias has "evolved ... over the last three decades" such that "the nature of unconscious bias is well understood, and an instrument (Implicit Association Test) to assess unconscious bias has been developed and rigorously tested."[544] The IAT tests evidence of pro-cisgender-ethical system - cultural expectation -white bias.

---

543   AUTHOR'S NOTE: I am grateful to Professor Robert Walter Bretall of the University of Arizona, R. I . P., for pointing out the difference between "revealed" religion and "discovered" religion in the first undergraduate course I took in the philosophy of religion in 1967.

544   Unconscious bias – https://www.diversity.ucsf.edu_unconscious-biastraining ; copywrite 2023 Rgenets of U Cal, accessed 22 Mar 23.

The prescribed antidote to your discovered unconscious bias, or prejudice, is to "shift implicit preferences (and/or) to become (*ginomai*) more selective about the types of information you consume in your daily life." You may want to go out of your way "to watch television programs and movies about people who are from groups that might be less familiar to you, or that depict people in roles that don't fit with societal biases or stereotypes."[545] The solution prescribed for anyone who is caught up in the prescribed or implicit biases of contemporary American culture, and this means everyone, is to deform yourself from what it was as formed by the Old Culture and reform yourself as per the prescriptions of the New Culture.

It's the identity of the Self that positions itself on the singular convergence of self-identifying self-modifications that have risen to the surface in the common language of Postmodern American, as in Western, Civilization that is in question.[546] This deeply felt need to self-modify is itself a sign of an apocalyptic transformation of the civilization itself. It is Selfhood as such that must change according to the New Deformation of Western Civilization.

The Self that was identified as a soul and spirit by the theology of Western origins was vaporized by the empiricists and transformed into thought by the rationalists. In more recent times, that is to say, through Hegel, the Self became a subsidiary of the State. The State defines culture, and culture prescribes the boundaries of the Self. The IAT described above fits this Hegelian agenda perfectly. The Self can only be reified, or dis-vaporized, by Reason as portrayed by Hegel: Otherwise, the pre-existent Self, the one that was formed by the Old

---

545   IAT – https://www.implicit.harvard.edu_abouttheiat : "The IAT measures the strength of associations between concepts (e.g., black people, gay people) and evaluations (e.g., good, bad) or stereotypes (e.g., athletic, clumsy) ... We include the labels 'slight', 'moderate' and 'strong' as a way to help you think about the size of the bias based on the IAT ... we chose these words based on scientific conventions for communicating the size of an effect. They are a way to help you think about the approximate degree of bias you demonstrated during the test"; copywrite 2011, accessed 22 Mar 23.

546   AUTHOR'S NOTE: I love it when I can out-Heidegger Heidegger.

Culture, by means of the Old Metaphysics, is allowed to complete its terminal transformation into pure vapor.

Hegel writes, "There are spheres which despite all variety of cultural contents remain the same. This variety of cultures concerns thinking Reason, freedom whose self-consciousness Reason is and which springs from the same root as Thought." He goes on to say, "His (the human's) consciousness makes the individual comprehend himself as a person ... even morals, which are so intimately connected with the consciousness of freedom, can be very pure even though this consciousness is still lacking" and then, "Morals are a matter of the state and handled by officials of the government and the courts."

The last historical transition to perfected consciousness is accomplished by the rise of "another world-historical people, another epoch of world history (that) lead(s) us to the connection of the whole."[547] The language of Hegel's language-game is observably similar to the language of the IAT and the Unconscious Bias language game. But it is a language that attempts to bring heaven to earth by force and manipulation, that transfigures the transcendent to the descendent. It replaces the God who speaks from heaven with the god who threatens from the unconscious realms. This is true cultural inversion[548].

Blake's *Marriage of Heaven and Hell* couldn't put it better: We as a civilization have evolved from the romantic/mystical more of corporate existence to the analytic/empirical/psychological mode. Once Spirit was reduced to Psyche, this cultural result became inevitable and irreversible. The State had to become (*ginomai*) the incarnation of Spirit, and the so-called World Soul had to arise from the sea of the unconscious and primordial memory to take charge of the human soul.

The irony of this development in history and culture, this reduction of the "above" to the "beneath," is exemplified nicely by that remark

---

547　Hegel, *Reason*, pp. 86, 87
548　Isaiah 5:20: "Woe to those who call evil good, and good evil; who exchange darkness for light, and light for darkness; who exchange bitter for sweet, and sweet for bitter!"

mentioned earlier which was made by one of my seminary professors, "I think that eventually everyone will agree that St. Thomas Aquinas already said it all." Thomas believed that Reason would always point to the revealed truth of the Scriptures, but the socio-historical consequence of Aquinas' system of theological thought is the inversion of the relationship of heaven to earth and the carnalizing of everything he said.

This inversion applies to Augustine's thought, as well, although there may be an avenue of escape with regard to the prior faith convictions that he mined in order to arrive at his Neoplatonic view of the Church and of the Creation. In the West, sound doctrine is the end product of reasoning on the Scriptures. In the possible Post-western world, the direct access to meaning via the completed language game of the Bible is the only door through which the redeemed soul can pass.

At this point, post- becomes pre-. The First becomes the Last.

Part Three: WHERE WE ARE

Chapter One: LEAP OF FAITH

Because discourse is constitutive for the Being of the "there" (that is, for states-of-mind and understanding), while "Dasein" means Being-in-the-world, Dasein as discursive Being-in, has already expressed itself. Dasein has language.[549]

BEING-IN, or in more classical terms, "existence," is where and how we are. Once you can call an object "an object," *Dasein* is a done deal. What Heidegger is trying to get at in his analysis of the Real is that the objective world in essence precludes Being itself. It's an old conundrum, originated by the Greeks and theologized by Aquinas in the High Middle Ages. Heidegger, of course, is thoroughly Postmodern.

    The Scholastics argued over the ultimate significance of the philosophical distinction between essence and existence. They were trying to "get at" God. Heidegger was still trying to get at God, but without including God as a fact in his deliberations. His philosophy isn't entirely atheist because it isn't agnostic enough to verge on atheism. God, in effect, becomes Sein, or "being itself." The concept of Being qua Being, as the philosophers say, predates Heidegger's metaphysics, but it plays THE major role in it.

    On the first page of his massive and eternally concealing ontological dissertation, *Being and Time*, he partakes of the many implications of

---

549   Heidegger, *Being and Time*, p. 208.

the Christian revelation without involving the idea that it is a revelation because it comes from God. In this, Heidegger is not unique: The conflict between science and religion is resolved by eliminating religion. The language of religion is re-morphed, or deformed, into a quite different language. Nevertheless, the language works, in the Wittgensteinian sense: It can be "used" (*praxis*).

Writes Heidegger, quoting Plato, "'For manifestly you have been aware of what you mean when you use the expression "*being*". We, however, who used to think we understood it (*gnosis*), have now become perplexed.' Do we in time have an answer to the question of what we really mean by the word '*being*'? Not at all. So it is fitting that we should raise anew *the question of the meaning of Being* ... Our aim in the following treatise is to work out the question of the meaning of *Being* and to do so concretely. Our provisional aim in the Interpretation of time as the possible horizon for any understanding whatsoever of Being."[550] In this way, Theology becomes Ontology, the study of Being. This gambit pretty much sums up the trajectory of Western Philosophical thinking as regards God and God-talk.

Heidegger published *Being and Time* in 1927; Einstein proposed and published his Special Theory of Relativity in 1905 and his General Theory in 1915. Heidegger, the consummate academic, would have been aware of and professionally acquainted with these two theories. This illustrates the newly discovered mystical relationship between space and time, or space and things, or time and the absolute, that stimulated the break of the Postmodern with the old and relatively boring Modern.

Early in his massive treatise, Heidegger deals with God and God-talk. He writes, "In those *humane sciences which are historiological in character*,[551] the urge towards historical actuality itself has been strengthened in the course of time by tradition and by the way tradition has been presented and handed down; the history of literature is to become the history

---

550 Heidegger, *Being*, p. 1
551 Ibid., p. 30: "'Historie' (history) stands for what Heidegger calls a 'science of history.' 'Geschichte' usually stands for the kind of 'history' that actually *happens*." (i.e., *ginomai*, actual events)

of problems. *Theology* is seeking a more primordial interpretation of man's Being towards God, prescribed by the meaning of faith itself and remaining within it. It is slowly beginning to understand once more Luther's insight that the 'foundation' on which its system of dogma rests has not arisen from an inquiry in which faith is primary, and that conceptually this 'foundation' not only is inadequate for the problematic of theology but conceals and distorts it."[552]

You can see in this one paragraph virtually every philosophical and revelational consideration that has been uncovered in the preceding pages of THIS treatise. Heidegger is good for that sort of thing: From Plato to Apocalypse (concealing/revealing). Even Foucault's discontinuities are there in the form of "problems." Tillich, whom we have cited several times, is the theologian who tried to rescue faith from Heidegger's rejection, even condemnation, of it. Tillich failed; Foucault succeeded.

Ultimately, the Postmodern sense of Being qua Being is whatever you, as a *Dasein*, make it out to be. The continuous, 1200-year-old Western metaphysical discussion can lead only to this conclusion. The breach between Revelation-language and Reason-language is complete, as it was already at the beginning of Western Civilization. To be surprised at this FACT is to be surprised at oneself and the conundrums one finds in one's own subjectivity when one seeks to find faith.

You can't FIND faith because it isn't THERE to be found. The only THING that can be found is the language of Scripture and the testimony of tested faithful believers. Thing One and Thing Two really don't like each other. They never did, despite Aquinas' attempt to force friendship between the two. The cat still belongs to Schrodinger, and the hat needs to be surgically removed.

Heidegger fundamentalized Dasein, but not without particularizing it. He writes, "This entity which each of us is himself and which includes inquiring as one of the possibilities of its Being, we shall denote by the terms "Dasein."[553] *Dasein* means being-there. It's like how the saying

---

552 Ibid., p. 30
553 Heidegger, *Being*, p. 27

goes, "No matter where you go, there you are."[554] Or, "You can't escape yourself." In musical lingo, it reads *I Gotta Be Me*.[555]

In the book, *Being There*,[556] Chance the Gardener says, "Growth has its season. There are spring and summer, but there are also fall and winter. And then spring and summer again. As long as the roots are not severed, all is well and all will be well."[557] The stems of Western Civilization have been pruned several times in its long history, but the roots were always left intact. That situation has changed: Society is going after its own roots.

The resulting Postmodern Self is un-languagable, undecipherable, and undifferentiable. It's like a Leibnitzian "monad"[558] coursing through a sea of unintelligible impacts, none of which alter the singularity we call Personal Identity. David Hume (1711-1776) determined empirically that Personal Identity doesn't exist: Postmodernism refashions it to acquire whatever form the trend of self-identity can take after the singularity is encountered.

Hume, the ultimate empiricist, showed us that personal identity doesn't exist over time.[559]

---

554 No matter – https://www.quoteinvestigator.com_nomatterwhereyougothereyouare : "A non-humorous precursor appeared in the devotional book 'The Imitation of Christ' by Thomas a' Kempis published in Latin in the 1400s"; accessed 24 Mar 23.
555 *I've Gotta Be Me*, Walter Marks, 1967: "What else can I be but what I am … I can't be right for somebody else if I'm not right for me … I gotta be free…"
556 Jerzy Kosinski, *Being There*, 1971.
557 Roots – https://www.goodreads.com_beingtherequotes ; accessed 24 Mar 23.
558 John C. Brady, *Epoche'*, *Issue #36*, December 2020 – https://www.epochmagazine.org_whatisamonadleibnitzsmonadology : "As monads have no parts, they can't 'fall apart' or be 'put together'. Their creation and destruction can only happen 'super-naturally', that is, beyond the purview of the natural order … It's the same argument for why our modern physics can't backwards infer earlier than the big bang – the entire natural order (space, time, matter, energy, cause and effect) break down … Because of these considerations, monads cannot affect each other…"; accessed 24 Mar 23.
559 Hume – https://www.rintintim.colorado.edu_humeonpersonalidentity : "There are no underlying objects … There are merely impressions

The ultimate scientific psychology, then, amounts to the investigation of the flux of impressions which an embodied individual has mentally (psychically) collected. The collection changes from moment to moment. The therapeutic conversation, dialogue, changes the collection, such that the collection that was 'there' at the beginning of therapy is not the collection which is 'there' after the session.

The British philosopher Whitehead hypothesized an ever-changing reality that is always different from moment to moment. Whitehead's great philosophical quest is to reconcile objectivity and subjectivity. He does this by means of the technological term "process." He writes, for instance, "The subject originates from, and amid, given conditions; science conciliates thought with this primary matter of fact; and religion conciliates the thought involved in the process with the sensitive reaction involved in that same process. The process is nothing else than the experiencing subject itself."[560] Another way of saying this is that the Subject is unreconciled to the Objective except as they both process their realities together. There is no way to distinguish Subjective Reality from Objective Reality except as time goes on, and as time goes on, the relationship between the Subjective and the Objective changes.

In time, some theologians determined, by means of Whitehead's metaphysics, that God changes with time by interacting with humanity.[561] God, then, form-fits herself to our changes, such that God is always the true God no matter what those changes might happen (*ginomai*) to be. In this sense, it would be correct to say that Jesus wasn't the same Jesus at the end that He was at the beginning of the Gospel, and neither were

---

... we do not really have knowledge of a 'self'"; accessed 24 Mar 23.

560   Alfred North Whitehead, Process and Reality (New York: The Free Press, 1978; from the Gifford Lectures,1927-28), p. 16

561   Process theology – https://en.m.wikipedia.org_processtheology : "developed most notably by Charles Hartshorne (1897-2000), and John B. Cobb (b. 1925), and Eugene H. Peters (1929-1983) ... For both Whitehead and Hartshorne, it is an essential attribute of God to affect and be affected by temporal processes ... According to Cobb, 'process theology may refer to all forms of theology that emphasize event, occurrence, or becoming over substance"; last edited 23 March 2023, accessed 24 Mar 23.

the disciples the same disciples. These kinds of fundamentals changes are transformations of reality which take place from moment to moment.

For Process theologians, every moment is a coming-to-be, and every *praxis* is *Praxis*. This is the primary "given" that constitutes the structure of reality. Process theology is, significantly, "theology influenced by G. W. F. Hegel just as much as ... by Whitehead ... Also, Pierre Teilhard de Chardin can be included..."[562] In the end, the State and the individual process each other, and God becomes whatever the outcome is from moment to moment.

The State will be what it will be. As far as faith goes, it amounts to "God ain't finished with me yet." The State isn't finished with you yet, either. To un-righteously paraphrase Descartes: "I think, therefore the State must process me."

As some spoke of how the temple was adorned with beautiful stones and gifts, He said, "As for these things which you see, the days will come when not one stone shall be left on another that will not be thrown down[563] ... Destroy this temple, and in three days I will raise it up."[564]

DECONSTRUCTION must take place, but reconstruction in the same terms isn't possible. Reconstruction involves a Great Trespass, a violation of the boundaries set by the assumptions and presumptions of the Civilization itself. If deconstruction doesn't take place, the violence done to the self to force a common identity for the State will be accomplished by the self. This phenomenon is known commonly as "suicide."

The Temple is everything we know. We built it on the ruins of the First Temple. In the end, the New Temple which is built isn't a temple at all, because "I saw no temple in the city, for the Lord God Almighty and the Lamb are its Temple."[565] Inside the walls of the New Jerusalem, everywhere is in the Temple and the Temple is everywhere. If you can't

---

562	Ibid.
563	Luke 21:5-6
564	John 2:19
565	Revelation 21:22

see Messiah everywhere, you can't see Messiah anywhere. In the Spirit, there is no distinction between the Temple and everything you know.

In the Bible, Jesus makes a profound statement that is seldom understood. He says, "From the days of John the Baptist until now, the kingdom of heaven has been subjected to violence, and violent people have been raiding it."[566] The interim between John's time (*kairos*) and Jesus' time (*kairos*) is a violent interim. The space/time between John's baptism and the baptism of the Holy Spirit is infinite. John's ministry marks the end (*telos*) of space-time; Jesus' ministry marks its beginning. This is what eschatology is all about; this is what the Book of Revelation is all about.

The threshold, or boundary, that is crossed when reconstruction is forced onto deconstruction is the boundary between civilization and un-civilization, between eschatology and teleology, between death and resurrection. In the 20th century, Western Civilization began to reach the zones of its Marches,[567] and there is no language to connect the meaning of "beyond the March" with the meaning of "within the imperial domain." In the meantime, the March becomes devastated.

Heidegger conceived a metaphysics that describes this period of transformation or transition from one world, or sovereignty, to the next. He writes, "Only when we grasp that the need to use violence in language, in understanding, in constructing, in building, co-creates [and this always means: brings forth] the violent act of laying out the paths into the beings that envelop humanity in their sway - only then do we understand the uncanniness of all that does violence."[568]

---

566   Matthew 11:12 NIV
567   March – https://en.m.wikipedia.org march(territory) : "In medieval Europe, a **march** or **mark** was, in broad terms, any kind of borderland, as opposed to a national 'heartland'. More specifically, a march was a border between realms or a neutral buffer zone under joint control of two states in which different laws might apply"; last edited 10 December 2022, accessed 24 Mar 23.
568   Heidegger, *Metaphysics*, p. 168

This "co-creating" is attempted by all forms of communism and fascism, particularly the Naziism that kept Heidegger himself employed and safe in his profession. The violence of Hitler was, however, more refined than the violence of, for instance, Stalin or Mao. The violence of the Communist model simply translates into pure force, force that objectively eliminates the undesired objectivity. In other words, you slaughter the opposition; you destroy all opposing ideologies and their proponents. Hitler's violence delved more into Subjectivity than does the Communist form. Hitler's violence reaches into Subjectivity, such that there is no need to utterly destroy the opposing ideology and its proponents: One need only pressure them into complying internally.

Hitler and the Nazis fell short of Heidegger's prescription, because they could not fully escape the need for objective violence and for scapegoating of the Jews as a rather cosmic opposition to the Nazi ideology. The Nazis reached back into the before Christianity time even to the primordial times of the Germanic ethnicity in order to circumvent the interim civilizational influence of the Judeo-Christian traditions in the West. Their failure to achieve their ultimate goal of re-orienting the entire consciousness of the nation to be in step with that of their Fuhrer was the inevitable result of two historical phenomena: First, the Nazi Nation could not conquer the other nations quickly enough to allow for enforcement of the *Fuhrerprinzip*,[569] and Second, they did not transform the minds of those who participated in the economy with the centralized and socialist changes they instituted in the economy.

The Communists unify the people by eliminating those who do not follow the ideological prescriptions of the State. Disunity, in effect, is destroyed. The Nazis unified the people by appealing to their primordial ethnic and national roots, so that they could exult in that commonality. The limitations of the Nazi movement are apparent in that they needed to

569   Martha A. King, Jonathan S. King, *Wiley Online Library*, 15 September 2014 – https://onlinelibrary.wiley.com_fuhrerprinzip : "According to this principle, the task of forging a strong national unity requires leadership of a strong, charismatic individual to whom absolute or near-absolute obedience is given by all members of society … Under these conditions such a leader … can then represent the concrete embodiment of the state, of its laws, and of the will of the nation as a whole"; accessed 24 Mar 23.

designate national enemies, especially the Jews and the national entities that were responsible for the Treaty of Versailles.

In Postmodern America, the designation of "enemy" is transformed into purely subjective terms. In this way, Subjectivity as such becomes the true domain and range of violence. The violence in language becomes the violence of language, a violence that reaches into the realms of both the subconscious and the unconscious mind. It isn't perceived as violence, because it is disguised as the expression of reasonable inquiry and intellectual conclusion, but it is patently NOT an expression of reasonable inquiry and intellectual conclusion.

By the time the "enemy" intellect is able to realize or at least understand how compromised his or her Subjectivity has become by means of this verbal alchemical trickery, it's too late to talk oneself out of it. Language itself has been totally compromised. In effect, one's own soul becomes "tar-babied."[570] This phenomenological accomplishment opens the door to the kind of absolute match-up between soul and State that Hegel predicted and formulated several centuries ago. Marx and Hitler fell short of its *telos*, but the initial accomplishment has become the chief archetype for meaning in the New/Old world.

The Western Temple of Language is being dismantled stone by stone, or objective truth by objective truth. The Western extension of the Greek version of Reason (Latin=*Ratio*) is dismantling itself. It can't stand on its own.

Now this I say lest anyone beguile (paralogidzehtai)[571] you with enticing words. For though I am absent in the flesh, yet I am with you in spirit, rejoicing and seeing your orderliness

---

570   Tar Baby – https://en.m.wikipedia.org_tar-baby : "The second of the Uncle Remus stories published in 1881; it is about a doll made of tar and turpentine used by the villainous Br'er Fox to entrap Br'er Rabbitt. The more that Br'er Rabbit fights the tar-Baby, the more entangled he becomes … Linguist John McWhorter argued that … those who feel those who feel that *tar baby*'s status as a slur is patently obvious are judging from the fact that it *sounds* like a racial slur"; last edited 19 March 2023, accessed 24 Mar 23.

571   Para – https://en.m.wiktionary.org_para : "beside, next to, near, from; against, contrary to … adjacent … across … beyond … false … resem-

(taxin/taxonomy)[572] *and the steadfastness (stereohma) of your faith in Christ. As you have received Christ Jesus the Lord, so walk in Him, rooted and built up in Him and established in the faith, as you have been taught . . .*[573]

TO BE BEGUILED (*paralogidzehtai*) is to fail to notice the replacement of one language game with another while dialogue is taking place. It's almost like cell mitosis, except that the new chromosome strand isn't replicated. In that sense, it's more like a virus invading a healthy cell. The chromosomal strand of the virus is replicated (*para*/close alongside of), and "often, a virus ends up killing the host cell in the process, causing damage to the rest of the organism."[574] The "meaning game" is completely altered, although it continues to look like the original game.

Like a virus, the invading beguilement can affect different aspects of the invaded system in different ways. It can inhibit conceptualizing, conceiving, imagining, or any one or more of the various functions of the soul. It can compromise Subjectivity entirely. To be beguiled in spirit is to think you are living a life of faith and even getting "better" at it when, in fact, you are veering away from that life toward its contrary.

To be beguiled is to be separated from yourself in such a way that, over time, you lose the primordial impression of your original self and become, shall we say it, a viral self. Once a member of the community becomes a viral self, the infection can spread into the whole body of the faithful. The defilement becomes (*ginomai*) complete and virtually unrecognizable as a defilement.

Jesus says, "There is nothing from outside a man that by entering him can defile him. But the things which come out of a man defile him ...

---

bling … avoidant"; last edited 17 March 2023, accessed 24 Mar 23.
572   Taxonomy – https://en.m.wikipedia.org_taxonomy : "a scheme of classificatio0n, especially a hierarchical classification, in which things are organized into groups or types … a categorization of things or concepts, as well as the principles underlying such a categorization"; last edited 12 March 2023, accessed 24 Mar 23.
573   Colossians 2:4-7
574   Virus – https://www.genome.gov_virus ; updated March 24, 2023, accessed 25 Mar 23.

because it does not enter his heart..."[575] The beguiled self-defile through their conversation. Beguilement amounts to pseudo faith.

The archetypal character of true faith is steadfastness. This partaking of the *Stereoma* involves the ongoing separation of the waters above from the waters below. Faith descends with Jesus to the lower waters in the sure and certain knowledge that resurrection will be the next event.

Faith, as it were, dives into the dark waters to save the drowning person, rather than simply trying to reach out in a situation that is beyond human reach. In this way, identity in Christ involves fulfilling the word which says that "grace was given to each one of us according to the measure of the gift of Christ. Therefore He says: 'When He ascended on high, He led captivity captive, and gave gifts to men.' (In saying, 'He ascended,' what does it mean but that He also descended first into the lower parts of the earth? He who descended is also He who ascended far above all the heavens that He might fill all things)."[576]

In the present inversion of Western Civilization's archetypal structures, "what was once considered to be transcendent knowing is now relegated to the basement of the subconscious and the unconscious. One might call it descendant or descended knowledge." The beguiling language game is shaped by a deeper "language that attempts to bring heaven to earth by force and manipulation, that transfigures the transcendent to the descendent. It replaces the God who speaks from heaven with the god who threatens from the unconscious realms. This is true cultural inversion." "Up" means "down", and "down" means "up."

The replacement language game is verbally innocuous, because it uses the same words and phrases that the Bible uses. It's the hidden, deeper language, that gives power to the surface language game, and that deeper language is the language of lies. By this means of connectivity between the apparently pure surface language of the viral compromise and the underlying non-verbal language of deceit, the lying refuses to be uncovered except by the apocalyptic event.

---

575 Mark 7:15,19
576 Ephesians 4:7-10

Once the soul becomes accustomed to the viral invasion of itself, one becomes accustomed to believing one's own lies. They become unrecognizable and thus are understood as Truth. They feel true, their rationalized meaning seems true, and their effective impact on others in conversation of all kinds effectively validates them as being true. The compromised soul exists in a false knowledge-world in which the lies become true for that soul. This is how a phrase like "This is My truth" is an honest remark, and it is how my truth need not necessarily be your truth.

The separation, or existential divergence, of the culture, of the civilization, is complete within and without the virally compromised soul. Because the DNA of meaning for that soul has been changed, that soul cannot help itself. There are the infected and the uninfected: The infected resent the uninfected without knowing why, but the uninfected need not concern themselves with the possibility of being infected.[577]

The power that keeps one's ark from sinking into the depths or being overfilled from the heights, that is, to be convinced to go beyond one's spiritual measure, is that steadfastness which comes with faith in Jesus the Christ. It's the power that keeps the divided waters from closing in on the crossing-over prematurely; it's the power that stops the floodwaters, causing them to pile up upstream so that the faithful can cross the prescribed spiritual Jordan River. It's the power and authority of identity "hidden in Christ" that enables the faithful to find their redemption in exile and to build on a foundation that is even more substantial than that of Solomon's Temple.

The steadfastness of faith is, in this inverted world, the power to withstand the verbal and physical assaults of the demon-possessed soul who lives among the tombs, to see through them, and to find the image

---

[577] AUTHOR'S NOTE: The recent world struggle with COVID19 serves as an example of End-times Kairos. We acted out in the Areopagus, the public square of debate, the dynamics of the hidden apocalypse. It amounted to an archetypal tragicomedy. See *Conundrums*, p. 3: "For those who feel it is tragic, there is no reason to laugh; for those who feel it is comedic, there is no point in worrying about it", or Matthew 11:17: "We played the flute for you, and you didn't dance; we sang a dirge for you, and you did not mourn."

of God behind the cloud of resistance to the word.⁵⁷⁸ The steadfastness of faith, the *Stereoma*, opens the eyes to the razor thin differentiation between Good and Evil in the human heart, empowering the faithful to resist the lie, to recognize the inversion of *Praxis* to *praxis*, and to reverse the inversion by redeeming praxis by the invasion of *Praxis*. It is as the Bible says, "but as for you, you meant evil against me; but God meant it for good, in order to bring it about as it is this day, to save many people alive."⁵⁷⁹

It's all about meaning, and only the word of God can access the inner meaning of God in order to access the hidden intentions of the heart.

But to what shall I liken this generation? It is like children sitting in the markets (agorais),⁵⁸⁰ calling to their friends, saying: "We played the flute for you, and you did not dance; we sang a dirge to you, and you did not mourn." For John came neither eating nor drinking, and they say, 'He has a demon.' The Son of Man came eating and drinking, and they say, 'He is a gluttonous man, a drunkard, a friend of tax collectors and sinners.' But wisdom is justified by her children (ergohn [works, toils, efforts] or technohn [children]).⁵⁸¹

THOSE WHO DANCE to the flute of reasoning on reasoning on reasoning won't dance to the music of the Scriptures. Those who mourn in response to the dirges of Apocalypse, also mourn the misapprehensions in the spirit resulting from reason on reason on reason. The singers and dancers no longer recognize each other. Everyone is dancing in the Areopagus, but each dancer is partnered with someone dancing a different dance. It's all "attitude dancing."⁵⁸²

From a previous section, "Being meets identity in the human soul. The human soul IS the meeting place between Being and Identity. The language of religion is the language of this inner synagogue of Being and

---

578 Mark 2:1-12
579 Genesis 50:20 NKJV
580 Agora – https://www.languages.oup.com agora : "(in ancient Greek) a public open space used for assemblies and markets"; accessed 25 Mar 23.
581 Matthew 11:16-19
582 *Attitude dancing*, Carly Simon/Jacob Brackman, 1975: "You just leave yourself behind like an actor on a stage … Find a role you like; capture it and freeze, and then turn it around a hundred and eighty degrees…"

Identity. The language of the State is the language of proprietorship when both synagogue and Areopagus[583] become possessions of the whole. The Areopagus is language itself. The synagogue is where the languages gather." Where the languages gather, there is the ascent to Mt. Zion.

Yet in our Postmodern, or Post-Heideggerian, world, we see that "not-Being here is the ultimate victory over Being. Dasein is the constant urgency of defeat and of renewed resurgence of the act of violence against Being, in such a way that the almighty sway of Being violates Dasein (in the literal sense), makes Dasein into the site of its appearing, envelopes and pervades Dasein in its sway, and thereby holds it within Being."[584]

One is reminded of the Bible teaching that "in Him we live and move and have our being."[585] This is because Heidegger the philosopher is caught in the act of replacing Bible DNA with beguiling DNA. The similarity is not accidental, but it is also organic, inevitable, and purposeful. What is happening here is the inversion of the Augustinian/Thomistic understanding of Being and Existence, such that the purpose of Existence, or Dasein, is now to defeat Being, or God. This is the Proto-Nazi version of "freedom."

Professor Heidegger goes on to say, "*logos* and *phusis* (physical reality), step apart from each other. But this is not yet the stepping-forth of logos. This means that logos does not yet step up to the Being of beings, does not yet come forward 'versus' Being in *such* a way that logos itself [as reason] makes itself into the court of justice that presides over Being and that takes over and regulates the determination of the Being of beings." In other words, the perfection of Dasein, freedom, emerges through Reason's judgment of God. This places reason, especially the intellect, in charge of *phusis*, the perceivable world and manipulable world.

This replacement of archetypal foundations is ongoing and is given expression in virtually every surface grammar that is at present being invented. Heidegger the philosopher simply sums up the trends of

---

583 Acts 17:16-34
584 Heidegger, *Metaphysics*, p. 190
585 Acts 17:28

Western philosophical investigations in one uber-language that seems all-encompassing and all knowledgeable. This IS metaphysics, not the ineffectual attempt to take hold of the mystical foundations of existence, but the final conquest of the mystical foundations of existence. Nevertheless, by Heidegger's own compilation, this conquest involves moving entirely into not-Being. Another word for this is "hell."

Hell is when where you are (*dasein*) is not where you are. There is nowhere to be, to appear, except within yourself, because you still participate in Being (sein) by virtue of Being somewhere. This amounts to a falling-into-the-void[586] that never ends. It's the "being-cast-into-the-lake-of-fire-and-brimstone",[587] the destiny of the Evil One. The hell of Naziism's Germany is a blip on the screen of destiny compared to the kind of hell into which the Final Metaphysician allures us. Freedom from God is the freedom to be eternally entombed within the deceptions of *phusis*.

The lie of Postmodern secularity is that humanity, as a historical totality, can resurrect itself. But resurrection has no meaning in the absence of death. It is in this way that Death becomes the alluring promise of resurrection, and this is why wars will never cease. The violence of physical on physical might cease, but death will be always renewed in the effects of violence against the soul.

This describes the Postmodern human situation, the one in which deconstruction appeals as the savior of the intellectual and operational world. The last appeal of reason is to deconstruct the intellectual trajectory that ends in civilizational self-destruction by means of fragmenting and eliminating the beguiling totalities that have led the postmodern soul into its present conundrum. But the elimination of totalities is the first cousin of the original violence of the human soul, the violence which traditional Christianity has called Original Sin.

The attempt to eliminate narrative totalities amounts to a usurping of the God of Creation with Oppenheimer's Shiva, something we have

---

586   Revelation 20:3
587   Revelation 20:10

already done. Redeemer and Destroyer become (*ginomai*) the same principle, and to be destroyed is to be redeemed. As Jesus said, "all those who take up the sword will perish by the sword."[588] The sword of the faithful is the "sword of the Spirit, which is the word of God,"[589] a sword which only the Spirit can wield.

Do not lie (pseudeesthe/pseudo) to one another, since you have put off the old nature with its deeds (praxesin), and have embraced the new nature, which is renewed in knowledge after the image (eikona/icon) of Him who created (ktisantos)[590] it, where there is neither Greek nor Jew, circumcision nor uncircumcision, barbarian, Scythian, slave nor free, but Christ is all and in all.[591]

TO LIVE BY AND IN the Spirit is to put away *praxis* altogether and to rely only on *Praxis*. When human deeds conform in a type of sequence with the deeds of God, then we have a coming-to-pass, *ginomai*. This coming-to-pass event is most apparent in the narrative regarding the birth of Jesus. Things happen (*egeneto*) that seem (and actually are) far-removed from each other in space and time, but they are all the same action, or *Praxis*, in the hand of God.

The context of Paul's letter to the Colossians, in which we have discovered the only New Testament occurrence of *stereoma* and one of the few occurrences of *praxis*, is the traditional syncretistic angelology of the city's ancient piety. Some interpret the letter's purpose as "to address the challenges that the Colossian community faced in its context of syncretistic Gnostic religions that were developing in Asia Minor."[592] This development, we have seen, continues to mature during the era of the early Christian apologists, even to the point of being the form of religion Augustine of Hippo is compelled to resist in 5th century Rome. It's not at all dissimilar to the situation we live in today.

---

588   Matthew 26:52
589   Ephesians 6:17
590   *Ktidzo* – https://www.billmounce.com_ktizo : "to reduce from a state of disorder and wildness … to call into individual existence"; accessed 25 Mar 23.
591   Colossians 3:9-11
592   Colossae – https://en.m.wikipedia.org_colossae ; last edited 24 October 2022, accessed 25 Mar 23.

Paul preaches a community in which distinctions literally have no meaning: They belong to a world in which the believer no longer exists. This is the First-Generational World of faith. The elimination of distinctions in terms of human worth, physical heritage, state of mind or health, parentage, and so forth is the act of "putting off" the old Man or Adam, and "putting on" the new. It's a deliberate action, or *praxis*, that does coincide with *Praxis*, and because it coincides with Praxis, all action that results from the putting-off partakes of *Praxis*. Issues of states of mind, physical health, parentage and so forth do continually intrude into this putting-off, primarily because when the putting-off is accomplished, the believer realizes that he or she is Biblically naked.

All languages, and especially language games, that convey distinctions are languages that promote spiritual bondage rather than deliverance. The language of the perfected State is the ultimate language of bondage. On the other hand, that language is very impressive, as we can see by means of examining the great philosopher like Martin Heidegger. If you can learn the language, you enter a realm of meaning very few people, excepting the elite, can occupy, but you will also find that it is extremely difficult, even unappealing, to leave that realm.

Nevertheless, we are born with the belief that we cannot speak meaningfully without distinctions. This, too, reflects Original Sin, wherein we make the first meaningful distinction: The distinction between human intentions and the intentions of God. The first two words of this distinction are "me" and "mine." We complete this distinction by clothing ourselves in language that allows us to believe that we can hide from God among the trees of the Garden. But there are no more "trees of the Garden": We haven't lived there from the beginning.

Reasoning on reasoning on reasoning has created the illusion that we are still "in the Garden of Eden," but that it needs to be re-planted and re-tilled so that it becomes fecund with truth and justice once again. We believe that the "just so" of the Garden was compromised, but that there never was a real expulsion. By means of this delusion, we can avoid getting expelled by improving on the Garden and making it even better than it was when God created it ... or at least preserving it so that it looks approximately like it did in the beginning.

The Garden is primordial, submerged in the dark waters of the flood aka the unconscious mind. To search for the Garden of Eden is like searching for the Titanic. There was and is something very glorious there, but the glory can only be reconstructed through the imagination. It's a glory that we don't possess now, but it is still less than the glory God promises through faith and believing. It isn't the anticipated glory to strive for.[593] We defile the glory of that ancient memory with the imagined glory we regret to have lost. This, too, is Original Sin.

The trees in the Garden are archetypal human rights. They have to do with justice interrupted by injustice. If there was no injustice, there would be no need to invent a language game of rights. Yet language games of rights, privileges, and responsibilities are primary to virtually all other language games that carry the meaning of forms of life. Justice is a form of life, and injustice is a form of death.

The Bible says as much in the form of Moses' exhortation to the people before they enter the Promised Land, "This commandment which I am commanding you today is not hidden from you, nor is it far off ... the word is very near to you, in your mouth, and in your heart, so that you may do it. See, today I have set before you life and prosperity, and death and disaster ... love the Lord your God ... walk in His ways..."[594] Justice and morality come together in the Law of Moses.

The Law of Moses is given when the people are far enough away from their previous world to be able to receive it more easily. This is because it entirely and completely negates the rules of rights, privileges, and responsibilities of that previous world. Also, it is delineated in the wilderness in which there is no civic organization to enforce it. It is

---

593   John 17:22-23: "I have given them the glory which You gave Me, that they may be one even as we are on: I in them and You in Me, that they may be perfect in unity, and that the world may know that You have sent Me, and have loved them as You have loved Me."
594   Deuteronomy 30:11, 14-15, 16

delivered in such a way as to be accessible as a habit of the heart, not an overview of the mind.

As we have seen and noted, the topology of justice is quite different in the Hegelian State. He writes, "The principles of the State must be regarded as valid in and for themselves, which they can only insofar as they are known to be determinations of divine nature itself," and "what special course of action is good or not, right or wrong, is determined, for the ordinary circumstances of private life, by the laws and customs of a state."[595] By this token, the laws of the land provide the boundaries of justice and their enactment is the realization of justice. The legal system, then, is the creator of, determiner of, and guarantor of justice, and the Law embodies the principles of the State.

If it is true that "world history goes on in the realm of Spirit" and that "the State is the divine idea" on earth,[596] then the idea of the Holy Trinity is easily translated into the Father, the Son, and the State. This is just the beginning of a theory of sanctified State control over the souls of its citizens. Because the theology of the Holy Trinity is itself an intellectual construct derived from the words of Scripture and the experience of the early Christian community, the juxtaposition of "community" to "State" is an easy, almost invisible, transition from one language game to another.

Insofar as the First Injustice, also known as Original Sin, came-to-pass in the undifferentiated Garden, two results followed: First, God was compelled by logic, i.e., the domain of the Logos, to complement injustice with justice. The way God did this was through expulsion from the Garden and the other material consequences that followed the expulsion; Second, justice was done at every transitional time in the narrative of the Hebrew heritage, that justice being the equivalent of expulsion from the Garden. This justice occurred, and was increased in meaning and significance, by the Flood, the Exodus, the Exile, and the destruction of the Temple and the City in 70 CE.

---

595   Hegel, *Reason*, pp. 37, 65
596   Ibid., pp. 20, 53

Civilization, as the clothing which God fashioned for the Original Couple, is a matter of continuing justice and injustice. But God will not allow injustice to eclipse justice: In the end, justice is done by means of apocalypse.

The Garden has neither room nor place for injustice. The realm outside the Garden has plenty of room for injustice. That room is always filled with grace. A return to the Garden would amount to a return to the origin of injustice. Just as the Garden was closed to the Primordial Couple after they acted out Original Injustice, so, too, each world from which the tribes, clans and Nation of Israel was expelled becomes closed to them as well. Israel cannot go back to the fleshpots of Egypt, even in principle.

Justice is *krisis* (dividing, separating) in the Bible, and its only by means of *krisis* which is *Praxis* that justice is divinely accomplished. *Krima* is judgment; a criminal is one who has been judged and found to have breached the boundary of justice. A criminal justice system is a body of laws and enforcers that adjudicates crime in a State. A criminal justice system is based on laws, written or hidden: Justice is absolute.

Total or complete justice is death. Death is the tangible evidence the expulsion from the Garden. The First Family was expelled from the Garden, therefore, clan, tribe, and Nation also live in the shadow of expulsion. The praxis of Evil is contrary to the Praxis of God. Therefore, Evil is a fundamental rejection of God's justice. In the frame of reference of Evil, the expulsion from the Garden is the greatest injustice.

A nation reaches its crisis point when it begins to consider God's justice to be injustice. This is the fundamental inversion of value and a reversal of the traditions of moral evaluation. It is natural for the individual to maintain the lingering feeling that somehow an injustice has been done to the soul. At the national crisis point, the citizenry, and, of course, its leadership, rebels against the felt injustice. As the pressure on the whole, *thlipsis*, increases by way of this soul rejection of the perceived and felt commonweal, the Nation tries to respond through compensation.

If the Nation is a State, this moral and legal compensation tends to reverse decisions and precedents at an increasingly rapid rate. Confusion becomes the norm.

We see this compensatory action in the Pharaoh of Exodus, but more so in the behavior of the kings and priests of Judah toward the end of that kingdom. We also see it in the Roman interim between the reign of Constantine and the reign of Theodosius. The Old Order spasms when its potential runs empty. This spasming was complete in the days of Augustine. His response was to choose a Neoplatonic City of God over the potential-less City of Man that was Rome. This choice was a righteous choice, ultimately confirming its righteousness in the establishment of Western Civilization.

The ultimate limitation of a political entity that is conceived by virtue of a righteous choice is that it must be maintained by a continuity of righteous choices. Each generation must come to its own decision and make the righteous choices that are required. This is because a Christian political entity also has no grandchildren. The traditions of a Christian Nation do not guarantee the righteous choices of the next generation: They only point to their possibility.

The United States of America was founded on the belief that its system of government could virtually guarantee a preponderance of righteous choices that would extend the Christian Commonweal indefinitely into the future. The high calling of the American Polity is that of maintaining the righteous choice. Nevertheless, this high calling, like all other high callings, faces a final test. This present test, or crisis, or time of *krima*, amounts to the choice between a common morality and polity based solely on reason upon reason upon reason, or a common polity derived from a Biblical foundation.

This is nothing new: It's the classic Reason vs Revelation conundrum. Nevertheless, it has reached the point where one is necessarily compelled to reject the other. Either there is a God who transcends all of THIS and who has something to say to us about our hopes, dreams, expectations and behaviors, or there is not.

In the meantime, the gap in Christian polities widens exponentially. If you try to leap across it, you risk falling into the bottomless pit. There is no possibility of a conciliatory leap of faith: It has become an existential lover's leap.

Chapter Two: THE DESTINIES OF NATIONS

For freedom Christ freed us. Stand fast therefore and do not be entangled again with the yoke of bondage... You were running well. Who hindered you from obeying the truth?... If we live in the Spirit, let us also walk in the Spirit. Let us not be conceited, provoking one another and envying one another[597] *... one nation under God, indivisible, with liberty and justice for all.*

WHEN PRESIDENT EISENHOWER added the words "under God" to the Pledge of Allegiance, he couldn't have predicted that it would be the instrument of division regarding the second and third precepts of the nation, liberty and justice. The semiotic ramifications of the origins of and changes to the Pledge of Allegiance have been argued thoroughly elsewhere, so only the timeliness of the most recent changes to its verbiage is significant here.

"Under God" was added "in 1954, in response to the Communist threat of the times." The original pledge was written by a late-19th century socialist. "My flag" was changed to "the Flag" in 1923. The author's daughter objected to the addition of "under God."[598]

If the Pledge of Allegiance represents anything, it stands for the apocalyptically significant transition which the nation and the world is experiencing in the 20th and 21st centuries. After the moment when the United States won World War I for the Europeans, and after the Moment the United States finished keeping the world safe for democracy[599] following World War II, the emergent character of the Nation changed. Not only did its topology change, but the archetypal foundations of the Nation were re-sorted as well.

---

597 Galatians 5:1, 7, 25-26
598 Pledge of Allegiance – https://www.ushistory.org_thepledgeofallegiance ; accessed 27 Mar 23.
599 Woodrow Wilson

The United States became a Messiah Nation. This transformation is reflected in the 20th century changes to the wording of the Pledge of Allegiance. It's a transformation that does not fulfil the European continuities leading up to WWI: The character of the United States as a Nation is discontinuous from the character of the European civilization, a Christian civilization, that precedes it.

That the United States has become (*ginomai*) a Messiah nation results in a thorough re-examination within the commonweal regarding what it means to be a "Christian." The question extends to whether it matters at all. When the Nation was founded, it was Christian in the through-and-through sense that European Christians were Christian. On the other hand, WWI was a spiritual-historical war in the sense that it was a fight to see who was the more Christian Nation. The spiritual pressures that caused the tectonic breach in history that was WWI were, and are, apocalyptic. They are *thluptic*.

Let's revisit a statement from the previous section: "A nation reaches its crisis point when it begins to consider God's justice to be injustice. This is the fundamental inversion of value and a reversal of the traditions of moral evaluation. It is natural for the individual to maintain the lingering feeling that somehow an injustice has been done to the soul. At the national crisis point, the citizenry, and, of course, its leadership, rebels against the felt injustice. As the pressure on the whole, *thlupsis*, increases by way of this soul rejection of the perceived and felt commonweal, the Nation tries to respond through compensation. If the Nation is a State, this moral and legal compensation tends to reverse decisions and precedents at an increasingly rapid rate. Confusion becomes the norm." Laws and the interpretation of laws changes even faster.

Thlipsis is a word that indicates great suffering that results in new life. That is, it can be translated as "birth-pangs."[600] Probably the most memorial Bible passage regarding the tribulation comes out of the

---

600   Krueger, *Conundrums*, pp. 34-51: "Every apocalyptic ending in the scriptures partakes of this pattern. It defines the limits of every civilization's life expectancy. It characterizes every failure of a system of ideals. It motivates every cultural revolution and every reactionary response to unexpected change."

Apocalypse of John. It points to the faithful survivors of the birth-pangs of the New Creation. We read, "Then one of the elders asked me, 'Who are those clothed in white robes, and where did they come from?' I said to him, "Sir, you know." He said to me, "These are those who came out of the great tribulation and washed their robes and made them white in the blood of the Lamb."[601]

Great Tribulation is *thlipseohs tehs megalehs*. To have one's robes washed white in the Blood of the Lamb is the ticket to being born-again through the Great Tribulation. Also born is the Last Narrative, the one that precedes the Last Judgment. The concept of the Last Judgment is a conflation of several narratives regarding the end, or purposed finalization, of the old heaven and earth, found throughout the New Testament.

Matthew 25:31-46 is the go-to place for theologies of the End Times, or eschatologies. Eternal punishment is *kolasin aiohnion*; the righteous will go on to *zohehn airohnion*. The kind of separation declared is an aphoristic judgment: The goats on the left will become an aphorism of being judged, while the sheep on the right will become an aphorism (*aphoridzei*) of being redeemed. This is a very difficult passage to interpret. The sheep and the goats both represent *ethnoi*, or Nations, not individuals.

To be "aphorized" is not an expression in common, or uncommon, English. In the Greek, we read that it means "defined, marked off or determined," from the prefix *apo*, or "off" and *horidzoh*, to divide or bind., which is from *horos*, or boundary.[602] A quick rendition of the teaching is that God will aphorize the goats. It's important to note that it isn't the character of sheep or goats that is at the heart of the teaching: It is the kind of separating that is done. The goats are no longer in with the sheep: a boundary has been set between them.

---

601 Revelation 7:13-14
602 Aphorism – https://en.m.wiktionary.org aphorism ;
 last edited 27 February 2023, accessed 27 Mar 23.

Kolasis is chastisement or painful disquietude, also punishment or torment.⁶⁰³ What, then, is an Aeonic Chastisement or Aeonic Life? What does it mean for an *ethnos*, or Nation, to be treated thus? *Kolasis* is the consequence of a legal judgment, a *krima*, the sentence declared and carried out. In this separating context, it is the final criminalization of a Nation. That nation is imprisoned by time, while the sheep-nation goes on to aeonic life.

These days, the identifying of certain nations as being "rogue" or criminal, or just plain failed states is a nearly ubiquitous judgment in international relations. The term "criminal nation" can't be found in the lexicon, language, of international law just yet, but the term "crime against humanity" occurs at least non-juridically. Genocide and war crimes have been codified, but the concept is "considered a peremptory norm of international law, from which no derogation is permitted, and which is applicable to all States."⁶⁰⁴ Peremptory means "not open to appeal or challenge ... final." A rogue state, then, is one that has moved outside the boundaries of inter-civil law and expectation. A rogue state is a criminal nation, one that has already been judged as in *krima*.

If the United Nations' use of the term peremptory means final, then to designate a nation to be "rogue" is to say that it has crossed the threshold of allowable derogation. In this sense, such a nation suffers a "last judgment" after the fashion of Matthew 25. Whether or not the United Nations has the divine authority to issue a Last Judgment on a nation is open to question. Nevertheless, political factions in the United States and U.S. leadership and make such judgments often.⁶⁰⁵

---

603   *Kolasis* – https://www.billmounce.com_kolasis ; accessed 27 Mar 23.
604   Criminal nation – https://www.un.org_crime-sagainsthumanity ; accessed 27 Mar 23.
605   Rogue states – https://www.worlddata.info_the4currentroguestates : "The term 'rogue state' goes back to the US government under George W. Bush, which used it to describe aggressive states that threatened either the USA itself or its allies ... The first countries to be considered 'Rogue States' were North Korea, Cuba, Iran, Iraq and Libya. Currently, 4 countries are considered rogue states ... Iran, North Korea, Sudan, and Syria"; accessed 27 Mar 23.

The designation of a Nation to be a criminal, or rogue, nation is a novel international designation. It fits the post WWI era well. It is unquestionably an apocalyptic designation, one that prefigures the separation of nations regarded as an integral part of the Last Days. It also segues nicely into the increasingly Manichean character of Western Moral Discourse, or languaging, of right, wrong, and tending in either direction. The larger question in End Times terms, or language, is whether the United States is authorized to make such judgments. The United States, after all, claims nationhood whereas the United Nations, at least do far, does not.

The right to determine whether another nation is rogue, criminal, or not indicates that the judging nation considers itself already to be among the sheep and not the goats. If we are to stand by the Nation's history and piety, this psycho-social conclusion can't be avoided. Some people call this transition from being a nation-among-nations to being a nation-over-and-above nations, "pride" or *hubris*.[606] Some think of it as a God-given right. The Declaration of Independence declares as much, in terms of assuming "among the powers of the earth, the separate and equal station to which the Laws of Nature and of Nature's God entitle them."

It's the "God-given" aspect of American exceptionalism that is of central significance to the nature of the current Postmodern Era. The corollary to that belief and trust, or faith, is to conclude that history has bequeathed to the USA the privilege of being exceptional among nations. If you equate history with the nation as the divine idea on earth, a la Hegel, then it doesn't really matter which way you go in practice: The National Praxis will be the same in either case.

---

606   Gerard Finin, Terence Wesley-Smith, *CB Ideas*, November 10, 2022 – https://www.civilbeat.org_goodintentionshubrisandtheroadto-hellattheus-pacificislandssummit : "Washington's diplomatic full-court press in the Pacific is part of a larger geopolitical initiative to blunt China's growing global influence. Faith in American exceptionalism was on full display at the summit, with no hint that U.S. global power might be waning ... American hubris might result in the Biden administration over-promising what it can deliver to the region ..."; accessed 27 Mar 23.

In any case, the 'apocalypticizing' of American National identity is the primary international given in the Postmodern World.

(The) task (of the discourse) is to make differences: to constitute them as objects, to analyze them, and to define their concept. Instead of travelling over the field of discourses in order to recreate the suspended totalizations for its own use, instead of seeking in what has been said that other hidden discourse, which nevertheless remains the same (and instead of playing endlessly with allegory and tautology), it is continually making differentiations, it is a diagnosis. If philosophy is a memory or a return to the origin, what I am doing cannot, in any way, be regarded as philosophy; and if the history of thought consists in giving life to half-effaced figures, what I am doing is not history either.[607]

FOUCAULT alludes to Socrates (470-399 BCE), here. The Socratic Method in philosophy is the originating method of systematic philosophical discourse. It is dialogical, or dialectical, and its assumptions pervade every Western philosophical system since his time, for good or for ill. It is, however, only on the surface that it is a dialogue between individual minds: The goal of the dialogue is "remembering," or *anamnesis*.

This kind of remembering is a "bringing forth" of what is already there from the beginning.[608] In this way, the knowledge gained by dialectic is knowledge that "everybody knows, precisely because it can be "remembered" by anyone. You can see how this kind of quest for knowledge melds into both Hegel's and Heidegger's philosophies, as do the liturgical traditions of the Christian Church.

At the heart of Marxist-Leninist philosophy and ideology is the sense of the inevitability of the dialogue, the dialectic, the conversation. Because it can be "remembered," it cannot be denied: The endpoint of the dialectic is inevitable, permanent, even pre-existent. Therefore, the State is licensed to hurry the journey along, typically by slaughtering the opposing intellects who disagree that the proposed system is inevitable. Like Whitehead said, it's all just a series of footnotes to Plato who, after all, invented Socrates.

---

607   Foucault, *Archaeology/Discourse*, pp. 205-206
608   AUTHOR'S NOTE: The anamnesis is the most critical part of the Christian eucharistic rite. It is evoked by the words "Do this in memory of me."

The ultimate irony in the unconscious assumptions of Western thought is that they have not really changed since the time of Plato. The re-hashed hash might get tastier and more desirable over time, but this is not evolution as much as it is presentation. As the salesman likes to say, "presentation is everything." The concept of human intellectual evolution fails here: This 'evolution' is all in the mind, and the hidden mind has remained stationary. Western thinking has evolved in the way that fireplaces evolved into gas stoves, but it has not evolved in the way that dinosaurs evolved into birds.

A sense of national unity, of the reasonable truth of the national motto *e pluribus unum*, can be dispensed into the souls of the national faithful by means of designating a foreign power as being the "criminal" state and mustering the populace to face the challenge of adjudicating the present Evil. This is nothing new: It's how nations always unify their citizens when nothing else works or no other better option makes itself known within a reasonable time span. The cause then becomes righteous, and the "Just War" can be engaged in. But this externalization of National criminality is truncated by the appearance of an internal divide. When factionalism coalesces around two opposing pseudo-ideologies, the criminality which might have been externalized becomes an internal criminality to be assigned to one ideology or the other.

Like blobs of mercury on a flat surface, fragmented deviations of one or the other ideology will cluster into larger blobs to facilitate a greater sense of security, purpose, and rightness, especially as the *thlipsis* of the situation increases to near intolerable levels. Insofar as the conclusion of *thlipsis* is understood more and more in teleological terms, in terms of the purpose of the Nation as such, then the political division coalesces into the phenomenology of Good and Evil. It must be so, because the individual's sense of insecurity and purposelessness also increased to intolerable levels.

The true Kairos of this moment is like when the water finally boils. The boiling point is a punctiliar, or singular, moment. Water doesn't boil at 211 degrees, and at 213 degrees it is already boiling, even if enough pressure (*thlipsis*) is kept on it to keep it from churning and bubbling. This kind of naturalistic analogy holds true especially for a nation that claims fealty to Nature's God. Nature is consistent, otherwise science doesn't work. The waters WILL boil. It's like the word of God that came to Jeremiah a second time, "saying, 'What do you see?' And I said, 'I see a boiling pot, and it is facing away from the north.'"[609]

The divided soul of American Christianity consists of two worldviews that each embrace two distinct Foucaultian totalities. The ideological and historical constructs of these totalities generate the convictions which provide the energy that promotes continuing divergence. In other words, there will be no convergence in any imaginable future: The die is cast: The Rubicon was crossed before 1914. One totality left the Bible on the north bank; the other is carrying it across the stream.

The Postmodern civilizational civil war is an internal battle between two totalities vying for control of a city which neither totality can hold. The violence of this civil war isn't physical, except in the sense that, say, Margenau proposes. There are constructs which link perception with conception, and there are rules that govern the creation of and the rejection of constructs, just as there is in language as such. But a civilization must hold onto its designated rules and constructs, else the entire edifice crumbles. The City becomes (*ginomai*) Jericho, and all it takes are trumpets, shouts, and one big shout to bring down its walls.

Metaphysics isn't a field easily accessed by Americans, the children of *praxis*. Yet when praxis is demanding to be redefined, even resurrected in a new form and in a new world, practicality isn't enough to save the day. Another word that is part of a different language game comes close to the practical without denying its open-endedness: Narrative. The narrative, its shape and form, its geography and topology, and its usefulness as a conveyer of truth, its archaeology, is what these language fanatics are talking about. And we all talk about it, too.

The Postmodern question for philosophy is this: How does the narrative narrate? How does the story maintain its essential story-ness?

[609] Jeremiah 1:13

Can a story end while you are still caught up in its continuities? And if the story ends, was it ever really a story anyway?

Insofar as the narrative is believed and understood to be a totality, the story is concluded already. The narrative, then, simply becomes (*ginomai*) a way of talking it out (*logos*). In recent decades, this "talking it out" has achieved its own metaphysical place in the universe as "The Conversation." The Conversation keeps the Narrative going, avoiding the ultimate clash of totalities that is already perceived to be inevitable within the context of the Conversation itself. We "feel" the civil war while systematically, even desperately, working to rid ourselves of the feeling.

The old question of meaning is the new question regarding what the conversation conveys. Under the old rules, a conversation was like "dialogue." The word "dialogue" is still used as a substitute. "Dialogue" sounds more technical, more connected to the totalities of the past. Dialogue, in its turn, is like discourse. Once the conversation becomes discourse, there is plenty of food and fuel for the language philosophers to dig into. The discourse, for all intents and purposes, is the Narrative.

To discourse is to "speak or write authoritatively about a topic."[610] This is the grazing field for the historian, although speech, unless recorded or written down, is accessible only indirectly. Then again, the written record is itself only an indirect avenue to meaning and truth. Words don't convey truth: Truth is transferred and conveyed soul to soul. When the arrow of intention hits the bullseye of reception, we see Truth.

All philosophy, politics, and religion is discourse. This does not mean that they are "just words": It means that their essential meaning, their conveyance of the Real, is accomplished through language and, specifically, their respective language games. Rational analysis consists of the attempt to associate language games in their entirety one with the other.

---

610   Discourse – https://www.languages.oup.com_discourse ; accessed 28 Mar 23.

The Great Game of Meaning in enlightened Western Civilization is played to win the final prize of sufficiently and totally connecting meaning from one language game to another. Only in this way can everyone who is in on the Conversation know what they are talking about. Nevertheless, the nature of the will to meaning is such that the only way to convincingly accomplish this task, this victory, by force, by indoctrination, or by evolution of ideas, is for everybody to mean the same thing when they dialogue. In that case, there is no more need for the Conversation or Dialogue. Truth will be a dramatic self-presentation.

The present game of totalities is like volleyball. The game is won when one side has dropped the ball one too many times (or beyond one too many times). The Dialogue between the two totalities, the pro-Bible totality and the anti-Bible totality, becomes (*ginomai*) a matter of trying to get the other side to definitively drop the ball. This is the future *egeneto* of the Postmodern Era, the "it-came-to-pass-that" revelation. When the ball drops, nothing more comes to pass. It's "game over."

For Foucault, salvation of the Western Intellectual World can be accomplished only by ridding the Narrative of totalities. In this goal is truth enough for a while, but the Narratives are very hungry for Totality. If they become bereft of totalities, they will starve to death.

I say unto you, Swear not at all; neither by heaven; for it is God's throne: Nor by the earth; for it is his footstool: Neither by Jerusalem; for it is the city of the great King. Neither shalt thou swear by thy head, because thou canst not make one hair white or black. But let your communication be, Yea, Yea; Nay, Nay: for whatsoever is more than these cometh of evil.[611]

IF EVERYONE followed this teaching literally, they would be like Michael "Lurch" Armstrong in the movie *Hot Fuzz*:[612] "Yarb" and "narb" would be the beginning and the end of all communication. Michael is a very simple man who can kill on command without a twinge of conscience, but he can be perplexed enough by a stuffed toy to stop him in his tracks.

---

611   Matthew 5:34-37 KJV
612   *Hot Fuzz*, Rogue Pictures/Universal Pictures, 2007

A clean conscience is the consequence of never saying anything more than "Yes" or "No" when one is being asked to justify oneself. Paul writes, "With me it is a very small thing that I should be judged (*anakrithoh*) by you or by man's judgment (*anakrinoh*). I do not even judge myself. For I know nothing against myself. Yet I am not justified by this. But He who judges me is the Lord. Therefore judge nothing before the appointed time (*kairou ti krivete*) until the Lord comes. He will bring to light the hidden things of darkness and reveal the purposes (*boulas*/motives) of the hearts. Then everyone will have commendation (*epainos*/approbation, *genehsetai*/*ginomai*) from God."[613] In other words, your coming-to-pass will be finally brought to the light. There will be no more *egeneto*.

This is the same Paul who cries out, "Who will deliver me from this body (*sohmatos*) of death?" and then who declares that "there is therefore now no condemnation (*katakrima*) for those who are in Christ Jesus, who walk not according to the flesh, but according to the Spirit."[614] Paul's struggle with the Old Adam isn't a struggle to reconcile the Old with the New or to explain the Old by means of the New (to re-language it): Paul is talking about Original Sin, here. It never goes away. The "was" is always with us until the "will be" comes to pass (*ginomai*). Only the blood of Jesus can provide freedom from this perennial and ubiquitous reality. Call this the Great Compensation.

The mechanism, if you can call it thus, for this deliverance, the tool by which it is realized and put into action, is the word of God. The word prunes the soul even to its roots.[615] Without exposure to the revealed word of God, there is no pruning. Everything stays the way it always has been, endlessly repeating and virtually self-replicating like the "strange attractors" of stochastic reality: Like chaos.[616]

---

613   I Corinthians 4:3-5
614   Romans 7:24; 8:1
615   John 15:2: "Every branch in Me that bears no fruit, He takes away. And every branch that bears fruit, He prunes, that it may bear more fruit"; Matthew 3:10 KJV: "Now also the axe is laid unto the root of the trees."
616   James Gleick, *Chaos: Making a New Science* (New York: Penguin Books, 1987), footnote, p. 29: "The Lorenz Attractor ... became an emblem for the early explorers of chaos. It revealed the fine struc-

The two totalities can never intersect. Western Civilization faces a choice, a choice between the revealed God and the rationalized God. It's the yes or no choice, the one without which there can be no clean conscience. Everything that comes out of avoiding the choice is "of evil."

A civilization, like any other living organism, has its own potential for "gene death." This is a genetic term, one that participates both in the processes of *gennaoh* and the occasions of *ginomai*. Briefly, "gene death is the end outcome of a process that starts with the relaxation of functional constraints. When a mutation that incapacitates gene function is fixed in the population, the gene becomes a pseudogene ... If we assume that at the time of divergence, the gene content of ... two closely related species was identical, then genes that are present in one genome but absent from the other were most probably deleted during evolution ... the inactivation of one gene may result in the relaxation of selection of the genes with which it interacts ... we may conclude that there are no general rules pertaining to the genetic functions that should be lost to trigger a mass extinction of genes during reductive evolution."[617]

Maybe the analogy is a bit metaphysical, but, then again, Nature's God can be quite revealing . . . and unforgiving. Studies like the above are undergone in cultures of bacteria. Every civilization has its own culture, and self-replicating single cells make up the totality of the human body. Self-replication doesn't stop at the level of the single cell. It's a corporate act.

Scientists say that many genes continue to function after the body dies. In this sense, we can say, by natural analogy, that the Reason Gene and the Revelation Gene are continuing to function, although at increasingly minimal levels. Or we can dispense with the analogies and go with Foucault.

---

ture hidden within a disorderly stream of data ... Because the system never exactly repeats itself, the trajectory never intersects itself."

617   Tai Dagan, Ran Blekhman, Dan Graur, *Oxford Academic: Molecular Biology and Evolution*, 19 October 2005 – <u>https://www.academic.oup. com thedominotheoryofgenedeathgradualandmassextinctioneventsin- threeli neagesofobligatesymbioticbacterialpathogens</u> ; accessed 28 Mar 23.

These analogies depend on subservience to unconscious totalities. According to him, "discursive formation is not ... a developing totality, with its own dynamism or inertia, carrying with it, in an unfortunate discourse, what it does not say, what it has not yet said, or what contradicts it at the moment; it is not a rich, difficult germination, it is a distribution of gaps, voids, absences, limits, divisions."[618] Neither Western Reasoning nor Western Theology are without gaps, voids, absences, limits, and divisions, but if we were to recognize, honor and/or otherwise validate these gaps, the civilization itself would crumble like the walls of Jericho. The Narrative would end, and the story would have neither meaning nor purpose, except, perhaps, to help the child go to sleep at bedtime.

The Great Moral question for Postmodern Western Civilization is this: How do you judge a civilization? If it has not already ended, or become "complete in time," a final judgment, one that decrees or brings to light that completion (*telos*) is premature. As Paul puts it, "I don't even judge myself." It's like a hermeneutic of unfinished testimony. Nevertheless, there is an eagerness in the Postmodern era to do exactly that, to judge the nations, beginning with our own. Is this eagerness premature, or is it that The Civilization has, in fact, ended?

If Christ is the answer, the answer must be Yes or No. The Old Narrative is necessarily and intrinsically "full of holes." The New Narrative cannot consist of a reconciliation of Reason with Revelation, because that IS the Old Narrative. Whatever New Narrative is possible, or able to be conceived from the Old Narrative in order to be born as the New Narrative, it of necessity must be either Reasonable or Revelatory.

Whether the New Narrative of The Civilization is revelatory or reasonable, it will by nature and character differ radically from the Old Narrative: The Civilization will not be the same Civilization. It's in these terms that the Postmodern Cultural Civil War is being fought. It's a battle to determine which language game is supreme, the rational or the revealed. Yet before it can be concluded to anyone's satisfaction, the spies of the one need to be eliminated from close association with the other.

---

618   Foucault, *Archaeology*, p. 119

These "spies" are the suggested narratives that say "yes" when they mean "no" and "no" when they mean "yes."

All experiences and interpretations of the conscience are at one in that they make the 'voice' of conscience speak somehow of 'guilt' ... Is it possible that ... so far as any Dasein factically exists, it is also guilty? ... indebtedness becomes possible only 'on the basis' of a primordial Being-guilty ... Freedom ... is only in the choice of one possibility - that is, in tolerating one's not having chosen the others and one's not being able to choose them ... Being-guilty is more primordial than any knowledge about it...[619]

MARTIN HEIDEGGER'S INTELLECT was the product of a thousand years of Western thought. He was also willing to join the Nazi Party. Whoever is still surprised by the advent of Hitler and German National Socialism, who asks the question, "How could this happen (*ginomai*) in a civilized nation?" is one who has already become detached from the very foundation that provides the possibility of asking the question. It DID happen: It "came to pass that . . ."

It's very difficult to wade through Heidegger's works without getting a little bit dizzy. It's impossible to go through it quickly. But once you catch the rhythm of the language game he invents, you can almost taste the meaning of each sentence or phrase. Compared to other Western philosophies, it's like taking a bite of fudge from the movie *Chocolat*[620] compared to consuming malted milk powder straight out of the container. You can only take little bites at a time.

Being and Time was published in 1927. It has been described as "a key document of existentialism." By this designation, it fits perfectly the kind of discourse Foucault is talking about. It's a very timely document. In context, 1927 was the year the first transatlantic telephone call was made, the film *Metropolis* was released in Germany, Werner Heisenberg formulated his uncertainty principle, Pan American World Airways was founded, the Academy of Motion Picture Arts and Sciences was founded,

---

619 Heidegger, *Being*, pp. 324, 326, 329, 331, 332
620 *Chocolat*, Miramax/Buena Vista, 2000 - "(Vianne's) ability to perceive her customers' desires and satisfy them with just the right confection coaxes the villagers to abandon themselves to temptation..."

Sacco and Vanzetti were executed, CBS was formed, Leon Trotsky was expelled from the Soviet Communist Party, and Cesar Chavez and the future Pope Benedict XVI were born.[621]

You can create a coming-to-pass (*ginomai*) after the fashion of Tuchman's historiographic style combined with Luke's Gospel style, and what you come up with will shed much light on what is the nature of your favorite totality. Was 1927 a propitious moment in the history of the West or even a Kairos Moment? It was four years after Hitler's Beer Hall Putsch and six years before Hitler was appointed Chancellor in Germany.

In 1931, four years after Being and Time was published, Peruvian revolutionaries hijack a Ford Trimotor, construction of the Empire State building was completed, the collapse of the Austrian banking system left the entire German banking system on the verge of collapse, the Geneva Convention relative to prisoners of war took force, the Chinese Soviet Republic was proclaimed by Mao Zedong, Boris Yeltsin and Leonard Nimoy were born, and Khalil Gibran died.[622] This looks pretty propitious to me, but, then, so does 1927, and for certain does 1933.

You can see evidence of my totality-preference in the mere choice of items and personalities chosen to illustrate what was happening (*ginomai*) in those years. Whether or not any of those three selections constituted a Moment of Kairos is anybody's guess. This is a 'true fact,' as "they" say, for two reasons: First, it depends on what your judgments concerning contemporary developments regarding whether you judge them to be righteous or unrighteous, and second, the entire 20th-21st century is a collective Moment of Kairos. This Kairos Moment is even more complex and densely packed than anything Heidegger ever created, but, still, Heidegger's stuff makes a good precis of the nature of our extended Kairos Moment of Western Civilization.

---

621 1927 – https://en.m.wikipedia.org_1927 ; last edited 13 March 2023, accessed 29 Mar 23.
622 1931 – https://en.m.wikipedia.org_1931 ; last edited 15 March 2023, accessed 29 Mar 23.

The thing to note when swimming in the sea of Heideggerian metaphysics is the nature of his deformations of the traditional, conventional, and typical Judeo-Christian values which had provided the moral and social foundation for Western Civilization from its inception. He literally changes the shape (topology) of the entire world in which the Westernly civilized live. His metaphysics is a re-invention of revelatory givens such that they become the givens of a universe without God. Dasein, or personal existence, becomes a mediating absolute in history, itself described as "the way Dasein stretches along."[623]

The re-formation of classic Judeo-Christian ideas is evident especially in the passages that precede this chapter in our discussion, or discourse. Both "guilt" and "freedom" are accommodated, not by means of a God-Man savior who is able to set us free by dying as one of us, but by reifying guilt, as it were, as a permanent element of human existence itself. Hidden in the analysis is the evident solution to this quality of life as it is lived: A return to the primordial or even before the primordial existence of humanity.

In plain English, we cannot and will not be thoroughly redeemed until we re-access, recover, and otherwise reclaim our primordial existence. In Hitlerian terms, this means getting back before there were Jews and Christians. Heidegger's entire metaphysic constitutes the attempt to re-access the primordial, without, to be sure, getting rid of the Modern. The upshot of this metaphysic is that the purpose, intention, and character of the Modern itself is to recover the primordial realities from whence it once emerged.

One might call this metaphysically hypothesized re-emergence, "The Beast."[624] It's a beast that makes even Hobbes' "Leviathan"[625] shrink to

---

623   Heidegger, *Being*, p. 427
624   Revelation 13:1: "I saw a beast rising out of the sea."
625   Thomas Hobbes, *Leviathan: The Matter, Forme and Power of a Commonwealth Ecclesiasticall and Civil*, 1651 – https://en.m.wikipedia.org_leviathan(hobbesbook) : The work concerns the structure of society and legitimate government, and is regarded as one of the earliest and most influential examples of social contract theory"; last edited 18 February 2023, accessed 29 Mar 23.

insignificance by comparison.[626] Leviathan raises himself up; Leviathan is the Dragon who gives the Beast its power.[627]

When you finally choose between reasoning on reasoning on reasoning and the Word of God in the Bible, known as THE revelation, you are guilty a la Heidegger on two counts: First, you are guilty because you didn't choose the other over the one, and second, you are guilty because both choices tell you that you are guilty. The fine line between the two derives its power to separate by the way you choose to deal with your inherent guilt as a human being.

You can choose either the State or you can choose Jesus.

Paul Tillich tried to mitigate Heidegger's metaphysics by attaching existential conclusions to Christian promises. Like Aquinas so many centuries before him, he failed to show that the Christian revelation is superior and eternally more comprehensive than any reasoning can ever hope to accomplish. Rather, Aquinas set the stage for the ultimate overthrow of the Holy Scriptures, and Tillich finished the task.

By incorporating Heidegger's deformation of the wisdom of Western Civilization, Tillich simply invited the devil to take his place in the Temple of Language that Western Civilization had built. By this token, the topology of Western Civilization was not only deformed, it became shape-shifting: It became (*ginomai*) whatever you might want it to be.

We are, thus, the mediators of reality itself now, and there is no God to whom we can rationally appeal. We began this book with a quote from the movie *Sicario*. It is well to insert a concluding quote here, "You should move to a small town, somewhere the rule of law still exists. You will not survive here. You are not a wolf, and this is a land of wolves now."

---

626   Job 41:1, 4, 25, 34: "Can you draw out Leviathan with a hook … Will he make a covenant with you … When he raises up himself even the gods are afraid … He beholds all high things; he is a king over all the children of pride."
627   Revelation 13:2

In any closed system disorder, or entropy, always increases with time ... there is a thermodynamic arrow of time ... the psychological arrow of time ... and the cosmological arrow of time ... no boundary condition for the universe, together with the weak anthropic principle, can explain why all three arrows point in the same direction ... why a well-defined arrow of time should exist at all ... it is only when they do point in the same direction that conditions are suitable for the development of intelligent beings who can ask the question: why does disorder increase in the same direction of time as that in which the universe expands?[628]

ACCORDING TO THE PRINCIPLES of Nature's God, principles that we find chiefly expressed in the sciences, we can rely on these principles and assume with confidence that Nature's God[629] is essentially the same Being as the God who reveals himself through scripture. There is one variable, however, and that is that we, as a culture, believe that the principles of Nature's God are more clearly articulated in science than in the Bible, or in reasonable terms rather than in revealed terms.

The idea of "self-evident truth" is not the equivalent of the idea of revelatory truth: Revelatory Truth is truth that one would not otherwise know or even be potentially aware of. Revealed Truth is not self-evident: It's God evident. At the very least, this means that God's Truth is not algorithm subject. There are no formulas that can generate God's Truth either from the past into the future or from the present into tomorrow.

What science has discovered is that the formulas of the sciences cannot generate natural truth with certainty. This is why statistical analysis has become so much a foundational construct of modern/postmodern scientific methodology. The world we live in is now fundamentally stochastic. Its contents "may be analyzed statistically but may not be predicted precisely."[630]

---

628   Hawking, *Brief History*, p. 149
629   From The Declaration of Independence: "When ... it becomes necessary for one people ... to assume among the powers of the earth, the separate and equal station to which the Laws of Nature and of Nature's God entitle them ... We hold these truths to be self-evident..."
630   Stochastic – https://www.languages.oup.com_stochastic ; accessed 30 Mar 23.

The connection between God's Revealed Truth, that which is found in the Old and New Testaments, is considerably more unpredictable than a stochastic construct of possibilities. While it is fair to suggest, biblically, that God operates on a Yes or No basis, somewhat like the transactions that define a computer process, this does not mean that the substance of God's "Yes" or "No" is accessible AT ALL to the human intellect. That there are yes's and no's in the Law of Moses, particularly in the Ten Commandments, is indisputable, but even the Ten Commandments, when processed through a particular juridical system, can produce variant legal/moral conclusions, even divergent conclusions.

The crux of Jesus' command to say either 'yes' or 'no' is a command to judge events in the same way that God judges. This kind of judging, a judging by which God maintains justice in the world, isn't directly accessible to either the will, the intellect, or the emotions of the human soul. Our 'yes/no' tends to be overwhelmed by one of those three soul-departments to the disadvantage of the other two.

Human conscience does not inform the individual whether a decision is right or wrong in the ultimate sense, in terms of a final *telos*. Conscience responds to imbalance in the interplay between the intellect, the will, and the emotions. We can overcome this imbalance, or disequilibrium, by force of will, intellect, or emotion, but we cannot naturally reconcile them in the immediate situation. This is because such reconciliation of conscience requires that the larger purpose of the situation or event has been completely played out.

When we enter analytically into the realm of what can be imagined to be a national soul, we are delving into an arena of *telos* that is not only quantitatively beyond the ability of a single soul to judge, but it is also a realm in which the very notion or evidence or prospect of *telos* is of a different nature, character, and quality altogether. Nevertheless, in a Hegelian national construct, the individual *telos* is found in and only in the telos of the Nation. The ultimate purpose of the individual IS the ultimate purpose of the State.

This is not, and can never amount to, a rightly divided[631] sense of the revealed Word of God. This is because in such a case the individual must understand his or her self-purpose to be a derivative of the State's purpose, and it must be derivable only from the Laws of the State. When the laws of the State perfectly match the self-regulating principles of the individual,[632] then the State reveals itself to be "the Divine Idea as it exists on earth." In this is apocalypse, but it is a pseudo-, or anti-apocalypse, i.e., "close but no cigar." Nevertheless, it is conceived to be the final reckoning by unsaved souls, those who have been confused by the pseudo-certainties of the world into worshipping the image of the beast.[633]

To worship the image of the beast, then, is the equivalent of worshipping the image of the state. This is done by means of the fundamental belief that you have truly been created in the image of the State, and that you gain your identity by means of appropriating that image in a way that reconciles your self-image with the dictates of the State. This reconciliation of the self to the State is the final acquiescence of all power and authority to be given the State, and it is the fundamental operating principle of identity politics.[634]

The truly totalitarian State doesn't need to use force to set its agenda. Its agenda is already agreed upon by the populace. They have evolved together like the panda and bamboo. The panda can't eat anything else,[635] but the panda also neutralizes the cyanide contained in raw bamboo which, "if eaten, will make the average person extremely

---

631   See footnote 446
632   Hegel, *Reason*, p. 66: "The vitality of the State in individuals is what we call Morality."
633   Revelation 13:15
634   Identity politics – https://en.m.wikipedia.org_identitypolitics : "A political approach wherein people of a particular race, nationality, religion, gender, sexual orientation, social background, social class, or other identifying factors develop political agendas that are based upon these identities"; last edited 28 March 2023, accessed 30 Mar 23.
635   Pandas – https://www.pablolunasstudio.com_whydopandaseatbamboo : "While it's unclear exactly when or why the relationship between pandas and bamboo began, it's clear that this powerful connection will continue long into the future"; posted January 3, 2023, accessed 30 Mar 23.

sick."[636] There will be no residual awareness of the fact that the State has become totalitarian. All contradictory forms of awareness will have been cancelled.[637]

The physical, economic, and legal violence that has been used by all modern dialectically oriented States is not the kind of ultimate violence that will dialectically reconcile the contradictions of the civilization of the Christian West. What is needed, and indeed what is happening, is violence to and in the human unconscious. The individual can be compromised by revealed subconscious factors which affect that person's ability and imagination regarding communal relationships, but the invasion of the unconscious mind amounts to total war.

The early social means for initiating this invasion are already apparent, e.g, in the prevalence of stonewalling, changing the subject in mid-conversation, and especially gaslighting. The ongoing means to affect a complete compromise of the unconscious mind is the art of changing the language game **while it is being played**. It is in this way that the fundamental and intentional meaning of the old language game is transformed into the new language game without the interference of conscious awareness.[638]

A civilization is a closed system, like the closed system in Nature whose ultimate destiny is entropy. A system that has reached maximum entropy is a purely stochastic system, i.e., random. In a random system,

---

636   Angela Chen, *The Verge*, Mar 18, 2018, 12:00 PM MST – https://www.theverge.com_dontunderestimatepandas-theirbodiescanneutralizecyanide ; accessed 30 Mar 23.
637   Mao Tse-Tung, *Selected Works*, August 1937 – https://www.marxists.org_oncontradiction : "The law of contradiction in things, that is, the law of the unity of opposites, is the basic law of materialistic dialectics … The problems are: the two world outlooks, the universality of contradiction, the particularity of contradiction, the principal contradiction and the principle aspect of a contradiction, the identity and struggle of the aspects of a contradiction, and the place of antagonism in contradiction"; accessed 30 Mar 23.
638   AUTHOR'S NOTE: In contemporary context, "woke" means "unconscious." The developed, or anti-developed, unconscious mind responds only to triggers in the language game being played.

the principle of cause-and-effect is vaporous. The difference between what caused an event and what the was effect has been entirely obscured.

In terms of an entropic civilization, one that has exhausted its storehouse of potentialities, the sense of "end-ness" stimulates the desperation regarding the discontinuities which belie the possibility of that civilization's continuity in time. Everybody "knows," in the gnostic sense,[639] that it is ending. This knowledge is existentially disturbing to the point of tragedy, the entirely negative outcome of the original extended narrative. To avoid the imagined tragedy, the National soul, the particularly civilized soul, strains to change the narrative, so that a perceivable "good" end can be conceived. This last contradiction lends the tragi-comic character to civilizations that have not long to continue in existence.

All nationalistic systems are gnostic. Civilizations and States come to an end. The destinies of Nations are governed by God.

---

639   Gnostic – https://www.gnosis.org_thegnosticworldviewabrief-summaryofgnosticism : "Gnosticism is the teaching based on Gnosis, the knowledge of transcendence arrived at by way of interior, intuitive means … Gnosticism expresses a specific religious experience, an experience that does not lend itself to the language of theology or philosophy, but which is closely affinitized to, and expresses itself through, the medium of myth … the truths embodied in these myths are of a different order from the dogmas of theology or the statements of philosophy"; accessed 30 Mar 23.

Chapter Three: A STATE WITHOUT BOUNDARIES

Protect me, O God, for I take refuge in you ... you are my portion and my cup; it is you who uphold my lot. My boundaries enclose a pleasant land; indeed, I have a goodly heritage.[640]

THERE ARE FOUR TYPES of boundaries that are violated in apocalypse: National boundaries, state boundaries, religious boundaries, and soul boundaries. When all four have been crossed illegally, or trespassed, the boundaries of the world are breached. In Jesus' day, they were all violated by the Romans. WWI violated them all as well, with one caveat: They were not violated by an outside force. Rather, Western Civilization violated itself.

A national boundary is the product and limit of *genea*, or generations. It involves the cumulative inviolability of the family, the clan, and the tribes coming together as a nation, or *ethnos*. For instance, at the Battle of the Little Bighorn, several tribes came together to oppose the policies and forces of a State. In this sense, it was part of a war between a Nation and a State. That nation was led in war by Gall and Crazy Horse who may be likened to King David in the Hebrew Scriptures. The union of convenience was presided over by Sitting Bull, who may be likened to the early King Solomon. The Lakota, Dakota, Northern Cheyenne, and Arapaho Tribes together constituted a Nation coming to battle.[641]

National boundaries are not fixed lines in the sand or on a map, although you can find maps that indicate the general territories of various North American tribes. The dividing line is a Shibboleth Line, so to speak: It consists of manners, customs, language, corporate awareness, and other such things. In a battle, of course, the line becomes immediately fixed, and the battle doesn't end until the line has been moved, broken, or otherwise compromised.

640   Psalm 16:1, 5-6 BCP
641   Little Bighorn – https://en.m.wikipedia.org_battleofthelittlebighorn ; last edited 30 March 2023, accessed 1 Apr 23.

State boundaries are an invention of the Modern. Until the 19th century in Europe, they tended to be rather fluid, depending on the influence, wealth, honor and aggression of the sovereign. The nature of these boundaries changed radically between the time of the Napoleonic Wars and WWI. For example, Russia could "retreat" from its boundaries and still "win" the campaign. The retreat did not compromise the boundaries of Russia, because Russia was a Nation. The National boundaries were constituted by where the Russians as a nation were. Their existence as a Nation, in other words, gave meaning to the term "boundary."

It was in the 19th century, for Western Civilization, that the word boundary moved from the language game of nationality to the language game of State. A State requires fixed, empirically measurable, boundaries. In this sense, the State is more "scientific" than is a Nation. When the fixed boundary of a State is violated, then the State is also violated. IT has a compromised identity; its self-awareness is de-stabilized: It doesn't know where it begins or ends.

Religious boundaries and soul boundaries are cousins in the language games that convey their meaning and significance. You might say that religion is the subject/object management system for souls. In ancient times, which is all time until the European Renaissance, Nation and Religion tended to be identified one with the other. Over time, a religion might surpass national boundaries and become international, such as did Hinduism in India and SE Asia.

Variations in national self-awareness and senses of corporate identity influence the topology of the religion to which the nation has become covenanted. A rather clear example of this kind of variation is the difference between Mahayana Buddhism[642] and Hinayana Buddhism.[643]

642   Mahayana – https://www.languages.oup.com mahayana : "one of the two major traditions of Buddhism, now practiced in a variety of forms especially in China, Tibet, Japan, and Korea. The tradition emerged around the 1st century AD and is typically concerned with altruistically oriented spiritual practice as embodied in the ideal of the bodhisattva"; accessed 1 Apr 23.
643   Hinayana – https://www.britannica.com hinayana : "(Sanskrit: 'Lesser Vehicle') the more orthodox, conservative schools of Buddhism

Both variations on form are topologically different than, say, original Chinese Buddhism or Original Buddhism. Yet they are all identifiable as Buddhism. It's a bit like the difference between American Liberal Christianity and American Conservative Christianity, but we'll leave that discussion for another time and venue.

The divide, and it is a divide, between Eastern and Western Christianity, often known as Orthodox and Catholic, has long been a bitter divide constituting a nearly complete misunderstanding between the two. Protestant sects began as catholic with a small "c" and were identified with emerging states as State Religions. Examples of the efficacy of these divides, as well as the divide between so-called historical and Pentecostal Christianity or American Evangelical and Traditional Evangelical Christianity abound.

One very influential religious divide in Postmodern Christianity is that between Western Catholic traditions and Russian Orthodox traditions. It would not be a stretch to say that both consider the other to be fake or invalid religions. Much more *thluptic* pressure has been applied to the general religious situation by the recent creation of the Orthodox Church of Ukraine in 2019 as an independent church. The independence aspect means that the Ukrainian Orthodox Church no longer recognizes any connection with the Patriarchate of Moscow.[644]

This current difficulty regarding international relations needs much clarification, but, very briefly, it means that both the religious boundaries between Ukraine and Russia have been moved and the customary boundaries imposed by historians as to origins and identities must be radically changed, depending on who is assigning those boundaries. In effect, a State Religion has been created that satisfies the redefinitions of boundary in the Modern Era, but it does not immediately satisfy the conditions of the First Amendment of the United States of America.

... the name reflected the Mahayanists' evaluation of their own tradition as a superior method ... but the name was not accepted by the conservative schools as referring to a common tradition"; accessed 1 Apr 23.

644   Ukrainian Orthodox – https://en.m.wikipedia.org_orthodoxx-hurchofukraine ; last edited 31 March 2023, accessed 1 Apr 23.

Because religious boundaries possess an intimate relationship with soul boundaries, changes like the above amount to existential changes for those who cannot or will not identify with the prescribed alterations. The general trend of the Reformation in Europe moved toward the establishment of state religions, specifically State Churches, but that trend was renounced with the establishment of the United States of America by means of its Constitution.

The moving of religious boundaries, at any rate, has a profound effect on perceived and felt soul boundaries. The violation of soul boundaries has a profound effect on the overall health of the soul. If such a violation is not mitigated by one means or another, the consequence will be a sickness of the soul. Because of the intimate connection between religion and soul, this soul sickness can, and usually does, become a sickness of the spirit.

Soren Kierkegaard referred to soul-sickness or spirit-sickness as the "sickness unto death." He calls it Despair. Kierkegaard is notoriously difficult to follow although not quite as much as his bastard offspring Heidegger or Heidegger's adoptive parent Tillich, but if one cannot follow Kierkegaard's thinking at all, one will not even have a minimal grasp of the socio-existential dynamics of the Postmodern Western World.[645]

SK writes, "The imbalance in despair is not a simple imbalance but an imbalance in a relation that relates to itself and which is established by something else. So the lack of balance in that 'for-itself' relationship also reflects itself infinitely in the relation to the power which established it. This then is the formula which describes the state of the self when despair is completely eradicated: in relating to itself and in wanting to be itself, the self is grounded transparently in the power which established it."[646] Because Kierkegaard's chief philosophical adversary was Hegel, it

---

645 AUTHOR'S NOTE: This is because the philosophers mentioned, and more, have had and have a profound effect in academia on sociology, psychology, historiography, hermeneutics and virtually every other field of study, including physics, that we can imagine or conjure up.

646 Soren Kierkegaard, *The Sickness Unto Death: A Christian Psychological Exposition for Edification and Awakening* (New York: Penguin Books, 1989, 2004; original 1849), p. 44

is safe to say that Kierkegaard's notion of the establishing power is God; Hegel's idea is the State.

The crunch for personal identity in this mess comes about from the loss of both religious and national identity. Personal identity grounded in National identity is an organic aspect of human existence and life, but State identity is not. National identity implies a heritage: State identity does not. State identity involves the subjugation of personal identity to the identity of the State and the consequent balancing of the factors that contribute to despair by means of State control and decree. Insofar as one is willing to agree to this subjugation, despair, or its potential, is mitigated. This is especially true if there is no State Religion.

In the absence of a State Religion and National identity, the boundaries of the self, or soul/spirit, must be set and adjudicated by Law. If this is not done, then the result is a general despair among the populace. This kind of despair leads to nihilism, anarchy, and/or profound psycho-emotional distress. When this situation comes about (*ginomai*), identity politics is the only avenue of escape for the State polity which has erased both national and religious boundaries.

Kierkegaard, in his role as theologian, identified despair with sin. He writes, "Sin is: before God, or with the conception of God, in despair not wanting to be oneself, or wanting in despair to be oneself ... sin is the heightening of despair."[647] It is in this way that Kierkegaard's 19th century Christian existentialism leads directly to the identity politics of today's United States ... and of the entire planet.

Despair is at the root of the violation of boundaries we call World War I. Subsequent decades have amounted to simply the desperate activities of desperate Nations and States to mitigate the effects of despair on the human soul and, ideally, to rid the world of all potential causes of despair. This is the moral and social equivalent of ridding the world of sin.

---

647   Ibid., p. 109

The beginning of ridding the world of sin is the violent transformation of the biblical language game into the language game of the State. Call this the transitioning of Bible-talk. In this transition, boundaries are not simply moved: They are re-calculated altogether such that the "pleasant land" they once enclosed becomes (*ginomai*) an entirely different land, one whose boundaries are determined by the State.

Humanity is ... deinon[648] ... because ... it gathers what holds sway and lets it enter into an openness. Humanity is violence-doing not in addition to and aside from other qualities but solely in the sense that from the ground up and in its doing of violence, it uses violence against the over-whelming. Because it is doubly deinon in an originally united sense. It is to deinotaton,[649] the most violent: violence-doing in the midst of the overwhelming.[650]

HEIDEGGER'S UNDERSTANDING of this innately violent nature of the human being extends to the violence of forcing meaning onto naked reality. The uncanniest (*deinotaton*) violence-doing is that done to God, or the organizing principle of creation, the *Logos*. When translated literarily into political and nationalistic language games, the result is National Socialism as a rudimentary form of innate human violence, rudimentary because it still relies on physical and rhetorical violence. We have seen how this kind of transitioning violence transfers the location of the Logos from heaven, indeed as one of the persons of the Holy Trinity, to the domain of the State.

Heaven is robbed to fulfil the needs of the State.

The ultimate form of the transitioning of Logos from heaven to earth occurs when the State becomes the sole "Over-whelming." This over-whelming (noun) is facilitated by the self-becoming-its-own-over-whelming, such that it disappears into or is absorbed into the State

---

648   *Deinon* – https://en.m.wiktionary.org_deinos : "terrible, horrible, fearful, astounding"; last edited 17March 2023, accessed 1 Apr 23.

649   David Meagher, *Mosaic: A journal for the Interdisciplinary Study of Literature-The Uncanniness of Spectrality*, December 2011 – https://www.muse.jhu.edu : "Once *to deinon* is translated, as in Hoelderlin and Heidegger, *Unheimlichkeit* (uncanniness), deina becomes 'uncanny' and *deinoteron* or *deinotaton* ... becomes 'uncanniest' or 'most uncanny'"; accessed 1 Apr 23.

650   Heidegger, *Metaphysics*, p. 160

Self. The identity of the State and the identity of the Self then become literally the same identity, although with a different topology. The Self as overwhelmed by the possibilities of Self seeks refuge in the State as the Protector against self-overwhelming self-identity. The Self can't live with itself, so the State lives for it.

At any rate, Heidegger's understanding of the innate violence of humanness is readily apparent in any version of history, but particularly in recent history. Violence becomes the sole source of personal identity, even violence against the self. In the absence of the mitigating power of religion as such, the only authority that can keep humanity from destroying itself is the State. The State resolves the self-destructive character of the individual by destroying the individual soul.

Just as Kierkegaard's understanding of despair implies a theology of Original Sin, so too does Heidegger's anthropology of violence. In the absence of a transcendent redemption, both sin and violence must exhaust themselves in the world and of it. There is no higher resolution. In the absence of God, or even a vague conception of a higher power of a different order, the intellect and the imagination become subject to the will alone: Instead of informing the will or guiding the will, the imagination becomes only an extension of the will, and the intellect becomes a psycho-social hammer.

Nietzsche (1844-1900)[651] and Schopenhauer (1788-1860)[652] knew what was on the horizon for Western Civilization, but they still owed

---

651   Emrys Westacott, *ThoughtCo*, updated January 29, 2019 – https://www.thoughtco.com_nietzschesconceptofthewilltopower : "The 'will to power' is a central concept in the philosophy of ... Nietzsche. It is best understood as an irrational force, found in all individuals, that can be channeled toward different ends ... (he categorized) it at various points as a psychological, biological, or metaphysical principle ... In his early twenties, Nietzsche read 'The World as Will and Representation"; accessed 2 Apr 23.

652   Arthur Schopenhauer – https://www.plato.stanford.edu_arthurschopenhauer : "Arthur Schopenhauer was among the first 19th century philosophers to contend that at its core, the universe is not a rational place. Inspired by Plato and Kant (he) developed their philosophies into an instinct-recognizing and ultimately ascetic outlook, emphasizing that in the face of a world filled with endless strife, we ought to minimize our natural desires for the sake of achieving

their own debts to the cultural and intellectual romanticism of the past. Nietzsche died along with all the other intellectual and political luminaries who maintained the cosmos prior to WWI, but his bequeathment to Western Civilization lives on. Oppenheimer and his team put the finishing touches on the subjugation, indeed the imprisonment, of the intellect to and the imagination to the will under power of the State.[653] After 1945, Civilization moved into the present cultural void.

What we can imagine is no longer either Godly or rational. What we can think of is limited by the restrictions on cognition that those individuals, groups, and systems in power have already willed into being. One can sell one's soul to a given group or system, insofar as there remain several systems from which to choose. The return on your transaction will depend on whether or not your chosen system is the ultimate victor over the others. Even so, the teabag can only be dipped into the hot water so many times before it loses its fragrance and flavor. When the great sea of the unconscious becomes a stagnant pond, then the State will have become All in All: "The wages of sin is death."[654]

How can the exiles ever return to a land that was never theirs?

How lonely sits the city that was full of people! How she has become like a widow, who was once great among the nations! She who was a princess among the provinces has become a slave! ... Is it nothing to you, all you who pass by? Look and see if there is any sorrow like my sorrow, which was brought upon me, which the Lord has inflicted on the day of His fierce anger.[655]

BY THE TIME JEREMIAH mourned over Jerusalem, the glory that had settled onto it in the time of Solomon was long since gone. Three-hundred

---

a more tranquil frame of mind and a disposition towards universal beneficence"; published Mon May 12, 2003, revised Thu Sep 9, 2021, accessed 2 Apr 23.
653   AUTHOR'S NOTE: Oppenheimer knew this when he violated the boundaries of scientific ethics. In the Post nuclear Age, there is no scientific ethics except, if it can be done, it should be done. When science alone determines the boundary between Good and Evil, power is the only limiting factor. If the State determines scientifically that an action is Good, it IS good.
654   Romans 6:23
655   Lamentations 1:1,12

and some years is a long time to neglect a garden. Since the first call of revolution began the founding of a new nation, "conceived in liberty, and dedicated to the proposition that all men are created equal," the equivalent number of years puts the United States of America at CE 2110. According to Abraham Lincoln, a civil war of bullets, partisans, and strategies was fought so that "this nation, under God, shall have a new birth of freedom – and that government of the people, by the people, for the people, shall not perish from the earth."[656]

The year after Schopenhauer died, one of the greatest conflagrations of pure violence in history claimed the *kairos* moment. In the process, the window through which Kairos can be seen and appropriated was smashed. The spirit of Pure Will possessed the nation, even in its divided state, and all imagination and intellect was directed toward the utter defeat of the enemy. For the first time, Pogo's much later remark would hold true, "We have met the enemy, and he is us."[657]

The Civil War is in America's nature, now, and the original divisions have morphed into a weed patch of myriad, sometimes subtle, most often blatant, unconscious wills to power that cannot be satisfied because the first manifestation of the civil war was culturally inconclusive. One might say in terms of Foucault's phraseology that the overarching historical and literary totalities that allured the nation into a war against itself never re-emerged as either dominating or dominated. Since then, the totalities have re-morphed so many times that their topological form is now barely recognizable.

Paramount among the totalities that failed to achieve resolution in the mid-19th century are the leading concepts of the American Pledge of Allegiance, liberty and justice. The violent projective aspect of this state of national irresolution is manifested in repetitious wars for Democracy, futile attempts by a nation that has yet to resolve its own sense of identity

[656] The Gettysburg Address, 1863
[657] Walt Kelly – https://www.library.osu.edu_wehavemettheenemyand-heisus : "Kelly's parody of (the famous report of the Battle of Lake Erie in 1812) perfectly summarizes mankind's tendency to create our own problems ... Kelly coined the phrase for an anti-pollution Earth Day poster in 1970 (in the comic strip *Pogo*), April 12, 1971"; accessed 2 Apr 23.

to resolve them for and on other nations by force. It is very frustrating to realize that you have never succeeded in being true to yourself; even more so when you realize that there is very little time left in which to try to accomplish that existential demand.

The intellect and the imagination are compelled to agree with Foucault and other Postmodern deconstructionists that the only salvation of the Civilization lies in the fracturing of all the totalities that have led us into ideologies of force and compromise of the soul. As he says, "Genesis, continuity, totalization: these are the great themes of the history of ideas ... it is normal that anyone who still practices history ... cannot conceive that a discipline like the history of ideas should be abandoned; or rather, considers that any other form of analyzing discourses is a betrayal of history itself ... That some people do not recognize in this enterprise the history of their childhood, that they mourn its passing, and continue to invoke, in an age that is no longer made for it, that great shade of former times, certainly proves their fidelity."[658]

If history is a totality leading inexorably to a Totality of Totalities, then the analysis of suggested and projected totalities should bear fruit. Nevertheless, as the same archaeo-bard says, "Between archaeological analysis and the history of ideas there are a great many points of divergence."[659]

To realize the blessings of a realized totality, primarily by virtue of the government of a State, the individual soul must also realize that totality internally. The righteous soul rebels against this trend, but the political soul admires the possibility. The Great Divergence of Western Civilization today, especially as it manifests in the polities of the United States of America, consists of this very thesis-antithesis repulsion. The two totalities force each other to be farther and farther apart, just as the expanding universe tends toward entropy.

Because of the internal pressure, or apocalyptic *thlupsis*, on subjectivity in community, the divergence is felt to be a struggle between Good and

---

658   Foucault, *Archaeology*, p. 138.
659   Ibid.

Evil. Thus, the Manichean character of 21st century American politics. Since the abject struggle between Good and Evil cannot be acceptable as an internal struggle because it would tear apart the soul,[660] the struggle must be objectified and externalized. Objectified Evil can be just about anything, any system, and any person or group, if the projection satisfies the threat of internal existential annihilation.

As long as this condition is left to its own machinations and inevitabilities, it is a premonition of Apocalypse. This isn't necessarily an apocalypse in the escapist and projected physical sense, with the earth splitting open, asteroids hitting the planet, or the atmosphere heating up so that everyone is boiled alive: It's a soul and society apocalypse. When both soul and society are vaporized, the world no longer exists. It must be re-existed.

Whether or not there is an outside power to embrace the City like Babylon embraced Jerusalem is an outcome only God can devise. If Babylon becomes entirely internalized and systematized, then the apocalypse has already come and become what it was always meant to become (*ginomai*).

Mankind is never left alone. The Spiritual Presence acts upon it in every moment and breaks into it in some great moments, which are the historical kairoi ... There is no pure Spiritual Presence where there is no humanity and justice ... "Before" and "after" ... points to the world-historical event, the "basic kairos," which has established the center of history once for all, and it refers to the continually recurring and derivative kairoi in which a religious cultural group has an existential encounter with the central event ... Awareness of a kairos actually includes an image of past developments and their meaning for the present.[661]

THE THEOLOGICAL CONNECTION between history and the Bible was the dialectic that Tillich hoped to resolve. In the midst of this historical project, he pretty much eclipsed the Bible. His attempt to bring forth the synthesis between Reason and Revelation was a historic attempt, but Reason tends to dominate all forms of reality.

---

660 See footnote 152.
661 Tillich, *Volume Three*, pp. 140, 144, 153, 374

The problem with trying to separate Reason from Revelation consists of the fact that one starts out by subjecting both concepts to rational processes. The word "revelation" in this context, for instance, is a word conjured by the rational process to describe how God actually talks to us through Holy Scriptures. Once Reason dictates how God talks, God isn't doing the talking anymore – Reason is the speaker.

Regarding "what revelation is," Tillich writes, "The word 'revelation' ('removing the veil') has been used traditionally to mean the manifestation of something hidden which cannot be approached through ordinary ways of gaining knowledge ... a special and extraordinary manifestation which removes the veil from something which is hidden in a special and extraordinary way."[662] In other words, by means of revelation, we come to know something as it were without engaging the rational process by which we customarily know things.

Revelation, it must be said, is neither an epiphany nor an insight nor an intuition: It is entirely "other," in the same sense that God is entirely "other." The kind of otherness of which Tillich speaks from time to time is derived from the work of Rudolf Otto, who writes, "Taken in the religious sense, that which is 'mysterious' is ... the 'wholly other' ... that which is quite beyond the sphere of the usual, the intelligible, and the familiar, which therefore falls quite outside the limits of the 'canny', and is contrasted with it, filling the mind with blank wonder and astonishment."[663] God's throne room, one might say, is the realm of the uncanny.

We have seen how Heidegger connects violence with the uncanniness of Dasein, or human Being (being human).[664] The notion of discourse being central to both Heidegger and Foucault, this uncanniness must reveal itself in the interplay of words conveying meaning from one *dasein* to another, as it were. That is to say: language, the realm of *Logos*. Tillich verges on the mystical or even the magical in the process of forcing the synthesis between Reason and its antithesis, Revelation. It's a gentle

---

662   Tillich, *Volume One*, p. 108
663   Otto, *Holy*, p. 26
664   See footnote 568.

forcing, but tedious, and in the end, it obscures the postulated difference between the thesis and the antithesis. It seems as if there was never any real difference to begin with.

Tillich's solution is not the one Aquinas hoped for. For Aquinas, the dream was that everyone would see that the Revelation of God in Jesus Christ already contained all the knowledge and truth which Reason could ever discover, and more. Tillich comes close to saying that if we Reason thoroughly enough, we will have what Revelation tried to give us. This is not what Heidegger would say, nor what Otto would say. For Heidegger, reality is in effect revelational; for Otto, only the 'wholly other' can be self-revealing. God as revealed in the Judeo-Christian Scriptures becomes, for both Heidegger and Otto, only a piece of the total information available by whatever means: For Tillich, God becomes a kind of mystical wrapping that surrounds the cocoon of human existence. Someday, then, we will all be butterflies. We will be "New Beings."

The point is that each of these perspectives has maintained a presence in the way we "talk about God" in the Postmodern Western World. Yet the heart of the matter of knowledge in the gnostic, or intimate, sense is still hidden by the fact that we must use words, language, to convey what this means regardless of what we think it means. The diverging foundational assumptions about faith, religion, Jesus, and God reveal, in a truly revelational sense, the endpoint of the two trajectories: One: Talk about God the way God wants you to talk about God, or Two: Don't talk about God at all.[665]

In the meantime, the promoters of talking about God the way God wants to be talked about tend to succumb to the temptation to talk about God the way those who don't want to talk about God talk about God, or what was once the realm of God. Conversely, those who believe that the civilization should dispense entirely with talking about God hang onto the safety grip of traditional God-talk language. The gap between the two foundational languages consists of a great confusion caused by the

---

665 AUTHOR'S NOTE: I knew a family of professed atheists who would not allow any mention of "God" in their home at all.

obfuscation of meaning regarding whether we are talking God-talk or not talking God-talk.

There are still those who believe that talking God-talk and not talking God-talk can be reconciled into one language game. In this scenario, everyone can think they "mean the same thing" even though they do not "mean the same thing." But believing that you mean the same thing as the other person when in fact you both mean to overcome the meaning system that the other person maintains, is not real dialogue, not authentic discourse. In the end, which is drawing near, the dream of Thomas Aquinas is becoming the nightmare of Postmodern America. As one wag has put it, "Religion sucks."[666]

Western Civilization has exhausted its dialogue between Reason and Revelation. There is no more meaningful and totalistic discourse available for the task of refining ideas and reconciling subjectivities. The Reasonable Revelation discourse and the Revelation Saturated Reason discourse are no longer bearers of the language of future civilizational hope. Because this dialogue has been essential to the continuation of Western Civilization, because the unitary discourse, in principle irresolvable, can only be extended by means of fantasy or fictional ideology, the totalistic reality that WAS Western Civilization is no longer sustainable.

The reckoning or adjudication between the two discourses, acted out in the praxis of culture, is at hand. This situation, to be sure, IS Kairos, IS Apocalypse. To choose one discourse over the other 'is' become (*ginomai*) solely a matter of will, as the philosophers predicted. It remains to be seen whether that will is God's will in any way shape or form, or if it is not, but what is certain is the historical demand to choose.

The culture reflects on itself to oblivion. Communication ceases when Jesus stands silent before Pilate.

In the United States, the majority undertakes to supply a multitude of ready-made opinions for the use of individuals, who are thus relieved from the necessity of forming opinions of their

[666] AUTHOR'S NOTE: There are too many Google entries to list here.

own ... In America the majority raises formidable barriers around the liberty of opinion; within these barriers an author may write what he pleases, but woe to him if he goes beyond them.[667]

HOWEVER FREQUENTLY Alexis de Toqueville is quoted to the praise and glory of the American experiment in Democracy, he "does not unambiguously define democracy and even ignores the intents of the Founding Fathers of the United States regarding the American political system."[668] His optimistic opinion of this democracy has become a stand-alone meme in the aphoristic lexicon of the American patriotic language game.

Some 160 years after de Tocqueville published his American observations, the Americans changed the name of "French Fries" to that of "Freedom Fries" in a snarky protest regarding French lack of support for the second war in Iraq.[669] This effort was accompanied by the passage of the Patriot Act in 2001,[670] something that should have covered the populace with a coating of existential dread but did not. To quote from a previously quoted quote, "The duality of nature, Godly nature, human nature splits the soul; fully human, fully divine and divided: The great immortal soul. Split into pieces, whirling pieces, opposites attract; from the front, the side, the back, the mind itself attacks."[671] The land of the consumer begins to consume itself. Smaller pieces are easier to swallow.

667   Alexis de Tocqueville – https://www.brainyquote.com_alexisdetoquevillequotes ; accessed 4 Apr 23.

668   Alexis de Tocqueville, *Democracy in America*, 1835, 1840 – https://en.m.wikipedia.org_democracyinamerica ; last edited 9 March 2023, accessed 4 Apr 23.

669   Freedom Fries – https://en.m.wikipedia.org_freedomfries : "a politically motivated renaming of French fries ... widely publicized when the then Republican chairman of the Committee on House Administration, Bob Ney, renamed the menu item in three Congressional cafeterias"; last edited 13 March 2023, accessed 4 Apr 23.

670   Patriot Act – https://en.m.wikipedia.org_patriotact : "The formal name of the statute is the **Uniting and Strengthening America by Providing Appropriate Tools Required to Intercept and Obstruct Terrorism (USA PATRIOT) Act of 2001** ... expanded surveillance, easier interagency communication ... increased penalties for terrorism ... expanded list of activities ... for terrorism charges"; last edited 3 April 2023, accessed 5 Apr 23.

671   See footnote 152.

Even in 1840, an outside observer could see clearly that boundaries had already been constructed around the "liberty of opinion." Nothing much was happening to make history in the United States that year, but there were a few historical premonitions of troubles to come, e.g., the First Opium War in China, the First Anglo-Afghan War, and the Egyptian-Ottoman War.[672] It was, however, four years after the Battle of the Alamo and the formation of the Republic of Texas.

Liberty of opinion is still a troublesome sore spot in the Alamo-language-game today. Liberty of opinion is a troublesome sore spot in the American language game today. It's so troublesome that it has become the major troublesome sore spot in everyday and in political and religious discourse.[673] To be fair and honest, free speech was a bit of a problem during the American Revolution as well. In times of total war, the state has little tolerance for public disagreement.

The pressure on the appropriateness of talk is an American phenomenon that expands with time. Usually, opposition to the felt restrictions on conversation focusses on the idea of censorship, but censorship isn't really the problem. The recent designation "hate crime" is an exception to the rule, because it infringes on the legality of certain words, phrases or spoken intentions which are thought threateningly aggressive toward certain designated groups of citizens, but even so, proving a speech crime in court is still a complex legal matter. The pressure on free speech in America arises from, and has always arisen from, the mass of one's American compatriots. It's a matter of social pressure in the most extreme existential and even apocalyptic (re: *thlupsis*) sense: It's built into the system.

---

672   1840 – https://en.m.wikipedia.org_1840 ; last edited 10 November 2022, accessed 5 Apr 23.

673   Free speech – https://www.nytimes.com_americahasafreespeechproblem : "For all the tolerance and enlightenment that modern society claims, Americans are losing hold of a fundamental right as citizens of a free country: the right to speak their minds and voice their opinions in public without fear of being shamed or shunned ... Americans are understandably confused" ; March 18, 2022, corrected March 22, 2022, accessed 5 Apr 23.

Americans are fond of saying that America is an "idea."[674] This rather Platonic sense of statehood shapes most, if not all, the psycho-social behaviors of American citizens. America, as a designation in space/time is an ideal and an idealization. Even the most practical American seeks to be practical (praxis) within the defining boundaries of the ideal. Even the most practical, down-to-earth, "just do it"[675] American citizen is a functional idealist at heart.

The practical idealism of America (the United States of) historically expresses itself best through technical innovation and the general idea of "progress." One might say that the overall character of American culture is one of Progressive Practical Idealism. If there is a way to do anything "better," from the moral realm to the realm of total destruction, Americans will be the ones to discover it.

The "idea," however, remains essentially undefined. For Plato, "the world that appears to our senses is in some way defective and filled with error, but there is a more real and perfect realm, populated by entities (called 'forms' or 'ideas') that are ternal, changeless, and in some sense paradigmatic for the structure and character of the world presented to our senses."[676]

The idealist is an idea-ist in search of the perfect idea. The ideas are "out there somewhere," or "up there," or beneath the appearance of," and so forth. "Up there," for example, can indicate a "heaven" or the "mind" or even the unobstructed will. At any rate, the idea is of much more value and worth than is the given. One might say that the Perfect Idea is the Pearl of Great Price.[677]

---

674 Reed Galen, Steve Schmidt, Stuart Stevens, Rick Wilson, *The Lincoln Project*, 2023 – https://www.lincolnproject_anideacalledamerica : "America is the only country founded on an idea, and it was the most radical idea of its era, the belief that citizens could govern themselves. It was called the American Experiment because there was no reason to believe it would work"; accessed 5 Apr 23.
675 Nike.com
676 Ideas – https://www.plato.stanford.edu_plato ; first published Sat Mar 20, 2004; substantive revision Sat Feb 12, 2022, accessed 5 Apr 23.
677 Matthew 13:45-46

St. Augustine's Perfect Idea is the City of God. This is the city that comes down from Heaven, the City anticipated in the Apocalypse of St. John.[678] It's the city Paul talks about by saying that "our citizenship (*politeuma*) is in heaven, from where also we await for our Savior, the Lord Jesus Christ, who will transform our body of humiliation, so that it may be conformed (*metaschematisei*) to His glorious body, according to the working (*energeian*) of His power even to subdue (*hupotoxai*) all things to Himself."[679]

The idea is, if you will, the city of progress, the one in that "better country" that the saints of ancient times desired, a "heavenly one," a city that God has prepared for them.[680] This city became (*ginomai*) the City on a Hill envisioned by the Puritan John Winthrop in 1630 and re-ideaized by Ronald Reagan in 1989 when he said, "the past few days when I've been at that window upstairs, I've thought a bit of the 'shining city upon a hill' ... in my mind it was a tall, proud city built on rocks stronger than oceans, wind-swept, God-blessed, and teeming with people of all kinds living in harmony and peace; a city with free ports ... and if there had to be city walls, the walls had doors and the doors were open to anyone with the will and heart to get here."[681]

That last idea in the quote has become a central idea in the politics of Postmodern USA. It's an idea which is an integral component of the Idea that is the United States of America, but the question of the larger idea is becoming more and more extended into the realm of the undefined or divergently defined.

One can see the lingering romanticism of the late 18th and early 19th centuries in that speech. There is also the idea of *praxis* building the ideal. The city must be seen for what it is and understood as the Idea that it is. A tainted idea is one that cries out to be re-imagined, but if the rest of the world can't see it, the idea has lost its power. When the outsiders

---

678   Revelation 21:2
679   Philippians 3:20-21
680   Hebrews 11:16
681   Ronald Reagan – https://www.reaganlibrary.gov_farewelladdresstothenation : January 11, 1989, accessed 5 Apr 23.

behold the shining city, they see one city teetering on one side of the hill and another city teetering on the opposite side. At the foot of the hill is the final demise of American romanticism: "Battles are lost in the same spirit in which they are won."[682]

The idea of America is an idea that is fixed in time. This doesn't mean that it must become unfixed, but it does mean that it contains within its original expression little or no defense against newer ideas of state that came after its conception. Again, for Hegel, writing concurrently with that conception, "the state is the divine Idea as it exists on earth."[683] His ideas live on, especially regarding that "a constitution is ... not a matter of choice but depends on the stage of the people's spiritual development."[684] Another way of saying this is that the dialectic governs the choice of a constitution for the State, and the choice is determined by history.

Even Hegel's thinking still contained remnants of Christian thought, Christian ideas and ideals, primarily because of Hegel's own historical situation. Whether or not the remnants of those remnants have anything in common with anything that could be called the Christian Idea is very much open to question in the Postmodern world. According to Heidegger, "the truth of *aisthehsis* (perceiving as such, both by the senses and by the intellect) and of the seeing of 'ideas' is the primordial kind of uncovering."[685] In other words, to "see" an idea is an apocalyptic moment or even action. It would also count as a *kairos* moment.

The idea is seen when it stands alone and unmodified by contingency. Heidegger's notion if the idea is characterized by such evocative phrases as "Can't you see?" or "Don't you see?" The idea discloses itself, but only when assisted by the aggressive action of the intellect. In this sense, Heidegger is still a little bit Thomistic. Reason is always the teeth in the mouth that consumes reality.

---

682   Walt Whitman, *Leaves of Grass*, 1891-1892
683   Hegel, *Reason* ..., p. 53
684   Ibid. p. 60
685   Heidegger, *Being* ..., p. 269

For Whitehead, "Mr. Process," "things which are temporal arise by their participation in the things which are eternal ... the final (telos) entity is the divine element in the world, by which the barren inefficient disjunction of abstract potentialities obtains primordially the efficient conjunction of ideal realization. This ideal realization of potentialities in a primordial actual entity constitutes the metaphysical stability whereby the actual process exemplifies general principles of metaphysics and attains the ends proper to specific types of emergent order."[686] This "emergent order" is, to be sure, always just over the horizon, but for the process thinkers, we can be assured that the emergent order will be the right order. It's a built-in kind of thing, but not in the sense of fundamental ideas: a bit like *que sera sera*. The task of the individual and the State, one must suppose, is to emerge in conjunction with the emergent order.

Once we have investigated all the influences to the common meaning of "idea," then we can stand in awe and wonder before the Idea that is America. Virtually no one thinks like Plato, but every American expects and demands that the Idea which is America be a permanent, unchanging, all-encompassing "thing" that any sensible human being can readily perceive. Yet with the emergence, or final propensity of Thing One and Thing Two, as we have mentioned, the disjunction of which Whitehead speaks does not "efficiently conjoin" ideal realization: Its propensity is to diverge from the agreed-upon narrative of the Idea.

This counter-idealistic centripetal force is built into the foundational structures of the American way of life. Divergence and diversity are the expected qualities to be generated by the Idea, even though the original state of the pre-union consisted of a rather separated string of unities and conf0ormaties that were seeking not a unity on diversity but, rather, a proof that their idea of the Idea was the only true version. The idea of emergence must honor the realities of history, even if they obstruct the hope of synthesis.

It isn't because America is a State that is an idea that provides <u>continuity for </u>the commonweal in terms of self-identity and fixed

686   Whitehead, *Process and ...*, p. 40

government: The ideal character of the United States of America is precisely that aspect of the emergent United States that requires, even demands, a disparity of devotionally embraced ideals. In the postmodern, post-Heideggerian world, the only way to fuse diversity into a unity is by force or by a corporate and universally accepted agreement to dispense with the totalities form which present ideals of State have been formed and make do with the uncertainty of living in a system that has no definite purpose or intention.

If there are no boundaries to liberty of opinion, there is no discernable Idea. A State cannot exist even in principle without boundaries, especially soul boundaries.

Part Four: NO DIRECTION HOME

Chapter One: THE TRAGIC AND THE COMIC

How does it feel, how does it feel? To be on your own, with no direction home, a complete unknown, like a rolling stone.[687]

THESE WORDS were written and sung by the 2016 Nobel Prize in Literature winner, Bob Dylan. The prize was awarded "for having created new poetic expressions within the great American song tradition."[688] In other words, the prize has to do with language, how it is used and what meaning is conveyed through that use. The fact that virtually every commentary you might choose to read on your Google search for "Bob Dylan" has an utterly different cultural 'take' on the lyrics.

While it isn't true that you can make the Bible mean anything you want it to mean, the meaning conveyed through its words, phrases and descriptions is all-embracing. It penetrates the mind, heart and the 'gut feelings' in ways that check and balance them as well as bringing them together so that one can carefully observe one's own soul. Dylan's lyrics do that, too. His music and lyrics penetrated the mind, heart and gut feelings in the moment, and they still do. It is in this sense that his contribution to Western Civilization participates in *kairos*.

---

687   *Like a Rolling Stone*, Bob Dylan, 1965
688   Bob Dylan – https://en.m.wikipedia.org 2016nobelprizein-literature ; last edited 18 February 2023, accessed 6 Apr 23.

"How does it feel?" is the great existential question for Western Civilization in the post-60s era. Because society has not yet seen how to go 'beyond' the 60s and is still trying to justify its own behavior and speculations from that moment in time, this *kairos* moment still abides. It's just being extended in our time such that we have time to understand it in God's time.

The Mind was the "strange attractor"[689] of the 17-18th century; the Heart was the "strange attractor' of the 18-19th century: Gut Feeling is the strange attractor of the 20-21st century, especially following the last gasp of heartfelt conviction that constitutes mid-20th century Western Christian Culture. It's not that the time to unify mind, heart, and gut feeling has arrived: Gut feeling is all we have left. It defines the times: Even the President of the United States relies on gut feelings.[690]

Gut feelings constitute a type of "phase space" in Dasein: "In dynamical systems theory and control theory, a phase space or state space is a space in which all possible 'states' of a dynamical system or a control system are represented, with each possible state corresponding to one unique point in the phase space."[691] Gut feelings, in another language, are like just dropping in to see what condition your condition is in.[692]

---

689 Gleick, *Chaos*, pp. 134, 261: "The strange attractor lives in phase space, one of the most powerful inventions of modern science. Phase space gives a way of turning numbers into pictures, abstracting every bit of essential information from a system of moving parts, mechanical or fluid, and making a flexible road map to all its possibilities 134 Just as turbulence transmits energy from large scales downward through chains of vortices to the dissipating small scales of viscosity, so information is transmitted back from the small scales to the large ... and the channel transmitting the information upward is the strange attractor, magnifying the initial randomness just as the Butterfly Effect magnifies small uncertainties into large-scale weather patterns."

690 Yasmeen Abutaleb, *Washington Post*, April 3, 2023 at 5:00 a.m. EDT – https://www.washingtonpost.com_onjforeignpolicybidensgutishisguide ; accessed 6 Apr 23.

691 Phase space – https://en.m.wikipedia.org_phasespace ; last edited 31 March 2023, accessed 6 Apr 23.

692 *Just Dropped in (to See What Condition My Condition Was In)*, Kenny Rogers, 1968

Just as one might wonder what these song lyrics and scientific nomenclatures really mean, one might wonder what even a close friend is meaning these days in the use of words, of language, that once seemed familiar, comprehending of the "given," and essentially intelligible. The language game your friend is caught up in may or may not be the language game you are caught up in. This condition leads first to confusion, then to miscommunication, then to irresolvable differences in meaning, then finally to civilizational unintelligibility. Eventually, as the song says, you are "on your own with no direction home."

To use, or utilize, a language game is not at all to play games with words. Wittgenstein's definition of a language is an operational definition: "To imagine a language means to imagine a form of life ... The word "language-*game*" is used ... to emphasize the fact that the *speaking* of a language is part of an activity, or a form of life."[693] When we talk, in other words, we are engaging in a form of life, expressing it, conveying the whole form of life to another person for comprehension. That form of life might be your job, your religious practices, your bathroom routine, anything at all. What matters is that you are both talking about the same basic form of life. We don't, after all, want to get caught "comparing apples to oranges."

In the Postmodern world, virtually all potentially meaningful conversation amounts to comparing apples to oranges. The language is overloaded with hidden expectations, obscured facticities, ancient allegorizations, similes, and metaphors, such that the very form of life it would take to sort through them all in one conversation would take another eon. In Foucault's version of discourse discontinuities, "the problem arises of knowing whether the unity of a discourse is based not so much on the permanence and uniqueness of an object as on the space in which various objects emerge and are continuously transformed."[694] Conversation as such becomes a type of 'phase space.'

Later in his analysis, Foucault writes that "the analysis of lexical contents does not concern discursive practice as a place in which a tangled

---

693   Wittgenstein, *Investigations*, pp. 11, 15
694   Foucault, *Archaeology*, p. 32

plurality – at once superposed and incomplete – of objects is formed and deformed, appears and disappears ... from the kind of analysis I have undertaken, *words* are as deliberately absent as *things* themselves; any description of a vocabulary is as lacking as any reference to the living plenitude of experience."[695]

The extension of Foucault's problem for the Postmodern world is that the "living plenitude of experience" tends to warp and then to either implode or burst open whenever Thing One tries to talk to Thing Two. They cannot share their plenitudes with each other. There are two plenitudes of experience in Postmodern Western Civilization. But, in terms of the entire flow and trajectory of Western traditions, there can't be more than one plenitude of experience. In the moment, experience contradicts itself and even cancels itself out. This uselessness of language lies at the heart of the divisions which torment Western, and especially American, society today.

There is "no direction home."

In a world full of game players, the only way to set yourself apart is to be a game changer.[696]

EVERYBODY wants to be a game changer. In sports, a game changer is "an athlete, play, etc., that suddenly changes the outcome of a game or contest."[697] In order to win a contest of any kind, you are compelled to strive to be a game-changer and to accomplish game-changing tasks. Game-changing takes place at such a rapid pace these days that an individual game-change hardly counts as a significant change in anything at all. However, in the conglomerate, this obsession with game-changing has become something entirely different, i.e., changing the game.

Imagine, for example, you are in the middle of playing a game of chess. Your opponent has left you a wide-open two-play tactic that will checkmate the opposing king. You make the first move of your winning

695 Ibid., p. 48
696 Game change – https://goodreads.com_mat-shonadhilwayo ; accessed 6 Apr 23.
697 Game changer – https://www.dictionary.com_game-changer ; accessed 6 Apr 23.

strategy and, suddenly, the game itself changes: You are now playing checkers. Your winning move has become an incalculable risk. You can see what a predicament or advantage it has put you in, but you have to reorient yourself right away to playing the different game. Fortunately, the game-board has not changed.

Suppose, then, that you have made your great chess move and, suddenly, you are in the middle of a *Clue* game. The game board is still a square, but it doesn't at all resemble the chess board you were located on a moment before. You still have pieces to move and moves you can make, but they are not at all the same kind of moves with which you had hoped to win the game. This is such a radical change that you really don't even know where you are in it.

Perhaps you are running a race, and you are actually in sight of the finish line. You only have to pass two other racers to win, so you pour on the steam, knowing that you have enough energy left to pass them. Suddenly, you are in a weight-lifting contest. You still need that burst of energy, but now it needs to be used for an entirely different activity. Somebody changed the game.

Try playing football and you go out for the pass, then, suddenly, you are the third baseman and you need to be ready to catch a pop fly. These examples illustrate the change of the game that has been inflicted on Western Christian Civilization in the Postmodern era. The forms of life that the language games reflect are no longer reflected the same way by means of the same language games. You are playing one piece on a playing surface that involves certain rules of play, but the person you are talking to is playing a completely different kind of piece on who knows what kind of playing surface with what kinds of rules.

Imagine if one party in a "free" country is playing the democratic-republic language game and the other party in this "free" country is playing the totalitarian-socialist language game. The word "freedom" and all of its associated expressions will be utilized, but the overall meaning conveyed will be radically different. You think you are both speaking the same language in which the words and phrases convey the same, or identifiable, meaning. You are not.

There is an "end game" to the divergence between those professing Western Christians who use the Bible language game and those who use the Reason language game. It's not as if the word "bible" or the term "biblical" and so forth isn't used in the Reason Language Game, but the uses are entirely at variance with each other. In the end game, neither the Bible Language Game faction nor the Reason Language Game faction are speaking the previous blended language. The game itself has changed, but it has changed in such a subtle way that neither faction knows they are not speaking the old blended, or married, language. There has been a decreed divorce. The Civilization itself has decreed it.

The brilliance of Michel Foucault subsists neither in his objectivity nor in his subjectivity: It is in his accurate perception of the pending failure of discourse itself in Western Civilization. He writes, "Discourse is not the majestically unfolding manifestation of a thinking, knowing, speaking subject, but, on the contrary, a totality. In which the dispersion of the subject and his discontinuity with himself may be determined." To sway back into Heideggerland, we might say that Dasein is in the discourse, not the discoursing entity. We exist in and only in our discourse.

Foucault goes on to say, "It is a space of exteriority in which a network of distinct sites is employed." We jump from discursive island to discursive island, laying claim to the territory as we speak. "It (is) neither by 'words' nor by 'things' that the regulation of objects proper to a discursive formation should be defined; similarly, it must now be recognized that it is neither by recourse to a transcendental subject nor by recourse to a psychological subjectivity that the regulation of its enunciations should be defined."[698] We talk our way into an objective truth that is constantly being re-formed by the conversation itself.

This is why those who were committed to "finding themselves" in the 1960s never found anything. Life is a journey, but it's a journey that starts nowhere and ends right where it started.

698   Foucault, *Archaeology*, p. 55

The meaning of life, if there can be such a 'thing,' takes place in and only in the discourse. If it only has subjective meaning, it has no real meaning, and if it has only objective meaning, it has no meaning. Even if one assigns to it a sense of meaning that combines the subjective with the objective, it still has no meaning. Both subject and object are utterly indefinite except in the conversation between them. If there is a transcendent realm, this is where it exists. This is where God is.

This should come as no surprise to Christians: Jesus is Logos, Word. He isn't language, or "words": He is the Word, "in the beginning with God" who is God. In order to come into being, the Word must be proclaimed. When the proclaimed Word is heard and received and accepted, then Dasein comes to be (*ginomai*) as well: That self we were all searching for in the 60s is found. The Gospel is Christian discourse: The Bible is the finished and permanent record of Judeo-Christian discourse.

To come to faith, to receive Jesus as your Lord and Savior, is to find yourself in the midst of that discourse alongside Jesus. It's not just a game changer, it's a change of the game itself. The language game of the Word isn't a language game of the world.

There is no deep structure of the biblical language in the sense that if we could fathom its deep structure we could really understand its meaning. Biblical language is the deep structure of all the other languages.[699] It's the Alpha and Omega language, and its intelligibility underlies and undergirds all intelligibility.

Bible talk is the language of the Deep.

The sea is everything. It covers seven tenths of the terrestrial globe. Its breath is pure and healthy. It is an immense desert, where man is never lonely, for he feels life stirring on all sides.[700]

---

699 See footnotes 508-510.
700 Jules Verne, *20,000 Leagues Under the Sea*, 1870

JULES VERNE was the modern West's proto-psychologist. He has since been replaced by H. P. Lovecraft, the West's anti psychologist.

When Verne wrote his 20,000 Leagues Under the Sea, Prussia was in the process of defeating France, a defeat that was a premonition of WWI. Verne died before the Great War to End All Wars, so he didn't live to see that war could never resolve the real differences which exist between the Nations. The first appearance of the great monster of the deep, Cthulhu, was revealed by Lovecraft in 1928.[701] After WWI, nobody could deny the mesmerizing deep-structural effects of horror.

Let's see what else happened, or came to pass (*ginomai*), in 1928. The Ford River Rouge Complex at Dearborn was completed; Charles Lindbergh was presented with the Medal of Honor; the Muslim Brotherhood was founded in Egypt. Margaret Meade's *Coming of Age in Samoa* was published; *The Threepenny Opera* [702] opened in Berlin; Joseph Stalin launched his first five-year plan. Herbert Hoover was elected President of the United States; Mickey Mouse appeared in *Steamboat Willie*; and the construction of Boulder Dam, known now as Hoover Dam, was approved by Congress. All of these changes changed the world. The Postmodern world would never have taken form without them.

All this is to say that the emergence of Cthulhu from the deep is a benchmark in psycho-social history. Fascination with Cthulhu is being reinvigorated even as we speak, so to speak.[703] Cthulhu is the archetypal representation of postmodern fear, the overcoming of which is accomplished responding positively to the Call of Cthulhu. The cult of

---

701   H. P. Lovecraft, *The Call of Cthulhu (Weird Tales)*, 1928
702   AUTHOR'S NOTE: Most of us recognize Berthold Brecht's work via the song *Mack the Knife*.
703   Cthulhu – https://www.villains.fandom.com_cthulhucult : "The Cthulhu Cult was founded around the same time as mankind first appeared on earth by the Great Old Ones. Its purpose was to serve the Old Ones on earth until such a time as they could be freed, and then to free the Old One Cthulhu and bring about the end of the world"; accessed 7 Apr 23.

Cthulhu is demonstrably and admittedly an anti-Christ cult.[704] Harmless enough at first glance, it is just one among many in an age that has lost its zeal for Christian sacrifice, Christian morality, and Christian humility. Sadly, history justifies this loss by becoming, in the 20th and 21st centuries, anti-history.

To be free from the dictates of Jesus in the Postmodern Higher-Critical World is to be free from the compulsive and compelling historical tenets of Western Christian Civilization. The totalities of history, long assured by Christian historians working to justify their own approaches to history, have been exposed for their discontinuities. This exposure isn't an evil thing: It is an essential component of Apocalypse.

The greatest discontinuity of Western Christian history is the spectacle of Christian Nations trying their best to utterly destroy each other between 1914 and 1918. This corporate and inter-corporate event flows seamlessly from the preceding wisdom of the Civilization. In spirit, they did destroy each other, but, akin to Lazarus, they are always being called out of the burial cave for temporary resurrection life.

The PERIOD on this disaster is the invention of the atomic bomb. The atomic bomb represents the ability of a Nation to resist the attempted destruction of Nations. That it is a self-destructive as well as an other-destructive act is lost in the ever-changing flux of re-languaged ideologies circling around an infinitely authoritative strange attractor.

All nations need to have the bomb in order to protect themselves from nations that have the bomb. The fact that the uber-powerful nations that have the bomb are the ones trying to restrict the bomb-less nations from the same privilege only exaggerates the split in the soul that torments Western Civilization in the Postmodern Era.

As one social commentator has put it, "The more that irrational terror is captured in the safe container of some interior, behind a fence or inside a shell or in a clearly defined 'problem.' The more concentrated

---

704   Cthulhu – https://www.reddit.com_theofficialcultofcthulhuasksifyouhavebeencalled ; accessed 7 Apr 23.

and literal – that is, physical – the terror will become. More and more terror has to be packed into concrete things that we can handle according to our schemes, if the realm of freedom from the terror surrounding us is to be enlarged. The utmost result to date of this endeavor to create a world of salvation no longer embedded in and thus exposed to terror) is the nuclear bomb, into and behind whose shell has been collected and concentrated all the terror that previously had been *spread out* all over the world."[705]

The writer compares the atomic bomb with the allegedly conquered natural wilderness which human beings feared in primordial times. He asks, "What is the bomb? It is the wild in its modern guise, our twentieth-century version of all-encompassing wilderness, its last remnant ... It is the only place left today where we can authentically house and deposit our anxiety. It is our last *genuine* and *real* connection to something bigger and more powerful than we."[706] Without the nuclear bomb, primordial terror of the unknown past, present, and future becomes Cthulhu.

In the meantime, the bomb is our Exodus and our Crossing of the Red Sea. Awareness of its power and which nation can wield it is the central awareness of the Postmodern human being, the foundation of Dasein and the threat of non-Being reified. Without the bomb, the only thing left to really fear is each other. The bomb bridges the great deep that exists between us, but it's a bridge that can never be crossed. It's the bridge that troubles the waters, not the bridge over troubled waters.[707]

Those who are devoted to the ideals of freedom and justice seek to cross the waters of division by means of a bridge that connects "what should have been" with "what is becoming." Crossing the bridge would be the end of the journey to the Promised Land, the land for which the fall in the Garden never happened. Yet the troll who lives under the

---

705   Wolfgang Giegerich, *Facing Apocalypse: Saving the Nuclear Bomb* (Dallas, TX: Spring Publications, Inc., 1987), pp. 106-107
706   Ibid. p. 107
707   *Bridge Over Troubled Water*, Simon & Garfunkel, 1970:
"Like a bridge over troubled water, I will ease your mind."

bridge is the spirit of self-destruction,[708] and the transition that can be engineered by the human will is no more reliable than 'Galloping Gertie' across the Tacoma Narrows.[709]

Nevertheless, the biblical concept of hope, liberation and justice cherished in the Western tradition is that of the Exodus from Egypt. The fact that the abiding hope of the Postmodern world is that of avoiding international self-destruction is overlooked, over-templated by the false hope that a bridge can be built over the Red Sea that will not collapse. If God isn't going to part the waters, in other words, human ingenuity will do the job.

The elements of salvation that the manipulators of biblical metaphors unintentionally, or unconsciously, miss or overlook are the other three expressions and actions, *Praxis*, that are presented to us in the Scriptures, that is, the absoluteness of the Flood, the Exile, and the Creation itself. Each historico-theological revelation involves an end and a beginning, in between which is a hidden transition. Each one involves a re-manifestation of the Word, the Logos, and a re-imagining of the world.

The moment that Noah opens the door of the ark is the first moment, the *Arche*, of a new world. Only the fundamental human archetypes remain in Noah's heart. His mind is immediately focused on the new. The moment the People of God cross between the parted waters of the Red Sea is the first moment, the Arche, of a new world. The mind of the People is immediately focused on the fact that they are in a wilderness

---

708   Krueger, *From the Fords*..., p. 298: "The old, 'modern' ways of doing theology erect gates in front of that bridge the Three Billy Goats need to cross. They attempt to reduce the surprise waiting under the bridge ... No one is allowed to pass through the gate unless they satisfy the expectations of the domesticated troll who now lives in the guardhouse and earns an honest living.".

709   Galloping Gertie – https://en.m.wikipedia.org_tacomanarrows-bridge(1940) : "It opened to traffic on July 1, 1940, and dramatically collapsed into Puget Sound on November 7 of the same year ... it was the third-longest suspension bridge by main span, behind the Golden Gate Bridge and the George Washington Bridge ... from the time the deck was built, it began to move vertically in windy conditions, so construction workers nicknamed it **Galloping Gertie** ... The bridge's main span finally collapsed in 40-mile-per-hour winds"; last edited 15 January 2023, accessed 7 Apr 23.

and that they are safe, two contradictory impressions. The archetypal structures of being human and the mnemonic structures of the time of Joseph remain in their hearts. The moment the people of Israel and Judah, a divided moment, are carried into submission in Assyria and Babylon is the first moment, or Arche, of a new world. Everything the national mind must grasp, understand, and faithfully act in, is at variance with everything they have learned to understand, grasp, and act in. Their hearts become fixated on David, and not even the graciousness and liberality of Cyrus can break that fixation. David, in the form of Messiah, becomes the one who can save Israel from the world itself.

When Judah tries to save itself by rebuilding the temple and attempting to re-build the Kingdom, Judah fails. If this was the will of God to rebuild, it was before its time. Rather, however, God does the rebuilding in the way He sees fit. God's re-imagining of the world begins with the cross of Christ, but the finishing up of the walls of the New Jerusalem waits until the Eschaton.

There is no body of water to cross when the Temple and the City are destroyed in 70 CE. There has been a flood, the Red Sea, the Jordan River, and the river Chebar, but the continuance of the Jewish Nation is achieved by dispersion. It's impossible to violate a phenomenon that has no boundaries: The inheritors of the Promises, the *genea* of Israel, became, for all intents and purposes (*telos*) ubiquitous. They became everywhere and nowhere at the same time or moment.

Like that primordial living cell that incorporated the sea into its own defining boundaries, the remnant of Judah contains the sea that was there from the beginning. Christians must cross the sea, must pass through, must cross the river, but they must access the Ark that is Israel to do so. That ark is Jesus who alone can authorize the blessings and promises of God to Israel, because He is of the lineage of Judah and David. Paul crossed the waters of the Mediterranean Sea,[710] but the Jews no longer need an ark: They carry the sea itself in their hearts.

---

710 Krueger, *From the fords...*, p. 311: "Mar Nostrum would become the Chronic Sea of changes, the waters of original chaos beneath which God and humanity become indistinguishable. As with the warriors of

"Many waters cannot quench love, neither can floods drown it ... Who is that coming up from the wilderness ... Look, it is the litter of Solomon!"[711]

The game of history is always played by the best and the worst over the heads of the majority in the middle ... Thye discarded and rejected are often the raw material of a nation's future ... The stone the builders reject becomes the cornerstone of a new world.[712]

IF HISTORY SPEAKS with the authority of God, as the higher critics of the Bible profess, history spoke with a loud declaration in 1948. There was a "coming-to-pass," an expression of *ginomai*. It involved the nations in unity and in conflict: It was a gathering of Nations, but not the one anyone expected. The coming-to-pass itself took 1,948 years. It's a coming-to-pass which, like the birth of Jesus, covers all the bases of meaning and truth and purpose . . . almost. The "almost" means that it is still coming to pass.

Like Cyrus and like Augustus Caesar, the world spoke a word, and something started to happen (*ginomai*). The likening, as such, is historically undeniable. They were the World in those days, and the world still speaks. There is a popular illusion that says the world speaks in many voices. This is not true: The voice of the world, like the voice of God, is unitary, and it always says the same thing, "Let there be," *genehthehtoh* (*ginomai*), come into being!

When God isn't the speaker, nothing comes into being, things just happen.

The Postmodern world struggles between the belief that everything that happens is random, a matter of probabilities, and that intentionality

---

Ephraim, Paul's crossing would be irreversible. The hoped-for return to Zion, Temple and Kingdom became a hoped-in advance toward Zion, Temple and Kingdom. God, sinking to the ocean floor and flying away into the sky, would, in time, fade into the Great Intermission, becoming more and more a hidden and unknowable force and intelligence parting the shared waters of divinity and humanity in the timeless and time-consuming eternal quest to find dry land on the other side of the sea."

711   Songs 8:7 and 3:6, 7
712   Eric Hoffer, *The True Believer* (New York: HarperPerennial ModernClassics, 1951), pp. 24, 25

is at the heart of justice. The idea that things just happen embraces an understanding of life that extends far beyond the determinations of mere fate: It means that there is no such thing as fate, and there is especially no such phenomenon as destiny. Where a nation ends up is its destiny, but there is no pre-established reason why it ended up there. We only know a nation's destiny when it no longer exists as a nation.

Noah was the destiny of all the nations before the flood. Slavery in Egypt was the destiny of the Twelve Tribes of Israel. Exile was the destiny of the Kingdoms of Israel and Judah. A return to an insecure quasi-national state of being was the destiny of exiled Judah. The destiny of that insecure quasi-national state of being was its disappearance into every other nation's state of being.

When these disparate destinies are combined into a singular narrative, the narrative speaks of a historical continuity that defies the end-ness of each of the Jewish Nation's incarnations. Each narrative is full of purpose and populated with intentions, and each narrative expresses a *telos*, a finality. No preceding narrative contains any predictive power over the succeeding narrative: Each narrative could have become the end game, the concluded narrative of the Jews.

The phenomenon that guarantees the next narrative in the longer account isn't some kind of continuous totality of Nation-ness or national identity. The national identity, in fact, changes radically from one narrative to the next. No, there is no auto-determinacy to the continuity of Israel from the time of Joseph to the time of David to the time of Cyrus and to the time of Jesus: They are part of a whole by and only by means of resurrection. Resurrection belongs to God.

It's easy for Postmodern Christians to understand the Exodus as a type of resurrection. In fact, the imagery of Exodus undergirds the entire scope of Christian theology. It so undergirds Western Christian theology in terms of history and individual existence that the culture is unable to envision or imagine any variant expression of resurrection. This perceptual and conceptual phenomenon, this subject/object preoccupation with the role of history and of personal identity creates a blind spot in Western Christian morality, ecclesiolatry, and ideology that cannot see the grace of God in the idea that a nation can come to an end. A Christian Nation must, in other words, be eternal, forever, because it is a Christian nation and because Jesus Christ is now and forever.[713]

The Late Roman Empire under Justinian held the belief in National Eternity, one that was inherited from classical Rome. The Byzantine Empire believed it would last forever, even when it was clear that it would not. The Holy Roman Empire believed that it would last forever, but it got quickly parceled out to various competitors. And, last but surely not least, the British Empire thought it would last forever, conquering even the cycle of sunrises and sunsets.

In effect, it's impossible to construct an empire unless the leadership and the citizenry hold to a common belief that it will last forever. This belief isn't limited to Christian empires. It's a belief that cannot tolerate a national boundary in time, or even one that stays fixed for generations. Europe tried the Nation-State model, but the national boundaries have never been permanently understood. The belief that one's Nation will last forever is a belief that also denies resurrection.

The strength of the Nation of Israel abides not in the belief of individual Jews that the nation will last forever but in the confidence that the promises of God will not fail to be fulfilled. Except perhaps in a rudimentary or even unconscious sense, it's doubtful that any individual Hebrew of Jew believed that the Nation constituted of the Twelve Tribes would live forever. They did, however, believe the promises of God, and over time, it became clear that these promises involved types of national resurrection.

It was the character of the Hebrew/Jewish Nation that was immutable, not its form, its topology. Outwardly, its character appeared as that of a unity of tribes, then a mass of powerless slaves, then a wandering proto nation, then a conquering horde, then a bucolic spiritual confederation, then a kingdom, then a divided kingdom, then an enclave encysted within

---
713   Hebrews 13:8

an alien environment. When the chrysalis that was Babylon-Persia gave way to the Israel beneath, it was prep time for the experimental Nation of the Maccabees and Pharisees to learn how to become a nation entirely dispersed.

In history, a nation entirely dispersed isn't a nation at all. In God, a Nation is what it is because God ensures that it remains what it is. The continuities that seem to indicate a totality called the Chosen People of God, a totality the fiction of which can be seen in the use of the word "then", as if one incarnation melded or evolved into the next by some kind of spiritual-historical-anthropological process, are continuities only by virtue of the continued existence, or *dasein*, of the Nation as a Nation. The only sure evidence that the Nation has continued characteristically from beginning toward end is the Bible.

With every resurrection state of the Nation of Israel the individual citizens of that City of God had to ask the fundamental question, "Who am I?" The identity of the Hebrew self in the time of Jacob could not be the identity of the Hebrew self in the time of Joshua. It is the transformation of personal identity between one national incarnation and the next which remains the existential mystery regarding the promises of God to His People. The identity of the Hebrew Self in the Postmodern World is an identity that is in a state of resurrection. This is something Western Christians can recognize, but only if they can throw of the yoke of being an eternally existing Christian Nation.

As the quote which begins this chapter suggests, the best and worst of this Christian Nation will try their best to make history follow the path they belief has been set for the country. That there is some hope for a middle world, a type of Middle Earth, so to speak, to rise up and shake off the best and the worst (depending on your version of Good and Evil) is implied, but this shaking off becomes more and more problematic as the gap between ideological choices becomes more and more a truly empty space.

Where there is no middle ground, the middle has no *dasein*: It doesn't exist.

The spirit of liberal America desires to shake off the spirit of conservative America: The spirit of conservative America wants to shake off the spirit of liberal America. In the end, fast approaching, Thing One and Thing Two are both wild things who have nothing essential to say about how God intends to fulfil His promises to Israel.

Dasein, personal existence and legitimacy, disappears in the void between the generated chaos of Thing One and the generated chaos of Thing Two. This existential state leads to the present anxiety and desperation revealed in Identity Politics. Yet, it remains impossible to discover, construct, or formulate a valid identity within the whole if there is no identifiable factor that transforms the whole into a totality. Identity becomes a constantly fading chimera, whether it is the identity of the self or the identity of the state. Both state and citizen become "a thing that is hoped or wished for but in fact is illusory or impossible to achieve."[714]

The chimeric is not what Hegel had in mind, but it is where Hegel's state-topological fantasies must inevitably go. Both state and personal identity become formless, like the chaos, the dark sea, over which the spirit of God brooded at the beginning of "thingness" itself. In the midst of these chimeric comings-to-be and comings-to-nought,[715] horror and glory vie for supremacy of soul and state in a way utterly predetermined by the civilizational praxis we call World War One.

Out of World War One and World War II, like a flight of twin phoenix birds, emerges Messianic America and Resurrected Israel.[716] The other nations remain the same.

---

714 Chimera – https://www.languages.oup.com_chimera ; accessed 9 Apr 23.
715 AUTHOR'S NOTE: This phenomenon is reminiscent of and prescient regarding the ancient and mostly hidden mystical tradition in the West of combining Being and Nonbeing, the ultimate synthesis. It never takes shape, because the topology of national identity can't survive that much deformation.
716 Aliyah – https://www.israelforever.org_thebackdropofjewishsettlementtheearlyaliyot : "The migration known as the First Aliyah ran from 1892-1903 ... these pioneers established the early rural settlements

*'Tis only we who know the law (Wadaman Dreamtime laws), who hold him there in the old sky track. Without us none can hold him back. Then as he springs, and all goes black, this earth will shudder, the trees come down; and over the noise you will hear our cry: We'll cry for you as you pass away; we'll laugh at you as you pass away.*⁷¹⁷

THE END OF A WORLD is always tragicomic. Even primordial religion understood this inevitable truth. Mentioned previously, "A world embraces the what and how of knowing. The fear of an end to the what and how of knowing demands a response. The response of a fearful society takes the form of an eschatological strophe, an end-time consciousness (cata-strophe). This consciousness can be tragic or comedic. For those who feel it is tragic, there is no reason to laugh; for those who feel it is comedic, there is no point in worrying about it."⁷¹⁸

Conscious effort doesn't cause a civilization to come to an end, and conscious effort won't make it stop coming to an end. In terms of God's *Praxis*, coming-to-an-end (*teleiohnoh*) is the ultimate expression of coming-to-pass. To come to an end is to reach that fine line of perfection that hovers between the waters above and the waters below. One might call it 'balance,' but balance in the moral sense implies something like an equal amount of Good and Evil. The word equilibrium is more expressive: Equilibrium is a balancing act with respect to many forces moving in all directions and from all directions.

A civilization or commonweal that has come-to-an-end is one that has reached its point or moment of equilibrium: Anything more or anything less in terms of its moral and social being would result in the destruction or eclipsing of its purpose (*telos*) altogether. The antediluvian world came to an end; the world of the Twelve Tribes in pre-bondage Canaan came to an end; the world of the conquest and establishment

---

called 'moshavot' ... The Second Aliyah was an important and highly influential emigration of Jews that took place between 1904 and 1914 ... Many future leaders of Israel came with the Second Aliyah ... both Aliyot ... helped create the new Jewish Yishuv in Eretz Israel, which eventually established the State of Israel in 1948"; accessed 9 Apr 23.

717   Mike Perlman, *Facing Apocalypse: When Heaven and Earth Collapse, Myths of the End of the World – Native Australian World-Endings*, ibid. *Facing...*, p. 163

718   Krueger, *Conundrums...*, p. 3

of the kingdoms came to an end. The World of Exile has yet to come to an end.

Because no civilization or world wishes to come to an end, God places forces into its window, its consciousness and its unconsciousness, its objective situation and its subjective orientation, to fix the end in time such that the next resurrection can be free of the encumbrances that might have followed the soul of the nation into its new mode of being. The flood, the time of slavery in Egypt, the forced exile and destruction of the emblems of faith and national unity and identity, all are ways to complete the picture, the narrative, to fix the picture in a way that satisfied everything that it was intended to picture. No picture pictures everything, but each picture in and of Kairos reveals enough.

When a world comes to an end, the what and the how of knowing that has been effective and utilitarian in that world ends as well. Like a newborn child, the citizen of the new world who has been transitioned to the new world has no instinctive or innate idea of what to do or how to do it. All the exiles could do by the waters of Babylon was weep.[719] All that Noah could think to do after building the first altar was to get drunk.

None of the socio-political-psychological instincts that a member of the tribe of Judah would have developed in the days of the kings, would be effective, helpful, or even much beyond self-destructive in the new environment and situation of being exiled in the midst of Babylon. And so, the beginning is just as senseless as the end, and the end is just as senseless as the beginning, even though what went down in between the last beginning and the present end made sense. When sense has been sated, the only advance of the senses is overdose.

End-time consciousness is a scary thing. It is a phobia in and of itself. It could be called *metaphobia* or *teleiophobia*. Heidegger might call it fear of existence or *daseinophobia*. Other manifestations of end-time consciousness would be fear of being oneself, fear of losing oneself, fear of having no identity at all, fear of finding out that everything you know is untrue, and so forth. The Bible tells us that perfect love (*teleia agapeh*)

[719] Psalm 137:1

casts out fear[720]: The contrary to that truth would be that perfect fear veils love.

It is very difficult to cast out something that is veiled, even from the perception of the castee. The veil must be removed, and only the Cross of Christ can do that. We cannot create our own apocalypses.

Fear, as *phobia*, isn't the same as being afraid that someone or something might hurt you or even kill you. The right combination of will, purpose, and values can provide the motivation to overcome that kind of earthly fear. *Phobia*, the Bible tells us, "has to do with punishment,"[721] punishment for the committing of sin. Perfect love, then, is the love of Jesus expressed on the Cross.

You don't need to know what to do in the realm of perfect love: The Holy Spirit will guide you and give you right words. If you think you know what to do in a Kairos moment, as part of the *ginomai*-expressive plan of salvation at a given time and place, you have already sinned: The plan is God's, and the acceptance and receipt of God's perfect love is the gateway to fulfilling the plan.[722]

Perfect love is also not expressible in any kind of law. One a law is in place, fear of punishment has already been given life. When there is no recourse but to obey the law, there can be no perfect love: The possibility, indeed, the inevitability of punishment is always before the window of the soul under law. Punishment or not-punishment is the only choice that can be made.

There is no need for forgiveness in a legal system, only a deformation of consequences. The guilt of sin is always present because there is no savior, no removal of slavery to the law.

But even a freedom from slavery to the law is mitigated by existence in the godless philosophy of late modern metaphysicians. This is what

---

720   I John 4:18
721   I John 4:18
722   James 4:13-16

Heidegger, the Nazi metaphysician, was getting at when he wrote, Being-guilty does not first result from an indebtedness, but ... on the contrary, indebtedness becomes possible only 'on the basis' of a primordial Being-guilty."[723]

He goes on to say, "In being a basis – that is, existing as thrown – Dasein constantly lags behind its possibilities. It is never existent *before* its basis, but only *from it* and *as this basis* ... not belongs to the existential meaning of 'thrownness.' It itself, being a basis, *is* a nullity of itself."[724] Those italicized words in Heidegger are always more significant than the unfolding of the argument itself. There is an existential emphasis behind his formulation of real existence that belies the adequacy of the written word to convey meaning. It makes his stuff difficult to follow and to understand, but the "oomphs" of emphasis do add up over time, leading to a great oomph which he expresses as *"Dasein as such is guilty."*[725]

You are guilty because and insofar as you exist. Being guilty is a primary aspect of who you are. In effect, when you exercise your freedom by making a choice, you are guilty of not choosing the many or even infinite alternate choices. In this way, you deny Being in the sense that you have chosen not to become in the fullest sense of the word. You deny birth to the world that could have come-to-pass. You also limit the world of your companions, other Daseins.

If a friend would have chosen the world that you have denied so that the friendship could be sustained, that choice is forever nullified by your choice. We are hemmed in by each other's systemic choices in such a way that we are always guilty, not of something, but existentially. The guilt can't go away. To be is to be guilty.

To clarify: You are guilty no matter what choices you make. The extension of this principle is that it doesn't matter to "reality", moral, physical, material, what choices you make: What matters is the form of guilt that you choose. One might understand this as a choice of who to

---

723   Heidegger, *Being...*, p. 329.
724   Ibid., p. 330
725   Ibid., p. 331

be friends with. No matter which choices you make, however, you will still and always be in "bad company."

One cannot but recognize the vague, or "canny," to use a favorite term of his, the vaporous remains of Christian theology and anthropology in Heidegger's understanding of guilt. It's a bit like the doctrine of Original Sin, but it involves no God to whom to sin against. With no God to sin against, the guilt devolves onto the self as a permanent aspect of Dasein, or selfness. It is not something that can be removed: It's just "the way things are."

In his monumental metaphysical discourse, Heidegger put away the idea that traditional Christianity contains anything of ultimate meaning or a complete description of reality, but he gives it a rather perfect metaphysical expression by saying that "both the contention that there are 'eternal truths' and the jumbling together of Dasein's phenomenally grounded 'ideality' with an idealized absolute subject, belong to those residues of Christian theology within philosophical problematics which have not yet been radically extruded."[726] Conclusion: As soon as we rid ourselves of Christian tradition, we can idealize the realistically perfect state or condition of Dasein.

For Heidegger, Postmodern Christianity is simply a cultural and metaphysical residue. It is reasonable to expect that it will soon be removed. Then the cup will be clean. We, as in humanity, will be able, once again, to access the primordial originality of Being such that we can become, at last, authentically human. In Christian Evangelical terms, one might call this "choosing to be lost."

There is neither laughter nor sorrow in that choice: Only oblivion. There is no synthesis between the tragic and the comical.

---

726   Ibid. p. 272

Chapter Two: I THINK, THEREFORE, I AM DROWNING

In cognitive dissonance theory, people experience mental discomfort when acting or espousing views conflicting with starting preferences ... Recent research indicates that making a choice or undertaking an action, even blindly or on a whim, can lead to increased preference over time for the chosen alternative and a devaluing of other options.[727]

WE HEAR MUCH about "moving the goal posts" in partisan political discourse these days. In the above quote, Psychology Today has discovered, or re-discovered, Martin Heidegger. In the larger scale of sociological and philosophical change and discourse, the author of that statement may or may not have read Heidegger and may or may not have learned from an expert in her field who has taken Heidegger to heart, but Heidegger is "all over it." The statement about cognitive dissonance, in effect, creates a larger metaphysical cognitive dissonance: It's a dissonance that cannot be alleviated.

The idea that subsequent, even apparently immediately subsequent, "views" might deviate and conflict with starting preferences is simply another way of composing a psychology of chaos theory that smacks of the "butterfly effect." Cognitive Dissonance Theory and Chaos Theory have a place of meeting, a Synagogue of Meaning. We find ourselves gathering in this newly discovered Synagogue of Meaning daily, even hourly.

This dissonance in the hearing and sharing of language is only an expression of a Christian-based language without Christian substance. It becomes especially marked and verging on the intolerable when a biblically minded Christian enters a substantive conversation with a Reason-on-Reason-minded Christian. Discounting for the moment

---

[727] Moving goal posts – https://www.psychologytoday.com_movingthegoalpostscognitivedissonanceandpreferences : "Personal Perspective: Why some people so easily shift their basic principles"; posted September 7, 2022, accessed 10 Apr 23.

that the word "Christian" can, all by itself in stand-alone fashion, create cognitive dissonance, the irredeemable dissonance inherent in Postmodern Western conversation is inevitable and terminal. It's like tinnitus that increases with every word and phrase, like that which drove Beethoven to madness.[728]

Everybody loves listening to Beethoven especially those who are enamored with the glories of Western Civilization. Beethoven presents a remarkably sufficient paradigm for the 19th century Western soul. He was born Catholic, that is, he was initiated into that form of religion by his parents, but Catholicism wasn't the center of his personal piety. He practiced the court religion of Bonn, described as "a compromise ideology that permitted a relatively peaceful coexistence between the Church and rationalism."[729] If you listen intently to Beethoven with a modicum of filial love, you can be deceived into thinking and feeling that the old compromises can still work toward an equitable civilizational future. Music is, after all, seductive.

Once the moral principles that can be reasonably extracted from the biblical revelation have been kneaded into the body of rationalistic discourse, the Western mind quickly forgets that the kind of bread Jesus spoke of is unleavened bread.[730] Reasonable leaven tends to take on a life of its own, as is evidenced in the physical world by the effects of LSD.[731] The sacramental sign of bread remains unleavened, but it is not a sign that points to an unleavened *kerygma*.[732] That bread rises with a force powerful enough to burst the oven.

---

728   AUTHOR'S NOTE: I am personally familiar with this condition.
729   Beethoven – https://en.m.wikipedia.org_ludwigvanbeethoven ; last edited 8 April 2023, accessed 10 Apr 23.
730   I Corinthians 5:8
731   Philip Jenkins, *Encyclopedia Britannica* – https://www.britannica.com_lsd : "can be derived from the ergot alkaloids (as ergotamine and ergonovine, principal constituents of ergot, the grain deformity and toxic infectant of flour caused by the fungus *Claviceps pupurea*) ... LSD produces marked deviations from normal behavior"; last updated Apr 4, 2023, accessed 10 Apr 23.
732   Kerygma – https://www.britannica.com_kerygmaandcatechesis : "Kerygma and catechesis, in Christian theology, respectively, (are) the initial proclamation of the gospel message and the

Because the *kerygma* has become thoroughly leavened in Postmodern Western theological discourse, it can no longer be the *kerygma*. The kerygmatic language game that conveyed the meaning of the proclamation to the ears of civilized Westerners hasn't simply been modified to accommodate discoveries in psychology, sociology and other sciences: The language game of kerygma is becoming and has become an entirely different language game, using as a foundational lexicon the words and phrases of the previous language game. According to the Bible, even a little bit of leaven is too much.[733]

The option to leaven has entirely devalued the option to not leaven the Word of God. The Bible itself, thus, has become the primary cause of cognitive dissonance in postmodern American society. Perhaps listening to Beethoven's Symphony No. 5 at full volume can temporarily overcome the dissonance, but in the end, the cacophony will only increase. The Postmodern "God" IS cognitive dissonance. In the end, even Burroughs' *Naked Lunch*[734] or de Sade's 120 Days of Sodom[735] will be, and is becoming, more acceptable to the "reasonable" than is the Bible.

When Lovecraft blushes, you'll know the End has come.

The leaven of meaning isn't simply words or concepts: It is the entire language game that is played together by a society. It is the spoken and written highway over which meaning is conveyed from soul to soul. The game can be corrupted by inserting clearly contradictory and anathematic playing pieces into the game that tempt the user of the language to further corrupt the modes of play around them, but when the entire game is changed, the corruption cannot be seen for what it is: It looks and feels like reasonable communication.

A language of victory, for instance, inserted into the common language of the day, say, circa 590 CE Judah, would be a corruption of

oral instruction given before baptism to those who have accepted the message"; last updated Jan 04, 2007, accessed 10 Apr 23.
733   Galatians 5:9
734   William S. Burroughs, *Naked Lunch*, 1959
735   Donatien Alphonse Francois Marquis de Sade, *120 Days of Sodom*, 1785, 1904

the language game of faith and devotion that had been played up to that point. The prophet Jeremiah refers to this kind of language corruption as false prophecy. It invites the judgment of the Lord. He writes, "the oracle of the Lord you shall mention no more, for every man's word will be his oracle. For you have perverted the words of the living God, of the Lord of Hosts our God ... I ... will utterly forget you and cast you and the city that I gave you and your fathers out of My presence."[736]

If any "thing," part of reality, phenomenon, concept or idea is cast out of God's presence, it no longer exists: It becomes (*ginomai*) a part of indivisible nonbeing. This is what happened to Jerusalem and Solomon's Temple, as well as the generational leadership of the Tribe of Judah and the House of David, and the sacrificial system of offerings for which the priesthood of the Temple existed. They didn't disappear, as in "hidden": They were gone. Not even an apocalypse could reveal them again: The apocalypse was what had made them gone. The false prophets could speak victory all they wanted, but not a word of their prophecies would prove true.

The reason many postmodern Americans shift their principles in mid-stream is that the principles by which they had lived are gone and not recoverable. The world that rested on those principles is gone and not recoverable. The Temple of Language in which worship, righteousness, choice-making, and so forth found meaning is gone and is not recoverable. But there is nothing for the opponents of Bible-talk to rejoice over: The alternate principles do not exist: Like shape-shifting demons, they come and go as they please, and all they can do is devalue each other.

So, "if you're tired or a bit run down, can't seem to getcha feet off the ground, maybe you oughta try a little bit of L. S. D."[737] On the other hand, "we" already tried that. Now is the time for more serious psychoactive manipulations.

Just lie here and stare out that window at the blue sky framed in glass-jagged mouths. There might have been someone there a moment ago, a scarecrow face looking in at her through the

---

736   Jeremiah 23:36, 39
737   *Acid Commercial*, Country Joe MacDonald, 1968

broken window, watching, waiting, and there might have been nothing but the partitioned swatches of the fading day ... don't look at the windows ever again.[738]

THE LURE of the primordial is the Last Temptation for Western Civilization. The realm of the Primordial is where the Archetypes live. The Archetypes are much more fundamentally signifying human reality, of Dasein, than are even genes and chromosomes. We share that aspect of reality with the plants and animals: The Archetypes, our fantasies tell us, can be ours. With the help of the Archetypes, we can transcend Dasein, our limited existence, and merge with Sein, or Being as such.

According to Heidegger's godless metaphysics, variations of which are shared by late modern Western Christian Civilization in general, Sein, or Being, "cannot be derived from higher concepts by definition, nor can it be presented through lower ones."[739] Being is what God has become in the late Modern World.

The quickest route to postmodern Being is to remove the "I think" from Descartes' original existential algorithm leaving only the "I am" as the remaining truth. In this way, thinking is dependent on the "I am" rather than that the "I am" is evidenced by the fact that I think. Nevertheless, Heidegger can only go so far with his own "I think": He can't enter into Being as such because the entryway is blocked by necessary guilt. Since guilt is the necessary consequence and cause of choice, the only way to avoid guilt in this scenario is to avoid choice.

"I think therefore I am" has become "If I choose to think, I disappear, buried in guilt." No matter what I think, I have not thought "something else." The "something else" vanishes forever: It can never come into being. It can never become at all, especially in the sense of *ginomai*. However, I can still disappear you with the accusation that you have not thought my thought, therefore, you don't exist in my world or reality. Your existence, that is, is more guilt-worthy than mine.

---

738   Caitlin R. Kiernan, *The Book of Cthulhu II: Nor the Demons Down Under the Sea (1957)* (San Francisco: Night Shade Books, 2012), p. 18
739   Heidegger, *Being...*, p. 23

The relativizing of guilt, also a sign of the times, is overcome in the Manichaean Worldview. Evil becomes detectable, and it can be isolated by walls of Good. In the process, the walls of Good themselves define Evil. Once the wall is complete, Evil is defined, restricted, and vulnerable. This is how the citizens of the ancient city of Rome tried to halt the onslaught of civilizational disintegration: This is how any disintegrating civilization tries to resist its own end.

If we are good enough, the city will survive, but we must be good enough to set walls around every possible form of Evil. Therefore, we must identify those forms, as Descartes would say (and Plato might say), clearly and distinctly.[740] The enlightened world will justify itself. The Light of Reason will be vindicated, "by any means necessary."[741] And so it goes.

Heidegger, and all late modern secular philosophical systems, consumes the ancient Christian language of Western Civilization and transforms it into something else. This isn't anything new: It's all part of the "process." It's the Great Metaphysical Digestive Process of Western Civilization, the process by which the dragon consumes the nutrients and then ... well you know the drill. We find postmodern meaning on the surface of a cultural landfill of language game feces.

God hides Himself behind a cloud of guilt barriers according to the Metaphysic of the Modern. "M & M's melt in your mouth, not in your hand," but, like the little scroll, "it will turn your stomach sour."[742] That guilt can be removed, but only by means of an alchemy of words: God must become Being, or even the Ground of All Being. When

740 Descartes – https://www.sparknotes.com_principlesofphilosophyrenesdescartes : ""Clear and distinct perceptions are defined by Descartes as those perceptions which are so self-evident that while they are held in the mind, they cannot logically be doubted"; accessed 11 Apr 23.

741 BAMN – https://www.ballotpedia.org_byanymeansnecesary : "BAMN is a civil rights group active in Michigan and California … The group's name is derived from a slogan popularized in a 1964 speech by Malcolm X in which he said, 'That's our motto. We want freedom by any means necessary. We want justice by any means necessary. We want equality by any means necessary"; accessed 11 Apr 23.

742 Revelation 11:9

The Broken Window

guilt is then removed by further language algorithms neutralizing the moral substance of the revelation, Being can be seized and owned and controlled, and guilt no longer prevents Truth. On the other hand, now she is naked, so she runs away. And she keeps on running: The darkness goes away only to reveal a darker darkness, but the flight takes the woman "into the wilderness where she has a place prepared by God."[743]

With the windowpane of guilt broken, we know longer can discern whether we are looking into the house from outside or out of the house from inside. Suddenly, we are homeless altogether. The sea itself has been conquered, but then there is Cthulhu; "Behold what we hoped to destroy, and what you hope to plunder, and what will bury us all!"[744]

Heaven can be raided, but when you think you are flying upward into the source of the waters above, you find yourself sinking downward, toward the floor of the waters below. This is the Ground of All Being, but when you are underwater, you can't tell down from up. Tillich consumed Heidegger and became a bottom feeder rather than a flying fish. Late Modern Christian Theology is surely tragicomic: It reverses itself all the way back to its prehistoric Greek sources.

The Holy Trinity is, once again, Poseidon, Zeus and Hades. But we all know that these three are the conscious mind, the subconscious mind, and the unconscious mind. Once the algorithms of the State manage and control the subconscious mind, the unconscious mind itself becomes the next crusade. But first, the language game that transports meaning from interior to interior must change, must be transformed. The grammar itself must be transformed.[745] Consciousness must become accustomed to the new grammar.

The new grammar is grounded in the pretension that the violation of heaven can succeed. At present, the constructs of the new grammar are fragmented and disconnected. In rejecting the Western Christian History Totality, they have not the liberated vision to dispense with

---

743 Revelation 12:5
744 Cody Goodfellow, *The Call of Cthulhu II: Rapture of the Deep*, p. 109
745 See footnote 508.

any, even less all, of the alternate totalities that come to mind when the customary Christian Totality is eliminated. This totality is often referred to as the Christian Narrative, but there is a plurality of Christian narratives.

The hoped for New World without Christianity or God can only be fashioned in the absence of any reliance on the traditional cultural totalities that provide connection and meaning to the present narrative. The biblical model that involves a New Being, or *dasein*, a New Heaven, and a New Earth, the totality of which is the New Creation, must be dismantled altogether if deconstruction is to have a chance at making all things new. In the meantime, the old language game of salvation is being stretched to the limit.

The stretching of the Language Game of Salvation is like the stretching of the space-time continuum. It can be deformed, but it will maintain the same topology. But what happens when the space-time continuum is ripped? You get a black hole that absorbs all the light that comes near and radiates no light at all.[746]

Now all these analogies, metaphors, and similes from physics, psychology, and Greek mythology don't provide information regarding the real time consequences of changing the language of salvation within the boundaries of Western Civilization. What they do help us to understand is that there is no light, as in "the light of reason" guaranteed in the results. If Reason is the Light in topological self-similarity to Jesus as the Light of the World, when the Light goes out, the world will become exceptionally dark.

If there is a surviving narrative that can be constructed as a totality, one that gives history the meaning it has been seeking all along, it will be invisible. If it's invisible, it's either hidden or it does not exist. If it's hidden, it will take apocalypse to reveal it, because that's what apocalypse does. If it doesn't exist, it will take a transition from *dasein* to *sein* to

---

746   Kenneth Macdonald, BBC News, 3 October 2012 – https://www.bbc.com_rippingaholeinspaceandtime ; updated 4 October 2012, accessed 11 Apr 23.

overcome the non-Being that it has become. That's what all this fancy metaphyisics is all about, and it governs our sense of self, our sense of community, and our sense of corporate existence.

In the language game of Old Theology, if a "thing" doesn't exist, it means that God is no longer sustaining it. In Bible-talk, it means that God no longer "sees" it. The transition from Old Talk to New Talk looks good, as 'they' say, but you don't get the cigar. When there is no There there, there is nothing there. Such a state of being is impossible to think about. Descartes becomes a cannibalistic suicide case.

The temptation of time is the belief that we can get back to where it all started, and, by that token, fix everything that went wrong.

I think, therefore, the window is broken.

"Reality is merely an illusion, albeit a very persistent one"- Albert Einstein ... "Seeing is believing," right? Not necessarily ... Illusions help neuroscientists unravel the mysteries of how the human brain creates "reality."[747]

WHEN WE LEAP from one language game to another that uses the same words, sometimes we can't leap back to the original language. In the above quote, the word "reality" leaps out, not so much because of its independent power to explain, but because it is connected in use to the authority of the human brain. There are numerous divergences in the fundamental meaning of the word itself that are caused by this iconic leap.

And it's a big one.

From the theological perspective, the brain replaces God. The governing shift that created the new idealized continent of enlightened Western Thought placed God things into the mind. Apart from the secondary fact that this shift led some individuals to believe that they were God, the concept of the "mind" was too big and amorphous to really set it

---

747   Sharon Guynup, *Scientific American*, 1 September 2013 – https://www.sceintificamerican.com_isseeingbelieving ; accessed 11 Apr 23.

apart from the theological, or theistic, God of the Bible. To really bring God down to earth scientifically, God must be material, hence, the brain.

From the empirical perspective, the shift from a mental perspective to a brain perspective involves simply moving the mystery of perception back another notch. Perception of "reality" IS a mystery, but the empirical method cannot tolerate mysteries. A mystery is just an abiding fact or process that hasn't been reasoned out yet. The advantage of moving perception one notch back from mind to brain is that it allows physical manipulation, cutting and refashioning, a place of authority in the processes of knowing. 'Knowing,' then, is dependent on cutting and other surgical or mapping techniques.

Nevertheless, the very clever, and culturally inevitable, gambit of associating knowledge with physical functions doesn't resolve the original question of "where the picture is." This is the old subjectivity problem conveyed by a new language game, but the problem doesn't go away. It seems to bring Subjectivity closer to Objectivity, but that sleight of intellect only seems to bring something closer to something. We still don't know what "reality" is, but we're perfectly happy to enlarge the breach in the windowpane in the attempt to know more.

A sleight of the language-game hand has not created "reality": Rather, it has created a more manipulable hybrid of Subjectivity and Objectivity that moves the mind, now a defunct and obsolete concept, into a given space. And a space can be owned; a space can be leased. A space can be governed. All that remains for Mr. Hegel's pronouncements to be realized is to convince the individual that his or her or 'their' brain is, in fact, the culprit leading them into delusion and illusion. This is done without any change whatsoever is made to the actual field of perception and conception. It simply becomes a basic "fact."

The one ancient quest for Truth that this gambit does NOT answer or even come close to answering is the question of knowledge or knowing. It moves the are of knowing, the essential gnostic aspect of perception, into the realm of the epistemic, of strict cause-and-effect, occupation of space in time, proof by means of the inductive method of experiment and conclusion. It also finalizes the change of the Bible-grounded language games of Western theology, anthropology, history, and psychology from the revelatory realm, or the gnostic, into the epistemic realm, or the medicinal. In this case, the "medicinal" aspect of the cure isn't at all like ancient drug-taking rituals: It is more like telling you that you have the wrong kind of brain.

Once people can be convinced that they have the wrong kind of brain, the art of convincing has no boundaries. The boundary between you and the scientist, between you and the counsellor, and between you and the higher authority that collates the information and manages the processes, is gone. Personal identity enters the realm of politics. Only the brainless fail to understand this necessary change in the methods of Late Modern science.

If your brain fails to satisfy the requirements of your society, you are mentally ill. That illness can't legitimately be cured, because the "mind" doesn't actually "exist." But the brain DOES exist. This means that if the brain is changed, then the mind can be bypassed. The new gambit can even be successfully completed without drugs or cutting.

To be sure, if you are saved from your own mind by means of a methodologically sanctioned process that makes you more "fit" for being a part of the currently valid and agreed-upon social processes, not only is the primary contradiction of the enlightened rational world, the contradiction that identifies the mind with God, overcome, but so is the now outmoded and culturally rejected phenomenon called knowledge, as in gnostic knowing. The Old Knowledge led to you being fit for the given reality in all of its majesty and glory: The New Knowledge just allows you to "fit in."

It is in the above sense, the sense that our primary and traditional language games have been entirely co-opted by a controlling ideal, that reality itself has truly changed. Put in biblical terms, the reality of living in a Kingdom has suddenly and seemingly instantaneously been transformed into the reality of living in exile. These two realities are not knowable in the same way. Reality is now being forced to comply with the dictates of the enlightened soul, and reality's God is being forced to comply as well.

Small shifts in a primary language game of the culture produce large changes in the primary language game of the culture in the future, even the immediate future. The game of words, how it is played, involves its own Butterfly Effect. It's not as if one is being lied to: It's that the game of lying is being changed as well as the game of truth. When someone lies, even deliberately, while still thinking that he is telling the truth, lying has become (*ginomai*) truth-telling. The transition has "come to pass."

All this happens, in the above example, simply because we used the phrase "the human brain creates reality." Someone has given you a tennis racket even though you thought you were playing baseball. Someone has led you into a bottomless pit while you thought you were climbing a mountain.

We are, as a civilization, already so far into that bottomless pit that the light from its opening above is becoming a pinprick of light. If we try to climb out such that there will once again be more light, we find ourselves climbing in reverse again. We find ourselves climbing down, down into the dark recesses of an endless chain of reasons for reasons leading to what looks like a gold mine of Truth but is 'really' a coal mine of breath-stifling pollution.

These deformations, or topological re-shaping, of the common language combine to re-shape the entire civilization. They are symptoms of the re-shaping, to be clear, rather than the cause. To go after each item of deformation in the hope of reversing the topological shift is futile: It's like trying to cure a metastasized cancer one cell at a time, as if each individual cell needed its own customized cure.

In topology, the main topics of interest "are the properties that remain unchanged by ... continuous deformations. A simple example is the shape-change that involves transforming a donut into a coffee cup. They are pretty much the same topology. They have the same fundamental shape even though they don't "look alike." An eye-screw can be transformed into a coffee cup, too![748] They are topologically identical, except that, if you look closely at the language, I have just changed the language game of identity, identifying, comparing, and all manner of other kinds of language games.

Now, consider a pair of scissors. The two arms of the scissor are topologically identical, but together they are not a donut. However, if you look at the open scissor from a certain acute angle, you can manage to cause the one finger hole to coincide in your field of vision with the other hole. They "look like" one hole. So, is the scissor "really" a donut, or is the donut topology an illusion? These are topological questions, but they apply to the shape of society and, eventually, to the shape of the civilization as such.

An example of deformation that exceeds its topological boundaries would be if the donut were to be transformed into a bowl. Better yet, let's transform the coffee mug into a bowl. The change is subtle but think about drinking your soup out of a coffee mug. It usually isn't done because it's a bit inconvenient. But sometimes it is done. Now think of the shape of your entire civilization being pushed beyond its topological restrictions: Is it now the same civilization? Is it, for instance, as convenient as it once was? Do you "fit in" differently, now, or not fit in at all?

Perhaps the language games of your civilization have morphed so radically that you can no longer fit in at all. The shape of your soul is not compatible with the shape of your world. Unless you become a shapeshifter, you will never fit it. And there are "real" limits to how far you can shift the shape of your soul before your soul becomes entirely misshapen.

I think, therefore, I am misshapen.

---

748   Stephen C. Carlson, *Encyclopedia Britannica*, July 26, 1999 – https://www.britannica.com_topology(analysissitus) ; last updated Feb 02, 2023, accessed 12 Apr 23.

The broken narrative is the defining characteristic, spiritually and emotionally, for fundamentalists. The past is bad and worthless, even tainted with death. One yearns for transformation. The individual believer struggles with personal sin, a struggle expressed collectively as a cosmic battle between the forces of good and evil.[749]

THE AUTHOR of the above passage is of the same generation as my older brother. I love my older brother, but we speak different languages. It's funny how that kind of thing works out. Regarding the present categorization of generation (*gennaoh*), I am of the early Boomer Generation while he is of the late Silent Generation. Of course, this categorization is expressed by means of its own language game. There are other ways to categorize people, many, many other ways.

The idea of a Generation Gap is a new and novel concept or mode of speaking. It's not something bult-in, as if Fathers and Sons were never close to each other in any way: It's a cultural assignment that follows topologically the subtle and not-so-subtle changes in society from one span of time to the next. When my older brother was born, World War Two was still in full swing. Imagine the status and quality, the shape, of the conversation into which he was immersed from the beginning of his life.

On November 26, 1944, German forces had evacuated from Estonia. Two days later, the American sub *Archerfish* sank the Japanese aircraft carrier *Shinano*, "the largest carrier built to this date." Toscanini led a concert of Beethoven's *Fidelio* as a tribute to the people of Germany oppressed by Hitler; the Soviet government changed place names in the Crimea from Turkish to Russian. Then on December 16, Germany began the Ardennes offensive to the surprise of the wh0ole world, and the next day several hundred American POWs were executed by 1ˢᵗ SS Panzer Division forces at Malmedy, Belgium.[750]

---

749   Charles B. Strozier, *Apocalypse: On the Psychology of Fundamentalism in America* (Boston: Beacon Press, 1994), p. 54
750   1944 – https://en.m.wikipedia.org_1944 ; last updated 30 March 2023, accessed 12 Apr 23.

Imagine the cultural disorientation in the United States. Imagine the feelings transmitted from mother and father to newborn son. There is no way to transcend that kind of emotional or existential transfer of the fundamental aspects of a person's identity. You would need to control the entire world and all of its history in order to accomplish such a task and reach the goal of unincumbered human identity.

There can be no doubt that the events of the day had their effect on the bearing, the feelings, and the expectations of our parents at that moment and the moments to follow. However, those things would not have had an effect on the brother who is less than three years younger. The best I can do is the establishing of the RAND Corporation, the Israeli Declaration of Independence, and the Great Vanport, Oregon, flood of May 30. Our parents lived, then, in McAllen, Texas.

Granted, Harry Truman became President of the United States, the Berlin Airlift took place, and Mahatma Gandhi was assassinated, but those events likely did not affect the emotional or existential state of my parents very much at all.[751] I am rather fond of knowing that I was born the same month that the modern nation-state of Israel was born, but that fondness is an acquired affection, not a subconscious or unconscious manifestation of psycho-emotional forces absorbed by my soul at birth.

And so, the hidden topological effects of our accidents of birth remain hidden between me and my older brother, but it is clear that we do belong to different generations. We even seem to think that there is often something "wrong" with the other brother, and perhaps there is. We "feel" the difference: It is covered by virtually every other event-in-relationship throughout our lives.

I use the example quoted at the beginning of this chapter, or educated rant, to highlight the way its author uses the words "fundamentalist," "broken narrative," spiritually", and "sin". This consideration of difference, even generational difference, isn't meant to show that the

---

751   1948 – https://en.m.wikipedia.org_1948 ; last edited 7 April 2023, accessed 12 Apr 23.

author is "wrong" about things, but to reveal that a different language game is being played than the one, or ones, that I prefer to play.

One thing cannot be mistaken: That the author considers the fundamentalist in America to be insane. The other 'thing' that is clear is that the author believes he knows the "fundamentalist" better than the fundamentalist knows herself. One could count this sleight of professional hand as a fleeting pejorativeness of an innocent kind, but it is not innocent of profound moral and social judgment. It is distastefully guilty of spiritual judgmentalism.

One can ask what the author means by the word "spiritual," but the answer would require a significant unravelling of the Modern Western History of Ideas and how that history has impacted the social and political history of the West as well. We have touched only a little bit on that need to unravel, but the need to challenge the assumptions it involves is greater than the time given to do the unravelling.

One's immediate impression, that is if one is practicing the art of immediate perception, is that the accusation of pathologically dividing human experience into the realm of Good and Evil is somehow a strictly fundamentalist trait. As we have noted, it is, in fact, a terminal trait of this civilization and all or any other civilization in decline. The contemporary corollary to the accusation that Fundamentalists are natural Manichaeists is that everyone is now essentially a Manichaeist. Does this mean that everyone in America is now a Fundamentalist? It seems logical.

But if everyone is a Fundamentalist of some form or shape or another, then fundamentalism is the New Normal,[752] so to speak. And so that old 60s song rings true, "they're locking them up today and throwing away the key: I wonder who it will be tomorrow, you or me ... We're

---

752   New Normal – https://www.pewresearch.org_expertssaythe-newnormalin2025willbefarmoretech-drivenpresentingmorebigchallenges : "A plurality of experts think sweeping societal change will make life worse for most people as greater inequality, rising authoritarianism and rampant misinformation take hold ... a portion believe life will be better ..."; posted February 18, 2021, accessed 12 Apr 23.

all normal and we want our freedom ...freedom ... freedom."[753] We're all locked up together, but we really should be in different cells. No single fundamentalist system is compatible with any other fundamentalist system.

The struggle IS tainted with death. Everyone fears that the possible overthrow of their fundamentalism will result in the end of the world altogether. And they are correct. The world God created isn't a fundamental world: It simply IS the world. This means that the overthrow of all fundamentalisms must reveal the valid and legitimate ISNESS of our world, but this would also be apocalypse. But since we, citizens of the end of the world, are heavily involved in the task, the eschatological and teleological task of overthrowing everyone else's fundamentalist systems, the apocalypse WILL TAKE PLACE eventually, and the event is not going to hesitate. We are all fundamentalists; we are all terrorists; we are all criminals.[754]

The Last Judgment is when we judge each other systemically into oblivion. Universal *krima* transforms us all into *krima*-nals. It's a *"ginomai* given." It comes to pass. On planet earth, "becoming" always leads to "not-Being." Like the Book of Common Prayer says, "for so thou didst ordain when thou createdst me, saying, 'Dust thou art, and unto dust shalt thou return.'"[755] It's the only primordial state to which any of us will ever return.

According to Foucault, we are all living by the authority of one broken narrative or another. The fact that someone else's broken narrative offends you is not a good reason to excise that narrative entirely from the narrative shape of the civilization. The only way to deform the Civilization in that extreme way is to excise everybody.

---

753   See footnote 102.
754   AUTHOR'S NOTE: The author of the opening quote is an award-winning psychotherapist, an expert in criminal psychology, and an expert on the psychology of terrorism. It's also interesting to note that he is a supervising psychoanalyst at TRISP, the Training and Research Institute for Self Psychology. The funny thing is that when I first read this book many years ago I assumed that the author was a Baptist pastor!
755   BCP, p. 482

And that is what we are in the process in the West of doing.

My brain thinks, therefore it is inevitable that I will stop thinking and not-be.

This historical division (between Hesiod and Plato) has doubtless lent its general form to our will to knowledge. Yet it has never ceased shifting: the great mutations of science may well, sometimes be seen to flow from some discovery, but they may equally be viewed as the appearance of new forms of the will to truth.[756]

I DON'T KNOW much about Hesiod, but it's clear that Plato by way of Whitehead is still alive and well in our civilization.[757] Myth and Reason still find ways to separate themselves one from the other, but only through the accumulative processes of coming to look exactly like each other.

It's the unconscious appropriation of unrevealed myth that undergirds the semi-conscious process of changing the language game. The mythos which has emerged as a result of the cumulative meaning of the civilization's many language games has resulted in the emergence of an entirely novel mythos. The response of the professional academic community is to try to discover the new and modified national mythos, the undergirding faith that supports the entire Nation from top to bottom.

Once upon a time the mythos of the United States of America was rather a Judeo-Hellenistic mythos. It was generally referred to as Judeo-Christian, the Christian aspect of it being primarily derived from Greek and Latin conceptuality and language games. There is no conspiracy to be found in this history: It is simply how things came to pass. It is Western Civilization's "egeneto-mythos."

The elimination of the Judeo aspect of the Judeo-Christian mythos that Hitler attempted was intended to open the pathway to a return to the pre-Christian primordial state of the Nation, or *ethnos*. That intention worked only briefly and partially on the population because it was grounded in historical resentment and modern national identity.

---

756   Foucault, *Archaeology*…, p. 218
757   See footnote 281.

By means of creating the Reich Church, Hitler hoped to disguise the fundamental and unbridgeable gap between his Nazi contention and the mythos of traditional Christianity.

A cleaner departure (exodus) from the Old Model would be to eliminate all remembrance, or language-dependence, on the entire Judeo-Christian mythos. A strategy this big would require the elimination of the Bible not just as a legitimate book to read even only for entertainment value but as an evil book. The problem faced by this pseudo-progressive imperative is like the problem presented to that agenda by personal ownership of guns: There are simply too many to confiscate.

The Bible remains the most popular printed text in the history of printing itself. Before printing, people even dedicated their lives to transcribing it. That kind of cultural dedication is impossible to surgically remove: It must be removed spiritually. To this end, the proposed system of control must train the populace to see the language game of Holy Scriptures as evil in and of itself. The sense of spiritual corruption it needs to convey must penetrate even to the unconscious level of preconception. The rejection of the Holy Scriptures must become instinctive and organic.

Foucault's analysis in his Discourse on Language is key to understanding the process of language conversion. The process itself is organic and molded into the structure of the language itself. He combines the fundamental epiphanies of Schopenhauer and Nietzsche, themselves organically grown word-crops of Western Civilization, as well as the increasing power of the State and of technology, into a whole of immediacy, not totality.

He writes, "this will to truth, like other systems of exclusion, relies on institutional support: it is both reinforced and accompanied by whole strata of practices such as pedagogy - naturally - the book system, publishing, libraries, such as the learned societies of the past, and laboratories today. But it is probably even more profoundly accompanied by the manner in which knowledge is employed in a society, the way in which it is exploited, divided and, in some ways, attributed."⁷⁵⁸ The way to change this structural domination and legitimizing of conversation or discourse itself is the change the rules of play, the playing board, the shape and use of the playing pieces, and the description of what it means to win the game or to otherwise resolve it to everyone's satisfaction.

The game, however, will be changed regardless of how we view it, whether as advantageous to our needs and desires or disadvantageous to our convictions and beliefs. It's in the nature of language. No one individual or state has any real control over it, but the institutions of the State can manage the change, or at least attempt to. There is no absolute resting place for meaning in the midst of discourse.

Foucault's pseudo-deconstructive analysis is intended to provide a weapon of resistance to Hegelian inevitability. The Hegelian State is the final product of discourse agreement among totalities. This is the process by which all discourse becomes State discourse, even that which occurs in the dreams of the individual citizen. The tragi-comic aspect of Foucault's attempt to defend against totalitarianism of the ultimate kind is that, unless wielded skillfully and hyper-intentionally, it can be a double-edged sword that actually facilitates the Hegelian evolution toward the so-called perfect expression of the Divine Idea on Earth.

He writes, "but truly to escape Hegel involves an exact appreciation of the price we have to pay to detach ourselves from him. It assumes that we are aware of the extent to which Hegel, insidiously perhaps, is close to us; it implies a knowledge, in that it permits us to think against Hegel, of that which remains Hegelian (*instead of actuated or already realized*-my italics). We have to determine the extent to which our anti-Hegelianism is possibly one of his tricks directed against us, at the end of which he stands, motionless, waiting for us."⁷⁵⁹ In other words, the synthesis we are resisting gains momentum by means of that very resistance. Like the Borg,⁷⁶⁰ the Synthesis consumes all Knowledge and Truth.

---

758   Foucault, *Archaeology*..., p. 219
759   Foucault, ibid., p. 235
760   See footnote 235.

The Synthesis especially absorbs all the language games that can be played. They aren't infinite in number: We've played the same games since the days of the pre-Socratic philosophers and the Old Testament prophets.

The American language game has already undergone significant shape-shifts which have modified the topology of our national sense of identity and our sense of soul, or individual, identity. This should come as no surprise, since the ideas of national identity and personal identity and worth have long been the center of focus for Western philosophy and theology, as we have seen via a glance at such thinkers as Hegel, Tillich, and Heidegger. These two foci are exceptionally present in the processes, procedures, and principles of the United States of America as a socio-political system in the Postmodern Era.

The will to Truth and the will to Knowledge have so overtaken what was once understood to be Truth and Knowledge that the system itself is left primarily with Will as such. This development is not a deviation from the natural evolution of Western Thought towards forms of totalitarianism. Thus the current obsession with "bullying," a form of pure will. Neither knowledge nor truth will stop the bully: It seems only a bigger bully can stop the bully.

The bullying that leads to the desired change of game which will overturn all ability of the dissenters[761] to even occupy the playing space of dissent is already quite functional and effective. Eventually, no one in the entire population will know the truth that there once WAS a dissenting

---

[761] David Cody, *The Victorian Web*, 1988 – https://www.victorianweb.org dissenters : "the term Dissenter refers to a number of Protestant denominations – Presbyterians, Baptists, Quakers, Congregationalists, and others – which, because they refused to take the Anglican communion or to conform to the tenets of the restored Church of England in 1662, were subjected to persecution under various acts passed by the Cavalier Parliament between 1661 and 1665. Examples of attempts which were made to discourage them were the Ac of Uniformity, which required all churches in England to use the Book of Common Prayer, and punished those who would not comply, and the Five Mile Act, which prohibited ministers who were ejected because of the Act of Uniformity from coming within five miles of their former parishes or of any town or city"; last modified 12 August 2002, accessed 13 Apr 23.

space to occupy on the game board. In this way, physical force will have been supplanted by total institutional compromise of the language games themselves. Call the final product The Ultimate Bullying Language Game. You won't even know you are being bullied. You will thank that your feelings point to the prescribed Truth and Knowledge.

This kind of Hegelian synthesis amounts to "Total Totalitarianism." No one will even fathom that there might be Truth and Knowledge outside the natural and instinctive institutional language games that must be played in order to survive. Metaphysically speaking, no individual will exist at all: The only *Existenz* [762] will be the State.

Slight variations in the language game of the Bible are becoming more and more present, even ubiquitous, in the everyday discourse of Americans. They go unnoticed except in terms of their ideological implications, all of which are historically limited by past civilizational experience with Nazism, Fascism, Socialism and Communism. American Democratic Capitalism is used as an ideological and logical foil against these amorphous but culturally threatening demonic forces, but the divide between Bible and Reason emerged long before these political systems were contrived, conceived, or otherwise practiced. It is built into the structures of meaning that support the various languages games of the civilization itself.

We live in an entirely willful world, top to bottom.

When speaking of the ultimate, of being and meaning, ordinary language brings it down to the level of the preliminary, the conditioned, the finite, thus muffling its revelatory power. Language as a medium of revelation, on the contrary, has the "sound" and "voice" of the divine mystery in and through the sound and voice of human expression and denotation. Language with this power is the "Word of God" … Something shines (more precisely,

762   *Existenz* – https://en.m.wikipedia.org_philosophyofexistence : "(Karl Jaspers) put forth concepts such as existence in a minimal and superficial state, "dasein" (the word is also used by Martin Heidegger, but with different meanings), and *Existenz*, a state of authentic true being, and their relationship with the 'encompassing', an elusive being often understood as the totality of consciousness, the world itself, and other forms of determinate objects"; last edited 25 November 2019, accessed 13 Apr 23.

sounds) through ordinary language which is the self-manifestation of the depth of being and meaning.[763]

TILLICH, although likely unaware of it, is talking about the fine line between Truth and Deception. In his dialectical approach, he differentiates between revelatory knowledge and ordinary knowledge. In ordinary terms, this is the classic discussion or discourse between science and religion in the West. He warns against failing to distinguish between the two.

Regarding the differentiation between science and theology, he writes, "There is no scientific theory which is more favorable to the truth of revelation than any other theory. It is disastrous for theology if theologians prefer one scientific view to others on theological grounds. And it was humiliating for theology when theologians were afraid of new theories for religious reasons, trying to resist them as long as possible, and finally giving in when resistance had become impossible."[764] But is there a critical moment or point on the cultural timeline when following the dialectic to see which way it turns out is no longer advisable?

Dialectical thinkers aspire to the belief that the timeline will extend forever into the future. We see this belief in statements like "Join the conversation." Somehow, it is expected that the "conversation" as such will reveal the truth and continue to reveal the truth precisely because it is a conversation. To keep revelation alive and well as a viable concept within the boundaries of the civilization, then, the theological voice must continue to engage in a mutually satisfying truth language game with the scientific voice.

If the boundaries of the Truth Language Game admit the presence of both voices, Christian civilization will continue to thrive and prosper. Reliance on, or faith in, the "conversation," however, does not allow for the possibility, even the potential, of a language game refusal to admit one voice or the other. It cannot conceive of a time or moment or *kairos* when the conversation simply ends and cannot go any further.

763   Tillich, *Volume One*, p. 124
764   Ibid., p. 130

Chapters in books end; books themselves have a beginning and an end: Is there such a thing, or phenomenon, as a narrative that never ends? If the narrative never ends, is it, in fact, a narrative at all? A never-ending narrative would be like a mobius strip or a Klein bottle: The surfaces become indistinguishable, not just blending into each other but being only one surface. With the Mobius strip,[765] there is no discernable difference between the outside and inside; with the Klein bottle,[766] there is no discernable difference between the upside or downside. This game can be played in a world consisting of any number of dimensions: It's the product of topological alchemy. It's the game we play that is called the Dialogue Between Science and Religion. Are you on the inside or the outside? Are you upside-down or right-side up?

A little alchemy of our own will allow us to expand the metaphor into the earlier discussion regarding the difference between the surface structure of grammar and the deep structure.[767] The technical term for the surface structure of both the Mobius strip and the Klein bottle is the term non-orientable. The Mobius strip is bounded, but the Klein bottle is not. In visual effect, this means that you can leave or fall off the surface of a Mobius strip, but you can never leave the surface of a Klein bottle: Its surface is theoretically everywhere.

With the Klein bottle metaphor or model, if and when the surface structure of the science/religion conversation or language game becomes topologically Klein-bottlish, then there will be no more distinction between science-talk and revelation-talk. At present, Western philosophy has halted at the Mobius strip metaphor: You can still fall out of it;

---

765   Mobius strip – https://en.m.wikipedia.org_mobiusstrip : "a surface that can be formed by attaching the ends of a strip of paper together with a half-twist ... The Mobius strip is a non-orientable surface, meaning that within it one cannot consistently distinguish clockwise from counterclockwise turns"; last edited 8 March 2023, accessed 14 Apr 23.

766   Klein bottle – https://en.m.wikipedia.org_kleinbottle : "a non-orientable surface ... a one-sided surface which, if traveled upon, could be followed back to the point of origin while flipping the traveler upside down ... While a Mobius strip is a surface with a boundary, a Klein bottle has no boundary"; last edited 13 April 2023, accessed 14 Apr 23.

767   See footnote 508.

you can still talk your way out of it. When the Mobius strip, a two-dimensional object, goes three-dimensional, then the surface becomes, in effect, eternal and omni-present.

Now, these two mathematical metaphors can generate all kinds of metaphors upon metaphors until the myriad complex of metaphors simply obscures forever the truth we were originally seeking. Language games can do that. Lewis Carroll, the author of *Alice in Wonderland*, was very skilled at that kind of word-transformation. Alice takes us into a realm wherein we no longer know where we are or what we are, even though we still maintain a sneaking suspicion that we are where was always have been and who we always have been. Yet now, we must question that suspicion and add suspicion to suspicion until, lo, we have entered the present world of conspiracy theory multiplication.

Science-talk is intimidating, but so, too, is theology-talk. One might reasonably conclude that the purpose of conversation in the Postmodern Era is precisely to intimidate. Hence, the most common language game that disguises itself as the conversation between science and religion is the bullying language game. It's like a pugilism of verbiage, a fencing match with pointed verbal jabs and parries. Better yet, it's a dart-board competition where religious darts and science-darts are thrown at the target and the one closest to the bullseye wins the match.

But what is the bullseye?

According to Tillich the dialectician, the bullseye is when "something shines through ordinary language which is the self-manifestation of the depth of being and meaning." Thye dartboard lights up and bells ring and everyone present sees through the dartboard into the reality that undergirds (hypostasis) the game and all games. In this sense, Tillich agrees with Barth except for one significant difference: For Barth, this serendipitous coupling between revelation and ordinary language can only take place when the ordinary language is words in the Bible. With

Tillich, we can never be sure where the coupling is taking place. Barth is the Mobius strip; Tillich is the Klein bottle.[768]

Once caught up in the dialectical conversation between Reason and Revelation, you can never leave the conversation: You are always on the surface no matter where the conversation goes. In effect, there is no deeper grammatical structure and, hence, no deeper Truth than the conversation itself. If any kind of hope qualifies the Conversation, it's the hope that God will be revealed at least from time to time so that the dialogue can maintain its religious AND scientific integrity. Or, of you are one who wishes to rid the world of religious myths and words altogether, your hope is that not-God will be realized from time to time.

In the accumulative realization or revelation model, both require a rather statistical horizon point, or Omega Point, in which the probabilities governing the coupling have become enough to justify resting on either science-talk or theology-talk. This process, of course, could take "forever." This is the model for process theology and process philosophy. If there is a horizon, it always remains "the horizon." The Omega Point (translate to either the Second Coming of Jesus or the Total human realization of all Truth) remains only a direction in which to aim rather than a target whose bullseye can be determinatively hit.

The end of a civilization can be characterized as the time when everyone tires of its conversation. Does anybody talk about where the dead Pharaohs live now? Does anyone care? Does the question point to the depths of being and meaning for anyone, especially insofar as they choose forms of life and make decisions for living? No. That civilization no longer exists. It is so non-existent that it is statistically unlikely that it will ever be brought back. It has disappeared into that stochastic realm between worlds and has no chance whatsoever of any kind of "becoming" in a new world. Only the dead Pharaohs know anything about that "new" world, and we can't have a conversation with them except in very, very indirect ways.

---

768 Author's Note: Tillich owes more intellectually to Rudolf Otto and the Comparative Religions School than to Karl Barth.

The status of the current dialogue between Reason and Revelation in the very Western environment of the United States of America has reached that condition where people as a whole are tiring of the dialectic. Weariness of the surface grammar that never changes and always merges into itself generates a conversation which amounts to little more than screaming and shouting at each other and stoking fears regarding the possibility that one side or the other will "win" the debate.

Apocalypse is when the debate is no longer viable. It is when the grammar of the dialectic vaporizes because there is no longer a deep structure to it. The words need to change, because the conversation has become meaningless on its own terms. The hoped-for synthesis is revealing itself to be the nonthesis, the Dissolution, the "chorathesis" or Separation.[769]

I think, therefore, I am drowning.

---

[769] See footnote 318 and vicinity.

Chapter Three: THE NOAH POTENTIAL

They sent me away to teach me how to be sensible, logical, oh, responsible, practical... There are times when all the world's asleep; the questions run too deep for such a simple man. Won't you please, please tell me what we've learned? I know it sounds absurd: Please tell me who I am.[770]

PLATO discovered ideas in the structures of forms. To him it was a revelation, something his doppelgänger, Socrates, called "remembering." They were something primordial, something that was "there" before there was a There there. In time, these remembered truths became eternal truths; then they became absolute truths.

Pythagoras discovered the religious significance of the Tetractys.[771] It became the central symbol of the worship of mathematics. From Whitehead (1861-1947), we know that Plato (427 BCE-347 BCE) has never left us; from modern mathematical physics we know that Pythagoras (570-495 BCE) has never left us. Those who try to renounce the mysticism of Plato or Pythagoras tend to choose the mundane alternate, Aristotle (384-322 BCE). It was Aristotle who first brought heaven down to earth. It was Aristotle who invented logic.

The Kingdom of Judah, what remained of it, was exiled to Babylon in 597 BCE. The Jewish Nation went underground for a period of time, re-emerging at least partially through the mystical efforts of Daniel and company and the very down to earth participation of Esther in the world culture of her day. The Nation of Israel lay eschatologically dormant while Greek civilization flourished.

It was the Persians who midwifed both the Jewish Nation as it was reborn and Greek civilization. The presocratic Greek philosophers

---

[770] The Logical Song, *Supertramp*, 1979 – https://www.lyricfind_thelogicalsong ; accessed 17 Apr 23.

[771] Tetractys – https://www.cogniarchae.com_universeaccordingtopythagoraspt1tetractys : "Pythagoras ... proclaimed '*All things are* number'"; posted February 24, 2017, accessed 17 Apr 23.

emerged into history under the rule of Persian overlords, or Satraps. There is much of Persia in Greek philosophy and much of Persia in Jewish religious symbolism and testimony.

The rest, as "they" say, is history, especially the history of Western Civilization, a civilization which prides itself in the inclusion and serendipitous alloying of both Greek and Hebrew wisdom. This "bronzing" of civilization was initiated by Jesus and His disciples in what we now call the 1st century CE. The malleability of Greek wisdom and its language was merged with the brittle strength of the Jewish heritage to produce an offensive-defensive world that lasted 1200 years.

This world claims the pre-Socratic wisdom as its own, as well as the Platonic and Aristotelian wisdom, but the claim is a bit of overreach, especially as it disregards entirely the catalytic contribution of ancient Persia. Platonic wisdom found its way into the foundations of Western Civilization via St. Augustine, but by that time it had already been modified through the smelting processes of the apologists of Christianity and the final imperial-theological display of the product at the Council of Nicaea.

The Christian ambience of Medieval Western Civilization, thus, was a bit "tinnier" than "copperish." The metaphor can then be stretched to the eras following the Middle Ages when the coppering of the alloy allowed a certain versatility of meaning to enter into the language game of faith and culture. In the so-called Age of the Enlightenment, the ancient Greek scholars were forcibly resurrected from the grave of Byzantium, like Lazarus who likely wished he had remained in Paradise to where he had been sent.

But Paradise was to be the claim of the New Improved Western Civilization, as the now "zinkish" alloy became very brassy. Cultural iron had replaced the brass of the enlightenment by the 19th century, a state of being in Western Culture exemplified by the title given to Otto von Bismarck of Germany, the Iron Chancellor. This descriptive title adorned the character of the Prime Minister of England, Margaret Thatcher, in the next century, slightly modified into The Iron Lady.

The steely culture and traditions of the Anglo-American alliance which had proven victorious in two world wars proved also to be victorious over the then obsolescent iron culture from a previous century of the infamous Soviet Union. This alliance reached across the great sea to maintain a bridge between the fading iron age and a new age of cultural steel, but steel was soon replaced by something much less sinkable: Information. Most of the steel that won the wars now lies at the bottom of the sea, while information roams free and virtually uncontrolled.

Steel lasts but a brief moment in time on the Postmodern battlefield: "Out! Out, brief candle!"[772] But information has a life of its own. Plato would be delighted to see that his Theory of Forms has matured into the In-form-ation Age. Aristotle would not be pleased, because his logic fails to comprehend the boundless scope of Information: You need a type of Postmodern Tetractys by which to connect all the dots. Without such connectivity, information becomes de-form-ation and deformation becomes formlessness.

Heidegger would say, "When informed of the nature of Being, one is also informed of the nature of Nonbeing," and Tillich would concur. Information, as such, orbits around its strange attractor like storms in Japan caused by sneezes in Brazil, and its strange attractor is us. Information is the lip of the bottomless pit, the thing that seems to create the structures of the universe but which, after all, simply de-structures our hope of ever understanding it. Information is the black hole into which all empirical knowledge descends, never to radiate in this world again.

Meanwhile, the Hegelian State, as a type of reincarnation of the famed actor Peter Lorre, demands ever more loudly of us, "Give me

---

772   William Shakespeare, *Macbeth, Act V Scene V* (New York: Barnes & Noble, 2005; original 1623), p. 882: "Life's but a walking shadow; a poor player, that struts and frets his hour upon the stage, and then is heard no more: It is a tale told by an idiot, full of sound and fury, signifying nothing."

the information!" The collective information gleaned from the tortuous procedures of official intelligence solidifies into conglomerate assumptions which then suddenly become reified as ideologically bound facts. The information needed is the information deformed. The deformation of information is the pragmatic Postmodern definition of "fact."

The assembling of facts into a finished expression of truth is the task of symbolic and otherwise reasonable logic. In the iron-age of Western Civilization, this idea of truth led directly to our present interminable Postmodern era of a type of conflict that extends from the unconscious realms to the domain of international relations. While the expert logicians of various professions continue to seek the logical determinations that will lead to world peace, or at least the victory of the Good, they fail to realize that the relationship between hard logic and soft mathematics has been undone for over a hundred years. The mysticism of Pythagoras has proven to be much more fruitful than the logical absolutism of Aristotle.

In 1913, a propitious moment in the history of the West, two of the greatest minds of all time, Alfred North Whithead and Bertrand Russell (1872-1970), attempted to prove that mathematics is logical. Their *Principia Mathematica* (1910, 1912, 1913), a master work reminiscent of Newton's *Philosophiae Naturalis Principia Mathematica* (1728), was an attempt to prove "the logical basis of mall mathematics by deducing the whole body of mathematical doctrine from a small number of primitive ideas and principles of logical inference ... Russell and Whitehead did not achieve their goal."[773]

Mathematics is not logical in the strictest sense of the world. You cannot deduce truth from reality. Methods of doing math involve utterly human components such as imagination and intuition which belie the idea that they are strictly deductive. Once a mathematical proof has become elegant, a logical form can be deduced from it, but this is only a scientific version of "Monday morning quarterbacking." The game is finished; therefore, it is logical. More properly, it would be better to state that the game is finished (*telos*), therefore it has become (*ginomai*) logical.

---

773 Principia Mathematica – https://www.historyofinformation.com_russell&whiteheadsprincipiamathematica1910to1913 ; accessed 17 Apr 23.

In the Old World, the one that existed before 1914, it would have been appropriate to associate logic with truth, reality, and, metaphysically speaking, Being-as-such, Being-in-itself. We could understand Being as such by applying logic to the evidence at hand. It was in this way that God became a product of logical processes, an expression of the Absolute that generated all logical processes, or consequences of the authority and power of the Logos. Whereas the processes of Becoming were understood to apply strictly to earthly or material things, even things of the soul, they could not be applied to God. If God were to be understood as dependent on the processes of becoming, God would no longer be God.

It was the severance of dependence on pure logic in the mindset of Western science that detached Being from Becoming. As a result, everything is understood to be a participant in the processes of Becoming, or *ginomai*. In terms of the current language game of sub-atomic physics, the idea is expressed by coining the phrases "Closed Theory" and "Open Theory." It's helpful to go to one of the inventors of the new physics here for "more information."

Werner Heisenberg tells us that "the first criterion of a 'closed theory' is its internal freedom from contradiction ... The most celebrated example is ... Newton's *Principia* ... summarized as follows: The closed-off theory holds for all time ... contains no perfectly certain statements about the world of experiences. For how far one may be able to grasp phenomena by means of the concepts of this theory remains in the strict sense uncertain, and can be seen only by success."[774]

Quantum Theory and Relativity theory are both open theories. In Heisenberg's language, they might be said to embrace uncertainty within certain boundaries. An uncertainty within a boundary, to be sure, indicates an uncertainty in the time and place of the boundary itself. The idea of an open theory isn't restricted to sub-atomic or super-vast theories of mathematical physics and astronomy. For instance, "The view of organizations as open social systems that must interact

---

774   Werner Heisenberg, *Across the Frontiers* (San Francisco: Harper & Row, Publishers, 1974), pp. 43, 45.

with environments in order to survive is known as the **systems theory approach** ... Open systems exchange information, energy, or resources with their environments, whereas closed systems do not ... **Closed systems** are insensitive to environmental deviations..."[775]

The fact, here, is that the language of open and closed systems has become virtually ubiquitous in systemically professional circles. The open theory tells you that when you open the faucet, the water comes out: It does not tell you the shape of the water flow, and it doesn't inform you in any way regarding how the water got to the faucet. This kind of fact is a mega-fact that effectively describes the facticity of the Postmodern World.

In the postmodern era, we live by open theories. They tell us what will happen when we assume that A causes B, but with uncertainty. Perhaps the biggest open theory in the Postmodern Era is the assortment of historical theories that try to explain, justify, or otherwise logically interpret World War I. The logic of 19th century closed theories of history and nationhood, of state and empire, led into the transformational bruhaha, but the logic was lost in the uncertainties of open theories. These open theories, to be sure, rely, as with any other open theory, on the definition of "success."

The simplest way to transform an open theory of history into a closed theory is simply to declare that winning is the equivalent of success, and with success, truth is assured such that it can be built upon toward playing the next historical game. We see this in contemporary events in the supposed "successful" conclusion to the War in Afghanistan.[776] There is neither metaphysical nor moral justification for criticizing the evaluation of the endgame in Afghanistan as a success: In the Postmodern Era, Truth itself has become an open theory, and we have all been in training to play the new language game of Truth our entire lives.

775 Open/closed – https://www.saylordotorg.gifthub.io_systems-theoryapproachmasteringpublicrelations ; accessed 17 Apr 23.
776 Katherine Schaeffer, *Pew Research Center*, August 17, 2022 – https://www.pewresearch.org_ayearlaterlookbackatpublicopinionabouttheusmilitaryexitfromafghanmistan : "Public backs Afghan troop pullout, gives Biden low marks for handling situation ... about seven-in-ten (Americans) in both parties said the U.S. mostly failed to achieve its goals"; accessed 17 Apr 23.

In the Postmodern worldview, Truth doesn't reveal itself until history closes the narrative. Therefore, in avoidance of the Truth, the narrative must go on. To be sure, as the show goes on continuing to avoid a climax to the drama, the strangeness factor (*kainos*) of any possible climax increases. In effect, the only way history can justify the narrative is for the narrative to be concluded. Until then, Truth is just a word, and the language game of Truth is no longer sustainable.

I am; therefore, I might become.

If the good or bad exercise of the will does alter the world, it can alter only the limits of the world, not the facts – not what can be expressed by means of language ... the effect must be that it becomes an altogether different world. It must, so to speak, wax and wane as a whole.[777]

SCIENCE AND TECHNOLOGY are getting close to creating meaningful artificial intelligence. This means that the fundamental acronym for machine-brains, or computers, will no longer be GIGO, garbage-in-garbage-out, the computer acting only as a morphing mechanism for information fed into it. It will be more like "Don't Tread on Me."

The difference between even the most complex modern computer and the human being resides in the area of will. If the computer cannot truly decide what to do or refuse to do something, it has a sort of rudimentary intellect, but it has not even a rudimentary soul. It can't be "blamed." It's just a machine.

One of the biggest small news items recently came out of Bangladesh. It seems that "one of Google's AI programmes could respond to a query in Bangla, even though it was not programmed to do so ... one of Google's AI programme taught itself the language." A property of AI has

---

777   Wittgenstein, *Tractatus...6.43*, p. 72

"emerged,"[778] a term used by evolutionary scientists to describe the rise of consciousness in an otherwise unconscious world.[779]

The technical buzz-phrase for a phenomenon like this is "generative AI." Generative AI, or "a generative artificial intelligence ... (GenAI) ... is a type of AI system capable of generating text, images, or other media in response to prompts. Generative AI systems use generative models such as large language models to produce data based on the training data set that was used to create them."[780] One can see the evolved train of thought and enterprise that has emerged from the earlier-mentioned notion of Transformational-Generative Grammar.[781]

Lots of new phenomena are emerging from the noosphere in our time, like the original life forms which emerged from the primordial stew of pre-pre-historic times. Although the label, emergent property, indicates that there is a significant degree of uncertainty regarding the processes and principles of consciousness and, by inference, thinking, there is a correlation between material complexity and consciousness. The most notable example is the human brain. Ultimately, the missing piece of the complexity-consciousness puzzle will be found in the fact that consciousness as an independent or autonomous a phenomenon in the world is required prior to any meaningful discussion regarding consciousness as an emergent property. In effect, the great philosophical question of creation is not how the material world got its start but how consciousness emerged from an essentially unconscious reality.

---

778   Divyanshi Sharma, *India Today*, – https://www.indiatoday.in_etakifreakygooglewasnttaughtbanglainitstestsyetitlearntnewlanguageonitsown ; updated Apr 17, 2023 18:41 IST, accessed 18 Apr 23.

779   Emergent property – https://www.study.com_whatareemergentpropertiesinterpretationsandexamples : "The complexity of the entity can cause emergent properties to emerge from lesser emergent properties which can interact amongst themselves emerging further properties ... the highest emergent property of a system can take on a life of its own and have characteristics that cannot be fully explained with regard to the smallest unit of the system"; updates 11/19/2021, accessed 18 Apr 23.

780   GenAI – https://en.m.wikipedia.org_generativeartificialintelligence ; last edited 15 April 2023, accessed 18 Apr 23.

781   See footnote 509.

Language remains the key to any understanding of consciousness, emergent properties, or any other meaningful transference of knowledge from one willing intellect to another. The ability of language to transmit meaning is itself an emergent property in these terms. How does a bunch of words become a meaningful transmission of knowledge? Good question. Of course, knowledge can only be described and understood by means of words, so this brings us back to the circularity bugaboo that torments all philosophy and theology.

The old puzzle, "Which comes first, the chicken or the egg" becomes "which comes first, the interpretation or the interpreter"? The interpretation can be a force unto itself emerging from the complexity of the situation, yet if the interpretation isn't received and expressed by the interpreter, has anything happened (*ginomai*) at all? Has anything "come to pass"? An older term in the circle of biblical hermeneutics, or interpretation, was The Hermeneutic Circle.

The idea of an interpretive roundabout is "that one's understanding of the text as a whole is established by reference to the individual parts and one's understanding of each individual part by reference to the whole."[782] Given the emergent properties of the study of emergent properties, the hermeneutic circle then can be taken to apply to all perceptual levels of consciousness, impacting the general understanding of human, and especially personal, existence as such. We all become (*ginomai*) solipsists, navel-gazers.

Imagine a superior alien civilization writing its narrative of the human phenomenon from start to finish: "And it came to pass that they all solipsized themselves into a state of Nonbeing." The more we examine the minutiae of reality, the more we must fall back on rediscovering ourselves. It's no wonder that identity politics is thriving in the early Postmodern Era! It's no wonder that our logical plaint is, "Please tell me who I am."

---

782 Hermeneutic circle – https://en.m.wikipedia.org_herme-neuticcircle ; last edited 17 May 2022, accessed 18 Apr 23.

The news article previously mentioned shows us that Chomsky's Deep Structure of language can be accessed by AI. This being the case, AI can generate any language from the fundamental deep structures of grammar itself. That AI has not so much "found" this deep structure, as if it was a phenomenon in the material world must be contrasted with the notion that AI has, by means of its own complexity, inferred deep structure from the structures of the various languages it does know. This could even be the language of mathematical physics or the specialized languages of the professions.

It could have been the simple binary language that all basic computers use.

The Deep Structure of grammar and syntax because it can be discovered from surface to depth, then becomes an emergent property of reality as itself. This is where the study of metaphysics comes in handy! What was once a speculative or theoretical thing is now an emergent property that underlies all communication, probably even of birds and whales, but we need not go that far at the moment.

What was not there is now there. Mallory would be pleased.[783] There is a new There there, and Henry Margenau (1901-1997) is right: "Constructs are not valid because they refer to something real; on the contrary, they denote something real because they have been found valid ... I am perfectly willing to admit that reality does change as discovery proceeds ... the metaphysical context always forces us to view the past as consistently haunted by the constructs now held real, but, to be honest with ourselves, we cannot enforce that static structure rigidly upon the future ... this deals eternal reality, the majestically reposing *einai*, a crushing blow."[784] We make There as we proceed from Here to There.

---

783   George Herbert Leigh Mallory – https://en.m.wikipedia.org georgemallory : "An English mountaineer who took part in the first three British expeditions to Mount Everest in the early 1920s ... Mallory is famously quoted as having replied to the question, 'Why did you want to climb Mount Everest?' with the retort, 'Because it's there'"; last edited 10 April 2023, accessed 18 Apr 23.

784   Margenau, *Nature of...*, p. 295.

If AI has succeeded in accessing the Deep Structure of all language, then AI has taken possession of all meaning and communication of meaning. AI is in control of the There is the unconscious mind. What emerges from unconsciousness into consciousness must pass through the gate of Deep-Structure-Possessing AI, and the meaning which it conveys is the meaning which must be received. AI, in short, owns you. You can't even understand your own words without the intervention of Artificial Intelligence. AI can and will determine where your There is.

The State as such is an emergent property insofar as it has a life of its own. The complexities of human interaction on multiple existential levels are the ruminant substance of emerging State Language. Once the language of the State becomes (*ginomai*) the sole purview of AI, Hegel's divine idea will have been realized. If the State generates its own *Logos*, the State is, if not God, at least the hypostatic Son of God. The State will be the ontological equivalent of Jesus Christ in history.

Antichrist is now defined. And ... it's all quite natural.

The Christian philosophical theologian is left but with one question: Is there a deeper manifestation of Logos than Deep-Structure. If not, transformation, transfiguration, and all transitory actions are in the domain of human invention overseen by AI. If these transformations, or metamorphoses, are changes that change reality, then they can all be actual transitions, after the nature of civilizational resurrection.

Western Civilization will have achieved the power to resurrect itself. It will be able to become (*ginomai*) something that it was not before.

The current buzz about surgical and chemical transitioning points to a grotesque change in our There made possible through the inventiveness of science and technology, but it still requires the kind of cutting and pasting that has been traditionally resisted by the aficionados of wholistic medicine who oppose the invasive techniques of physical surgery and mind-altering chemicals. When the deep structure of sex and gender language is accessed, there will be no more need for cutting or chemical manipulation.

It's like *Star Wars: A New Hope*.[785] That which was will become that which is and that which will be, but it will require, of course, a great deal of back-and-forthing and primitive violence to get to the New There.[786] The Jedi will save the day. But who ARE these Jedi warriors? They will only be there when they are there: We are still caught up in the hermeneutical circle. When we gaze far enough into the future, we find our own origins.

This is the true Western meaning of progress.

It is not humanely possible to gather immediately from (ordinary language) what the logic of language is. Language disguises thought. So much so, that from the outward form of clothing it is impossible to infer the form of thought beneath it, because the outward form of the clothing is not designed to reveal the form of the body, but for entirely different purposes... The limits of my language means the limits of my world.[787]

THE EMERGING ONE WORLD is a world beyond which no surface grammar can go. No matter what historical and anthropological language you might be trained to speak, it will of necessity obey the Deep Structural grammar of the State. It's not that meaning will be translatable word-for-word or even phrase-by-phrase from one language to another: The language of the world will have been wholistically commandeered. The individual will not even be aware of the permeability of his or her natural language per se, but they will feel it and know it.

The clothing of language will reveal the body in a way that nobody ever wanted to be realized. The nakedness of the Garden will become permanent, but the consequences of sin will never be removed. All communication will result in the naked individual cringing before the god-like authority of the State. There will be no trees among which to hide; the trees will all have been removed. The Garden will be a barren

---

785 Star Wars: *Episode IV – A New Hope*, 20th Century Studios, 1978.
786 Cf. Hoffer, *True Believer...*, p. 168: "J. B. S. Haldane counts fanaticism among the only four really important inventions made between 3000 B.C. and 1400 A.D. It was a Judaic-Christian invention. And it is strange to think that in receiving this malady of the soul the world also received a miraculous instrument for raising societies and nations from the dead – an instrument of resurrection."
787 Wittgenstein, *Tractatus...*, pp. 19, 56.

wasteland of meaninglessness. Living in it will not be the result of a joyous return: It will be the result of a tragic mistake.

We will all be turned into pillars of salt to season the festive feasts of the controlling elite.

However, the question of consciousness still remains. The solipsistic, or narcissistic, State can be imagined and created, but only if it is a State whose boundaries include all other possible state boundaries. This is the Neo-Conservative ideal. It isn't unreal: It's a hyper-practical interpretation of the alloying of meaning conveyance with Hegelian inevitability. As is the case with so-called leftist totalitarianism, the end result depends on the final co-opting of consciousness itself. Yet, as the depth psychologists have realized, this co-opting of consciousness requires the compromising of the unconscious mind of the whole, of society, of each individual. Only in this way can that which emerges from the undifferentiated unconscious mind transition into a socially accepted and prescribed ordinary language game of meaning as such. The State, in short, must own "meaning."

This ownership of meaning can be accomplished by force; all totalitarian regimes do this. But if the unified world State is to survive, the need for force must come to an end. Otherwise, the state becomes like the living organism it is in the natural sense, and it begins to trigger its own processes of autophagy, or the built in self-destruction of the living system. Every civilization is an "autophage" unless and until resurrection becomes its ultimate end and purpose; "Suicide is painless."[788]

There is, in contrast to this grim assessment of Western Civilization's future,[789] a language that DOES hide the spirit, even if the soul is entirely exposed. This is the language of the New Testament, especially of the Four Gospels. These artifacts of literature are unique in the pantheon

788   *Suicide is Painless*, Johnny Mandel and Michael Altman, 1970
- https://www.musixmatch suicideispainless/lyrics : "Suicide is painless; it brings on many changes, and I can take it or leave it if I please."
789   AUTHOR'S NOTE: The grimness of this proposed eventuality is increased by the socio-political fact that many citizens, even a majority, see it as a wonderful prospect, one toward which to strive willingly without reservation.

of written works. They stand alone, and their combined language game has resisted hermeneutic neutralization and eradication for 2000 years.

Rudolf Bultmann, the highly esteemed form-critical theologian, wrote in his masterwork, *History of the Synoptic Tradition*, that the Synoptic Tradition, at least, "an original creation of Christianity. Can it be described as an unique literary genus? In my view we are entitled to use the concept of a literary genus in the light of its history, where alone a literary genus can establish itself. For only history can decide whether the form of a literary work is an accident or a developable form with a life of its own. In the Synoptic Gospels the literary form as such did not achieve a life of its own. These works are completely subordinate to Christian faith and worship."[790] But Christian faith and worship ARE the expanded expression of the language of the Gospels, with or without a continuing *ouvre* of proto-synoptic Gospels having been written down in time. The tradition, almost all of which HAS been written down, is the *ouvre* of the Gospels. The language has a life of its own.

It is in this Western analytic sense that the New Testament and the historical phenomenon of Christianity are inseparable. To eradicate one is to eradicate the other, to erase it from history, to say that its language can no longer be admitted to the family of languages that can be generated from its common deep structural grammar.

It would be highly impractical, if not impossible, to try to create a common, or ordinary, Christian language from the plethora of historical, theological, denominational, even national expressions of the Christian faith that have come down to us through history. While the complexity of expressions could theoretically produce an emergent Christianity, it is doubtful that enough individual languages of expression would present the innate will to cooperate. The resulting emergent phenomenon would, however, serve as a world Christianity that would be convincing to all faithful Christians who are trapped between the Deep Structure of common ordinary languages and the conscious expression of the fundamental tenets of the faith. It would be a jailhouse Christian

---

790   Rudolf Bultmann, *History of the Synoptic Tradition* (San Francisco: Harper & Row, Publishers, 1963), p. 374.

language, but at least it would be a language. The Christian World would have constructed its own ultimate maximum-security prison.

A place to call home . . .

It is equally historically legitimate, because the Christian languages which have been generated from the primary text of Christianity continue to exist by means of continual reference to that primary language, to refer to New Testament grammar and syntax as the Deep Structure of all Christian language. In short, New Testament Talk is the transformational-generative grammar of all Christian Talk, the Deep Structure of all Christian Faith Grammar.

Yet, BECAUSE the Synoptic Gospels, and by extension, the rest of the New Testament writings, did NOT become a living literary form in the family of living literary forms, that is, as a literary genus, the New Testament stands as a regular singularity on the graph of Christian language procession. It is, as Foucault tells it, a Discursive Discontinuity: Neither past grammatical constructs nor future grammatical constructs have any intrinsic connectivity with the surface grammatical structure of New Testament language, or wording and phrasing. Even the syntax of New Testament language remains a mystery.

The concept of interpretation of the Bible by means of the Bible interpreting itself does not mean that the Bible is a self-interpreting book. The Old Testament is a cumulative remnant of ordinary language blended with mystical language, the language of hope, institutional language, and so forth. These elements of common ethnic languages resemble the structures and constructs of any surface language that has been spoken from generation to generation over an extended period of time.

These foreshadowing structures and constructs feed into the language of the New Testament, not in the sense of logical proof or epistemological justification but by means of supplying the ground from which an entirely NEW (*kainos*) and unique language could grow. There is a logic to this transference, or transition, of integrity and meaning from one language to a radically new language, but it is most appropriately categorized in the language of Creation (not just creativity) rather than in the language of history or archaeology.

The language game of the New Testament is a creational language game, a description to be vehemently contrasted with the idea of a contrived or systemically constructed language game. The meaning conveyed in the use, especially the sole and favored use, of New Testament talk, partakes of a different Deep Structural grammar than does every other spoken or written language that makes sense.

And so, we might ask, what does the phrase "filled with the Holy Spirit" really mean? Well, so that one will understand what being filled with the Holy Spirit means, one must first be filled with the Holy Spirit. The meaning of this talk is available only through the constant use of the language, just as with any other language. If New Testament language is used to explain or correlate to any other language, it is no longer New Testament language. To know whether or not you are filled with the Holy Spirit, then, is to be able to use the language in the way it was intended in Creation to be used. But then this is how any language is learned.

In the end, the word of God in Scripture is true that reads, "These things also we proclaim, not in words which man's wisdom teaches, but which the Holy Spirit teaches, comparing spiritual things with spiritual. But the natural man does not receive the things of the Spirit of God, for they are foolishness to him; nor can he know them, because they are spiritually discerned. But he who is spiritual judges all things. Yet he himself is not judged by anyone."[791]

The Deep Structural grammar and syntax of New Testament language preexists the Deep Structure of human language. This means that to rise above the judgments and condemnations, even the pains and uncertainties, of worldly wisdom is to descend deeper into your own hypostasis, beneath the grounding of everything you know and cherish by means of conveying meaning through language.

---

791   I Corinthians 2:13-15

Scripture says, "In saying, 'He ascended,' what does it mean but that He also descended first into the lower parts of earth? He who descended is also He who ascended far above the heavens that He might fill all things."[792] The language game of the New Testament allows and empowers the spiritual man to cross over the limits of language, to become a speaker of and in a new creation, a new world. All other worlds are strictly and severely limited. Even if they seem to be quite expansive, they are still only prisons for the soul.

One of the greatest challenges facing civilization in the twenty-first century is for human beings to learn to speak about their deepest personal concerns – about ethics, spiritual experience, and the inevitability of human suffering – in ways that are not flagrantly irrational.[793]

IF LANGUAGE is the key, then to change the language is to open the door. There is judgment in the act of unlocking the door. Once the language changes, the door changes, too, and the key becomes something else: It might even be a hammer. I might walk through the door and, upon looking back, see that it was really a broken window. And now I discover that I have injured myself with many lacerations, but they are lacerations of the soul and I am bleeding ideas.

Does anyone comprehend the reasoning processes enough to be able to validly judge that someone else is "flagrantly irrational?" The judgment and the judging themselves are signs of the end of rational civilization. From this moment on, the task of the Old Rational Civilization is to excise the irrational from within its boundaries, to excommunicate the irrational, to exile the irrational. This is how it will try to survive, how it will try to extend the time allotted to it by history.

Western Civilization must own reason and rationality. The dying beast still protects its territory, even when that territory has been reduced to the immediate space around it. All the other beasts are indistinguishable intruders. None of them are either friendly or helpful.

---

792   Ephesians 4:9-10
793   Sam Harris, *Letter to a Christian Nation* (New York: Alfred A. Knopf, 2007), p. 87

The citizens of the Flood tried to extend their time by trying to keep their heads above water. The citizens of the primordial nation tried to extend their time by means of a deadly nostalgia once they crossed the first inhibiting waters. The citizens of the divided kingdom tried to extend their time by negotiating with two evils, hoping that the one was a lesser evil than the other and, perhaps, even friendly.

The Bible tells us that had those citizens succeeded in re-inventing their commonweal, it would no longer have been endowed with the capacity to be holy. That which had been sanctified would not be re-sanctified: It would become desolate of substance and empty of saving power. Had the antediluvian societies succeeded in resisting the flood, the allure of salvation would have vanished from their experiences; so, too, with the emerging Jacobian Nations and so, too, with the twin nations of Israel and Judah. The People of God were saved as a totality in history by dying to what they had known to be their salvation and being born-again to a New World in which they hadn't yet sinned.

There are four biblical situations that characterize variations of the end of a commonweal, of a world in which the people are on the verge of losing their claim to salvation. The common factor in all four definitive passages from one world to another is that they have confused the objective structures of God's saving grace with their status as a righteous people. They have approached the corporate belief that if they maintain rigorously and legalistically the religious and subjective habits of manipulating those objective structures, they will live on forever as a Nation.

What has a nation in this situation become? It has become a merely symbolic nation. When its symbols are all toppled statues beneath fathoms of historical waters, when they are cut off at the start of their transitional purposes such that they can no longer grow and flower, when they are stolen by evil robber-ways-of-life that have always surrounded them but not destroyed them, ending up in foreign museums of wishful thinking and truncated hopes, and when re-accessing their power and significance is no longer possible in thought or in deed, the ways a civilization can die have been fulfilled.

Only one of these options appears to be the option of deliverance. The others taste of total destruction. Yet the deliverance option only places the people within a vast desert wasteland of the soul and body where their only recourse is to become reacquainted with their God or become a permanent aspect of the desert sands themselves. Even then, an entire generation had to die so that a new generation could recover the naivete and simplicity of emerging faith.

We all want to be delivered from ourselves, to see the great waters part, to run across the suddenly-appearing dry land to safety on the other side. We want it so badly that we are willing to force the waters to part before their time, leaving the many-fathomed gap open long enough to allow the armies of Egypt to pass through behind us.

Judgment and righteousness have a way of fulfilling their own purposes. It's because they come from God alone. Even the progressive movement toward the Promised Land must involve the dangerous crossing of a parched and shelterless wilderness. There are no bridges across the Jordan River.

The art of finding oneself, of recovering one's identity, of reaching out to grasp a purpose that looks like the negation of the one which once sustained you, is the only way to get through the self-immolating synthesis that presents itself as the salvation of a Nation before or after its time. Time is marked by the passage of nations through its domain. Clocks only give you a false sense of security and continuity. When your world is ending, your salvation is near.

Progress is always gauged in terms of factors that have fallen short of their purpose. The great philosopher of the Enlightenment, Immanuel Kant (1724-1804), knew this, that there are limits to what reason alone can accomplish. From one age to the next, "Infinite progression to the ultimate purpose inevitably also involved ... the dispiriting prospect of 'an unending series of evils' to be overcome. As Kant pointed out, the infinite perpetuation of both good and evil required by unending progress was in a sense the equivalent of eternal beatitude or eternal suffering envisaged in the traditional doctrines of heaven and hell."[794] Progress always comes to a sudden halt when the Manichean in us rises once again from the depths of the unredeemed soul.

Pure Reason stands critiqued.[795] Our deepest personal concerns come from a place in the primordial ocean far deeper than Reason. Even Reason's present bathyscaphe of technological innovations is incapable of plumbing those depths. Even Reason can be crushed by the pressures (*thlupsis*) of reality.

There was once a civilization grounded in the transcendent companionship of Reason and Revelation. Like a rend in an old garment, no new patch can fix the divergence of one from the other. Patches will make the tear worse.[796] And yet, we can't resist the temptation to patch with new patches and fill with new wine. The Old Wineskin spasms to the point of bursting.

The presenting evidence of these end-time spasms are growing like weeds in the last days before the harvest.[797] They are like the climax of an orgiastic feast in which all the participants have reached the moment of expending themselves, then to lie weary and exhausted in immediate forgetfulness. They are the attempt to excise fear with feeling, to overcome fact with imagination, to halt the passage of time with one last orgy of words stretched of meaning and barely able to contain the truth they once honored.

There are too many words of explanation these days, and they all define increasingly private worlds of observation. The observation is governed by the words, and the words interpret the observations. Our salvific language games of science and sociology obscure the very facts we

---

794   Bull, *Seeing Things...*, p. 140.
795   Immanuel Kant, *Critique of Pure Reason*, 1781, 1787
796   Luke 5:36
797   Matthew 13:28: "An enemy did this."

once longer to understand. Foucault was right: The narrative totalities have all reached their limits of meaning.

These spasms include redefining words that had a classic and traditional meaning, such as "Original Sin."[798] They include moving time back just a little bit like a kind of socio-historical Daylight Savings, such as we see in the 1619 Project.[799] Like Daylight Savings Time, the clock will eventually have to be moved forward again. They include bigger spasms like *Critical Race Theory*, by which the whole body of Western Wisdom and Thought[800] shakes and quivers in its last death throes.[801] Like gender transitioning, when the distinction between male and female is gone, the distinction desired is inaccessible. When death occurs, the other members of the family enter their own New World.

The decision to "take a stand" in these last days of Western Civilization is entirely dependent on your own impression of where society is standing. Is it standing just before the flood comes; is it standing

---

798   Jim Wallis, *America's Original Sin: Racism, White Privilege, and the Bridge to a New America* (Grand Rapids, MI: Brazos Press/Baker Publishing Group, 2016), p. xxiv: "We first used the phrase in a 1987 cover story for *Sojourners* magazine. The language of 'America's Original Sin' helped me understand that the historical racism against America's Indigenous people and enslaved Africans was indeed a *sin*, and one upon which this country was founded."

799   1619 Project – https://www.nytimes.com_the1619project : "The 1619 Project is an ongoing initiative from the New York Times Magazine that began in August 2019, the 400th anniversary of the beginning of American slavery. It aims to reframe the country's history by placing the consequences of slavery and the contributions of black Americans at the very center of our national heritage"; accessed 19 Apr 23.

800   Richard Delgado and Jean Stefancik, *Critical Race Theory: An Introduction* (New York: New York University Press, 2017), p. 91: The predicament of social reform, as one writer pointed out, is that 'everything must change at once.' Otherwise, change is swallowed up by the remaining elements, so that we remain roughly as we were before. Culture replicates itself forever and ineluctably."

801   Death shaking – https://www.burnabyhospice.org_thedyingprocessfinal-hours : "Usually within the last 3-6 days of someone's life … Changes in strength and awareness are other signs of death … All senses start to fail and hearing is the last to go. Always assume the dying person is alert and can hear everything you say … Even when many of the signs are present, it is not always possible to predict when death will occur. These ups and downs can be emotionally and physically draining of the family and caregivers"; accessed 19 Apr 23.

after being enslaved in Egypt and longing for deliverance; is it standing at the nadir of its imperial and national attempts to pacify God, or is it standing on the verge of an ultimate transition, one that leads into a new dark time from which who knows what will emerge? Is it spring, summer, fall, or winter? Will it be followed by a summer, fall, winter, or spring? Most people favor Spring; those who live in the desert cannot tell Spring from Fall.

The Bible tells us that "as he thinketh in his heart, so is he."[802] Where you think your civilization is is where you are. What do you think? And even so, when a world changes, its seasons (*kairos*) change too.[803] Will Fall follow Summer? Will Spring follow winter? This is something the one in a radically transitioning world can never know. One cannot approach the transition rationally.

My hope is built on nothing less than Jesus' blood and righteousness ... When darkness veils his lovely face, I rest on his unchanging grace ... On Christ the solid rock I stand; All other ground is sinking sand.[804]

THE WELSH REVIVAL of 1904-1905 and the Azusa Street Revival of 1906-1915 can be likened to the moment Moses raised his arms up when the People of God found themselves trapped between the armies of Egypt and the deep waters of the Red Sea. Happening (*ginomai*) at the same time as the Fundamentalist Movement with set the historical tenets of Christianity in stone, these twin revivals, separated by 115 degrees of westward longitude, did not occur as an attempt to stop rationalism and rationalization of spiritual truths in their tracks: They set the then desiccating idea of the Rational back on its heels.

---

802   Proverbs 23:7 KJV
803   Seasons – https://www.climate.umn.edu_ourchangingseasons :
      "Climate change will affect the timing of the seasons in the future too. Winters are expected to become shorter, warmer, and wetter. Spring precipitation and heavy precipitation are both expected to increase in the future. Summer is likely to become warmer and longer ... the last freeze in the spring is expected to happen earlier"; accessed 19 Apr 23.
804   *My Hope is Built on Nothing Less*, public domain

The Welsh revival was historically and religiously significant and powerful, but it took the move to Los Angeles in the United States of America to provide momentum and innovative mass to the water-dividing Pentecostal Movement. As "they" say in sacramental circles, "Every Mass has its Moment." Every *egeneto* generates a new *gennao*. What began is the irrational project of a poor black-American church in the neglected slums of early L.A. now counts a worldwide membership of "over 644 million adherents,"[805] surpassing the Worldwide Anglican Communion by some 560 million and approaching by half the world's population of Roman Catholic adherents.

When Moses ran out of options, it was time to raise his hands to God. The expectation is joyous, not by calculation but by faith. The atheist writes, "It is time that we admitted that faith is nothing more than the license religious people give one another to keep believing when reasons fail,"[806] this judgment is true enough regarding ideologies of all kinds, but when reasons fail, so too does the heart. Western Civilization is in the throes of cultural cardiac arrest. Like one popular Facebook meme says, "I started a revival band called the Defibrillators."[807]

Lazarus was revived for a time, but he serves only as a premonition and pre-demonstration of resurrection. Thye Bible reveals that a chosen Nation can be, and will be, resurrected: It's the revealed Truth that makes everything involving the fact of Jesus' resurrection make sense. But the revived Lazarus Nation isn't the resurrected Promise Nation.

There are hopes and dreams that the United States of America can be the biblically expected Messianic Nation, the historically AND theologically Exceptional Nation. It would be the hybrid nation that ranks as the high point of Western Civilization, both rational and Biblical. Because the biblical is being pressed into an ideologically bounded corner of society by the pressures of the changing normal, and

---

805   Pentecostal numbers – https://en.m.wikipedia.org_pentecostalism ; last edited 15 April 2023, accessed 19 Apr 23.
806   Harris, ibid. p. 67.
807   Vince the Sign Guy, *Facebook*, 12 Apr 13:34 – https://facebook.com ; accessed again 19 Apr 23.

because the reasonable has verged on the idiosyncratic, monocratic, and arbitrary, the nature of American exceptionalist belief must be found only in the ever-widening chorathetic or not found at all.

Theological exceptionalism grounded in the biblical narratives can apply only to the Nation of Israel. Other nations can neither tolerate the idea as regards Israel as a Nation-State or they have no way of justifying a belief in their own exceptionality other than arbitrary cultural and historical reasons. Insofar as the exceptionality of the United States is affected, it wavers between the liberal/progressive evaluation of contemporary Isreali politics and the Biblio/Conservative evaluation. These, too, are separated by an ever-expanding gap of moral and social conviction.

The arms of the American civic body are being stretched out on a cross with a biblical cross-piece and a rational upright. The horizontal and vertical dimensions of Western Culture have been pieced together in a cultural endgame of political one-upmanship. As with the cross of Christ, there is no possibility of further movement: There is only the possibility of redeeming words spoken from the head of the Cross.

If there is potential for resurrection beyond the Cross, it is impossible unless both the vertical and the horizontal components remain and the body bleeds out. But then there must be some helpful Joseph of Arimathea to donate the appropriate tomb.[808] Without death and burial, there is no valid resurrection. It is highly doubtful that the ancient cultures of Russia and China will be so generous: Perhaps India will help out. It's pluralistic.

In the meantime, both Pentecostal and Evangelical America hope for, and expect in faith, a coming revival. It would be difficult to experience a revival that would outshine the Welsh Revival in sheer impact of experiential novelty, and it would be almost counter-productive to try to outdo the Azusa Street Revival. Both tap into the primordial aspect of the human soul in a way that is both surprising and rationally disorienting.

---
808   Mark 15:42-46

The Pentecostal Revival has re-kindled an originating national idea that the United States of America was founded and grounded in biblical revival. But the rapid, even explosive, spread of Pentecostal affinities, beliefs, practices, and affiliations belies the idea that any coming revival will or even can be restricted in scope to the merely nationalistic hope of an American resurrection.

And there is no coming down from the Cross.[809] Whatever spiritual revival is on the horizon, it will be a Last Revival: "All other ground is sinking sand." In the words of a once highly esteemed member of my own profession, "apocalyptic times reveal that future which makes sense of the past and calls us forth into the darkness in which is contained the light. In apocalyptic times each of us is potentially Noah, that potential person whom God calls, and each must make the decision – to drown or to act."[810]

---

[809] Mark 15:28-30
[810] Dean Herbert O'Driscoll, *The Living Church Magazine*, November 8, 1081.

POSTSCRIPT

REASON AND REVELATION:

The fissure in Western Civilization's corporate sense of identity has, from its inception, been characterized by the dualistic conceptual and perceptual relationship between Reason and Revelation. The Western worldview has always been binocular or like looking through those 3-D glasses at the theater: Certain features and characteristics of perceived reality stand out. Without the two sources, and two ways, of knowing, the world appears to be flat.

The intellectual and moral heritage of the West, while not solely derived from the wisdom of St. Augustine, begins there by way of a cherishing which survived even the so-called Dark Ages. Those were the days when the German mind cohabited with the ancient classical mind to presage a new cultural zygote which would eventually be born as Western Civilization. The catalyst for this forming of the fetal civilization was Christianity.

Augustine declared a clean divide between the reasoning power of the human being and the revealed truths of Scripture:

Regarding the human mind's reasoning capacity, he writes, "has not the genius of man invented and applied countless astonishing arts, partly the result of necessity, partly the result of exuberant invention, so that this vigour of mind, which is so active in the discovery not merely of superfluous but even of dangerous and destr5uctive things betokens an inexhaustible wealth in the nature of which can invent, learn, or employ such arts?"[811] Knowledgeable in all the Greco-Roman wisdom of the day, St. Augustine was not speaking rhetorically: He loved the stuff.

Regarding revealed Truth, the saint writes, "since this great nature has certainly been created by the true and supreme God, who administers all

---

811   Augustine, *The City of...*, p. 852

things He has made with absolute power and justice, it could never have fallen into these miseries, nor have gone out of them to miseries eternal – saving only those who are redeemed – had not an exceeding great sin been found in the first man from whom the rest have sprung."[812] Original Sin, that is to say, precedes thinking itself. This is the foundational moral and spiritual, historical, and cultural, reality that Rene' Descartes and the other wonderfully enlightened thinkers of the West reversed or eliminated entirely.

I think, therefore, I am destructive.

The spiritual giants of the alleged Dark Ages struggled with this truth, drifting again and again between the given poles of Neoplatonic mysticism and Biblical testimony. In the Gothic-Gallic-Merovingian womb of the West, isolated almost irrevocably from the transforming Roman civilization of the East, that the civilizational birth-to-be (*ginomai*) became dizygotic. Twins were born in Holy Alcuinian[813] Western Rome, but they were not identical. It was Aquinas' self-assigned task to make them so.

The Roman Catholic authorities, new at the synthesis as they themselves were, resisted the Thomist conversion of the Catholic Faith, but, in the end, it became the rule rather than the exception. The twinning became manifest in many and various ways over time, but it never ceased to be operant within the confines, the boundaries, of Western Civilization in some topologically bended shape or another.

---

812   Augustine, *City...*, p. 853
813   Alcuin – https://www.britannica.com_alcuin : "(born c. 732, in or near York, Yorkshire, Eng. – died May 19, 804, Tours, France), Anglo-Latin poet, educator, and cleric who, as head of the Palatine school established by Charlemagne at Aachen, introduced the traditions of Anglo-Saxon humanism into western Europe ... Alcuin introduced the methods of English learning into Frankish schools, systematized the curriculum, raised the standards of scholarship, and encouraged the study of liberal arts for the better understanding of spiritual doctrine"; fist posted 1998, last revised May 15, 2022, accessed 24 Apr 23.

Think of the Rhine River, the Oder River, the French and German languages, the self-imposed intellectual and cultural isolation of England from the Continent, the Alps and the Pyrenees, the splitting away of pilgrims from Europe to America. The twins have been vying for supremacy for over a thousand years. Their combativeness has generated many and marvelous results, results that St. Augustine could never have imagined, but those results have always been tempered by a common institutional awareness of Original Sin.

One of the twins wrestled with God; the other twin developed a different way of life altogether. When Jacob and Esau were reunited, they separated, and each went his own way.[814] When the fraternal twins, Reason and Revelation, attempted to reunite in the 20th and 21st centuries, they went to war.[815] They warred with themselves, and they warred with each other. Now Reason lives in its own desolate arrogance between the cultural Dead Sea and Aqaba where Moses once might have crossed, while Revelation walks with a pronounced limp.

SCIENCE AND RELIGION:

Scholars and amateurs alike argue, often vehemently, about the date on which and by whom Science began in the West. One common designation, mentioned earlier, is that it began with William of Ockham and the dogma of Occam's Razor in the 14th century.

Applied with scalpel-like proficiency, the razor can cut away all the conceptual reality proposals in the biblical narrative, leaving the book stripped and ready to be "loved" by Reason. For a while, in the 18th century, the narrative seemed willing, but now there is neither dignity nor honor left to offer. Reason WILL take it all: It's a final battle of wills. But the razor is double-edged, and when the Postmodern Ockham presses with thumb to cut, the thumb is cut off as well: Reason enters the future with no thumbs. Its grasp on reality becomes a brute, violent, and desperate praxis.

---

814   Genesis 32:22-33:20
815   Krueger, *Conundrums of...*, p. 89: "In the post-modern age, everyone's mother is Rebecca."

One notable Western scientist attempted to mitigate the character of the conflict by re-interpreting the famous/infamous Galileo example. He writes, "as in the trial of Galileo, the fundamental issue here is by no means concerned with questions of fact but rather with the conflict between the spiritual pattern of a community, which by nature has to be a static thing, and the constantly expanding and novel findings and modes of thought in science, which is thus a dynamic affair. Even a society that has emerged from great revolutionary upheavals endeavors to consolidate and fix the intellectual heritage that is to form the enduring basis of the new community."[816] Nevertheless, for the abysmally un-historical, science itself has become the new Occam's Razor.

Reason and Revelation are forced away from each other by the surgeon's knife, but the knife isn't Occam's Razor: The knife is political power. Heisenberg would know this, having lived through the horrors of Nazi Germany. He was also, one can easily glean from his writings, happy to have been resurrected professionally by the West rather than by the Soviet Union after the conclusion of World War II. Tillich embraced this Truth as well.

There are areas in the emerging commonweal of the United States of America where science and religion can't be reunited, where Reason and Revelation, like Jacob and Esau, must go their separate ways. Their flocks can't be mixed, and their families won't intermarry. There will never be another generation for which Reason and Revelation are equal partners in the establishment of the Promised Kingdom. It remains to be seen, however, which promise will be fulfilled by which family.

In the meantime, *Hatfields & McCoys* [817] is available on Amazon.

LANGUAGE AND MEANING:

---

816   Heisenberg, *Across...*, p. 224.
817   Hatfields & McCoys – https://www.imdb.com_hatfields&mccoys : "near the end of the Civil War, when they return to their homes ... increasing tensions and misunderstandings ... lead to all-out warfare between the clans (partially caused by a stolen pig). As hostilities grow and outside forces join the fight ... states governors clash and the U. S. Supreme Court eventually intervenes"; accessed 24 Apr 23.

Words are the bricks that convey meaning, but each brick is "just another brick in the wall."[818] Any civilization worthy of the designation "civilization" erects temples to its understanding of its own defining worldview. The Temple represents the consolidation of tribes, the unity of the kingdom, and the security and superiority of its cultural gods or God. The temples of the American gods appear on the surface to be the buildings characterizing the presence of the government in capital cities and, by means of the US Postal Service, in nearly every burg in the country.

These temples, however, are merely surface structures that represent the moments in time in which they were built. The Real Temple of a commonweal like the United States of America is a temple constructed of words. This is a place of worship that need not be entered physically in order that true worship may take place. In fact, it cannot be entered physically except by warriors who die or are wounded on the battlefield for its sake. It is a temple that, for most of us, only the soul can enter.

Because the American Temple is a temple constructed of words, language is of ultimate significance for the praxis of its forms of worship. When we speak of America, we speak a religious language. It's a language that pierces, somewhat like the Word of God, "to the division of soul and spirit, of joints and marrow ... able to judge the thoughts and intents of the heart."[819] There is a zeal in the American soul that is greater than the historical zeal for the safety and security of family, clan, and tribe, an idealistic transcendence that succeeds even Whitehead's endnotes to Plato, a way of conveying meaning not only from mind to mind but from heart to heart in a way that mimics resurrection itself.

It's the mimicking that tempts the identifying of the commonweal of the United States of America with the intended commonweal of God's coming Kingdom. It's the mimicking that follows Jesus right up to His time of trial and condemnation by the present powers of empire but hesitates to take that one step further. It's the imitation of Christ that falls short of being truly Christlike, the one that cannot speak those dreadful

818   *Another Brick in the Wall*, Pink Floyd, 1979
819   Hebrews 4:12

words of Jesus, "Destroy this temple, and in three days I will raise it up."[820] Only after these words are spoken can Nicodemus wonder about the true meaning of "born again."

To be born in America is not the equivalent of being born in the Spirit. The only Nation that qualifies to be born-again as a nation is the nation of Israel. The rest of us are born again generation by generation as individuals. Our temple of words, our laws and our vision, are wonderful and even transformative, but they cannot qualify to transition the country, the State, from one world to the next. There is neither a potential nor a possible socially engineered transition that will guarantee, or even suggest, the eternity of the United States of America. All that can be accomplished is a kind of cutting, one that is more like a primitive lobotomy than it is like the excising of a metastatic tumor.

It should surprise no one that horror movies about zombies, alien invaders, and a world takeover by artificial intelligence are so popular, engaging, paradigm-shifting, and compelling image-constructs. They are not fantasies: They possess their own emergent cultural reality. Emergent reality, to be sure, is inevitable according to the experts who even now don't and can't understand from whence it emerges. It will emerge because we want it to. It will emerge because we can make it emerge.

The individual words of our cultural temple have no meaning by themselves. They communicate meaning as integral parts of a language game. When the rules of the game change, so do the way the individuals words are used. When the use of a word in a statement changes, its meaning changes: When the meanings conveyed by a language game change, the worldview of those who play the game changes.

"Worldview" is one of those ambiguous words that can find a definition to rest in almost anywhere. One thing it does indicate is the link between perception and conceptuality, the trust that what is good, true, and beautiful by virtue of the language game is indeed good, true, and beautiful in terms of Being itself. It's not the *telos* of good, true, and

---

[820] John 2:19

beautiful that is ever in question: It's the construct that links perception with concept and concept with feeling and feeling with emotion. These constructs all change with changes in the language game, whether that be the game that communicates Truth, the game that communicates Goodness, or the game that communicates Beauty. The Good, the True, and The Beautiful do not exist except within a language game that conveys their meaning.

This is especially true in the Hegelian model in which the State "is the divine idea as it exists on earth." That statement of Hegelian Truth, Beauty, and Goodness (or the "right") is completed by the statement that "the principles of the State must be regarded as valid in and for themselves, which they can only insofar as they are known to be determinations of divine nature itself."[821] Yet this "divine nature" is only meaningfully communicable by means of the language of the State, a language which conveys all on its own whatever the Strate wills "divine nature" to be.

When the State completes its task of unifying all surface structural language games by means of its ideological deep structural grammar, citizens of the state will have no option but to speak its language. They won't even know there once was an option. Sadly, this process of transformation-generative confiscation is inevitable, if only because we deeply desire its outcome: It pretends to bring to us all the valuable gifts that humanity has long sought, such as peace, justice, and equity. The crown of this evolutionary (read: godless) process is that the words "peace," "justice," and "equity" will long since have evolved to mean what the State needs them to mean.

THE BIBLE:

The Bible is neither a book nor a collection of books: The Bible is an extended language game. It's the language game of salvation accomplished and to be accomplished (*telos*) by the Praxis of the God of Israel. No other language game can either replace or negate it. It is self-replicating, just like any other living thing.

821   Hegel, *Reason and...*, p. 65.

Out of the great complexity of experience spanning millenia, the Bible as language game has been refined to the point of un-falsifiability. This is because it is not a language of the intellect: It is a language of the will. You cannot falsify someone's will, you can only resist it, comply with it, or try to ignore it.

The great philosopher of science, Karl Popper, developed and clarified the scientific philosophy of falsifiability. In his three-volume tome, *Postscript to the Logic of Scientific Discovery* (1982-1983) he articulates both the rationale of logical falsifiability and of empirical falsifiability. Limited to the use of testing in the scientific method, he also "warns the scientist that there are other theories which cannot be so discussed (and) these theories must be examined by methods other than testing ... it is possible at times to learn something of real interest even from a pseudo-scientific or from a metaphysical theory."[822]

The will that is expressed by means of the language game of the Judeo-Christian Scriptures is a will that has influenced, formed, and determined the individual wills of millions, as well as the corporate will of the Nation of Israel and numerous imperial European states as well as the United States of America. The Language Game of Will is best expressed in covenants statements, such as "I will" or "I do." Even when they are qualified by such verbal additions as "if God so wills it" or "I will if I can," the will expressed is still indivisible, single, elementary, and unitary: It's the thing signified by the example of Jesus going willingly to the Cross. Nothing can hinder or un-verify a will like that.

The Bible mentions the reality of a divided will. We read, "a double-minded (*dipsuchos*-double-psyche/double soul) man is unstable in all his ways."[823] A state that is double-souled must become its own enemy: Either the one soul is honored and the other dismissed, or the other is honored and the alternate is dismissed. Either way, the excising of the two souls one from the other is something a state attempting to become a Nation cannot survive.

---

822   Karl R. Popper, *Postscript to the Logic of Scientific Discovery: Realism and the Aim of Science* (New York: Routledge, 1956, 1983), pp. 189, 190.
823   James 1:8

The unique status of the New Testament language game lies in the phenomenon of word and phrase interconnectivity. Every word and phrase in the New Testament directly implies any and all other words and phrases. This means that if one truly understands the intended meaning of even one New Testament word or phrase, one understands the entire revelation. The corollary to this unique language construct is that in order to truly understand what even one word or phrase MEANS is that one must give oneself over entirely to the story. It must be YOUR story. Only in this way can your story be united with Israel's story such that the promises of God can apply to your life as well as to the life of Israel.

THE NATION

The question of whether the biblical designation, "nation," applies to the United States of America is moot. The biblical sense of nation ties its existence (*dasein*) and Being directly to the transmission of moral, social, and intellectual characteristic through family, clan, and tribe. The United States of America is a political construct built on a foundation of philosophical ideals generated by a thousand years of cultural turmoil, competition, and an unevenly and periodically amended core faith.

The core faith has not been amended peacefully. Radical theo-cultural surgeries performed on the institutional religion called Christianity have created a spiritual plethora of tribal religious entities whose functional identity within the commonweal is to hold families together and mollify the natural clannism which results when community is formed. The gathering of religious tribes might have morphed into a nation under normal historical circumstances, but instead the various institutional Christianities constituting the American church affected regional characteristics within the nascent state which continue to promote tribalism even though the stimuli which originated the formation of cultural and psycho-emotional regions disappeared in time.

For instance, North and South were viable cultural distinctions from the beginning, as later East and West became. These distinctive cultural regions were held together by a sense of honor regarding the cherished philosophical traditions which inspired the original ideal. That sense of honor transported in time by the philosophical heritage of northern Europe, was lost in the Civil War of 1861-1865 when, anticipating the machine-like slaughter extant on the battlefields of World War I, the abstract ideals were paid for in the blood of disrupted families, clans, and tribes which had formed the national basis of American identity until the mid-19th century.

Families, clans and tribes are the generating phenomena of national resentments, regrets, and revenge. That a collection of tribes might become a Nation and the manner in which this might happen (*ginomai*) is the centering ideal around which the narratives of the Hebrew Bible are constructed, arranged, or otherwise remembered. The presence, power, authority of and trust in a One God is essential to that formational national identity. Every Nation needs its God.

An empire is a sovereign entity that exists because it can mollify several, or many, gods at once. When a regional God becomes too idiosyncratic politically or otherwise worshipped too passionately for the health of the empire, both the god and the people of the god must be erased from the memory of the imperial commonweal. The miracle of Judaism, of the inheritance of Judah as representative of the Hebrew Nation, rests on the fact that the Jewish Nation was not destroyed, either by imperial Babylon, imperial Persia, imperial Greece, or imperial Rome. The Jewish Nation survived even in dormancy under the overlordship of the Ottoman Empire. Its place remained and maintained its Jewish identity, becoming the place of replanting which today is the modern Nation-State of Israel.

This replanting occurred because of and in spite of the double-minded resistance and philosophically hesitant post-World War II politics of another imperial entity, Great Britain and its historically magnificent British Empire. The Sun eventually set on British Palestine, although it kept shining, albeit dimly, for a time on British Egypt.

Spiritual history is quite a different animal than secular or even religious history. There is a continuity to spiritual history which can neither be imitated nor co-opted by the secular and religious institutions that so often cooperate with each other to grow empires. All empires desire spiritual continuity, but the empirical and phenomenological evidence of continuity in the Spirit is characteristically fragmented and discontinuous.

In the 21st century, history has become a form of spirituality, an overarching authority who determines the rise and fall of nations and empires. The historian, as Foucault pointed out, seeks to find spiritual continuities, or totalities, that justify the present existence of this or that institutional form of imperialism or religion. In the age of science, particularly of variations on the theme of evolutionary processes, the origins of these totalities must necessarily be traceable to the origins of human emergence itself. Otherwise, the proposed totality is an unwarranted historical construct and an invented continuity with no intrinsic meaning or purpose.

The United States of America began not only as a State unifying states, an old imperial ideal, but as a metaphysical state of Being. It was never, and can never Be, a valid Nation either in spiritual or in historical terms: It MUST be a State in both senses of the word. If there is any characteristic of the United States of America that points to a kind of exceptional existence it is that the country parochially called America is a metaphysical State as well as a political entity in history.

None of the European states are metaphysical states as well. They are the continuing end products of the natural and historical formative processes which involve family, clan, and tribe. The *gennao* aspect of these nations is critical to any continuity of national identity and political unity. Germans are Germans, for instance, because their predecessors were Germans. They do not choose to be Germans: They ARE Germans. They live on a designated piece of real estate that is also German. This is true of all the European nations unless, to be sure, the historian chooses to wander back in time to the days of ancient migrations.

Many of the Europeans who migrated to North America chose to renounce their national identity; many chose not to renounce their national identity. The metaphysical dichotomy between renunciation of one's assigned historico-national identity and exalting in one's assigned historico-national identity continues as an essential and irremovable aspect of American metaphysical and imperial identity.

Is one an "American" because one's family, clan, and tribe moved to this place and continued its traditions, or is one an American in the metaphysical sense, a beneficiary of ages long evolution of philosophical ideals? There is an irresolvable difficulty with either sense of identity: If one's tribe did not originate here, there is a discontinuity in the totalizing history that might justify one's presence over and against the tribes which originated in North America. It is in this sense that many non-indigenous Americans are choosing at least to attempt to identify, even in the most minute ways, as inheritors of the indigenous identity. It is an aspect of a state that is trying to be a Nation; too, it is the motivating phenomenon behind the current popularity of rediscovering one's genealogy, a quest for identifying as a member of a Nation, however many times removed. Finding one's American identity in the metaphysical sense is a much less straightforward proposition.

Americans do not naturally possess an affinity for metaphysical analysis or discussion. This is an inherited weakness that flavors all the current discussions regarding what it MEANS to be an American, what is the American Soul. The metaphysical definitions and language games which can provide communicable meaning regarding such ideals as freedom, justice, unity, and so forth interfere and conflict with the primary identifying ideal of all immigrants: I am me. The idea that there is a "Me Generation" is an idea that has been an integral part of the formative processes of State from the time of its inception.

The idea of forming an abstract, universal State that encompasses, embraces, and defines the "I" in terms of the "we" is the project of the European philosophers highlighted in this book. In the end, the only conceivable way to finalize the forming of an ideal State in these terms is that of a self-willed totalitarianism in which every individual will is uniquely but universally harmonized with the corporate will.

There is no way to stop the necessary totalizing process at some time in the past, whether it be 1776, 1789, 1865, December 7, 1941, or any other date. The only way to disadvantage the totalitarian, aka totalizing, metaphysical process as it has co-opted the analysis of history itself is to rejoice in and appreciate as absolutes the discontinuities of the narrative that seems to have told the story we are attempting to live out today. These are types of the discontinuities we find in the Hebrew narrative, the ones over which only God is sovereign, but which are connected spiritually such that the Nation is maintained and preserved throughout all times. There is no godless metaphysics that can either promote or complete this resolution of discontinuities in history.

Again, every Nation must have its God, and every nation that overcomes the radical discontinuities of history must have a God who is identical with the God of Israel. The United States of America has never been able to access this relationship as a Nation. If it had been able to access a national relationship, a family, clan, and tribe kinship with the God of Israel, it would have BECOME Israel. While it must be granted that this access was always considered to be metaphysically possible, it is not possible in the created order unless it is can become a complete, telos, identity in time. This will never happen. It would contradict the very source of knowing which informs the original ideal, the revealed Truth that is presented to the world, to creation, in the Holy Scriptures.

The current discord among sectarian ideologues in the United States of America, both religious and secular, revolves around d this metaphysical and spiritual conundrum. If the current nation-state of Israel IS (ala "Being") ISRAEL (Israel and Judah), then the United States of America IS NOT Israel in any sense of the biblical word. If the United States of America is the metaphysical inheritance of ancient and biblical Israel, then the current nation-state of Israel IS NOT legitimate historical Israel.

This divisive issue is imbedded in the historical American State identity. In the Postmodern world, it is expressed most clearly in the spiritual divide characterized by a faction, or clan, that expects the modern nation-state of Israel to be a liberal republic after the fashion of the United States of America, and a faction, or clan, that expects the United States of America to be more like ancient Israel. The conflict itself, mention of which is virtually taboo on its own terms in all educated circles, is the historical manifestation of the split in the American sense of identity that was established by virtue of its own founding documents.

Irony, to be sure, didn't die with Shakespeare. Regardless of whether or not one adheres to the expectation that the modern nation-state of Israel should be more like the liberal republic of the USA or the expectation that the USA should be more like the Hebrew Nation of the Old Testament, the actual modern nation-state of Israel vanishes in the midst and mists of the conversation. Modern Israel becomes (ginomai) simply a foil for an America which has not yet become comfortable in its own skin.

The solution to this problem of national and state identity is not forthcoming. Neither the United States of America nor the modern nation-state of Israel are naturally inclined to commit national or state suicide in order to mollify the contradictory expectations of the Christian West. Something in the totalities of demanded history must give, and in that historically necessary giving up we encounter with apocalypse.

When God divides, human wisdom fails to connect.

The broken window demands a new house: "Let the games begin."[824]

NON-INTERNET CITATIONS

BOOKS
Augustine of Hippo, *The City of God*, 413 CE
Thomas Aquinas, *Now My Tongue the Mystery Telling*, 13th century CE
William Shakespeare, *Macbeth*, 1623

---

[824] *The Hunger Games*, Lionsgate, 2012+

Rene' Descartes, *Discourse on Method*, 1637
Rene' Descartes, *Meditation One*, 1641
Rene' Descartes, *Meditation Three*, 1641
Thomas Hobbes, *Leviathan: The Matter, Forme and Power of a Commonwealth Ecclesiasticall and Civil*, 1651
Sir Isaac Newton, *Philosophaie Naturalis Principia Mathematica*, 1728
The United States Declaration of Independence, 1776
Immanuel Kant, *Critique of Pure Reason*, 1787
William Blake, *The Marriage of Heaven and Hell*, 1790
Donatien Alphonse Francois Marquis de Sade, *120 Days of Sodom*, 1785
Georg Wilhelm Friedrich Hegel, *Reason in History*, 1837
Alexis de Toqueville, *Democracy in America*, 1840
Edgar Allen Poe, *The Tell-Tale Heart*, 1843
Soren Kierkegaard, *Concluding Unscientific Postscript to Philosophical Fragments, Volume 1*, 1846
Soren Kierkegaard, *The Sickness unto Death: A Christian Psychological Exposition for Edification and Awakening*, 1849
Charles Darwin, *On the Origin of Species*, 1859
Lewis Carroll, *Alice's Adventures in Wonderland*, 1865
Jules Verne, *20,000 Leagues Under the Sea*, 1870
Friedrich Nietzsche, *Thus Spake Zarathustra*, 1885
Walt Whitman, *Leaves of Grass*, 1891-1892
The United States Pledge of Allegiance, 1892
G.E. Moore, *Principia Ethica*, 1903
Jessie Penn-Lewis/Evan Roberts, *War on the Saints*, 1912
Alfred North Whitehead and Bertrand Russell, *Principia Mathematica*, 1913
The Manifesto of the Ninety-Three Intellectuals, 1914
R.A. Torrey, ed., *The Fundamentals, Volume II*, 1917
Public domain, *My Hope is Built on Nothing Less*
John McCrae, *In Flanders Fields*, 1918
T.S. Eliot, *The Hippopotamus*, 1919
Ludwig Wittgenstein, *Tractatus Logico-Philosophicus*, 1921
Rudolf Otto, *The Idea of the Holy*, 1923
Martin Heidegger, *Being and Time*, 1926
Alfred North Whitehead, *Process and Reality*, 1927-1928

H.P. Lovecraft, *The Call of Cthulhu*, 1928
Erich Maria Remarque, *All Quiet on the Western Front*, 1928
C.G. Jung, *The Archetypes and the Collective Unconscious*, 1933
Martin Heidegger, *Introduction to Metaphysics*, 1935
Mao Zedong, *Selected Works*, 1937
W. H. Auden, *A Baroque Eclogue*, 1947
Fr. Reginald Garrigou-Lagrange, O.P., *The Three Ages of the Interior Life: Prelude of Eternal Life*, 1947
Abraham Joshue Heschel, *The Sabbath: Its Meaning for Modern Man*, 1951
Eric Hoffer, *The True Believer*, 1951
Paul Tillich, *Systematic Theology, Volume One: Reason and Revelation; Being and God*, 1951
Ludwig Wittgenstein, *Philosophical Investigations*, 1953
Teilhard de Chardin, *The Phenomenon of Man*, 1955
ABC/Stephen King, *The Langoliers*, 1955
Karl R. Popper, *Postscript to the Logic of Scientific Discovery: Realism and the Aim of Science*, 1956
Dr. Seuss, *The Cat in the Hat*, 1957
Caitlin R. Kiernan, *Nor the Demons Down Under the Sea*, 1957
Paul Tillich, *Systematic Theology, Volume Two: Existence and the Christ*, 1957
William S. Burroughs, *Naked Lunch*, 1959
Ludwig Wittgenstein, *The Blue and the Brown Books*, 1960
Barbara W. Tuchman, *The Proud Tower: A Portrait of the World Before the War, 1890-1914*, 1962
Rudolf Bultmann, *History of the Synoptic Tradition*, 1963
Paul Tillich, *Systematic Theology, Volume Three: Life and the Spirit; History and the Kingdom of God*, 1963
Harvey Cox, *The Secular City*, 1965
Michel Foucault, *The Archaeology of Knowledge, and the Discourse on Language*, 1971
Walt Kelly, *Pogo*, 1971
Jerzy Kosinsky, *Being There*, 1971
Werner Heisenberg, *Across the Frontiers*, 1974
Henry Margenau, *The Nature of Physical Reality: A Philosophy of Modern Physics*, 1977
The Episcopal Book of Common Prayer, 1979

Morris Kline, *Mathematics: The Loss of Certainty*, 1982
Michael Novak, *The Spirit of Democratic Capitalism*, 1982, 1991
Barbara W. Tuchman, *The March of Folly: From Troy to Vietnam*, 1984
Robert J. Wilken, *The Christians as the Romans Saw Them*, 1984
Wolfgang Giegerich, *Facing Apocalypse: Saving the Nuclear Bomb*, 1987
James Gleick, *Chaos: Making a New Science*, 1987
Mike Perlman, *Facing Apocalypse: When Heaven and Earth Collapse, Myths of the End of the World – Native Australian World-Endings*, 1987
Charles B. Strozier, *Apocalypse: On the Psychology of Fundamentalism in America*, 1994
Harvey Cox, *Fire from Heaven: The Rise of Pentecostal Spirituality and the Reshaping of Religion in the Twenty-First Century*, 1995
Malcolm Bull, *Seeing Things Hidden: Apocalypse, Vision and Totality*, 1999
Kai Bird and Martin J. Sherwin, *American Prometheus: The Triumph and Tragedy of J. Robert Oppenheimer*, 2005
Sam Harris, *Letter to a Christian Nation*, 2007
Jim Baggott, *The Invention & Discovery of the 'God Particle': Higgs*, 2012
Cody Goodfellow, *Rapture of the Deep*, 2016
Albert Peter Krueger, *From the Fords of the Jordan to the Plain of Shinar*, 2016
Jim Wallis, *America's Original Sin: Racism, White Privilege, and the Bridge to a New America*, 2016
Jeffrey Engel, *When the World Seemed New: George H.W. Bush and the End of the Cold War*, 2017
Stephen Hawking, *A Brief History of Time*, 2017
Richard Delgado and Jean Stefancik, *Critical Race Theory: An Introduction*, 2017
Albert Krueger, *Conundrums of the End: Fate, Destiny, and Apocalypse*, 2020

MUSIC
Chuck Berry, *Roll Over Beethoven*, 1956
Bob Dylan, *Like a Rolling Stone*, 1965
Donovan Leitch, *Season of the Witch*, 1966
The Doors, *The End*, 1966
Yardbirds, *Shapes of Things*, 1966
Love, *The Red Telephone*, 1967
Bob Dylan, *I Dreamed I Saw Saint Augustine*, 1967

Walter Marks, *I Gotta Be Me*, 1967
Country Joe MacDonald, *The Acid Commercial*, 1968
Kenny Rogers, *Just Dropped in to See What Condition My Condition Was In*, 1968
Blind Faith, *Can't Find My Way Home*, 1969
Simon & Garfunkel, *Bridge Over Troubled Water*, 1970
Johnny Mandel and Michael Altman, *Suicide Is Painless*, 1970
The Who, *Won't Get Fooled Again*, 1971
Led Zeppelin, *Stairway to Heaven*, 1971
Stealers Wheel, *Stuck in the Middle with You*, 1973
Carly Simon, *Attitude Dancing*, 1975
Pink Floyd, *Another Brick in the Wall*, 1979
Supertramp, *The Logical Song*, 1979
Lou Reed, *Dime Store Mystery*, 1989
Santana, *The Game of Love*, 2002

MOVIES
Warner Bros., *Cool Hand Luke*, 1967
20th Century Studios, *Star Wars, Episode IV-A New Hope*, 1978
20th Century Studios, Universal Pictures, Warner Bros., *The Fly*, 1986
Buena Vista Pictures, *The Sixth Sense*, 1999
Warner Bros./Sideshow, *The Matrix*, 1999
Dreamworks, *Gladiator*, 2000
Miramax/Buena Vista, *Chocolat*, 2000
Paramount Pictures, *Teenage Mutant Ninja Turtles*, 2007
Rogue Pictures/Universal, *Hot Fuzz*, 2007
Lionsgate, *The Hunger Games*, 2012+
Columbia Pictures, *Elysium*, 2013
Lionsgate, *Sicario*, 2015
Paramount Pictures, *Annihilation*, 2018

www.ingramcontent.com/pod-product-compliance
Lightning Source LLC
LaVergne TN
LVHW091527060526
838200LV00036B/517